The Keynesian Revolution
in the Making, 1924–1936

'We can conquer unemployment': the cover of Lloyd George's 1929 proposals on unemployment, as defaced in the official Treasury copy

The Keynesian Revolution in the Making
1924–1936

PETER CLARKE

CLARENDON PRESS · OXFORD

This book has been printed digitally and produced in a standard specification in order to ensure its continuing availability

OXFORD
UNIVERSITY PRESS

Great Clarendon Street, Oxford OX2 6DP

Oxford University Press is a department of the University of Oxford.
It furthers the University's objective of excellence in research, scholarship,
and education by publishing worldwide in

Oxford New York

Auckland Cape Town Dar es Salaam Hong Kong Karachi
Kuala Lumpur Madrid Melbourne Mexico City Nairobi
New Delhi Shanghai Taipei Toronto

With offices in

Argentina Austria Brazil Chile Czech Republic France Greece
Guatemala Hungary Italy Japan South Korea Poland Portugal
Singapore Switzerland Thailand Turkey Ukraine Vietnam

Oxford is a registered trade mark of Oxford University Press
in the UK and in certain other countries

Published in the United States
by Oxford University Press Inc., New York

Database right Oxford University Press (maker)
First issued in paperback (with corrections) 1990

Reprinted 2011

ISBN 978-0-19-820219-6

Printed and bound in Great Britain by CPI Antony Rowe,
Chippenham and Eastbourne

In memory of
JOHN WILLIAM CLARKE
4 January 1908–25 May 1987

PREFACE

This book is chiefly addressed to my fellow historians. I hope that it will be intelligible to others. It represents a quest for the historical Keynes, whose part in giving the economic role of the state a wholly new political salience in the twentieth century few historians would deny—yet few have properly explained. For there remains a hole in the middle of the picture, where Keynes's own ideas ought to be. Economic historians of this period have usually focused rather closely upon 'policy', leaving 'theory' to the economists. Political historians, conversely, have been too readily content with a question-begging acknowledgement that something important must have been going on, but have circumspectly declined to elaborate. As historical explanation, this is hardly better than saying 'with one bound Jack was free'.

In seeking a proper explanation, I have spent a fair part of the last few years in learning enough to follow a debate over Keynesian economics which has been in progress on a number of levels. I have been encouraged to continue by the helpful response I have encountered from many economists, and I would particularly like to thank Neville Cain, Selwyn Cornish, Partha Dasgupta, Elizabeth Durbin, Geoffrey Harcourt, Susan Howson, Peter Kriesler, Murray Milgate, Donald Moggridge, Thomas Rymes, Donald Winch, Richard Wright, and Warren Young.

The making of this book has been a tortuous process. An early result of my work was my essay 'The politics of Keynesian economics, 1924–31', published in Michael Bentley and John Stevenson (eds.), *High and Low Politics in Modern Britain* (Oxford, 1983). (Since parts of it are recapitulated in the present book, I have taken account, notably in Chapter 4, of subsequent criticisms of its contentions.) One theme of the essay was the importance of the political context in understanding the theoretical position Keynes adopted in his *Treatise on Money* (1930). I intended to match this with an essay along the same lines, covering the years in which Keynes produced *The General Theory of Employment, Interest and Money* (1936). But as my work progressed, it became clear that the story was more complicated than I had supposed.

My decision to write a book was due in part to the belief that this was the only way in which a crucially important dimension of economic theory could be satisfactorily explained to non-specialists. It was also due in part to the richness of the historical sources which I discovered. Finally, however, it was due to a growing sense that economists might benefit from what I had to say.

It was borne in on me that many disputes over Keynesian economics revolved around a construct. (This is apart from the related problem about subsequent 'Keynesianism'.) The figure confidently referred to as 'Keynes' often turned out to be an ahistorical abstraction, located not in the context of actual arguments over policy or of actual debates over theory, but with citations from his various writings, of various dates, pressed into service in senses which could hardly have been intended. In view of Keynes's own use of the label 'classical economist'—to which his friend and critic D. H. Robertson raised pointed objection—it is ironic that the whirligig of time should have brought in one of his revenges by making the name Keynes into what Robertson called a 'composite Aunt Sally of uncertain age'. I concluded that only by telling the story of the argument at some length could I make it comprehensible, and thereby retrieve the historical Keynes.

I was helped by discussion with Professors Lord Kahn, James Meade, and Sir Austin Robinson. I should like to thank the librarians and archivists who assisted my research, especially Judith Allen at the Marshall Library, Cambridge, Henry Gillett at the Bank of England, Michael Halls at King's College, Cambridge, and Angela Raspin at the British Library of Political and Economic Science. For permission to quote from unpublished writings of which they control the copyright I am grateful to: Professor D. E. Moggridge; Professor T. K. Rymes; the Bank of England; the British Library of Political and Economic Science; and the Provost and Scholars of King's College, Cambridge (for unpublished writings of J. M. Keynes copyright 1988). Crown copyright material in the Public Record Office is reproduced by permission of the Controller of Her Majesty's Stationery Office. Illustrations are reproduced by permission of Dr W. M. Keynes.

Over many years I have accumulated many debts. This work effectively began during my tenure of a Visiting Fellowship in the History Department of the Research School of Social Sciences at the Australian National University, Canberra, in 1983. Early drafts were tested out as seminar papers or lectures for the ANU; Sydney University; the Combined Victorian Universities seminar in modern British history, Melbourne; Churchill College, Cambridge; the Institute of Historical Research, London; the University of Essex; the annual conference of the Historical Association; and the Beesly Society, University College London. My research has been supported throughout by the Master and Fellows of St John's College, Cambridge. The final draft was expertly prepared in the History Faculty Office by Lorraine Ostler and Elizabeth Murray. I am also grateful to Sarah Blackhall for compiling the bibliography. In Ivon Asquith, who commissioned the book, I found the ideal publisher. What I owe to my family is reserved to the dedication of my books. Beyond that, my final debt is to those scholars, world-wide, who read substantial parts of my penultimate draft: Eduardo da Fonseca, Ewen Green, Susan Howson, Donald Moggridge, Mary Short, Duncan Tanner, Philip Williamson, and Donald Winch; and, above all, to Stefan Collini, Barry Supple, and John Thompson, who read every word.

P. F. C.

St John's College
Cambridge

CONTENTS

LIST OF PLATES

'We can conquer unemployment': the cover of Lloyd George's 1929 proposals on unemployment, as defaced in the official Treasury copy. Crown copyright: Public Record Office (T 175/26).

frontispiece

PART I

Introduction

PROLOGUE

The story of an argument

This book tells the story of an argument. The argument arose out of the performance of the British economy in the period of depression between the two World Wars. In the first place it was an argument about policy, and as such it naturally involved assessing what it was administratively feasible and technically sensible for government to attempt. Secondly, it was at crucial stages a political argument, challenging the conventional view of the economic role of the state and bringing political parties into electoral competition over their rival approaches. Thirdly, it became an argument about economic theory, as the analysis of unemployment itself emerged as a professionally contentious matter.

Keynes played a central role in each of these overlapping disputes and this book is conceived as an effort to understand his ideas. It is not, however, a systematic analysis of his thought in its fully developed form but rather a historical account of his thinking. Thus it follows the course of the argument in which he was engaged—into the province of government, into the arena of politics, and into the discipline of economics—over a period of about twelve years. His own ideas changed a good deal during that time; so did his opponents and allies; and so did the level of debate. But there was always an argument going on, and it is impossible to understand what Keynes meant—or what his opponents meant—except in that context.

The book's structure is broadly chronological. It is often more concerned with what was happening to Keynes at any one time than with what he did in any one field. I hope never to lose sight of the fact that it was the same man who, in the same week, had an exchange with Treasury officials, contributed a polemical article to the *Evening Standard*, and drafted a chapter of the *Treatise on Money*. While it is obviously necessary to appreciate the different levels on which Keynes was working, there is much to be learned from moving between them—as he did himself. Yet this book is neither a biography nor a history of economic doctrine. A study of Keynes's thought may properly consider itself bound by the strict conventions of the doctrine-historical discipline, especially over which texts

constitute admissible evidence; but in studying Keynes's thinking I
have relaxed these criteria and refused to segregate his activities or
his writings into separate compartments.

The ideal source material for this project would be a verbatim
record of Keynes expounding and discussing his ideas at a formative
stage in their development. Fortunately two such sets of records
survive. One is the transcript of the evidence given to the Committee
on Finance and Industry which sat under the chairmanship of Lord
Macmillan between 1929 and 1931. Professor Sir Austin Robinson
correctly sensed the existence of buried treasure here forty years ago
in his obituary notice of Keynes:[1]

The pages of the Volumes of Evidence of that Committee, particularly his
exchanges with Professor Pigou and D. H. Robertson when they appeared as
witnesses, provide what is probably the best published record of Keynes's
thinking in that period. And among the unpublished papers of the Committee
there is understood to exist a record of Keynes's exposition of his ideas to his
fellow-members, in which he followed the main lines that he later published
in the *Treatise on Money*, but expanded many points in more detail under
cross-examination.

I have therefore drawn extensively upon not only the double-volume
of officially published evidence, which scholars have often referred
to, but also the set of unpublished minutes which are naturally less
widely known. Indeed, Chapters 5–9 are a contribution towards a
history of the Macmillan Committee—running parallel to the
exemplary account of the work of the Economic Advisory Council in
the same period by Susan Howson and Donald Winch.[2] The other
source which I have found illuminating in this respect is the series of
lecture notes by students who attended Keynes's university lectures
in Cambridge in the years 1932–5, while the *General Theory* was
taking shape, and Chapter 11 benefits particularly.[3]

Up to the end of the 1960s, the tone of much writing in this field
was set by Keynesian triumphalism.[4] The great man's ideas had

---

[1] E. A. G. Robinson, 'John Maynard Keynes, 1883–1946', *Econ. Jnl.*, 57 (1947),
1–68, at 38.

[2] *The Economic Advisory Council, 1930–9* (Cambridge, 1977).

[3] In using them, I have relied upon the scholarly labours of Professor T. K. Rymes,
who first drew my attention to the availability of these transcripts; see below, ch. 11
n. 9.

[4] It would be unfair to set up the first edition of Michael Stewart's widely read
Penguin, *Keynes and After* (Harmondsworth, 1967) as the straw man of triumphalism,
but it bears characteristic marks of the period in which it was written.

apparently won wide acceptance and the Keynesian revolution had done its beneficient work in eliminating unemployment, which seemed not only controllable but fairly well under control. Since then, it hardly needs saying, many of these callow certainties have been called into question, both in practice and in theory, as a formidable economic literature serves to testify. The new historiography about Keynesian economics has accordingly turned sceptical—perhaps too much so. The original Keynesian account was of the eventual triumph of the forces of light (personified, almost single-handed, by Keynes) over the forces of darkness (often represented at the level of policy by the Treasury and of theory, above all, by Professor A. C. Pigou). Not only was Keynes always right: the Treasury and Pigou seemed merely silly. Some recent examples of revisionist historiography, however, have simply turned this version upside down, so that it is now Keynes who seems merely silly.[5] I think the time has come to present an account of an argument which involved Keynes and the Treasury and Pigou—as well as many others—without diminishing the stature of any of the participants by caricaturing their ideas.

In reconstructing the position adopted by the official monetary authorities, I have gained a good deal from the archives of the Bank of England and the Treasury papers at the Public Record Office. I am conscious of my debt to other scholars who have worked in these archives, even though I may disagree with some of their conclusions. I have been lucky in discovering a hitherto closed file (T. 172/2095) which only became accessible at a late stage in my research. This turned out to be of fundamental importance in understanding the formulation of the so-called Treasury View in the late 1920s, and thus forms the main support for Chapter 3. If it modifies the conclusions of some existing accounts, which were necessarily written in ignorance of its contents, I am conscious that, by the same token, I may have missed other valuable needles in the haystack of Treasury papers. And until the task of cataloguing the Bank's archive is complete, historians will not be sure how much gold lies in its vaults.

Consistent with the approach of this book, I have read many Treasury papers with an eye to the thinking that lay behind them

[5] The volume edited by Sean Glynn and Alan Booth, *The Road to Full Employment* (1987), which contains the fruit of some excellent research, e.g. the essays by Forrest Capie, Roger Middleton, and by the editors, may be counterpoised against Stewart's book.

rather than simply looking to their formal conclusions. I have often found the hastily scribbled internal comment as illuminating as the fully corrected typescript of the final draft. In this sense I have treated Treasury officials like Sir Richard Hopkins, Sir Otto Niemeyer, and Sir Frederick Leith-Ross in the same way as I have treated Keynes, whose *obiter dicta* likewise sometimes provide clues which are missing in his finished writings. In short, I have not been afraid to use inference from inevitably incomplete and sometimes fragmentary sources. I have acted on the maxim that the surviving evidence is rarely bespoke to the requirements of the historian, who must be satisfied if it fits where it touches.

The sheer mass of evidence, it must be said, is plentiful enough; and the most important part of it is published. In general, I have only quoted at length from sources which are unpublished (like the Treasury papers) or not readily accessible (like the Macmillan Committee evidence). I have tried to abbreviate my quotations from works in print, especially from the wonderfully comprehensive edition of Keynes's writings, to which I provide references wherever possible. My indebtedness to the editors, and especially to Donald Moggridge, will be obvious. I hope that I either bring the evidence which is necessary to support my account into the public domain, or give citations which can be followed up without difficulty.

There is an enormous and still burgeoning economic literature on Keynes and Keynesian economics; and a distinction between the two has become commonplace. Some of the most fertile contributions have come from economists who have acknowledged that their concern is primarily with the relevance of 'Keynesian' analysis to their current preoccupations. Thus Axel Leijonhufvud warns that the 'doctrine-historical objective is strictly secondary' in his work.[6] Likewise the fruitful adoption of 'an historical method of approach' by Murray Milgate is, as he explains, 'in order to reveal analytical rather than historical conclusions and insights'.[7] As a historian, I am content to reverse these priorities. Yet I think it is important that historians should show a fuller appreciation of a continuing

[6] Axel Leijonhufvud, *On Keynesian Economics and the Economic of Keynes* (1968), 9. See 'Schools, "revolutions" and research programmes in economic theory' in Leijonhufvud, *Information and Co-ordination* (1981), 291–345, esp. 318, which subsequently withdrew some of the historical claims; and Richard Jackman,'Keynes and Leijonhufvud', *Oxford Econ. Papers*, NS 26 (1974), 259–72, for a doctrine-historical rebuttal.

[7] Murray Milgate, *Capital and Employment* (1982), 6.

economic debate of which they have often seemed innocent. The work of Moggridge and Winch, of course, has been informed by an understanding of economic theory without becoming inaccessible to a non-technical readership;[8] and their work was an indispensable starting-point for my own. But the sort of doctrine-historical research which has been carried on with such impressive professionalism by economists like Patinkin and Milgate has not entered into the mainstream of historians' studies of the period.

I have accordingly followed the practice of referring to economists by name fairly often in the text of Part IV; whereas in Part III I have been much more sparing in mentioning my fellow historians. In case this is felt invidious or disproportionate, let me record my sense of how much I have learnt from previous historical research in this field, especially on matters covered in Chapters 2, 3, and 7. Let me say also that in offering a revised chronology of the making of the *General Theory* in Chapters 10 and 11, I am conscious of building upon the solid foundations laid by distinguished predecessors like Robinson, Klein, Harrod, Lambert, Moggridge, Milgate, Cain, Patinkin, and Kahn.[9]

Finally, the plan of the book should be explained. Chapter 1 provides an introduction to those themes in Keynes's career up to 1924—and to the economic assumptions of the time—which are salient in understanding what happened subsequently. This prefaces the substantive treatment in Part II, which offers a general explanation of the principles of sound finance as upheld in the 1920s and an empirical examination of the provenance of the 'Treasury View' of

---

[8] Donald Winch, *Economics and Policy*, revised edn. (1972); D. E. Moggridge, *Keynes*, 2nd edn. (1980).

[9] E. A. G. Robinson, 'John Maynard Keynes, 1883–1946,' *Econ. Jnl.*, 57 (1947), esp. 39–46; Lawrence R. Klein, *The Keynesian Revolution* (New York, 1947; London, 1952), esp. ch. 2; Roy Harrod, *The Life of John Maynard Keynes* (1951), ch. 11; Paul Lambert, 'The evolution of Keynes's thought from the *Treatise on Money* to the *General Theory*', *Annals of Public and Cooperative Economy*, 40 (1969), 243–63; D. E. Moggridge, 'From the *Treatise* to the *General Theory*: An exercise in chronology', *Hist. of Pol. Econ.*, v (1973), 72–88, and reformulated to some extent in the 2nd edn. of *Keynes*, pp. 91–119; Milgate, *Capital and Employment*, and 'The "new" Keynes papers', in John Eatwell and Murray Milgate (eds.), *Keynes's Economics and the Theory of Value and Distribution* (1983), 187–99; Neville Cain, 'Cambridge and its revolution: A perspective on the multiplier and effective demand', *Economic Record*, 55 (1979), 108–17; Don Patinkin, *Keynes's Monetary Thought: A study of its development* (Durham, NC, 1976), chs. 7–9, and *Anticipations of the General Theory?* (Chicago, 1982), Pt. I; see also Don Patinkin and J. Clark Leith (eds.), *Keynes, Cambridge and the General Theory* (1977), 3–25; Richard F. Kahn, *The Making of Keynes's General Theory* (Cambridge, 1984).

1929. Part III considers the challenge which Keynes mounted to this conventional wisdom at the level of policy in the years 1924–31. After Chapter 4, which has a directly political focus, this debate is primarily followed through the deliberations of the Macmillan Committee. The relation of Keynes's policy advice to the theoretical analysis of his *Treatise on Money* is kept in view throughout. The break between Part III and Part IV is not just chronological: it marks the shift from policy to theory which characterized Keynes's concerns in the early 1930s when he came to formulate the theory of effective demand. This is not essentially an analysis of the *General Theory* but an historical account of how and why it came to be written. As such, however, it bears upon the appropriateness of the term 'Keynesian revolution'; and the nature of Keynes's endeavour and achievement is a final theme.

1

Keynes before Keynesianism, 1883–1924

By 1924 Keynes had turned forty. He was already rich and famous. He was rich because, starting from a position of ample bourgeois comfort, he built up a personal fortune through speculation. He did this not once but twice, having lost most of his money in 1920. Though his net assets touched sixty thousand pounds in 1924, they were to dip below ten thousand in 1929, before climbing to a peak of half a million pounds in 1936—truly his *annus mirabilis*. (Equivalent values in the late 1980s might be fifteen or twenty times higher.) Keynes's other activities in the City added to his income, which fluctuated in this period around five thousand a year. For comparison, Professor Alfred Marshall in his prime had managed perfectly well on a stipend of £700 per annum.[1] Less than half Keynes's income can be classified as 'academic' and his regular stipend was only the loose change—£100 per annum, for example, on his appointment as Second Bursar of King's College, Cambridge, in 1920. Even his academic income, therefore, coming largely from his royalties and other literary earnings, stemmed from his fame. With the publication of *The Economic Consequences of the Peace* (1919), Keynes had acquired instant recognition in educated circles on both sides of the Atlantic. His was the voice which spoke with eloquence and authority against the Versailles Peace. He capitalized upon his position in the succeeding years to keep his name almost constantly before the public.

When he came to compose his *Treatise on Money* (1930)—and *a fortiori* the *General Theory of Employment, Interest and Money* (1936)—he was not just 'some academic scribbler',[2] whose *magnum opus* might fall, in an unpropitious hour, stillborn from the press. His problem, if anything, was to be that of establishing his scholarly credentials, since he already had a platform as a publicist. Keynes's

---

[1] *JMK* x. 225 ('Alfred Marshall', as reprinted in *Essays in Biography* from *Econ. Jnl.*, 34 (1924)). For Keynes's finances, see *JMK* xii. 1–29, esp. Tables 1–3.

[2] 'Madmen in authority, who hear voices in the air, are distilling their frenzy from some academic scribbler of a few years back.' *JMK* vii. 383 (*General Theory*).

importance in this period stemmed from his combination of roles in three overlapping areas: politics, policy, and theory. To appreciate what he gave to each of them, it must first be established what he brought to each of them.

Politics

Keynes brought an outlook instinct with the values of English Liberalism and one which took for granted its characteristic methods. Partly this was a product of the parental home in Harvey Road, Cambridge, where his family tradition fused high-minded non-conformist scruple with open-minded worldly improvement, not least of their own position. His father became Registrary of the University of Cambridge; his mother the city's first woman mayor. Sir Roy Harrod's classic biography made much of 'the presuppositions of Harvey Road', pointing to an implicit paradigm of ordered progress, animated by moral earnestness and furthered through rational persuasion.[3] If the young John Maynard Keynes did not accept his heritage without putting up a fight, it bears some marks of being a put-up fight.

When Keynes subsequently recalled his early beliefs, he spoke of his circle of undergraduate friends as having had 'a religion and no morals'—meaning that they were preoccupied with abstract ideals and introspectively absorbed in their own states of mind to the exclusion of the consequences of actions or the larger problems of the world outside.[4] The philosophy of G. E. Moore has, somewhat indiscriminately, been compounded into this picture. Yet the aspects which Keynes chose to stress when talking to his Bloomsbury friends some thirty years afterwards have too often been regarded as a literal account and a rounded picture, as though 'religion' had in fact wholly displaced 'morals'. Keynes's rebellion against 'Victorianism' was real enough, and it was his friend Lytton Strachey who delivered the *coup de grâce* with *Eminent Victorians* (1918); but Keynes clung to more of the wreckage than he always disclosed in the superficial manner he affected. The Keynes of the inter-war period will be understood better if one bears in mind the comment of another

[3] Harrod, *Life*, 2–3, 183, 192–3.
[4] *JMK* x. 436 ('My early beliefs', read to the Memoir Club, 12 Sept. 1938); see Anne Olivier Bell (ed.), *The Diary of Virginia Woolf*, v (Penguin edn., 1985), 168–9.

biographer (Austin Robinson) who knew him in those days: that 'beneath a Georgian skin there peeped out from time to time an almost Victorian sense of moral purpose and obligation'.[5]

It is now notorious, in one sense or another, that Harrod's biography is less revealing about the young man Keynes in one respect: his homosexuality. Now that this can be acknowledged, a much fuller picture has emerged of Keynes's intense relationships with many of the Cambridge undergraduates who were, like him, members of the 'Apostles'—several of whom maintained a lifelong association as part of 'Bloomsbury'. Strachey is important here, and later the artist Duncan Grant; and there were others in the years before the First World War. Homosexuality was the hidden ingredient in a 'Kingsy-Bloomsbury' style of high aestheticism. Robert Skidelsky justifiably dwells upon this theme in dealing with Keynes's life up to 1920;[6] but how far it can be made to yield insights for his later career is another question.

Charles Hession has gone furthest in extrapolating an answer. In his interpretation, the Keynes who was a product of 'Jocasta mothering' was dogged throughout his life by a homosexual identity which constituted his 'dreadful secret'. His bisexuality was in this sense linked to his heightened imaginative powers, displayed in a creative flowering which, *pace* Harrod, did not wait until the mid-1920s to come to bloom. Thus it was Keynes's ambivalent position as at once outsider and insider which opened him to reformist political influences; and a keen eye can discover homosexual allusions in, for example, his lecture on 'Economic possibilities for our grandchildren' and in the *Treatise on Money*, both published in 1930.[7]

Now there may be something in this, especially in the ideological overtones of a challenge to social respectability; but it is ultimately a matter of which perspective seems right for the whole picture. In the period covered by the present work, Keynes was married (from 1925) to the ballerina Lydia Lopokova, with whom he evidently formed a close rapport. Although a startling match for a Cambridge don, it seemed less anomalous in *outré* King's than it would in an anaesthetically undemonstrative college—the ballet, so to speak, gave Keynes a foot in the other camp. This was the Keynes seen by younger

[5] 'John Maynard Keynes', 25.

[6] Robert Skidelsky, *John Maynard Keynes*, i, *Hopes Betrayed, 1883–1920* (1983), esp. chs. 5, 8, and 10.

[7] Charles Hession, *John Maynard Keynes* (1984), esp. 106–7, 203–4, 219, 244, 252, 310.

colleagues who could perfectly well spend these years wholly oblivious to bisexual predilections on his part. The fact is that the issue simply has not obtruded, explicitly or implicitly, into a consideration of his thinking on public affairs and economic theory. Readers must judge whether, in this perspective, the ensuing story of the argument makes adequate sense without such references.

In common with his Bloomsbury friends, Keynes was dismissive about conventional morality: but mainly on account of its conventionality. He once told Virginia Woolf: 'I begin to see that our generation—yours & mine V., owed a great deal to our fathers' religion.' Christianity had, he came to think, underpinned a good deal of what he accepted without question as wholesome and right. 'We had the best of both worlds,' he reflected. 'We destroyed Xty and yet had its benefits.'[8] So far as Keynes himself was concerned, the Bloomsbury style of expatiating upon love and personal relations and states of mind did not preclude a wider social concern. For the years before the First World War, however, there is plainly scope for differences of interpretation. Is Robinson right to say 'Keynes' absorbing interest at this stage of his life was politics', or Skidelsky to describe his attitude as 'political indifference'?[9]

In the first place, what threshold of political commitment seems appropriate? Clearly Keynes was not on the road to a career as a professional politician—he had resisted blandishments to this effect—and it was chiefly an *intellectual* commitment to the cause of Liberalism that he manifested. If he had simply sat in his armchair and written about his political views, this would at any rate have provided a serviceable record of what they were: but he did significantly more than this. He spoke frequently in political debates at the Cambridge Union Society, of which he became President; he was concurrently President of the University Liberal Club. His forte, not unnaturally, was Free Trade, which, from the inception of Joseph Chamberlain's campaign for Tariff Reform in 1903, had become the major political issue of the day (and was thus in no sense an esoteric fad). In the two General Elections of 1910, Keynes played an active part, notably by going to Birmingham for a week of speech-making in support of his friend Edward Hilton Young, the Liberal candidate for East Worcestershire. (The victorious Unionist candidate was

---

[8] Anne Olivier Bell (ed.), *The Diary of Virginia Woolf*, iv (Penguin edn., 1983), 208 (19 Apr. 1934).
[9] Robinson, 'John Maynard Keynes', 10; Skidelsky, *Hopes Betrayed*, 229; cf. 233.

Austen Chamberlain.) It is interesting that, in the following year, Keynes went to Ireland for a fortnight's tour with some fifty Liberal MPs. Keynes may, at this juncture, be judged to fall short of some notional standard of strenuous citizenship, but, even so, the concept of political indifference seems somewhat stretched by his recorded activities.[10]

Secondly, the substance of Keynes's views needs to be placed in context. What did it mean to identify with the party of Asquith and Lloyd George? This was the period in which the New Liberalism gave the party a new rhetoric in responding to a new predicament, proclaiming a need to move beyond the agenda of Gladstonianism. If the Old Liberalism of the nineteenth century had been associated with the achievement of political democracy, it was suggested, the New Liberalism of the twentieth should identify with social democracy. The end of *laissez-faire* was pronounced; the politics of collectivism, state intervention, and redistributive taxation were enunciated. Just as there was no necessary antithesis in theory between liberalism and socialism, so, it was claimed, there was no need for conflict in practice between the Liberal party and Labour. Instead, both should work together in a progressive alliance which alone could match the force of vested interests, united behind Tariff Reform in the Conservative and Unionist parties.[11]

Such was the happy vision which beckoned many Edwardian Liberals; and there are indications that Keynes was ready to countenance some shocking suggestions—'the progressive reorganisation of Society along the lines of Collectivist Socialism' or 'the confiscation of wealth'—as ones which Liberals might conceivably entertain.[12] He was certainly flirting with such propositions; whether he was wedded to them is another matter. A further issue may be mentioned, since it often served to differentiate New Liberals from Fabian Socialists, with whom they otherwise held much in common. Whereas Fabians

[10] This paragraph defends the interpretation in Peter Clarke, *Liberals and Social Democrats* (1978), 131, against Skidelsky, *Hopes Betrayed*, 241; but it does so almost entirely by drawing on examples in his rich account, to which the whole of this section is much indebted.

[11] Clarke, *Liberals and Social Democrats*, esp. chs. 2–5. For an alternative view, which brings out, instead of the broader political trends of the period, a more rigorous and schematic interpretation of the New Liberalism as a holistic, organicist, and Idealist philosophy or ideology, see Michael Freeden, *The New Liberalism* (Oxford, 1978). Obviously I am not seeking to identify Keynes with these particular conceptions; see also below, ch. 4.

[12] See Skidelsky, *Hopes Betrayed*, 241.

can be characterized as 'mechanical reformists', believing that state collectivism had to be engineered from above in the interests of the working class, New Liberals can be characterized as 'moral reformists'. They should not be confused with 'moral regenerationists', who typically believed that the only thing that mattered in effecting improvement within society was a change of heart and a remoralization of individual character. But moral reformists did stress the need for the minds and hearts of the people—leaders and led alike—to be infused with the proper social spirit, because this alone sanctioned a democratic collectivism and checked the slide into an illiberal version of statism.[13] Such conceptions, it will be suggested, though sometimes deeply buried, were likewise deeply rooted in Keynes's mind. Looking at the pre-war evidence, then, it may be a moot point how much Keynes had really absorbed from the New Liberalism; but the point of lasting significance, as will be seen, is how much was to resurface in his later thinking.

Policy

In the field of policy, Keynes came with a formidable reputation behind him and a range of personal contacts which gave him an unusual entrée to the highest echelons of government. For in the First World War he had held an influential post in the Treasury, with a heavy responsibility for financing the war effort, culminating in his role as Treasury representative at the Versailles Peace Conference. The beginnings of his administrative career went further back—to 1906, when, having come second in the Civil Service examination, he went to the India Office as a junior clerk. Although he left after two years, his experience set him up for authorship of his first book, *Indian Currency and Finance* (1913), and membership of his first Royal Commission, that on Indian Finance and Currency. In doing so, moreover, it established him as an expert on the workings of the Gold Standard.

It was, however, Keynes's wartime stint in the Treasury which gave him first-hand knowledge of the making of economic policy at a high level, just as it gave him exemption from conscription, to which he maintained a conscientious objection. He rose to become the chosen adviser of Reginald McKenna as Liberal Chancellor of the

[13] For these concepts see Clarke, *Liberals and Social Democrats*, 5, 14–15, 65.

Exchequer; through McKenna he was naturally drawn into the circle of Asquith, the Prime Minister, and equally naturally drawn into factional conflict with Lloyd George, whose *bête noire* McKenna had become. It was Keynes who briefed McKenna in taking a cautious, prudent, well-buttressed view of Britain's finite economic resources; it was Lloyd George who argued instead for a bold *dirigiste* strategy to drum up further resources out of thin air.[14] When, in the late 1920s, Keynes joined Lloyd George in contesting the Treasury View, he knew whereof he spoke. On Asquith's displacement as Prime Minister by Lloyd George in December 1916, Bonar Law succeeded McKenna as Chancellor in the new Coalition Government. Perhaps unexpectedly, Keynes found that he got on well with the Conservative leader, and also with Austen Chamberlain as Chancellor in 1919.

It was not just that Keynes got to know the top politicians; he also worked cheek by jowl with Treasury colleagues, from Sir John Bradbury, the Joint-Permanent Secretary, downwards. If Keynes cannot properly be called an establishment figure, he cannot conceivably be called an anti-establishment figure. He tended to identify with the upper-crust institutions he knew—Eton, King's, Cambridge—with a team spirit that depended partly on which team he was playing for at the time. Hence his love–hate relationship with the Treasury: he loved it when he was there, he only hated it when other people were in charge. It was an élitist milieu with a distinctive style which he came to relish: 'very clever, very dry and in a certain sense very cynical; intellectually self-confident and not subject to the whims of people who feel that they are less hidden, and are not quite sure that they know their case.'[15]

Harrod defined one of 'the presuppositions of Harvey Road' as 'the idea that the government of Britain was and would continue to be in the hands of an intellectual aristocracy using the methods of persuasion'.[16] Now Keynes did not work out a formal theory of power; and if he had, it is not likely that this notion would have been more than one aspect of it—which is, to be fair, all that Harrod claimed. Although such a presupposition does help explain his view of a powerful institution like the Treasury, Keynes well recognized that 'the efficacy of intellectual processes' could not be relied upon

[14] See Skidelsky, *Hopes Betrayed*, ch. 13.
[15] *JMK* xvi. 299 ('The civil service and Treasury control', lecture, given 26 July 1921). Henry Roseveare, *The Treasury* (1969) is the standard authority.
[16] Harrod, *Life*, 192–3.

to determine the political outcome. 'Everything is always decided for some reason other than the real merits of the case, in the sphere with which I have contact,' he wrote on one occasion while still in the Treasury—betokening a condition for which the perfidy of Lloyd George can hardly have been solely responsible.[17] Keynes had more than an inkling that many things were done in the real world 'by means of the bad fairies—always so much more potent than the good',[18] Harvey Road notwithstanding.

It was over Lloyd George's policy that Keynes resigned from the Treasury in protest at the scale of reparations demanded from Germany under the Versailles Peace Treaty. In writing *The Economic Consequences of the Peace*, he made himself at a stroke the Government's most articulate critic. He spoke for the Opposition—Asquithian and Labour alike—against Lloyd George. With stinging irony, Lloyd George was admonished for his initial efforts to bamboozle—and derided for his belated attempt to debamboozle—the self-deceiving President Wilson. At the heart of Keynes's indictment was an argument about Germany's capacity to pay which was lifted from the Treasury memoranda which he had earlier prepared. He brought the issue here down to a fundamental economic point which was to reverberate through the debates of the 1920s. For the only way that Germany *could* pay—even if it were expedient to exact such payment or right to demand it—was by a transfer of resources in the form of goods. This implied that she would have to achieve a permanent surplus of exports over imports, with attendant distortions upon international trade. 'Germany can pay in the long run in goods, and in goods only,' Keynes insisted, directing attention to the centrality of the 'transfer problem'.[19]

Keynes resigned from the Civil Service in June 1919, but he remained steadfast in his support for financial rectitude. He had deplored the breakdown of Treasury control over expenditure under Lloyd George, castigating 'a government which habitually put finance last of all the relevant considerations and believed that action however wasteful is preferable to caution and criticism however justified'. This was an attitude which he deliberately reaffirmed after the war: 'Personally, I think one receives the higher possible praise in

[17] Quoted in Skidelsky, *Hopes Betrayed*, 347 (Keynes to his mother, 14 Apr. 1918).

[18] *JMK* iv. 138 (*Tract on Monetary Reform*).

[19] *JMK* ii. 118; Skidelsky, *Hopes Betrayed*, 384–91, gives a good appraisal of the book.

being described as Treasury-minded.'[20] When Keynes cited Lenin as saying that the best way to undermine the capitalist system was to debauch the currency,[21] he was not simply playing with words. That he evidently meant it can be seen from the advice he offered the Chancellor when Chamberlain sought his opinion early in 1920. Faced with an inflationary threat, Keynes opted for a stiff dose of dear money. 'K. would go for a financial crisis (doesn't believe it would lead to unemployment),' Chamberlain noted. 'Would go to whatever rate is necessary—perhaps 10%—and keep it at that for three years.'[22] Whether this had been good advice under the circumstances, Keynes himself was subsequently not sure—or, rather, sure in 1930 that he had overstated his case and equally sure in 1942 that he had not.[23] It was, at any rate, only towards the end of 1922 that he came to see deflation as the protean enemy.

Theory

Just as it needs close scrutiny to perceive that Keynes was not simply orthodox in financial policy, so it needs singular prescience to discern a departure from orthodoxy in economic theory. *The Economic Consequences of the Peace* conveys a vivid sense of the end of an era of peace, cosmopolitanism, and Free Trade: a world whose passing Keynes observed with mixed feelings but without apprehension of an economic alternative. Starting with Schumpeter, some writers have glimpsed here 'the origin of the modern stagnation thesis' and 'the embryo of the *General Theory*'.[24] For Keynes looked back on the nineteenth century as an age when the inequality in the distribution of wealth permitted a vast aggregation of capital—'like bees they

[20] *JMK* xvi. 294, 306 (Keynes to Beatrice Webb, 11 Mar. 1918; 'The civil service and Treasury control', 1921); and see Kathleen Burk, 'The Treasury: From impotence to power', in Burk (ed.), *War and the State* (1982), 84–107.

[21] *JMK* ii. 148.

[22] Quoted in Susan Howson, '"A dear money man"? Keynes on monetary policy, 1920', *Econ. Jnl.*, 83 (1973), 456–64, at 458.

[23] Contrast his comments in the Macmillan Committee, PRO, T. 200/5, private session, 31 Oct. 1930, 9; and those of 7 Jan. 1942 in T. 172/1384, quoted in Howson, '"A dear money man"?', 461–2, where the case is made that it is too simple to dismiss Keynes as 'orthodox', as Harrod does (*Life*, 294).

[24] Joseph A. Schumpeter, 'John Maynard Keynes, 1883–1946', reprinted from *Am. Econ. Rev.*, 36 (1946) in his *Ten Great Economists* (1952), 260–91, at 268; see also Schumpeter, *History of Economic Analysis* (New York, 1954), 1171; this is followed by Hession, *John Maynard Keynes*, 170.

saved and accumulated, not less to the advantage of the whole community because they themselves held narrower ends in prospect'.[25] Thus the working class was denied the possibility of consumption while the capitalist classes, who had the possibility, denied it to themselves through an ethic of deferred satisfaction. Keynes certainly hinted that these conditions could not be perpetuated, but chiefly because the poverty of the many and the puritanism of the few could no longer be relied upon to sustain the function of saving, not because that function was no longer necessary. As he wrote in 1922, in the articles from which his *Tract on Monetary Reform* was shaped, 'a growing population requires, for the maintenance of the same standard of life, a proportionate growth of capital. The favourable conditions for saving which existed in the nineteenth century, even though we smile at them, provided this proportionate growth.'[26]

Keynes had initially become an economist with the encouragement of Alfred Marshall, who held the chair of Political Economy at Cambridge from 1885 to 1908, during which time he played a paramount role in establishing the discipline in British universities and in launching the Cambridge Economics Tripos as the flagship of the enterprise. If Keynes remained a fairly faithful Marshallian until the old man's death in 1924, it was with good reason. One of Marshall's last acts before retiring had been to bring Keynes back to Cambridge from the India Office to lecture on the subject; it was from this invitation that Keynes's subsequent academic career as a Fellow of King's College and as Editor of the *Economic Journal* (1911–45) directly flowed.

After the War, to be sure, Keynes chose to become a Supernumerary Fellow of King's (unpaid), spending only part of the week in Cambridge (usually Saturday, Sunday, and Monday), and the rest of the time at his London home, 46 Gordon Square, Bloomsbury (with a country home, too, at Tilton in Sussex, after his marriage). He was not a full-time don, busy with routine teaching; he never became a Professor and used a standard disclaimer—about not accepting the title without the emoluments—to fend off this style of address. (That it was sometimes used, however, shows how he was perceived, and it is a solecism perpetrated in the course of this book.) Cambridge, moreover, was not then a university with a strong

---

[25] *JMK* ii. 11.
[26] *JMK* iv. 28 n. (*Manchester Guardian*, Reconstruction Supplement, 27 July 1922); cf. the final text of the *Tract*, ibid. 6, 16, 29–30.

institutional association between colleagues working physically alongside each other in departmental offices. For Keynes, Cambridge meant, above all, King's, to which his most immediate service was as First Bursar from 1924. (The endowment fructified.) It was there that his Political Economy Club met on a Monday evening. Earlier the same day, Keynes might have delivered a university lecture—he generally gave a course of eight each year—which was his only formal contribution to the teaching of the Economics Faculty.[27] If he was less often *in* Cambridge, however, he was quintessentially *of* Cambridge—and seen as such.

Throughout his life, the way Keynes referred to his early training in economics was as an orthodoxy on which he was 'brought up'. It was a slightly playful term, allowing him to reprimand others who had not been properly brought up, as well as implying a sense of filial piety. For his father J. N. Keynes was also an economist, and a Fellow of Pembroke College, Cambridge; in a sense, young Maynard absorbed his earliest understanding of the subject at his father's table, to which Professor and Mrs Marshall were frequent visitors. It was 'a small cultured society of great simplicity and distinction', Keynes recalled. 'This circle was at its full strength in my boyhood, and, when I was first old enough to be asked out to luncheon or to dinner, it was to these houses that I went.'[28] When Marshall retired from the chair, he was succeeded by A. C. Pigou, Fellow of King's College, then a youthful and athletic figure, in contrast to the physically broken donnish pedant who was still 'the Prof.' in the 1920s and 1930s. The books of Marshall and Pigou were, as Keynes explained to German readers in 1933, 'those English works on which I have been brought up and with which I am most familiar'.[29]

Marshall's *Principles of Economics*, first published in 1890, was intended and received as an authoritative exposition of 'neo-classical'

---

[27] This paragraph draws particularly on Robinson, 'John Maynard Keynes', 26–35, 49–50, and the percipient (Canadian) perspectives on the Cambridge academic environment in Patinkin and Leith (eds.), *Keynes, Cambridge and the General Theory*, 65–6 (D. E. Moggridge) and 98–114 (Harry Johnson). Like the *General Theory*'s allusions to 'classical' economics (*JMK* vii. 3 n.), the solecism of 'Professor Keynes' is deliberately and unrepentantly perpetrated below when it serves the purposes of this book.

[28] *JMK* x. 213 ('Alfred Marshall').

[29] *JMK* xiii. 409 ('A monetary theory of production'). See the useful essay by David Collard, 'A. C. Pigou, 1877–1959', in D. P. O'Brien and John R. Presley (eds.), *Pioneers of Modern Economics in Britain* (1981), 105–39, and the *DNB* entry by E. A. G. Robinson.

economics. How Keynes viewed his mentor's *œuvre* is made clear in
the obituary essay which he wrote in 1924. In it he noted 'the
painstaking,   complete,   ultra-conscientious,   ultra-unsensational
methods of Marshall'. Yet this characteristic method—'The author
furnished his ideas with no labels of salesmanship and few hooks for
them to hang by in the wardrobe of the mind'—had serious disadvantages when it came to impressing the heuristic force of the
concepts upon the student. Pigou notoriously used to claim that 'it's
all in Marshall', with a self-deprecating gesture of deference towards
his mighty achievement. Keynes, even in 1924, took a rather
different view—in effect, that if everything is in Marshall, nothing is
in Marshall: 'How often has it not happened even to those who have
been brought up on the *Principles*, lighting upon what seems a new
problem or a solution, to go back to it and to find, after all, that the
problem and a better solution have been always there, *yet quite
escaping notice!*'[30]

Only after Keynes had taken the Mathematics Tripos—he was
Twelfth Wrangler in 1905—did he formally turn to economics. (Even
thereafter his own research was on the theory of probability.) Keynes
had eight weeks' supervision from Marshall but did not take the new
Economics Tripos. He picked up the subject somewhat unsystemati-
cally, and as much through personal contact as close application to
the literature. As Keynes put it in 1924, 'there grew up at Cambridge
an oral tradition, first from Marshall's own lectures and after his
retirement from those of Professor Pigou, different from, and (I
think it may be claimed) superior to, anything that could be found in
printed books until recently.' Moreover, when it came to the crucial
theory of interest, the *locus classicus*, beyond Marshall's *Principles*,
was his printed evidence before the Royal Commission on Gold and
Silver in 1887–8. 'It was an odd state of affairs', Keynes conceded,
'that one of the most fundamental parts of Monetary Theory should,
for about a quarter of a century, have been available to students
nowhere except embedded in the form of question-and-answer before
a Government Commission interested in a transitory practical
problem.'[31] (It was as though Keynes himself never actually
published his *Treatise* and modern readers were left to glean his
insights only from his evidence to the Macmillan Committee.) In
arguing over these dog-eared texts—'I have my copy still, scored all

[30] *JMK* x. 184, 212 (emphasis supplied).
[31] Ibid. 189, 192.

over!'—the Keynes of 1936 ultimately wearied of his colleagues' response 'that Marshall related it all to a Royal Commission in an affirmative sigh';[32] but this state of affairs was indicative of the dependence of Cambridge economics upon a doctrine which had been more often handed down than written down.

Even in his encomium of 1924, Keynes did not seek to found the superiority of the Cambridge oral tradition upon the lucidity of Marshall's lectures—'Certainly in 1906, when I attended them, it was impossible to bring away coherent notes.' Instead, he claimed that Marshall propagated a humane conception of the subject which did not suppose that 'the bare bones of economic theory' were sufficient in themselves: 'The whole point lies in applying them to the interpretation of current economic life.' Hence the *combination* of gifts— as 'mathematician, historian, statesman, philosopher'—which made a good economist such a rare bird. 'An easy subject, at which very few excel!'[33] It should be appreciated that, at the time of this comment, Keynes's only substantial scholarly work was in another field—his formidably rigorous *Treatise on Probability* (1921).

Specifically, Marshall had made his 'general theory of economic equilibrium' into a strong and effective 'organon of thought' by generalizing from his ideas about the determination of value. In his most famous metaphor, it may be recalled, Marshall had shown that supply and demand *jointly* determined market price at the margin by intersecting like the two blades of a pair of scissors—the basis of many a subsequent diagram at the academic chalkface. Keynes claimed, in his essay, that it was Marshall's achievement 'to discover a whole Copernican system, by which all the elements of the economic universe are kept in their place by mutual counterpoise and interaction'.[34] The process of equilibration, in short, could be discovered working through the economy, subsuming the parts in the whole. This is what Keynes suggested in 1924, at a time when he accepted that, given flexible prices, there were deep-rooted and pervasive natural tendencies working towards equilibrium. It is what

[32] *JMK* xiv. 94 and n. 4 (Keynes to Robertson, 13 Dec. 1936).

[33] *JMK* x. 216, 196, 173. 'Marshall's imperial vision of the subject'—too grandiose even for his own pupils—is brought out well in Stefan Collini, Donald Winch, and John Burrow, *That Noble Science of Politics* (Cambridge, 1983), 309–37, at 336.

[34] *JMK* x. 205–6. This is not to say that Keynes found in Marshall the rigorous conception of general equilibrium associated with Walras; and the impressionistic account of Marshall here can be corrected by reference to the excellent introduction to his thought in Winch, *Economics and Policy*, 36–50, 54–7.

he meant, looking at this conception from another angle in 1933, when he pointed to 'the fact that all our ideas about economics, instilled into us by education and atmosphere and tradition are, whether we are conscious of it or not, soaked with theoretical presuppositions which are only properly applicable to a society which is in equilibrium, with all its productive resources already employed'.[35]

It is always hazardous to articulate implicit assumptions, but a simple version of the Marshallian model may be understood as follows:

All resources are employed because markets clear—every willing seller finds a buyer. So everything that is for sale or hire is in fact sold or hired—or, if it is not, it is because of some obstruction which prevents these transactions from taking place. This is achieved through flexibility of prices. The higgling of the market is axiomatically capable of finding a point at which supply and demand are brought into equilibrium. If there is excess supply, it simply means that the price is too high, and that it will have to be reduced to the going rate in order to take up the slack. Thus, other things being equal, unemployment is a signal that the price of labour is too high: it is axiomatic that, at lower wages, the market will clear. If the reward of labour is constrained by the current level of productivity, so is the reward of capital. Investment depends on saving. It is the job of interest rate to find a level which offers sufficient stimulus to each of them so as to bring their levels into equilibrium—a rate which will constitute at once an affordable burden to productivity and an adequate incentive to thrift. Without saving, investment cannot take place; but with thrift, enterprise will flourish.

In view of his upbringing, it is not surprising that Keynes's own ideas, until well beyond the First World War, were soaked with the theoretical presupposition of equilibration through compensating adjustments of price within a self-righting system. But theoretical presuppositions govern theory; they do not necessarily prescribe policy in the real world of practical experience. In his *Tract on Monetary Reform* (1923), Keynes referred to the quantity theory of money—the doctrine that, provided the public's behaviour about holding money does not change, the price level will rise and fall with the money supply. 'This theory is fundamental,' he wrote. 'Its correspondence with fact is not open to question.' Yet he saw no inconsistency in coupling a citation of Marshall on the way it ultimately operated with an advocacy of immediate policy measures of his own devising. 'Economists set themselves too easy, too useless

[35] *JMK* ix. 350 (*The Means to Prosperity*).

a task,' Keynes commented, 'if in tempestuous seasons they can only tell us that when the storm is long past the ocean is flat again.' This is the context for his most frequently quoted—and most frequently travestied—dictum: that 'this *long run* is a misleading guide to current affairs. *In the long run* we are all dead'.[36]

Obviously Keynes did not mean that economists should ignore the long-term consequences of their advice—harping on the 'economic consequences' of policy acts was practically his stock in trade. But in the real world of hard choices, under conditions which rarely approximated to the frictionless postulates of theory, Keynes maintained that painful difficulties could not be wished away by describing them as short-run problems of adjustment. A doctrinaire might wash his hands—exalting economic theory into what Weber calls an 'ethic of ultimate ends'—but this was alien to the Cambridge school's 'ethic of responsibility' in political economy, shared by Marshall and Pigou and Keynes alike.

The *Tract* was a plea for monetary stability through a managed currency. Whereas the conventional view was that such stability could best be assured through a return to the Gold Standard, Keynes favoured engineering stability in internal not external values. Internal price stability, in a changing world, implied that the parity of sterling would be subject to adjustment through constant intervention by the central banks. Keynes was confident that the currency could be managed. The alternative was to fix the parity, as under the Gold Standard, and rely on a natural process of adjustment to bring all domestic prices into line. But could this be managed? 'Theoretically, of course, the pre-war method must be able to make itself effective sooner or later,' Keynes conceded, 'provided the movement of gold is allowed to continue without restriction, until the inflation or deflation of prices has taken place to the necessary extent.'[37] But such price movements, he now maintained, were capable of inflicting great injuries. The effect of inflation was worse upon the distribution of wealth, that of deflation worse upon its production. The sharp inflation of the immediate post-war years had driven this point home; and the succeeding deflation had accordingly become the debilitating problem of the period since 1920.

---

[36] *JMK* iv. 61, 65. On the persistence of a Marshallian framework in Keynes's thought right up to the *Tract* see D. E. Moggridge and Susan Howson, 'Keynes on monetary policy, 1910–46', *Oxford Econ. Papers*, NS 26 (1974), 226–47, esp. 226–7, 232–3.   [37] *JMK* iv. 130.

Keynes was beginning to draw together several strands of analysis, faced with the persistent under-performance of the British economy. Throughout the 1920s, Britain was exporting capital. The only means by which such resources could be physically transferred abroad was in the form of surplus exports—goods or services for which no immediate remittance was received in Britain because instead their value was left to accumulate abroad as an investment. Surely, in a well-ordered system, this should have stimulated her export industries to operate, like those of pre-war Germany 'continuously and at full blast'?[38] Yet the fact was that, after the collapse of the inflationary boom in 1920, unemployment was rife. The official figures showed over 20 per cent out of work in the spring of 1921, and at the beginning of 1924 the proportion was still over 10 per cent. Did Britain perhaps have her own transfer problem? Was the flow of capital abroad at the expense of investment at home? By 1924 such questions were in Keynes's mind, and he directed attention particularly to the workings of the Trustee Acts which, he alleged, through their discriminatory provisions, artificially siphoned off British capital in loans to the Empire.[39]

At the same time, Keynes broadened the issue by publishing in the *Nation* an article entitled, 'Does unemployment need a drastic remedy?' Harrod was surely right to claim that Keynes here gave 'the outline of the public policy which has since been specifically associated with his name'.[40] For the thrust of these proposals was to advocate a reorientation which amounted to hardly less than a revolution in economic policy. Why?

[38] *JMK* ii. 7.

[39] The nub of this argument is stated in the *Nation*, Aug. 1924, and reiterated in Keynes's evidence to the Colwyn Committee on National Debt and Taxation, Oct. 1924: see *JMK* xix. 279, 317.

[40] The articles are quoted at length and discussed in Harrod, *Life*, 345 ff., comment at 350; see *JMK* xix. 219–30, and below, ch. 4 nn. 9–10.

PART II

Sound Finance

PROLOGUE TO PART II

Even after the disruptive experience of the First World War, the economic role of the state was conceived in terms which had become canonical in the late nineteenth century. The Treasury and the Bank of England saw themselves as guardians of sound finance—a Gladstonian heritage which they invested with moral rectitude as well as economic rationality. Budgets had to be balanced; the parity of the pound sterling had to be maintained so that it was 'as good as gold'; Free Trade had to be preserved. Only by elevating these interlocking policies into matters of principle could they be rendered 'knave-proof'—that is, made safe from the meddling of opportunistic politicians and from short-sighted attempts to snatch illusory benefits. For sound finance depended on taking a long view and giving the market mechanisms time to adjust. Much the same conception can be found in the Treasury View of the late 1920s, as promulgated by Churchill as Conservative Chancellor of the Exchequer. The idea of using public works to alleviate unemployment presented an obvious temptation; but the Treasury, under the tutelage of its house economist R. G. Hawtrey, maintained that such a course embodied a demonstrable fallacy. The strength of the doctrine is shown by the fact that it was not only deployed against the proposals of the Opposition, notably the Liberal party, but also enforced against true-blue Conservative initiatives for development schemes. The authorities' principled commitment to sound finance in the late 1920s is thus no myth and the Treasury View was, as Keynes suggested, a crucial barrier against the adoption of an active policy to tackle unemployment.

2

Rigid doctrines and flexible prices

Balanced budgets

In his Romanes Lecture at Oxford in June 1930, Winston Churchill took the opportunity of reflecting upon the recent intrusion of the economic problem into politics. 'Before the War the issues fought out in Parliament were political and social,' he claimed. 'The parties fought one another heartily in a series of well-known stock and conventional quarrels, and the life of the nation proceeded underneath this agitated froth.'[1] In taking a retrospective view of the sudden end of a golden age, Churchill was to some extent vulnerable to a common hazard: that of the dissolving perspective which telescopes and exaggerates discontinuity. After all, in the pre-war years, he had himself prominently championed the New Liberalism as bringing 'a reality and a seriousness' into politics because of the new issues—'They are great class and they are great economic and social issues'—which it took up.[2] Yet the welfare politics of the Edwardian period, with a rhetoric of social justice and redistribution, were essentially micro-economic (apart from Hobsonian under-consumption). It was the new macro-economic dimension, concerning the functioning and performance of the economy as a whole, to which Churchill now rightly drew attention.

Churchill was in a unique position to appreciate the political impact, having held ministerial office for all but five years of the previous quarter-century; he had served promiscuously in Liberal, Coalition, and Conservative Governments, culminating in a tenure of the Treasury for the length of a full parliament—more than twice as long as any other Chancellor since 1914. His account of the prevailing conventions thus reflects the seasoned judgement of a shrewd and versatile insider, with comparable experience of half a dozen government departments from the point of view of more than one party interest:[3]

---

[1] 'Parliamentary government and the economic problem', in W. S. Churchill, *Thoughts and Adventures* (1932), 174.

[2] See P. F. Clarke, *Lancashire and the New Liberalism* (Cambridge, 1971), 358–60.

[3] *Thoughts and Adventures*, 176.

The classical doctrines of economics have for nearly a century found their citadels in the Treasury and the Bank of England. In their pristine vigour these doctrines comprise among others the following tenets: Free imports, irrespective of what other countries may do and heedless of the consequences to any particular native industry or interest. Ruthless direct taxation for the repayment of debt without regard to the effects of such taxation upon individuals or their enterprise or initiative. Rigorous economy in all forms of expenditure whether social or military. Stern assertion of the rights of the creditor, national or private, and full and effectual discharge of all liabilities. Profound distrust of State-stimulated industry in all its forms, or of State borrowing for the purpose of creating employment. Absolute reliance upon private enterprise, unfettered and unfavoured by the State.

Churchill was surely right to say that these principles were 'all part of one general economic conception', to which the authorities—the Treasury and the Bank—were fundamentally committed. They therefore worked together to safeguard, with vigilance and steadfastness, the three pillars of sound finance: balanced budgets, the Gold Standard, and Free Trade.

Official advice reached the Chancellor of the Exchequer from a select group of senior officials. The Permanent Secretary to the Treasury throughout the 1920s and 1930s was Sir Warren Fisher, who saw his role as that of head of the home Civil Service, which he largely succeeded in unifying and subordinating to overall Treasury control. The result was that he became the confidant of the Prime Minister rather than of the Chancellor, and, in Churchill's first year in office, as much as three months might pass without them even meeting. Churchill, who had clearly been unprepared for this conception of the Permanent Secretary's responsibilities, responded by dismissing Fisher's occasional efforts to formulate Treasury policy on the grounds that 'I do not consider that such fitful interventions on your part rest upon a sufficiently solid foundation of aid and guidance.'[4] The crucial post for advising the Chancellor on all financial matters was therefore that of the Controller of Finance, held from 1922 by Sir Otto Niemeyer. Niemeyer had had a gilded career since coming out top in the Civil Service examinations in 1906—Keynes came second—and was only thirty-nine on appointment. The fly in the ointment was that Fisher was a mere four years older; the masterful Niemeyer could hardly hope to succeed him yet

---

[4] Churchill to Fisher, 1 Dec. 1925, in Martin Gilbert, *Winston S. Churchill* v, Companion Pt. I (1979), 600–3; and see E. O'Halpin, 'Sir Warren Fisher, head of the civil service', Ph.D. thesis (Cambridge, 1982).

chafed under his suzerainty. In 1927 this incipient conflict came to a head and Niemeyer left to join the Bank of England, with which he had formed notably cordial relations.

Niemeyer's successor as Controller of Finance (with which Supply was now combined) was Sir Richard Hopkins, widely known as 'Hoppy', and an altogether less abrasive figure. Instead of Niemeyer's doctrinaire views on sound finance, Hopkins exhibited a layman's readiness to learn from the economists while diluting their propositions with wholesome draughts of pragmatism. 'It seems useless to endeavour to follow professional economic teaching,' he once minuted, 'for there is no criterion for determining the proper economists to follow, and whoever one chooses, one is apt to find oneself led into actions which are either repugnant to common sense or incapable of practical achievement.'[5] Hopkins's experience had been in the Inland Revenue department, where he had worked fruitfully with the taxation expert Sir Josiah Stamp, and it seems to have taken him a little time to find his feet at the Treasury. Not until 1930 did he fully establish his authority, and there are indications of a suppressed rivalry with his deputy F. W. Leith-Ross, which was only finally resolved with the latter's appointment as the Government's chief economic adviser in 1932. For Leith-Ross, Niemeyer was the great model public servant, to be bracketed alongside Sir John Bradbury (Lord Bradbury from 1925), who had been Fisher's predecessor as Permanent Secretary.[6] When Bradbury held office as Principal British Representative on the Reparation Commission, 1920–5, Leith-Ross had happily served under him as an interlude in his Treasury career. With Niemeyer and Leith-Ross, Keynes was never wholly easy, whereas Hopkins escaped many of his characteristic strictures upon the Treasury.

These were the men principally responsible for advising Churchill as Chancellor. They were later joined by F. W. Phillips, who rose to be Assistant Controller in 1931 and was thereafter Hopkins's closest

[5] Quoted in Susan Howson, *Domestic Monetary Management in Britain, 1919–38* (Cambridge, 1975), 91, which is an extremely helpful and reliable guide. For Niemeyer, see the *DNB* entry by Lord Cobbold; for Hopkins, the *DNB* entry by Wilfrid Eady and the anonymous appreciation by a former colleague in *Public Admin.*, 34 (1956), 115–23; G. C. Peden, 'Sir Richard Hopkins and the "Keynesian Revolution" in employment policy, 1929–45', *Econ. Hist. Rev.*, NS 36 (1983), 281–96, is invaluable on his later career.

[6] See F. W. Leith-Ross, *Money Talks* (1968), esp. 106, 144–5; and *DNB* entry by Harold Parker. For Bradbury see *DNB* entry by R. G. Hawtrey.

coadjutor. In addition, R. G. Hawtrey was employed as Director of Financial Inquiries. An old friend of Keynes as an Apostle at Cambridge, Hawtrey was the only professional economist in the Treasury; he was used as a consultant, and his lack of administrative talent meant that he was somewhat patronized by his colleagues. One of them, however, has recalled that the restless autodidact Churchill wanted Hawtrey given more scope and would periodically demand 'that the learned man should be released from the dungeon in which we were said to have immured him, have his chains struck off and the straw brushed from his hair and clothes and be admitted to the light and warmth of an argument in the Treasury board room with the greatest living master of argument'.[7] In this and other reminiscences, P. J. Grigg conveys an instructive impression of the tone and manner of the informal exchanges between the authorities and their political master, the Chancellor, whose private secretary he became in 1924. The somewhat testy Grigg established a strong rapport with Leith-Ross, with whom he shared a Gladstonian Liberal outlook and a passionate attachment to the principles of sound finance. Much Treasury advice in the late 1920s was mediated through these two.

The Treasury saw its task in terms of public finance not economic management. In a memorandum of 1925 Niemeyer declared:[8]

The objects of our financial policy since the Armistice have been:
1. To balance the Budget out of revenue.
2. To reduce the debt.
3. To reduce public expenditure and in consequence to remit taxation.

In fact, the Treasury's priorities ran in inverse order: the point was to achieve a balanced budget on Gladstonian lines, by retrenchment, not on Lloyd Georgian lines by piling up ingenious new taxes. In enforcing this strategy, the Treasury's secret weapon had been the concept of the 'normal year'. First evolved in 1915, when McKenna was Chancellor, the normal year was initially defined by the level of expenditure considered normal during the pre-war period. This had

---

[7] P. J. Grigg, *Prejudice and Judgement* (1948), 82; *DNB* entry on Grigg by H. F. Oxbury and on Hawtrey by R. D. C. Black. There are useful biographical notes in Howson and Winch, *EAC* 371–81.

[8] Draft for the Prime Minister, 26 June 1925, T. 176/21; and see G. C. Peden, 'The Treasury as the central department of government, 1919–39', *Public Admin.*, 61 (1983), 371–85. The rest of this section is heavily indebted to the important study by Mary Short, 'The politics of personal taxation: Budget-making in Britain, 1917–31', Ph.D. thesis (Cambridge, 1985), esp. chs. 1, 4, and 5.

to be covered by taxation, as did debt charges; but the costs of the war were to be met by borrowing. The normal year was thus a means of clinging to Gladstonian principles in a world turned upside down, by ensuring that within a grossly unbalanced budget lay a balanced one. In the spring of 1919, however, the definition of the normal year was shifted from the historic expenditure of government during the last peacetime year to the projected revenue from that historic level of taxation during a hypothetical post-war year. Instead of it setting the amount of taxation to be raised—with any expenditure above this floor being financed from borrowing—it now set a ceiling on the amount of revenue available, with the implication that spending programmes must be cut to balance the budget. Austen Chamberlain may have entered 11 Downing Street in 1919 confiding that 'the old Gladstonian Treasury tradition was quite unsuited to the moment',[9] but in making the normal year the standard for post-war expenditure he soon belied his words. Treasury control, in short, shackled the Lloyd George Coalition from its earliest months after the Coupon Election.

There was, however, a significant twist in the story, which came when Sir Robert Horne succeeded Chamberlain in 1921. Horne was primarily a businessman in politics, an ideological Coalitionist who, despite his Conservative party label, owed his rise to Lloyd George. Faced with the fact that the slump was more than a temporary recession, he prepared a budget for 1922 which deliberately rejected the precepts of the normal year. Debt charges were an inescapable burden for all post-war Chancellors, eating up more than a third of their revenues. Horne's radical proposition was to cut taxes rather than give priority to the redemption of the debt through the sinking fund. The Treasury officials regarded this as budgeting for a deficit by resorting to an expedient which they deeply regretted. Niemeyer later explained that he did 'not want to have elasticity' over the provision for the sinking fund: 'It is putting temptation in the way of the Treasury to which they had much better not be subjected.'[10] In overruling his officials in 1922, Horne was impressed by the contrary argument, of which the ex-Chancellor McKenna had made himself the mouthpiece, that the limit of taxable capacity had been reached; under the circumstances of depression, the 1922 Budget statement

---

[9] Quoted in Short, 'Politics of personal taxation', 29.

[10] Quoted in Howson, *Domestic Monetary Management*, 42; and see Short, 'Politics of personal taxation', ch. 4.

declared that it would 'offend against no sound canon of finance' to reduce the burden on industry in this way.[11] In fact, the out-turn of the budget was an unexpected surplus of over £100 million, which satisfied everyone.

Well might Horne assure Neville Chamberlain in 1931 that 'balancing yr budget is not everything: you must balance it in the right way'.[12] Phillips of the Treasury admitted in 1936 that 'there is no great technical difficulty in producing for a series of years budgets which are balanced at the end of the year to the nearest penny'.[13] It was in this spirit that Churchill approached budget-making. He had been against 'financial prudery' in the 1922 Cabinet, and from 1924 to 1929 he indulged a positively Victorian taste for licence under the cover of humbug. There was little real effort to wipe out the debt, and a series of revenue dodges—a windfall from Schedule A, a raid on the Road Fund, another raid on the Road Fund—helped him paper over the cracks. Churchill was capable of washing away his financial sins, however, by simultaneously preaching to the bankers about 'those sound principles that you have to pay your debts, you have to balance your Budget'.[14] Philip Snowden, Chancellor in the two Labour Governments, would no more have dreamt of budgeting for a deficit than of going into a public house; Churchill was constantly taking the pledge because he knew himself to be so susceptible to temptation. Niemeyer's aim was to paint the Chancellor into a corner with ineluctable commitments. If the balanced budget convention was ultimately an ideological constraint rather than a financial discipline, it was one to which the Treasury firmly clung in the late 1920s and with which they periodically chastised their profligate master. They knew, moreover, that they could appeal from Winston drunk to Winston sober.

The Gold Standard

Before 1914, sterling had been 'as good as gold' for three reasons. In the first place, the pound could be freely converted into gold at a

---

[11] Quoted in Short, 'Politics of personal taxation', 184.   [12] Ibid. 168.
[13] Quoted in Howson, *Domestic Monetary Management*, 123; also in Roger Middleton, *Towards the Managed Economy* (1985), 82, which has a perceptive discussion of budgetary orthodoxy, 83–92, largely reprinted from his earlier article, 'The Treasury in the 1930s: Political and administrative constraints to acceptance of the "new" economics', *Oxford Econ. Papers*, NS 34 (1982), 48–77.
[14] Quoted in Short, 'Politics of personal taxation', 176, 209.

fixed official price of £3.17s.10½d. an ounce (and gold into pounds at £3.17s.9d. an ounce). Second, private citizens were free to import and export gold, thus ensuring that the authorities could not flout 'the rules of the game' by sitting tight. Finally, the domestic money supply was directly linked to the Bank of England's gold reserves. As Bradbury put it: 'The "gold" pound pre-supposes an automatic increase in the number of pounds in circulation whenever gold is worth less than £3.17s.10½d. an ounce and an automatic diminution whenever it rises above that figure.'[15] The exchange rate was thus fixed to that of any other country which was similarly on the Gold Standard: notably against the American dollar at $4.86 to the pound.

If total British receipts were insufficient to meet total payments due across the exchanges, there would be an outflow of gold; and likewise if British capital investment abroad exceeded the level of export surplus required to transfer it. The Bank of England would thus be required to take corrective action, notably through changing its discount rate ('Bank rate'). An outflow of gold should in principle reduce the quantity of money in circulation, and hence have some effect in deflating sterling prices. More important, the Bank rate would be raised to protect the reserves, by attracting gold from overseas. Before the First World War, the Bank managed this system with little difficulty, basically because of Britain's strong international market position; as long as there was an underlying surplus, changes in Bank rate tended only to trim its size by temporarily repatriating funds. The fluctuations were small ones, easily adjusted within the margin on international financial flows.

In the post-war situation, when the decline of British exports had eroded the surplus, the effects of the Bank rate upon the domestic economy were more far-reaching. By 1931 the Macmillan Report provided the received version of a four-stage process whereby a deficit was corrected through dear money.[16] First, a higher Bank rate attracted funds which would otherwise have gone abroad, and had an immediately favourable effect on the balance of payments and the reserves. In the second stage, the real economy was affected, through

---

[15] Quoted in D. E. Moggridge, *British Monetary Policy, 1924–31* (Cambridge, 1972), 275; this is the standard work, on which I have implicitly relied. See also the useful guide by Barry Eichengreen (ed.), *The Gold Standard in Theory and History* (1985), esp. 3–4, 9–12, 16–19; and R. S. Sayers, *The Bank of England, 1891–1944* (Cambridge, 1976), 47 ff.

[16] *Macmillan Report*, Cmd. 3897 (1931), par. 215; and see below, ch. 5 n. 20.

a reduction in demand which made room for more exports and directly curtailed imports—both tending to reinforce the move towards a payments surplus. In the third stage, moreover, there was further assistance to the balance of trade from the reduction in prices which the curtailment in enterprise had brought about, meaning that goods in production were sold off at the expense of profits. The fourth stage, however, was crucial. For production at lower prices would only be continued at a loss on a temporary basis, and a corresponding reduction in costs, especially wages, was necessary to put the improvement upon a more durable basis. The Gold Standard mechanism thus depended upon correcting disequilibrium through a flexible adjustment of prices, notably wages, instigated by changes in Bank rate.

Responsibility for managing this system rested with the Bank of England. 'Before the outbreak of the War,' Bradbury recollected, as the former Permanent Secretary to the Treasury, 'we certainly never regarded ourselves as entitled to meddle or even ask questions.' Niemeyer was characteristically trenchant in saying that 'a change in bank rate was no more regarded as the business of the Treasury than the colour which the Bank painted its front door'.[17] Although this was the formal position, informal contacts between the authorities had often been a good deal closer, depending on personal relations. Leith-Ross chose to stress the asymmetrical nature of this consultation—that it was only 'on Treasury matters'[18]—but it is clear that these links were steadily institutionalized in the late 1920s under the governorship of Montagu Norman.

Norman held office for the unprecedented span of twenty-four years. First elected in 1920, his appointment was repeatedly renewed despite the psychosomatic difficulties which crippled him at times of stress. Fastidious and aloof, he was seldom in the public eye until the return to gold in 1925, and made little effort to appease the curiosity of the press thereafter. When his habit of booking his frequent trans-atlantic passages under the name of his secretary, Skinner, became known, it fostered his image as a man of mystery. Under Norman, the Bank moved decisively towards a central banking role, but it

---

[17] Bradbury to Phillips, 18 Feb. 1929; Niemeyer to Phillips, 18 Feb. 1929, T. 176/13; this is a useful file on Bank–Treasury relations.

[18] Macmillan Committee, private session, 30 Oct. 1930, 29, T. 200/5; see also Sir Ernest Harvey's statement of the position, *Macmillan Evidence* (1931), Q. 454. Sayers, *Bank of England*, esp. chs. 6–9 and 22, is the authoritative history.

was part of his conception of a central bank that it should have private shareholders, to insulate it from government control. His view of 'the advantages of benevolent despotism over democracy' was convincingly interpreted by a friendly financial journalist:[19]

The situation can best be compared to that of the shareholders of a company, who would like to obtain the distribution of the full profits in dividends, while the board, which is aware of the possibility of lean years, favours the distribution of a moderate dividend. Although the directors may not be popular among the rank and file of the shareholders, in reality they safeguard the shareholders' interests against the latter's own short-sightedness. In our case the shareholders are the electorate, and the dividends are the prospects of increased business activity through the adoption of an inflationary policy.

So far as Norman was concerned, he was the trustee of the public interest, which ultimately rested with a return to the principles of 'unadulterated sound money' as soon as post-war exigencies allowed.[20] 'The Gold Standard', he assured Churchill, 'is the best "Governor" that can be devised for a world that is still human, rather than divine.'[21] He may not have been indifferent to the effects of his policy upon unemployment, but he did not regard this as falling within his responsibilities. 'Social and political matters are no direct concern of the Bank,' was how one of his colleagues put it. 'The Bank disapprove of all the politicians but can't do anything about it.'[22]

Such feelings were heartily reciprocated by Churchill, whose private suspicion of 'that man Skinner' and his policy was fed by his crony Lord Beaverbrook, the proprietor of *Express* newspapers. But Norman was not without friends in the Treasury. His relations with Bradbury, Niemeyer, Hopkins, Leith-Ross, and Grigg were all notably cordial. Indeed this explains why a berth was found for Niemeyer at the Bank in 1927 when the Treasury became un-congenial, and his translation opened new channels since he continued to receive a number of official papers from his old

---

[19] Paul Einzig, *Montagu Norman* (1932), 82, 171; for Einzig see his autobiography, *In the Centre of Things* (1960), esp. 136–8 and the *DNB* entry by C. Gordon Tether. On Norman see the hostile account in John Hargrave, *Professor Skinner alias Montagu Norman*, n.d. (?1939), the official life by Henry Clay, *Lord Norman* (1957), and the more subjective study by Andrew Boyle, *Montagu Norman* (1967).

[20] Clay, *Norman*, 122.

[21] Quoted in Moggridge, *British Monetary Policy*, 272.

[22] J. A. C. Osborne, questions (?July 1930), Bank of England, EID 1/2; cf. Clay *Norman*, 166–7.

colleagues. The Governor's diary shows that he would have lunch every Friday with either Hopkins or Leith-Ross to settle Treasury Bill tenders; and Norman took to dropping in virtually every day to see Hopkins—and Grigg, too, two or three times a week—so that the sight of his car outside the Treasury at about six o'clock each evening became routine. Under Philip Snowden, whom the officials regarded as their favourite Chancellor, the circle of mutual confidence and respect between the Bank and the Treasury became complete.

Less formally, the Tuesday Club, which met monthly to discuss financial topics, was a select forum in which the official mind (Niemeyer, Hopkins, and Leith-Ross all belonged) could encounter 'a good many heterodox opinions' from other members like Keynes and McKenna.[23] This was, in fact, much the kind of group in which Churchill liked to subject the advice he was proffered to independent scrutiny, as indicated by the manner in which he approached the crucial decision over the Gold Standard in 1925. Grigg has left an account of a dinner party in March 1925 at which the Chancellor got Niemeyer and Bradbury to state the case in favour of return, while Keynes, supported by McKenna, argued against. Bradbury's phrase about the Gold Standard being 'knave-proof' made a great impression on Grigg, who helped put it into general currency.[24]

From his close observation of Churchill at work, Grigg concluded that he manifested 'a great hankering to be considered orthodox';[25] but his method was to thrash out the pros and cons in the rough and tumble of argument rather than simply bow to official opinion. Thus he presented his advisers with a string of searching criticisms of the Gold Standard orthodoxy while declaring himself 'ready and anxious to be convinced as far as my limited comprehension of these extremely technical matters will permit'.[26] The official advice he received was such as no prudent politician—certainly not one still conscious of carrying the can for Gallipoli—would have overridden.[27]

[23] Niemeyer to Hopkins, 19 Apr. 1928, Bank of England, OV/9; cf. Leith-Ross, *Money Talks*, 147–8.

[24] Grigg, *Prejudice and Judgement*, 182–3; for these discussions see Moggridge, *British Monetary Policy*, ch. 3.

[25] Grigg, *Prejudice and Judgement*, 195.

[26] Quoted in Moggridge, *British Monetary Policy*, 262.

[27] As First Lord of the Admiralty in 1915, Churchill was responsible for the Dardanelles operation, which was pursued despite lack of support from Lord Fisher as First Sea Lord—the proper source of professional advice. Perhaps unfairly, Churchill was widely held personally culpable for the ensuing casualties at Gallipoli. It was a major setback to his career and the taunt pursued him.

The small but distinguished committee set up to examine the issue in 1924 had included Austen Chamberlain (as a former Chancellor), Bradbury, Niemeyer, and Pigou. Their final report, unanimously in favour of an early return to gold, reached the Chancellor in February 1925, supplemented by supporting memoranda from Niemeyer, Norman, Bradbury, and Hawtrey.

'I firmly believe that a balanced Budget is the beginning of sound credit and currency,' Niemeyer wrote; 'but it is equally true to say that unless you have a sound credit policy you can't maintain a balanced Budget.' Under the Gold Standard, the necessity of using the Bank rate to discipline the domestic economy would be inescapable. A return to gold at $4.86—the only parity seriously considered—would no doubt involve squeezing down British prices through dear money, which industry would not welcome. (Sir Robert Horne had impressed this point upon the Chamberlain–Bradbury committee.) But both Niemeyer and Norman rejected Churchill's suggestion of a conflict of interest between industry and finance. 'The real antithesis is rather between the long view and the short view,' Niemeyer explained. 'Bankers on the whole take longer views than manufacturers.' Norman considered that 'the merchant, manufacturer, workman &c, should be considered (but not consulted any more than about the design of battleships)'; and gave his view that cheap money was important 'more for psychological, than for fundamental reasons'.[28] These were the arguments to which Churchill, despite his misgivings—'I would rather see Finance less proud and Industry more content'—could see no effective alternative. 'You and the Governor have managed this affair,' he told Niemeyer. 'Taken together I expect you know more about it than anyone else in the world.'[29] Beaverbrook made a further effort to disabuse the Chancellor but, as Churchill afterwards told him, 'in the end the counter-arguments prevailed'; in his Budget speech in April 1925 Churchill announced Britain's return to the Gold Standard at the pre-war parity, and subsequently defended the Government's decision to 'shackle themselves to realities'.[30]

Keynes used Beaverbrook's *Evening Standard* for an attack on this

[28] The memoranda by Niemeyer, Norman, and Bradbury are printed in Moggridge, *British Monetary Policy*, App. 5; quotations at 267, 266, 271, and for Horne's evidence, 46–7; see also Pigou in *Macmillan Evidence*, QQ. 6070–109.

[29] Moggridge, *British Monetary Policy*, 76; for the handling of the decision see also Henry Pelling, *Winston Churchill* (1974), 300–3.

[30] Martin Gilbert, *Winston S. Churchill*, v (1976), 99, 119.

policy, subsequently published as *The Economic Consequences of Mr Churchill* (1925). He claimed that the Chancellor was 'committing himself to force down money wages and all money values, without any idea how it was to be done'. His point was that the dear money mechanism which would now have this task could attain its result only '*by the deliberate intensification of unemployment*' in the hope of squeezing down money wages. 'The gold standard,' he concluded, 'with its dependence on pure chance, its faith in "automatic adjustment", and its general regardlessness of social detail, is an essential emblem and idol of those who sit in the top tier of the machine.' The mistake lay in continuing 'to apply the principles of an economics, which was worked out on the hypothesis of *laissez-faire* and free competition, to a society which is rapidly abandoning these hypotheses'.[31] As Keynes wrote in a private letter to Leith-Ross, 'if the Treasury goes on advising on the basis of the orthodoxies of a generation ago, which orthodoxies assumed a competitive wage level and an effective mobility of labour—partly existing then and now not existing at all—we are in for much worse things yet'.[32]

It is worth observing the stance of the other leading sceptic, McKenna. As chairman of the Midland Bank, he could not be ignored; yet there was no one whom the authorities more wholesomely despised. Grigg reports him as telling Churchill, 'There is no escape; you have got to go back; but it will be hell'; and cites his annual chairman's speech in January 1925 as evidence of his pusillanimity. Admittedly, this made out a case for the Gold Standard 'on psychological and not on economic grounds', so long as nine out of ten people believed it best[33]—a level of support easily surpassed in the Treasury. As McKenna later put it, 'the return to the gold standard, under proper circumstances, was a most meritorious act'.[34] But were the circumstances of 1925 appropriate? His public position, upon which Niemeyer sought to capitalize, was read by Churchill as 'a deliberately weak defence of the gold policy'—an interpretation

[31] *JMK* ix. 212, 218, 224.
[32] Quoted in Leith-Ross, *Money Talks*, 93.
[33] Grigg, *Prejudice and Judgement*, 184–5; Reginald McKenna, *Post-War Banking Policy* (1928), 102–3. R. S. Sayers, 'The return to gold, 1925', an able defence of the rationality of the decision, is ready to accept Grigg's account at face value: Sidney Pollard (ed.), *The Gold Standard and Employment Policies between the Wars* (1970), 85–98, at 89.
[34] Macmillan Committee, private session, 23 Oct. 1930, 22, T. 200/5. McKenna's position is put in context in L. J. Hume, 'The Gold Standard and deflation: Issues and attitudes in the 1920s', in Pollard (ed.), *Gold Standard*, 122–45.

backed by his private information that McKenna regarded it as 'unnecessary and unwise'.[35] Whatever McKenna's dissimulations, he was to remain a consistent critic of deflationary policies throughout the 1920s.

It has long been a controversial question, how far the authorities understood the nature of the adjustments that the return to gold required, how far they underestimated their difficulty, and how far they subsequently regretted their policy. The proposition that sterling was overvalued in 1925 at a parity of $4.86 eventually became accepted. Indeed the strongest ground for querying it is by turning the Keynesian analysis on its head and arguing that it was not the exchange rate that was 'wrong' but the level of real wages[36]— essentially the orthodox position in 1925. It was commonly accepted that some adjustment at some stage was necessary to bring British costs into line with the Gold Standard parity for sterling. This issue was discussed by the Macmillan Committee in 1930.[37]

McKenna: Up to April 1925, before we went back to the Gold Standard, there was obviously a policy to drive down prices, in order to bring us back to the Gold Standard. There is no question about that.
Bradbury: That is true.
McKenna: The further question I ask is: was that policy continued after April 1925?
Bradbury: I never heard of the suggestion that it was, after at any rate the price level had been brought to the point which enabled parity to be maintained.

The official Treasury line remained that of defending the Chamberlain–Bradbury Committee's judgement 'that only a small *additional* strain would be entailed by the restoration of the gold parity, as compared with the strain required to hold sterling at its then exchange value'. A Cabinet paper of 1929 conceded that 'the adjustment of prices had been a longer and more difficult process than was anticipated', but asserted that 'the process of adjustment did not impose an impossible strain on the national economy'. It followed that 'the transitional difficulties' and 'the unpleasant jolt necessitated by the reversion to the gold standard' were a price worth

[35] Moggridge, *British Monetary Policy*, 73; cf. 263.
[36] K. G. P. Matthews, 'Was sterling overvalued in 1925', *Econ. Hist. Rev,* NS 39 (1986), 572–87.
[37] Private session, 7 Nov. 1930, 21–2, T. 200/5.

paying.[38] Privately, Churchill seems to have been less certain. He harboured a sense of having been over-managed in the affair by Norman, whom he increasingly distrusted, and Niemeyer, whose departure from the Treasury was not unwelcome. Their 'rough and pedantic handling of the problem' disturbed him.[39] But it was only in much later years that he fell into ruminating about the return to gold as 'the biggest blunder of his life'—according to Grigg in 1948, a legend which 'obtained such currency that Winston himself has almost come to believe it'.[40] As long as Churchill remained at the Treasury, the Gold Standard was firmly defended as essential to the policy of sound finance to which he had nailed his colours.

Free Trade

When the Keynesian proposals for public works became a live political issue, they notoriously encountered resistance from within government—the so-called Treasury View. This episode may have helped feed a left-wing conspiracy theory that obstruction of radical policies came from crucially placed Civil Servants who were closet Conservatives. Their reputation for political impartiality was admittedly to be seriously compromised by the Baldwin Government's decision to publish a White Paper countering the Liberal manifesto in 1929, including a Treasury Memorandum which was not even signed by the responsible minister.[41] In fact, however, there was no easily identifiable Conservative in the top echelon of the Treasury and the leanings of Bradbury, Leith-Ross, and Grigg were plainly towards old-fashioned Liberalism. There was nothing new or unusual in this. In the pre-war period, both the Treasury and the Board of Trade were looked at askance by many prominent Conservatives, for the obvious reason that it was their own outlook which challenged the ingrained Cobdenite maxims of British fiscal policy.

[38] CP 53 (29), pars. 21–2, 28, 23 Feb. 1929, CAB 24/202; for the provenance of CP 53(29) see below, ch. 3 n. 29.

[39] Moggridge, *British Monetary Policy*, 75 n. 4; cf. 96 and n. 4; see also Howson, *Domestic Monetary Management*, 72 n.

[40] Lord Moran, *Winston Churchill: The struggle for survival, 1940–65* (1966; Sphere edn. 1968), 330 (diary, 10 Sept. 1945); Grigg, *Prejudice and Judgement*, 180. It is regrettable that, in the thousand pages of vol. v, Martin Gilbert's biography could not find space to address this issue.

[41] See below, ch. 4 n. 74.

Whereas the Liberals were immemorially Free Traders, from 1903 the Unionists were identified with the Chamberlainite programme of tariffs, which found its highest expression as a system of national economy.[42] Of all the principles of sound finance, Free Trade was politically the most delicate for the authorities to champion.

'Nineteenth-century Liberalism was greatly concerned with the establishment of certain economic principles, which were, a hundred years ago, highly controversial, novel, and intellectually difficult,' Keynes wrote in 1923. 'These found their chief embodiment in the doctrine of free trade.'[43] It was more than a party cry: it was the orthodox presumption of the economics profession. The committee of economists of the Economic Advisory Council (comprising Keynes, Pigou, Stamp, Hubert Henderson, and Lionel Robbins) provided an authoritative summary of the argument in 1930. The normal effect of a tariff, they agreed, 'must mainly be to divert the productive forces of the community from one occupation to another, and not to increase their total activity'. Hard cases aside, the argument was that 'tariffs will tend to divert production from the channels where we are relatively more efficient into channels where we are relatively less efficient; that is to say, the play of natural forces will be more successful in discovering the occupations in which we can employ ourselves most profitably, than any system of tariffs will be'. Tariffs introduced an inelasticity into the distribution of resources, protecting the relatively inefficient; thus 'the effect will be seen in a higher cost of living relatively to the money-wages, and consequently in a lower standard of life'. This encapsulation of the professional consensus was approved by Keynes, Pigou, Henderson, and Stamp. Robbins dissented only because it did not go far enough in emphasizing that 'in the past, the so-called exceptions to the general presumption in favour of Free Trade have been regarded by economists as academic playthings—interesting as illustrating remote analytical points, but, from the point of view of practice, completely insignificant'.[44]

The connection of free trade with the Gold Standard was histori-cally strong. Although it is true that the Gold Standard mechanism

---

[42] See E. H. H. Green, 'Radical Conservatism in Britain, 1899–1914', Ph.D. thesis (Cambridge, 1986), esp. ch. 4; for the Gladstonianism of the Treasury, Bruce K. Murray, *The People's Budget, 1909–10* (Oxford, 1980), 77–9.

[43] *JMK* xix. 118 (*Nation*, 11 Aug. 1923).

[44] Howson and Winch, *EAC* 202, 209; and see below, ch. 9 nn. 27–9.

could work with any given level of protection—as in the USA—regarded as a once-for-all addition to prices, in principle it was an alternative way of responding to an imbalance of trade. A tariff was a short cut out of a deficit position; free trade was a means of restoring equilibrium on an optimal basis in the long run. Keynes explicated the process in 1930, starting from the example of increased motor car imports:[45]

From that point onwards the free trade argument would be, that would lead to a loss of gold, the loss of gold would lead to an increase in Bank rate, the increase of Bank rate would lead to unemployment, the increase of unemployment would lead to pressure for a reduction of wages; when wages had been reduced we should be able to produce cars in competition or to make some other article which we now import. When the final position had been reached, while money wages would be lower than before, real wages would not be lower, in fact they would be higher than under protection, because we should be producing those articles for which we are distinctly better suited.

On this reading, all effects are those of displacement; aggregate employment is not ultimately affected; and resources thrown idle in one direction can be absorbed in another, provided that prices—especially that of labour—are sufficiently flexible. The role assigned to the Bank rate in initiating the process is crucial—indeed from this point onward *the 'automatic adjustments' required by free trade are exactly the same as those required by the Gold Standard.* But there is no sign that Keynes appreciated the significance of this point in the mid-1920s.

In the First World War, just as the Gold Standard and the balanced budget convention were *hors de combat*, so the pure doctrine of Free Trade was peremptorily infringed. In 1915 McKenna imposed tariffs on a number of luxury items, on the plea of rationing shipping space. In practice, the McKenna duties were retained after the War by the Coalition and thereafter treated as a political football; they were abolished by the first Labour Government in 1924 and restored by the incoming Conservative Government in 1925. There were also 'safeguarding' duties, introduced under the Lloyd George Coalition in 1921.[46] The Conservatives, however, were restrained from going further in a protectionist direction by their discouraging performance

---

[45] *JMK* xx. 114 (private evidence, 28 Feb. 1930).
[46] Forrest Capie, *Depression and Protectionism* (1983), ch. 3.

in 1923, the only post-war General Election when they put Tariff Reform to the fore. In the General Election of 1924 they found a better platform in anti-socialism and Baldwin sealed the issue by appointing Churchill, a Free Trader of long standing, as his Chancellor.

Keynes had not taken a particularly prominent part in the 1923 elections and what he did say was hardly novel. The two articles he contributed to the *Nation* are worth scrutiny precisely because they present 'the *general* argument for free trade', the 'familiar outlines' of which were retraced (as Keynes later confessed) by a 'faithful pupil of the classical school who did not at that time doubt what he had been taught and entertained on this matter no reserves at all'.[47]

'Free trade', he proclaimed, 'is based on two fundamental truths which, stated with their due qualifications, no one can dispute who is capable of understanding the meaning of words.' One was that it was better to specialize at what one did most efficiently. The other was that it was good to receive useful imports in return for exports, since 'the exchange would not take place (subject to the necessary exceptions just stated) unless there was an advantage in it'. Through free exchange, it was thus axiomatic that utility was maximized on both sides. 'Every export, which·is not paid for by an import,' Keynes added, 'represents a decrease in the capital available within this country.' Presumably, then, it was better to maintain a balance of payments by allowing in the imports which paid for exports rather than using an export surplus to transfer capital abroad. Keynes threw in his opinion that there was already 'too much encouragement to the export of our capital'.[48] The implicit assumption behind all his reasoning here was that Britain would have no fundamental difficulty in generating an export surplus if she chose to do so—a proposition which it might have been difficult to defend explicitly as the 1920s wore on.

Keynes spurned a further general argument for free trade—'the *laissez-faire* argument which appealed and still appeals to Liberal individualists'—preferring to rest on the specific economic case that it was 'the only policy which is technically sound and intellectually tight'.[49] He suggested that 'whilst protectionists have really wanted protection for its own fallacious sake', they characteristically began

[47] *JMK* xix. 152 (*Nation*, 1 Dec. 1923); *JMK* vii. 334 (*General Theory*).
[48] *JMK* xix. 147–9 (*Nation*, 24 Nov. 1923).
[49] *JMK* ix. 298 ('Am I a Liberal?').

by invoking the hard cases without recognizing that they made bad law. In making an appeal for protection to relieve unemployment, Baldwin had plunged 'headlong into pure error of the 2+2=5 variety' and showed himself 'a victim of the protectionist fallacy in its crudest form'.[50] If it was snobbery that kept Keynes out of the Labour party, it was surely intellectual snobbery that kept him clear of the Conservatives—still manifestly the stupid party.

Free trade, then, was regarded by Keynes in the 1920s as an open-and-shut case, self-evidently true to anyone who could follow its reasoning. It demonstrated that 'if there is one thing that protection can *not* do, it is to cure unemployment'. But Keynes had to qualify this blank assertion in a potentially significant way. 'If protectionists merely mean that under their system men will have to sweat and labour more, I grant their case,' he conceded. 'By cutting off imports we might increase the aggregate of work; but we should be diminishing the aggregate of wages.'[51] It was a traditional free trade argument that protection would have the effect of cutting real wages. Which way would this argument point if Britain became locked in a position where unemployment persisted because real wages were too high?

One response to such a question was given by the Bank official J. A. C. Osborne in 1930, acknowledging that protection could serve as a furtive means of reducing real wages: 'The chances of deceiving the working class in this manner would seem to be practically nil, and if so the alternative advantages of telling them the truth will have been lost.'[52] The more elevated argument for Free Trade was that it abjured the chicanery of tariffs, whereby indirect gains and losses were visited upon different sections of the community through a process all too open to political manipulation. Protection opened the door to an irreversible corruption of public life. To some extent Free Trade manifested its Liberal pedigree even here, with the Gladstonian propensity to regard policy not as 'a social means to a social end, but a campaign of Good against Evil'.[53]

Keynes continued to advocate free trade but not, as it were, with capital letters; he had already shed much of the Free Trade mentality.

---

[50] *JMK* xix. 150–1, 154.
[51] *JMK* xix. 151, 155.
[52] 'Bank of England's Views', ?May 1930, F.ID 1/2.
[53] Sidney Webb quoted in Peter Clarke, *Liberals and Social Democrats* (Cambridge, 1978), 87.

In his *Tract on Monetary Reform* (1923) he commented that 'many conservative bankers regard it as more consonant with their cloth, and also as economising thought, to shift public discussion of financial topics off the logical on to an alleged "moral" plane, which means a realm of thought where vested interest can be triumphant over the common good without further debate'.[54] The case for balanced budgets, for the Gold Standard, and for Free Trade had a clear economic consistency; in particular, each rested upon the premiss that the economy was self-righting if only a process of adjustment which depended upon the flexibility of prices were allowed to run its course. It was, however, upon the moral plane that these precepts achieved full communion, as different expressions of the nostrum that the principles of sound finance had to be immutable and 'knave-proof'—a conception open to subversion by the *Tract*'s view that in 'the realm of State action, *everything* is to be considered and weighed on its merits'.[55]

[54] *JMK* iv. 56.   [55] *JMK* iv. 56–7.

3

The formulation of the Treasury View, 1925–1929

'Radically fallacious'

'The orthodox Treasury view', as described by Churchill in his Budget speech in April 1929, purported to be an official consensus upon one crucial topic: the feasibility of state borrowing and state expenditure as a possible cure for unemployment. The term rapidly became established in this restricted sense, which was reinforced by the appearance of a White Paper in May 1929 embodying the Treasury's public critique of the Liberal proposals for tackling unemployment by means of loan-financed public works. Keynes notoriously depicted the Treasury View as dogmatic, but the findings of research in the public records in recent years have tended instead to bring out the pragmatic way in which Treasury officials sought to judge particular schemes on their merits at different times.[1] Was there really a principled and well-entrenched Treasury View of the kind which Keynes affected to suppose? This question will be addressed by taking account of new evidence from the public records which illuminates the context in which the Treasury View was formulated and promulgated.[2] It is now clear that the Treasury was not simply reacting to a plan sprung upon it by Lloyd George in March 1929; nor was Churchill speaking beyond his brief. Rather, a series of developments during the last year in office of the Baldwin Government induced the Treasury to exercise considerable care in

---

[1] See especially G. C. Peden, 'The "Treasury View" on public works and employment in the interwar period', *Econ. Hist. Rev.*, 2nd ser., 37 (1984), 167–81, which ably draws together this line of research, much of which is well grounded. The starkest rejection of the importance of the Treasury View as a theoretical position is in Jim Tomlinson, *Problems of British Economic Policy, 1870–1945* (London, 1981), 80, 84, 87–8, 91. A recent restatement is Roger Middleton, 'Treasury policy on unemployment', in Glynn and Booth (eds.), *The Road to Full Employment*, 109–24.

[2] The crucial document is a bound Treasury file, 'Cure for unemployment memoranda of 1928 and 1929', T. 172/2095, which had been kept in the library of the Treasury instead of the archive and was therefore not recognized as a public record for release under the thirty-year rule until 1986. It is quoted extensively below and forms the documentary spine of this chapter.

preparing its position, of which Churchill's Budget speech was a well-considered representation.

In the first place, the role of Keynes in galvanizing the Treasury into action is apparent. His salience in this debate is not a retro-spective trick of the light. Admittedly, it should not be overlooked that Sir Otto Niemeyer had, as early as 1921, provided a reasoned case against post-war proposals for public works, which had the effect of drawing out the implicit assumptions which the Treasury held. His argument was that if government spending were properly funded (through taxation or borrowing), its effects would be merely those of displacement; and if it were met through inflation, its effects in raising employment would probably be cancelled out by wage rises.[3] These may have been good arguments which Niemeyer found no subsequent reason to repent;[4] but the Treasury understandably felt no call to rehearse them in a vacuum in subsequent years. When the International Labour Office asked about official policy in 1927, however, it was informed that 'the decision taken by the Government at the end of 1925 to restrict grants for relief schemes was based mainly on the view that, the supply of capital in the country being limited, it was undesirable to divert any appreciable proportion of this supply from normal trade channels.' Since this statement, which was not published until 1931, was then promptly quoted in the Macmillan Report, it can be taken that Leith-Ross, as the Treasury's observer on the Committee, accepted it as accurate.[5]

The public silence was broken, so far as the Treasury was concerned, by the resuscitation of the issue at the hands of a man already marked out as a prominent critic. In July 1928 Keynes published an article under the title, 'How to organise a wave of prosperity', in Beaverbrook's *Evening Standard*, the same paper he had used for his attack on the return to gold in 1925. Since then, he claimed, the situation had turned out as he had predicted. 'The fundamental blunder of the Treasury and of the Bank of England has been due, from the beginning, to their belief that if they looked

[3] Robert Skidelsky, 'Keynes and the Treasury View: The case for and against an active unemployment policy, 1920–1929', in W. J. Mommsen (ed.), *The Emergence of the Welfare State in Britain and Germany, 1850–1950* (London, 1981), 170–3. Skidelsky makes the point: 'The Treasury View, like Conservatism, became identifiable as such only when it started to be contested' (p. 167).

[4] See his lecture in Cambridge, 22 Feb. 1929. Niemeyer Papers, Bank of England OV 9/480.

[5] International Labour Office, *Unemployment and Public Works* (Geneva, 1931), 30; cf. *Macmillan Report*, Add. I, Cmd. 3897 (1931), 203–4; also in *JMK* xx. 302.

after the deflation of prices the deflation of costs would look after itself.' As a first step, he urged, the Bank ought itself to liberalize credit and simultaneously to encourage other central banks to do likewise. Finally, Keynes maintained, 'the Chancellor of the Exchequer must remove and reverse his pressure against public spending on capital account'.[6]

Keynes's gibes hit home in the Treasury. 'I am sorry to see that Keynes is renewing the Press propaganda which has done him little credit as a politician and considerable harm as an economist,' Leith-Ross commented.[7] As Chancellor of the Exchequer, Churchill had long shown himself sensitive about the level of unemployment, continually pressing his officials for facts and figures, and refusing to minimize its gravity. It is no surprise, therefore, to find him asking Hopkins, Leith-Ross, and Hawtrey to comment on Keynes's article. Since Niemeyer's departure to the Bank of England in 1927, these three constituted the natural source of expertise on issues of principle in economic policy. Hopkins was content to forward to the Chancellor the separate memoranda which the other two produced.

On one issue the two memoranda disagreed. Keynes had claimed: 'When we have unemployed men and unemployed plant and more savings than we are using at home, it is utterly imbecile to say that we cannot *afford* these things.'[8] His point was that the idle resources themselves supplied the requisite means; and the distinction he was to develop between saving and investment became his standard way of explaining this. But the drafts of his *Treatise on Money*, on which he was working that summer, reveal no evidence that this distinction was given prominence before October 1928.[9] Even in his own mind, therefore, Keynes may not have been entirely clear; and to the mind of Leith-Ross a reference to 'more savings than we are using at home' appeared unhelpful in the extreme. 'To me, this seems to be sheer perversion of the facts,' he commented.[10] Hawtrey, however, was

---

[6] *JMK* xix. 762, 765.

[7] F. Leith-Ross, memorandum, 3 Aug. 1928, T. 172/2095; also in T. 175/26.

[8] *JMK* xix. 765.

[9] Compare the draft table of contents for 22 Sept. 1927 with that for 6 Oct. 1928. which first introduced the chapter, 'Digression on savings and investments', ultimately ch. 12 of the *Treatise on Money. JMK* xiii. 48–50, 78–82.

[10] Leith-Ross memorandum, 9 Aug. 1928, T. 172/2095. This is a revision of his memorandum of 3 Aug. 1928, with amendments by Hopkins. An extended criticism of the National Insurance scheme was omitted in the version sent to Churchill. This memorandum is mistakenly cited from T. 176/16 by Skidelsky, 'Keynes and the Treasury View', pp. 177–8, 180–1, and attributed to Niemeyer, who is thus identified as 'the principal architect of the "Treasury View"' (171 n.). Plainly this was not the View of Niemeyer alone.

inclined to allow Keynes this point, in so far as it could simply be assessed by reference to the existence of capital exports in the external trade statistics.

Leith-Ross remained unimpressed. 'Mr Keynes' remedy seems to me peculiarly unsound,' he wrote for Churchill's eyes; and he concluded that 'it is really absurd of Mr Keynes to suggest that we have savings which are available and are not being used.' He found it significant that new lending abroad was now running below the level of income from past investments (so no further accumulations were taking place). He stressed that foreign loans were desirable in that they necessarily generated equivalent exports. His analysis thus pointed in another direction altogether—to the problem of competitiveness.

> The result of our high labour costs and social services is to encourage consumption and reduce savings so that the margin of capital available for production and development schemes tends to be inadequate. All that Mr Keynes' policy would achieve would be the transference of labour and capital from exports to internal development works. It would tend, therefore, to increase imports and restrict exports—about the last thing that we want. There might *in theory* be something to be said for taxing wages or articles of prime necessity such as food, with a view to restricting consumption, and using the proceeds for development schemes; but there is no point whatever in trying to finance such schemes by diverting our inadequate capital resources from economic to uneconomic schemes of development.

Leith-Ross was prepared to acknowledge that Keynes was now offering 'an analysis of the industrial situation which states the case against the Treasury policy more fairly than his articles a couple of years ago', that is, after the return to the Gold Standard. He thought, however, that Keynes exaggerated the degree of resistance to wage cuts and he contested the proposition 'that labour costs are now the main obstacles to our economic revival', which he identified instead in 'defective organisation at home and lack of capital abroad'. Leith-Ross persisted, therefore, in hoping that existing policies would at last bring their due reward. 'What we must aim at', he concluded, 'is a cautious credit policy, a bold industrial concentration policy and a reduction, as and when possible, of excessive labour costs.'[11]

Hawtrey's memorandum could afford to deal with the central issues of public works more concisely because, as he told Leith-Ross,

[11] Leith-Ross, 9 Aug. 1928, T. 172/2095. The words in italics were inserted into his draft.

'I think you already know my views.'[12] He attached a copy of the article on this topic which he had published in *Economica* in 1925. It is not clear whether this was also forwarded to the Chancellor. Churchill would not have found its eleven pages more abstruse than the economic tracts he digested in his youth while mugging up the fiscal issue. Hawtrey's treatment did not assume numeracy in its readers, making no use of equations, statistics, diagrams, or tables. It is an elegant and well-polished version of a talk which Hawtrey had given at the Economic Club in February 1925, examining the principle of public works proposals from the time of the Minority Report of the Royal Commission on the Poor Law in 1909. Hawtrey was not concerned with the immediate administrative practicability of such schemes, nor with commending or disparaging a particular proposal. What he set out to do was to specify in a logically water-tight way the conditions which had to be satisfied before public works could be associated with a net increase in employment.

Hawtrey cited Pigou's pre-war objection to the view that 'any resources which the State or private persons turn to the purchase of extra labour at one point are necessarily taken away from the purchase of labour at some other point.'[13] Pigou, he noted, had since shifted his ground in this argument, though without departing from his original conclusion. Hawtrey argued that this conclusion was fallacious, basically because the sources of the funds received by those newly employed had not been properly identified. Such balances, he maintained, 'can only be provided at the expense of the people already receiving incomes'; because their unspent margin between income and outlay (their savings balances) would come under pressure. 'If all simultaneously try to increase their balances, they try in vain.' Under these conditions, it was 'this limitation of the unspent margin that really prevents the new Government expenditure from creating employment.'[14]

Because Hawtrey was seeking an exhaustive analysis, not a quick answer, he then explored possible alternatives. One was that, through

[12] R. G. Hawtrey, memorandum, 4 Aug. 1928, T. 172/2095.
[13] R. G. Hawtrey, 'Public expenditure and the demand for labour', *Economica*, 5 (1925), 38. The significance of this article has been suggested in K. Hancock, 'Unemployment and the economists in the 1920s', *Economica*, ns 27 (1960), 311; and Howson and Winch, *EAC* 27. On the development of Hawtrey's thought see Susan Howson, 'Hawtrey and the real world', in G. C. Harcourt (ed.), *Keynes and His Contemporaries* (London, 1985), esp. 149.
[14] Hawtrey, 'Public expenditure', 41–2.

increased velocity of circulation, the same stock of money might do more work. Now it was conceivable that this might happen, if the outlook for industry were so grim that idle balances, which private enterprise had not utilized, were to be taken up by public borrowing. But this was presented as an exceptional case or limiting condition. The entire argument, however, rests on the hypothesis—'This assumption is fundamental, and must be applied very carefully, and the effects of removing it must be examined equally carefully at a later stage'—that there is no expansion of bank credit. Relax this assumption, and the case is transformed. Hence by a sufficient increase in bank lending, new enterprises *can* be accommodated without diminishing balances elsewhere and 'they *will* give additional employment'. But the cause lies in the relaxation of the fundamental assumption, for 'the same reasoning shows that a creation of credit unaccompanied by any expenditure on public works would be equally effective in giving employment'. Public works in themselves were 'merely a piece of ritual'.[15]

Indeed, having reached this conclusion, Hawtrey was tempted to extend it to 'the exceptional case where there is an extreme stagnation of balances', and argue that even here it was the Government's borrowing not its expenditure that did the trick. In practice he did not suppose that these alternatives would have to be faced since he had 'no doubt' that through a low Bank rate it was 'possible to find an escape from any depression, however severe'. Hawtrey's analysis was now complete so far as a closed economy was concerned. He had further to allow for the international aspect. Given the Gold Standard, an import of capital (or a decrease in capital exports) acted like a protective tariff: as 'a device for bringing about inflation without depreciation'. It was like a tariff, too, in that it could mitigate unemployment for one country but not for all at once. Again Hawtrey had brought the argument back from public works to the conditions of credit. Hence his summing-up: 'The original contention that the public works themselves give additional employment is radically fallacious.'[16]

When Hawtrey was asked for his advice in 1928, he was content to reiterate these conclusions.

Such spending can only increase employment if accompanied by the appropriate monetary or credit expansion, and this latter would in any case

---

[15] Hawtrey, 'Public expenditure', 40, 43   [16] Ibid. 44–6, 48.

increase employment whether accompanied by increased public spending or not. If, however, the public spending diminishes the export of capital, it permits of a monetary expansion which would not otherwise be possible without making the foreign exchanges adverse.

He chose to elaborate on the implications for international capital movements, an aspect which had become more conspicuous in the period since 1925, though only to illustrate his contention that some temporary gain for Britain might be possible. He now added that a way in which 'any of these makeshift expedients might be beneficial' was by enabling the Bank of England to lower its discount rate. This remained the heart of the matter. Thus his attitude is well caught by his dismissive remark that 'it is hardly worth while to consider elaborate and roundabout devices for giving the Bank of England an opportunity of relaxing credit.'[17] This was, so far as he was concerned, the hidden agenda in all proposals for public works. The extent to which the Treasury accepted Hawtrey's view in this regard is shown in Leith-Ross's memorandum. After three pages of exegesis of 'How to organise a wave of prosperity', he tore aside the veil in which he took the scheme to have been decently draped: 'What Mr Keynes is after, of course, is a definite inflation of credit.'[18]

Whether Keynes was right to suppose that Churchill himself was 'not ... naturally unsympathetic' to a new initiative on unemployment, except when ensnared by 'the timidities and confusions of the so-called "sound" finance',[19] is a moot point. Had he shown signs of wavering, however, the stern tutelage of the Treasury would have been hard to escape. Though 1928 seems to have been the first occasion on which official scrutiny of Keynes's ideas on public investment was called for, his record as a critic of the Treasury was hardly one which seasoned campaigners like Leith-Ross were disposed to forget or forgive. Hawtrey may not have been fired by any personal animus but his long-standing friendship with Keynes was marked by a kind of professional symbiotic rivalry. They were in many ways closely attuned in their economic thought, able and ready to engage in prolonged bouts of mutual criticism from which both benefited. On the one hand, Hawtrey guarded his independence and integrity from Keynes's incipient intellectual hegemony; on the other, his own status in the Treasury depended partly upon how seriously

[17] Hawtrey, 4 Aug. 1928, T. 172/2095.
[18] Leith-Ross, 9 Aug. 1928, T. 172/2095.
[19] *JMK* xix. 766 ('How to organise a wave of prosperity').

Keynes was taken. So far as the Treasury was concerned, Hawtrey was the one man who ought to know whether Keynes was talking nonsense. With Keynes's growing prominence in the economic debates of the 1920s, Hawtrey found himself in a position where his advice was more earnestly solicited. It was in this context that his highly academic specification of the relationship between public expenditure and unemployment became the corner-stone of the Treasury's argument that public works meant inflation.

CP 53 (29)

Since the publication of the Liberal 'Yellow Book' *Britain's Industrial Future* in February 1928, it had been clear that a scheme of public works would be part of the Liberal programme at the next General Election. 'How to organise a wave of prosperity' was Keynes's own effort at keeping the issue alive. So far as Lloyd George was concerned, the theme was developed in a speech in the House of Commons in November 1928. By the New Year of 1929, therefore, with thoughts already turning to the General Election due by the end of October, the issue of unemployment was bound up with Lloyd George's bid to spearhead a Liberal revival. Until 9 February, however, he was himself convalescing from a Christmas illness in the Mediterranean.[20] Just before his return, there was an attempt *within* the Government to launch an initiative on unemployment, which was suppressed at the time and never made public, but which none the less inspired the formal statement of the Treasury View of 1929.

The proposal came from the somewhat unlikely figure of the Home Secretary, Sir William Joynson-Hicks. 'I have thought over this matter for some little time,' he wrote to Churchill on 6 February, 'and have stolen L.G.'s thunder and have prepared the Memorandum because I am seriously worried as to the effect of the present position on the General Election.'[21] The memorandum which he enclosed made no effort to dissimulate its blatantly electoral rationale, which was spelled out in its opening paragraph.[22]

[20] John Campbell, *Lloyd George, The Goat in the Wilderness, 1922–1931* (London, 1977), 219–20.

[21] Joynson-Hicks to Churchill, 6 Feb. 1929, T. 172/2095.

[22] CP 27 (29), 'Unemployment', memorandum by the Home Secretary, 7 Feb. 1929, CAB 24/201, also in T. 172/2095.

It is no part of my purpose to discuss in this memorandum the broad national and economic aspects of the problem presented by the unemployed: these are only too familiar to us all. I have, however, been considering lately the problem in relation to its reactions on the fortunes of the Party at the General Election, and I must confess that despite the remedial measures already applied, in preparation or contemplated, I find the prospect most disquieting. There is not lacking evidence that the Government during the Election will be vilified on all the Opposition platforms not only for having done nothing to improve the unemployment situation during their term of office, but for having allowed it to become even more acute ... We cannot disguise from ourselves the fact that an attack on the Government's unemployment policy is inevitable and will evoke considerable sympathy in the country, and it is necessary for us to use our utmost endeavour to render the attack abortive.

What he proposed was a scheme of public works—railways, dams, irrigation works, power stations, harbours—in the Dominions and Crown Colonies, with the threefold aim of stimulating British exports, encouraging migration, and increasing the economic strength of the Empire. Joynson-Hicks suggested that the funds could be found from a Government-guaranteed loan, despite professing himself 'aware that in many quarters the raising of such a loan would be regarded as an abuse of Government credit and as a concealed measure of inflation'. He then added a significant argument about mitigating the cost, maintaining that 'there would be some immediate return to set off against such expenditure; increased employment and migration would relieve the unemployment fund and the rates, which between them provided in benefit and out-relief some £50 millions during last year for the unemployed and their dependants, and there would, of course, be an increase in the national revenue'. Such contentions were to resurface in the middle of the polemical whirlpool in the disputes of the coming months.

Before hailing (or deriding) Joynson-Hicks as a proto-Keynesian, it should be remembered that his own purposes were unashamedly party political. Thus he further proposed to bridge the gap before an imperial scheme could become effective—'if we are to survive politically'—by anticipating the sort of road programme for Britain which Lloyd George intended to put before the country. He acknowledged that the Industrial Transference Board had deprecated the creation of artificial employment, but appealed to the keener imperatives of electoral politics.

... it is my firm conviction that unless we are prepared to create work during the intervening period we shall suffer for our neglect at the polls. This may seem to be placing the question on too narrow a Party basis, but if a Labour or Liberal Government is formed as the result of the General Election, there is no doubt that the projects they will conceive for meeting the situation will inflict far more injury on the State than will the creation of artificial employment for 50,000 or 100,000 men. I do therefore urge my colleagues to reconsider their refusal to embark on road construction on a fairly large scale. It is the only work suitable for the unemployed and has the advantage that it makes a good show throughout the country. In effect I want a reply to the question which will be hurled at us on every platform, 'Where can I get work?'

When Joynson-Hicks referred to the Cabinet's 'refusal to embark on road construction on a fairly large scale', he doubtless had in mind the tepid reception which had recently met the Minister of Labour, Sir Arthur Steel-Maitland, when he expressed impatience over the slow pace at which local authorities were bringing forward proposals.[23] Steel-Maitland had long been sympathetic to public works, which, as an old Chamberlainite, he regarded as an antidote to socialism. Before the Cabinet could consider Joynson-Hicks's memorandum, Steel-Maitland weighed in with his own comments. He suggested that the Home Secretary had got the problem somewhat out of perspective; that the present unemployment figures were likely to improve; but that scope undoubtedly existed for a business-like programme. The question was, what must be its features 'if it is to make a bright enough fly for us all to go a-fishing with in murky water'?[24] Industrial transference, he held, was a necessary policy of philanthropy which prosperous areas of the country must be asked to swallow: 'one of those items of the white man's burden which any decent administration is bound to undertake occasionally.'[25] Schemes for trunk roads at home—the eight-million-pound plan he had put to the Cabinet in the previous month—as well as for imperial development received his endorsement. At this point, however, Steel-Maitland recognized that the wider economic aspect of the problem had to be faced. 'The Treasury is like nature itself,' he wrote benignly: '*Expellas furca, tamen usque recurret.*'[26]

[23] Cabinet 2 (29) 6, 23 Jan. 1929, CAB 23/60.
[24] CP 37 (29), par. 8: 'Unemployment', memorandum by the Minister of Labour, 16 Feb. 1929, CAB 24/201, also in T. 172/2095.
[25] CP 37 (29), par. 10.
[26] CP 37 (29), par. 14. The sense is: 'Though forcibly expelled, it will none the less reassert itself.'

Tariff Reformers had always had an ambivalent attitude towards the canons of sound finance as representing, on the one hand, the hoary fallacies of Cobdenism and *laissez-faire*, but on the other, a necessary discipline against the menace of socialism. Steel-Maitland was thus well placed to act as candid friend of the Chancellor, whose penchant for Free Trade and trust in the efficacy of the market mechanism was historically well attested. Steel-Maitland identified two criteria by which public works schemes were always judged: the first being ('and quite rightly, too')[27] a test of businesslike economic return. The second constituted the key paragraph in his memorandum.[28]

The other question is that of the diversion of credit. Is it or is it not true that if capital be directed to such schemes it will not be forthcoming in the same abundance for more natural and more fruitful ordinary business? This question concerns a cardinal principle of finance and financial policy, on which, of course, my Department offers no opinion. The Home Secretary's memorandum, however, has raised the question definitely. And after 8 years of financial orthodoxy and 8 years of unabating unemployment, ought we not to ask for a reasoned proof, for some foundations of belief that the financial policy by which we guide our steps is right?

Getting into his stride as devil's advocate, the Minister of Labour listed some layman's questions. 'Is it not possible to give a fillip to public confidence and thus start business on the up-grade rather sooner?' he asked. 'Or does the strict orthodox theory of credit forbid?' Why, he demanded, could shortage of goods and lack of employment in supplying them not be eased by manipulation of credit? He then posed his potentially most embarrassing charge.

We have all of us supported the Chancellor of the Exchequer in his return to the gold standard. It was practically the last and an almost inevitable move on a course previously fixed and definitely set. But did those on whose initiative it was commenced foresee the results of the rapid deflation occurring in a country in which workers had the will and the power to resist strenuously a reduction in the nominal rate of their earnings, even though the real value would remain unchanged, a country also in which imports were free?

The author of these heretical questions hastened to reassure his colleagues that he was no advocate of inflation or of abandoning the Gold Standard. His point was that 'we should have a full case stated, subjected to criticism and substantiated, for the financial policy

---

[27] CP 37 (29), par. 15.   [28] CP 37 (29), par. 16.

which we are asked to continue'. Hence his plea that the Cabinet should face the issue of whether 'the settled financial policy of the country' had 'dominated our actions unduly and prevented us from adopting ameliorative measures which would have reduced the numbers unemployed, and, if so, is it expedient to continue to acquiesce in that domination?'[29]

Meanwhile, in the Treasury, work had already been put in hand on meeting this challenge. Frederick Phillips, the Principal Assistant Secretary, and G. C. Upcott, Deputy Controller of Supply Services, were the officials nominated by Churchill as presumably 'able to show the fallacies underlying the idea that a great loan for Colonial development would be a permanent remedy for unemployment'.[30] Had Hawtrey not been at Harvard, on special leave from the Treasury for the academic year 1928–9, the task would probably have fallen to him. As it was, Phillips and Upcott collaborated with Leith-Ross in producing a memorandum which was a rejoinder not only to the Home Secretary but also to the Minister of Labour. This became the Cabinet paper CP 53 (29).

Part I dealt with development loans. The heart of it lay in four taut and closely linked paragraphs, rather in the manner of Hawtrey. The initial proposition was that, if inflation were ruled out, the Government could only obtain the necessary resources from taxation or borrowing. 'Thus, in all cases the question is whether £1,000 spent by the Government will give more employment than if the £1,000 had been left to the public to spend. This will be so only if the Government is skilful enough to find ways of spending £1,000 which give more employment than the spending of £1,000 by the public would do.'[31] The cause of business depression was put down to high costs of production rather than any scarcity of credit. The conclusion followed: 'If there were no artificial inflation of credit (which, in present circumstances, would inevitably produce depreciated exchanges and carry its own revenge), a policy of large loans for development would probably be quite nugatory as regards the general employment position, the resources directed by the Government to the employment of extra labour being taken away from the resources of private persons, the investment of which would have led

[29] CP 37 (29), par. 17.
[30] Churchill memorandum, 13 Feb. 1929, T. 172/2095.
[31] CP 53 (29), par. 5: 'Unemployment', Note prepared in the Treasury, 23 Feb. 1929, CAB 24/202, also in T. 172/2095.

to the employment of labour at other points.'[32] The 'crowding-out' thesis could hardly have been stated in more directly hydraulic terms. Here was a simple assertion that Archimedes could not take a bath without the water he displaced spilling over the side.

As it happened, the current issue of the *Nation* carried an unsigned article, almost certainly by Keynes, which sought to counter precisely this case against public works. 'The objection which we hear most frequently', it claimed, 'is that any money raised by the State for financing productive schemes must diminish *pro tanto* the supply of capital available for ordinary industry.'[33] In a last-minute addition to CP 53 (29), the arguments of this article were explicitly countered. Its opportune publication by the *Nation*, indeed, may well have been prompted by informal contacts with Steel-Maitland. He was already in touch with its editor, Hubert Henderson, who provided him with a summary of the arguments against the Treasury View, partly paralleling Keynes's article. Over the next few weeks, Steel-Maitland brooded over these issues. After examining the case for expansion on the one side, and 'the extreme view that £1,000 raised in loans means £1,000 denied to business' on the other, he was confirmed in his opinion that 'both these extremes seem to me absurd'.[34]

In the *Nation* Keynes indicated two sources (other than inflation) from which resources could be drawn: first, a surplus of savings over investment and, second, an excessive rate of foreign lending. CP 53 (29) swept aside these two possibilities, both of them embodying contentions which Leith-Ross was notoriously unable to swallow.[35] On a third point, too, the *Nation* was taken to task. It had claimed

[32] CP 53 (29), par. 7.

[33] 'The objections to capital expenditure', *Nation*, 23 Feb. 1929, 710–11. Notwithstanding the rigorous procedures followed by Moggridge in editing *JMK* xix, which does not include this piece, there appears to be both internal and external evidence pointing to Keynes's authorship: (1) stylistically it is consistent, especially with contemporary *Treatise* drafts; (2) the Treasury took it as by Keynes (see Phillips to Leith-Ross, 11 Mar. 1929, T. 172/2095) and this at a time when they were in direct personal contact. For both points, see below, ch. 4 nn. 50–1, 54.

[34] Steel-Maitland to E. R. Peacock (a Director of the Bank of England), 22 Mar. 1929, copy; cf. Henderson, 'Answer to the argument that capital expenditure promoted directly or indirectly by the State would divert capital from ordinary industry', 22 Feb. 1929. Steel-Maitland Papers, Scottish Record Office. I am indebted to Dr E. H. H. Green for copies of this material, which is also cited in Rodney Lowe, *Adjusting to Democracy* (Oxford, 1986), 202 ff.

[35] CP 53 (29), p. 2 n.; on authorship cf. Leith-Ross to Phillips, 7 Mar. 1929, and Phillips to Leith-Ross, 12 Mar. 1929, T. 172/2095.

that the Archimedean argument, if valid, must apply not only to state undertakings but to any new business enterprise by, say, Morris or Courtaulds. Upcott had tried to meet this point by claiming that it all depended on whether there were a trade revival: 'But State schemes will do nothing in themselves to create a trade revival (which must depend on an expectation of increased profits), and without a Trade revival, capital expenditure (whether by the State or by Messrs Morris) on one scheme merely reduces the capital available for other schemes.'[36] This bleak and rigorous view did not find its way into the final text, presumably by Leith-Ross, whose rebuttal of the *Nation* rested instead upon a more optimistic reading: 'If the capitalist system is sound, private enterprise is more likely than the Government to direct investment to purposes which are economically justified and will tend to increase the wealth of the community.'[37]

If the argument of CP 53 (29) were accepted, it followed that loan-financed public expenditure on projects yielding less than the prevailing rate of return could not produce any permanent increase in employment; and private enterprise would already have identified which the productive projects were. But it went on none the less 'to consider the more *immediate* effect of the proposals advocated by the Home Secretary and the Minister of Labour', even though a sufficient reason for rejecting them on principle had already been advanced. This section naturally dwelt upon the doubtful administrative practicality of achieving appreciable results soon enough to redound credit upon the Government and to relieve it of the imputation of 'a death-bed confession of failure'.[38] Part II then turned to the 'Doubts and Queries about the Gold Standard' which Steel-Maitland had raised. It seems likely that Phillips was responsible for drafting this section, which expressed scepticism that 'any economic *exposé* [would] have much effect in silencing the Government critics who are only interested in economics in so far as it supplies them with political ammunition'.[39] The world-weary tone certainly echoes memoranda which Phillips and Hopkins had written the previous month in response to press criticism from Keynes.[40] CP 53 (29) concluded by inviting the Government to assume a brusque

[36] Comment by Upcott, n.d., T. 172/2095.
[37] CP 53 (29), p. 2 n.
[38] CP 53 (29), pars. 8, 17.
[39] CP 53 (29), par. 19.
[40] 'No doubt Mr Keynes writes as a journalist and as a currency heretic.' Hopkins to Churchill, 31 Jan. 1929, T. 172/2095; commenting on *JMK* xix. 775–80.

attitude in defence of its own actions and also those of the Bank of England. The last thing that was needed, *pace* Steel-Maitland, was a committee of industrialists sitting in judgement on these matters!

At its meeting on 26 February, the Cabinet had before it the memoranda from Joynson-Hicks and Steel-Maitland.[41] On the eve of the Cabinet, Churchill decided to set his own seal upon the critique in CP 53 (29) by prefacing it with a clear-cut statement of his advice.[42]

I do not advise my colleages in the closing months of a Parliament, and possibly of an Administration, to challenge the basic arguments upon which our monetary policy stands. That policy has been pursued by all British Governments; and it seems to me very unlikely that a Conservative Government would be well advised in abandoning it or throwing doubts upon it ... It is to be hoped that we shall not let ourselves be drawn by panic or electioneering into unsound schemes to cure unemployment, and divert national credit and savings from the fertile channels of private enterprise to State undertakings fomented mainly for political purposes. The devastating nature of the criticism which could be applied to a policy of curing unemployment by large loan expenditure of an unprofitable character, whether on the roads or elsewhere, would only become apparent after a Government was committed to that policy and to the promise based upon it.

There is every indication that Baldwin, with his control of the Cabinet agenda, backed Churchill's judgement on this point. The Cabinet of 26 February found no time to explore the issue and it was remitted instead to a Cabinet Committee, membership of which was to be nominated by the Prime Minister. It is pretty clear that Baldwin thus took Joynson-Hicks's proposal into his own hands, only to let it wither on the vine. When he was asked on 13 March whether his committee had yet been established, he used the absence of Churchill and Steel-Maitland as an excuse for inaction. Pressed again on 26 March, he claimed to be in communication with his colleagues and promised to raise the question after the Easter recess. Then came the preparations for Churchill's Budget in April. Baldwin again reported that he was in touch with his colleagues, though no Cabinet Committee had been set up. Finally, armed with a promise of funds from

[41] Also circulated was a plaintive appeal from Sir Philip Cunliffe Lister, the President of the Board of Trade, for financial assistance from the Government over rationalization. Its lack of backbone cut no ice with the Treasury. 'Surely all this need not be regarded seriously!' Leith-Ross minuted. Leith-Ross memorandum, 25 Feb. 1929, T. 172/2095; commenting on CP 57 (29), CAB 24/202.

[42] CP 53 (29), Memorandum by the Chancellor of the Exchequer, 25 Feb. 1929.

Churchill if the Government were returned, Baldwin proposed to include a vague reference to Empire development in his major speech on 18 April, but 'the Prime Minister deprecated discussion of the various detailed proposals that had been circulated to the Cabinet'.[43] CP 53 (29) had carried the day.

'A sound principle is proclaimed'

So far as the history of the Treasury View is concerned, Joynson-Hicks's initiative was instantly eclipsed, just as he had feared, by the Liberal scheme as launched by Lloyd George on 1 March 1929. He offered a pledge to reduce unemployment to 'normal proportions' within a year of the inception of the programme. How this transformed the polemical climate can be seen from a speech by Joynson-Hicks on 8 March: 'I cannot understand how a man of his ability could put such a proposal before the people of this country and think it really possible. Is he the only man of brains in the world? Do you think we have not thought our schemes of transport and road work during the past few years?'[44] No doubt these words were uttered more feelingly than his audience appreciated; but they are a clear indication of the Government's strategy. 'We should not try to compete with L.G.', was how Churchill put it in private, 'but take our stand on sound finance.'[45] As far as the substance of Lloyd George's proposals went, a memorandum was quickly prepared by the Minister of Transport stating his administrative obstacles to the realization of the pledge within a year—a timetable dismissed as 'preposterous'.[46]

Churchill was already busy adapting the relevant paragraphs of CP 53 (29) as a statement of 'the orthodox argument against a policy of large Government loan expenditure to give increased employment'.[47] There is a direct continuity not only of argument but of

[43] Cabinet 17 (29) 1, 17 Apr. 1929; cf Cabinets 9 (29) 4, 11 (29) 13, 13 (29) 8, 26 Feb., 13 Mar., 26 Mar., 1929, CAB 23/60. The salience of empire development proposals is brought out in Philip Williamson, '"Safety First": Baldwin, the Conservative party, and the 1929 General Election', *Hist. Jnl.*, 25 (1982), 398–400, 403–6.

[44] Campbell, *Lloyd George*, p. 225.

[45] Jones, *Whitehall Diary*, ii. 175–6 (6 Mar. 1929).

[46] CP 67 (29), Memorandum by the Minister of Transport, 5 Mar. 1929, CAB 24/202, also in T. 172/2095.

[47] Churchill's draft with Leith-Ross's alterations, n.d. but between 25 and 28 Feb. 1929, T. 172/2095.

phrasing, running through successive drafts from the end of February to his Budget speech as delivered in the House of Commons in the middle of April. In this work of drafting, which Churchill supervised personally, he was principally assisted by Grigg, Leith-Ross, and Hopkins. The biggest addition to the line taken in CP 53 (29) was an elaboration of the case in favour of foreign lending, for which Leith-Ross was initially responsible. But the main effort was to tighten up the exposition rather than to modify its thrust. Thus Grigg assured Churchill that he had 'thought over it a good deal and discussed it with Leith-Ross from the point of view of seeing whether the argument would stand the fierce light of public discussion'. The more they returned to first principles of economic theory, the more satisfied they became 'that the argument is unimpeachable'. Grigg's mind ran back over Hawtrey's old publications which would, he trusted, resolve any arcane difficulties—'I can't see my way through to the second order effects but perhaps Hawtrey clears up all these points'—and was relieved to find it so. Back numbers of *Economica* were ferreted out for the Chancellor to inspect himself, with Grigg to remind him that 'Hawtrey (in 1925) wrote an article (of extreme obscurity) proving that relief works were an absolute delusion unless they were accompanied by an expansion of banking credit, which would relieve unemployment without any intervening relief schemes.'[48]

Churchill's interpretation of the economics of the Liberal plan was constrained by this theoretical analysis. He told Leith-Ross on 3 March that he had 'no doubt that Mr Lloyd George has at the back of his mind a definite inflationary purpose in accordance with the general Keynes view'.[49] Three days later, the Cabinet was informed of how the Chancellor would respond to a deputation from the motor industry, pressing for loan-financed expenditure on roads.[50]

Mr Churchill proposed, in his reply, to base himself on the general attitude assumed in the Treasury Memorandum attached to C.P. 53 (29). He would show that State borrowing for purposes like a road programme could only be drawn out of the general fund of available credit, and consequently at the expense of private borrowers; that the employment to be obtained from road construction was limited, both in amount and in time, and compared unfavourably with permanent industries that might be established by private

---

[48] Grigg to Churchill, 2 Mar. 1929, T. 172/2095.
[49] Churchill to Leith-Ross, 3 Mar. 1929, T. 172/2095.
[50] Cabinet 10 (29) 4, 6 Mar. 1929, CAB 23/60. The words in italics were added.

borrowing; that if inflation were resorted to the immediate result would be a movement of gold out of the country, involving the raising of the Bank Rate and further restriction of credit. While adopting these general lines, Mr Churchill intended to leave the door open for such reasonable expenditure, *in minor ways and as exceptional measures*, whether financed by Loan or otherwise, as the Government might decide it was wise to make with a view to relief of unemployment.

The Cabinet approved his general line, subject to the italicized proviso. The fundamental economic objection to public works as a cure for unemployment was repeatedly rehearsed and reinforced. Leith-Ross, for example, assured Churchill that 'any loans raised by the government must either attract existing savings or entail inflation. If the loans are to be raised out of existing savings, they can add nothing to the total volume of employment in the country, but will merely divert resources from private to Government employment (see the arguments set out in Treasury Memorandum in CP 53 (29)).'[51] In the Treasury draft of a major speech prepared for the Prime Minister the essentials of the argument were restated as simply as possible.[52]

We must *either* take existing money *or* create new money. Suppose we take existing money. Does anybody happen to have a few hundred millions lying idle? Not much! All the existing money is already being used to the full by trade and industry, and if we are going to take it away from them, we tend to create unemployment at one point while curing it at another.

Leaning on this text when he addressed his followers at Leicester, Baldwin added, 'you merely then may make something on the swings which you will certainly lose on the roundabouts'. In concluding that it was 'a very simple problem, really', the Prime Minister set his seal upon the formulation of the issue in CP 53 (29), as 'whether a thousand pounds spent by a Government is going to give more employment in the country than a thousand pounds left to the individuals to spend and use for that purpose.'[53] It is notable that Steel-Maitland was egregious in maintaining a different tone—that of commending the Government's own efforts in this direction. 'Every single thing which has been advocated by the party of ideas opposite,'

---

[51] Leith-Ross memorandum for Churchill, 11 Mar. 1929, also incorporating Upcott, 8 Mar. 1929, T. 172/2095.

[52] Draft by Upcott, revised by Hopkins, n.d., T. 172/2095.

[53] *The Times*, 22 Mar. 1929.

he said in the House, 'is a thing which we have been doing for years.'[54] He might have added: on a modest scale.

When the Liberal plan was published as *We Can Conquer Unemployment* in the middle of March 1929, Churchill contemplated issuing in reply a written memorandum, of which the first part would be 'the orthodox view as already drafted by me'. There would follow a reasoned case for some flexibility in application. 'A sound principle is proclaimed, and modifications in practice are admitted,' Churchill summarized his theme. 'These modifications are inevitable; but they must be looked at with a critical eye, and kept within strict bounds.' Indeed, he then added a query as to 'whether we have not gone too far along the path of laxity', which his officials prudently decided to omit.[55] The form in which Churchill's statement was eventually to appear was governed by the Prime Minister's decision to collect memoranda from other Departments affected by the Liberal proposals. This was the origin of the White Paper published in May 1929, essentially the product of an interdepartmental official committee. The Treasury Memorandum had been set up in print as part of a Cabinet paper by 2 April—a fortnight before Budget day. Meanwhile, Churchill decided to use his Budget speech for his own pre-emptive declaration of the Treasury position.

In preparing his remarks on public works, Churchill had before him a paper from Leith-Ross which had been endorsed by both Hopkins and Fisher as his immediate superiors. Though it was an arrangement under which Leith-Ross chafed, as not recognizing his own special competence, he acknowledged in his memoirs that Hopkins rarely took exception to his drafting. The evidence is that they were of one mind, and Hopkins was content to append a final comment after discussion at the Bank of England.[56] The well-thumbed Treasury copy of *We Can Conquer Unemployment* survives in the public records; to Lloyd George's appeal on the cover, 'Let us Mobilise for Prosperity', the words 'Extravagance, Inflation, Bankruptcy' have been added.[57]

Churchill showed himself still fascinated by the issue of principle

[54] 5 *Hansard* (Commons), ccxxvi, 2160 (25 Mar. 1929); cf. his speech at Exeter, *The Times*, 16 Mar. 1929.

[55] Churchill to Grigg, 15 Mar. 1929, T. 172/2095.

[56] Leith-Ross for Churchill, 12 Mar. 1929; Hopkins's endorsement, 15 Mar. 1929, apparently following his regular lunch with Norman and a meeting with W. W. Stewart. See Norman diary, 15 Mar. 1929, ADM 20/18.

[57] In Hopkins papers, T. 175/26.

which had been raised. 'You will see for yourself the delicacy of an argument which on the one hand declares that all Government borrowing simply withdraws money from ordinary enterprise, and then proceeds to boast that we have done it, and are doing it on a gigantic scale,' he commented to Leith-Ross. 'I do not say that these arguments cannot be reconciled, and I am trying to do so; but pray, address your mind to the subject also and let me have the result in the course of a few days.'[58] Leith-Ross, who had taken the example of railway improvements in East London as a potentially permissible public utility project, made one further effort to meet the Chancellor's difficulties. 'It is surely quite reasonable', he responded, 'to maintain that the Government has not stinted the finance required to carry on in full efficiency the public services for which it is responsible: but that it is not prepared to embark on a grandiose programme of borrowing without due regard for economic return.'[59] The crux of the Treasury View was that public works competed for finite resources with private enterprise; hence 'crowding-out'; but it was still possible to argue that *some* public projects might show a better return than the private projects which they presumably displaced. The final draft which Leith-Ross submitted via Hopkins attempted to stake out this path, taking CP 53 (29) as its starting-point.

'There is no evidence', it claimed, 'to suggest that in Great Britain the volume of money savings is not fully absorbed by real investment.' Stringent criteria must therefore be satisfied before Government was justified in entering the market for funds. There followed a passage examining the argument—in fact, Keynes's—that the necessary funds could be obtained by diverting money from foreign loans. This was deprecated as either impracticable or, if practicable, uneconomic. Armed with this critique, the analysis pointed to lack of competitiveness as Britain's real industrial problem. The ground was thus prepared for the counter-attack on the 'humbug' of the 'sudden outcry' over unemployment. 'The remedy is easy enough to find,' it was stated. 'If our workmen were prepared to accept a reduction of 10 per cent in their wages or increase their efficiency by 10 per cent, a large proportion of our present unemployment could be overcome.' The attachment of

[58] Churchill to Leith-Ross, 31 Mar. 1929, T. 172/2095.

[59] Leith-Ross to Hopkins and Grigg, 3 Apr. 1929, T. 172/2095; marked by Churchill: 'Keep by handy. I shall want soon.'

organized labour to present conditions showed 'that they would prefer that a million workers should remain in idleness'. This was the issue that could not ultimately be balked. The Treasury had no difficulty in agreeing on the words to put in Churchill's mouth: 'The orthodox argument is, I believe, unanswerable and I feel little doubt that even Mr Keynes would admit that, in the long run, it holds good.'[60]

On Budget Day Churchill found his own way of putting the matter, though one that remained faithful to official advice. The Treasury View, as he stated it, was that Government borrowing had the effect of crowding-out private enterprise by raising the rent of money. While no absolute rule could be laid down, he continued, experience suggested that the results of public capital expenditure upon unemployment had been disappointing. 'In fact,' *The Times* reported him as saying, 'they have been so meagre as to lend considerable colour to the orthodox Treasury dogma, which is stead-fastly held, that whatever might be the political or social advantages, very little additional employment and no permanent additional employment can in fact, and as a general rule, be created by State borrowing and State expenditure (hear, hear).' This was the form subsequently quoted by Keynes, notably in *Can Lloyd George Do It?*[61] In *Hansard*, however, the text refers to 'the orthodox Treasury *doctrine* which *has* steadfastly held'[62]—a variant reading which circumspectly distances the officials from too close a public identification with an entrenched position.

Adroit, intelligent, and politically sensitive, Hopkins and his colleagues had no wish to be thrust into the arena of controversy, nor to have it said that any preconceptions on their part might impede fair consideration of proposals from whatever quarter. But in assessing the effect of public borrowing and expenditure, they necessarily worked with some kind of model of how the economy behaved. Their particular model had been explained most clearly and consistently by Hawtrey, and on re-examining it at the beginning of

[60] Final draft, by Leigh-Ross with amendments by Hopkins, T. 172/2095; partly used in 5 *Hansard* (Commons), ccxxvii, col. 53 (15 Apr. 1929).

[61] *The Times*, 16 Apr. 1929; cf. *JMK* ix. 115, beginning: 'It is the orthodox Treasury dogma, steadfastly held, that whatever ...' etc. Keynes first quoted this passage in 'A cure for unemployment', *Evening Standard*, 19 Apr. 1929 (*JMK* xix. 809).

[62] 5 *Hansard* (Commons), ccxxvii, col. 54. It is, of course, possible that the proof had been 'tidied up' in accordance with Members' prerogatives; or perhaps *The Times* man misheard. The *Evening Standard*, 15 Apr. 1929, prints 'doctrine'.

1929 they still found it uniquely compelling. Keynes may have been
right to suppose that 'Treasury Officials are naturally far too much
occupied with other forms of economy to have much leisure for the
political variety.'[63] Maybe their confidence in their colleague
Hawtrey was rather uncritical as a result; but they compensated with
an amateur enthusiasm for any deficiencies in professional scholarship.

There is every sign that the Chancellor shared their sense of
intellectual conviction on this point. He refused to parrot the conventional noises about sound finance without first pressing his
officials to justify their case; but having dissected it, he made it his
own. Leith-Ross understood Churchill's methods, having watched
him make the decision to return to gold, 'partly, as he himself said,
because he knew that if he adopted this course Niemeyer would give
him irrefutable arguments to support it.'[64] On the sidelines in 1925,
Leith-Ross aspired to fill Niemeyer's shoes after his departure to the
Bank of England; and in 1928–9 it was, above all, Leith-Ross who
marshalled the irrefutable arguments for the Chancellor, albeit with
Hopkins's approval. On the face of it, public works offered—even to
a capitalist party—obvious electoral temptations, such as Lloyd
George showed himself unable to resist. Within the Conservative
Government, as is now apparent, there were advocates of an active
policy; indeed the Treasury View was articulated as the decisive
economic objection to their proposals. The impeccably Conservative
auspices of these proposals, in short, did not protect them from
exactly the same refutation later deployed against the Liberals.
Convinced that state intervention to reduce unemployment was bad
economics, Churchill had no difficulty in arguing that it was bad
politics too. Faced with the spectre of Extravagance, Inflation,
Bankruptcy, the Conservatives would be better advised to invest their
political capital in financial rectitude.

The party line for the General Election of 1929 was summarized
in the Conservative speakers' handbook: 'Liberal Proposals Purely
Palliative', 'Relief Works Always Uneconomic'. This was so because
'they deflect from profitable and useful investment large sums of
money which would be better employed in normal economic development'.[65] When the Cabinet approved the Prime Minister's election

[63] *JMK* xix. 820.   [64] Leith-Ross, *Money Talks*, p. 92.
[65] National Union of Conservative and Unionist Associations, *Election Notes for
Conservative Speakers and Workers* (1929), 152. On Baldwin's choice of political
strategy see Williamson, '"Safety First"', 400–8.

address on 6 May, it was decided to omit a paragraph boasting of the success of the Government's public works programme on the grounds that it was 'inconsistent with the Treasury contention that public works could only be carried out by taking money from the aggregate sum available for expenditure, and which would in any event have been used to give some form of employment'.[66] The Treasury View may have served ideological functions in propping up a case for sound finance which appealed to sectional self-interest and extenuated the Conservative record; but that did not absolve its critics from the requirement to find an equally effective counter-argument. 'I say that the Treasury dogma is fallacious,' Keynes proclaimed just after the Chancellor's speech. 'It is neither plausible nor true.'[67] True or otherwise, it had proved highly plausible, as Keynes would have done better to acknowledge rather than resort to rhetorical overkill. At any rate, it was far from unreasonable in the spring of 1929 to suppose that the Treasury View represented a proposition which it would be necessary—though perhaps not sufficient—to confute before the case for public works was likely to gain acceptance.

[66] Cabinet 20 (29) 3, 6 May 1929, CAB 23/60.
[67] *JMK* xix. 809.

PART III

A Revolution in Economic Policy?

PROLOGUE TO PART III

With Lloyd George's pledge to 'conquer' unemployment, public works became a central policy issue. There was an economic legitimation for Keynes's support of the Liberal proposals—the 'special case' envisaged under his *Treatise on Money*, when, because of the Gold Standard, interest rates could not come down far enough to do the trick. This is the story Keynes subsequently told himself; but there is a fatal inconsistency in it over chronology, pointing instead to a political explanation of the origins of Keynes's commitment. The late 1920s were the most active period of Keynes's political career and his initiatives in policy dragged along a justifying body of theory in their wake—sometimes improvised on the spot. These efforts culminated in the 1929 General Election, when the Liberals failed to break through, and a minority Labour Government took office under Ramsay MacDonald.

One result was the appointment of the Macmillan Committee, with Keynes in a key role. By the time he gave his 'private evidence' to it, he had a coherent analysis, soon to be expounded in his *Treatise*, which underlay all his policy proposals. By the spring of 1930, Keynes had established an ascendancy within the Committee, in alliance with Reginald McKenna and Ernest Bevin. The authorities, by contrast, were pushed on to the defensive. The Bank of England had to work hard to retrieve the position after the acknowledged fiasco of Montagu Norman's evidence. The Treasury, however, under the capable direction of Sir Richard Hopkins, reformulated its position in an adroit and plausible way—shifting the argument against public works from economic doctrine to administrative feasibility. With worsening economic conditions, too, the prospects for a radical departure looked less hopeful, and they were probably harmed as much as helped by the advocacy of Sir Oswald Mosley.

The establishment of the Economic Advisory Committee, and particularly its committee of economists, meant that expert advice on policy acquired a new prominence. Keynes was at the heart of all these discussions. With a widespread recognition of the structural problems of the British economy went a growing willingness to

consider interventionist expedients. If public works could be represented as a special case under the *Treatise*, so, on much the same
reasoning, could tariffs. Moreover, Keynes shared a good deal of
common ground with his neo-classical colleagues, notably Pigou.
They were developing, albeit in slightly different terms, an approach
to Britain's persistent economic disequilibrium which was at once
pragmatic, cogent, and sophisticated. Keynes was not egregious
through any fundamental differences with orthodox economic
analysis. His distinctiveness was that he was 'in favour of practically
all the remedies which have been suggested in any quarter'—
including tariffs.

Ultimately the choices were political as much as economic. The
failure of the Labour Government to opt for a viable strategy, faced
with a mounting wave of difficulties, meant that it was swept away in
August 1931. A financial crisis fed on a Budgetary crisis, exacerbating
a sterling crisis and provoking a political crisis. The Labour Cabinet
split but MacDonald was persuaded to continue as Prime Minister,
now in a 'National' Government dominated by the Conservatives, as
a ploy to restore confidence. Within weeks, however, the Gold
Standard was abandoned—and with it disappeared the premiss for
the 'special case' on which the consistency of Keynes's argument for
a revolution in economic policy had hitherto depended.

4

The politics of Keynesian economics, 1924–1929

'A drastic remedy for unemployment'

'It is difficult to reconcile Mr Keynes the politician with Professor Keynes the economist,' wrote the Conservative Cabinet minister, Sir Laming Worthington-Evans, in the midst of the 1929 General Election campaign.[1] He had been primed with a series of statements made by Keynes during the previous few years, generally suggesting that excessive costs were Britain's real economic problem. Yet Keynes was now proposing to tackle unemployment by raising a public loan, which surely meant raising interest rates too. When Sir Laming arraigned Keynes for inconsistency he was out to score an immediate political point, but the underlying issue is one which has provided a long-standing puzzle for economists familiar with Keynes's *Treatise on Money* (1930).

The analysis of the *Treatise* clearly pointed to cheap money as the cure for unemployment; but Keynes was simultaneously lending his advocacy to a different cure—public works—when the problem was debated in the political arena. It hardly seems enough to say that Keynes simply acted in different ways in the different roles he played.[2] There is, indeed, a resolution of this difficulty which has rightly won general acceptance in the recent literature. This is to identify public works as a special case in terms of the *Treatise*, when defence of the currency at a fixed parity *prevented* interest rates from falling sufficiently to restore domestic equilibrium.[3] Abundant evidence will emerge later that this had become the basis of Keynes's policy advice by February 1930. But was this true a year earlier, when he endorsed Lloyd George's proposals? And did Keynes's

---

[1] Letter to the *Evening Standard*, 6 May 1929.
[2] Cf. Don Patinkin, *Keynes's Monetary Thought* (Durham, NC, 1976), 132.
[3] See D. E. Moggridge and Susan Howson, 'Keynes on monetary policy, 1910–46', *Oxford Econ. Papers*, NS 26 (1974), 236; D. E. Moggridge, *Keynes* (2nd edn., 1980), 85–8. This interpretation focuses on 1930–1 and my point is simply that it cannot be stretched backwards to cover the 1920s.

espousal of public works actually stem from the return to gold, as one of the economic consequences of Mr Churchill?

On examination, the verisimilitude of such an explanation turns out to be logical not chronological. It was a legend which Keynes himself propagated, claiming in April 1929 that 'I began advocating schemes of National Development as a cure for unemployment *four years* or more ago—indeed, as soon as I realised that, the effect of the return to gold having been to put our money rates of wages too high relatively to our foreign competitors we could not, for a considerable time, hope to employ as much labour as formerly in the export industries.'[4] He repeated the claim a couple of weeks later, asserting that, since the return to the Gold Standard, 'I have spent the *four years* trying to find the remedy for the transitional period and to persuade the country of its efficacy.'[5] There is only one snag in this account, but a crucial one: the actual order of events. Churchill announced the return to gold in April 1925; Keynes's article, 'Does unemployment need a drastic remedy?', had been published in the *Nation* nearly a year previously, in May 1924—not 'four years ago' but five.

It may be said, of course, that the structure of interest rates already anticipated the return to gold, since this had been a declared objective of British policy since the Report of the Cunliffe Committee in 1918. The key point is really how Keynes saw things at the time. In April 1924 he acknowledged that a return to gold was the Government's stated intention but commented that 'fortunately they are not so foolish as to take any active steps in that direction'. Given time, he thought it 'certainly quite possible that we shall return to our former parity of exchange without resorting to deflation'.[6] At this point, therefore, he did not suppose that return was imminent and the appointment of the Chamberlain–Bradbury Committee a few

---

[4] *JMK* xix. 812–13 (letter to the *Evening Standard*, 30 Apr. 1929); emphasis supplied. Robert Skidelsky follows this line in making 1925 the watershed in Keynes's analysis of unemployment: 'Keynes and the Treasury View', in W. J. Mommsen (ed.), *The Emergence of the Welfare State in Britain and Germany, 1850–1950* (1981), 178–80. This misconception may originate in Robinson, 'John Maynard Keynes', 34–6.

[5] *JMK* xix. 824 ('The Treasury contribution to the White Paper', *Nation*, 18 May 1929); emphasis supplied.

[6] *JMK* xix. 212–13 (discussion at the Royal Economic Society, 14 Apr. 1924). Murray Milgate suggests that Keynes may have professed these hopes of a return to parity as 'a sop to the advocates of the return to gold': 'Keynes and Pigou on the Gold Standard and monetary theory', *Contribs. to Pol. Econ.* (1983), 39–48, at p. 45. But this seems to be purely speculative.

weeks later did not pre-empt the decision. It was not until January 1925, it should be noted, that Montagu Norman shifted from being 'greatly in favour of a return to gold at an early date, but a date which I could not be brave enough to define', to declaring that 'I am now greatly in favour of a return during this year.'[7] Keynes's own evidence to the committee in early July 1924 shows that he shared the general expectation that American prices would rise—'I am really at one with almost everybody on that point'[8]—and therefore did not regard a British deflation as a necessary concomitant of a return to gold. His inflationary expectations at this stage may seem surprising or even inconsistent, but they reflect his state of mind when he broached his 'drastic remedy' for unemployment.

Taking his cue from an initiative by Lloyd George, Keynes outlined proposals for 'national development'—primarily public works—as a cure for unemployment, which currently stood at 770,000. The seeds of some of his most fruitful notions were planted here, in words which his later writings were to echo. He advanced the claim that 'we must look for succour to the principle that *prosperity is cumulative.*' He contended that 'the mind must be averted' from wage cuts, in favour of seeking 'to submerge the rocks in a rising sea'. In response to his critics, he defied them to 'maintain that England is a finished job, and there is nothing in it worth doing on a 5 per cent basis'.[9] As for finding the money, Keynes pointed to an excessive outflow of foreign investment and hinted at using the Sinking Fund for productive capital expenditure at home.

Keynes was surely right in 1929 to look back upon these articles as the inception of his new policy agenda, even if he fudged the chronology to give them an economic rather than a political rationale. For the alternatives, as Keynes saw them, demanded an essentially political choice. 'A drastic reduction of wages in certain industries, and a successful stand-up fight with the more powerful trade unions might reduce unemployment in the long run,' he conceded. 'If any party stands for this solution, let them say so.'[10] It was no accident that these proposals were first published in a Liberal

[7] D. E. Moggridge, *British Monetary Policy, 1924–31* (Cambridge, 1972), 62.
[8] *JMK* xix. 250 (evidence of 11 July 1924); and see Moggridge, *British Monetary Policy*, 43, esp. n. 6, 96.
[9] *JMK* xix. 221 ('Does unemployment need a drastic remedy?', *Nation*, 24 May 1924); ibid. 228 ('A drastic remedy for unemployment', *Nation*, 7 June 1924).
[10] *JMK* xix. 230–1.

journal, subsequently discussed under Liberal auspices, and increasingly identified as the policy of the Liberal party in the late 1920s. If Keynes had relied only upon his economic theory to guide him, his activities would never have taken this turn. In his early drafts of the *Treatise* he maintained that capital expenditure financed by public borrowing could 'do nothing in itself to improve matters' and might 'do actual harm'.[11] As he wrote in 1925, after the return to gold, 'I am trying with all my wits, now in this direction and now in that, to face up to the new problems, theoretically and practically, too.'[12] But theory and practice seemed to pull him in different directions at this stage, and the drastic remedy for unemployment which he suggested in 1924 relied heavily upon intuition. Mr Keynes the politician, though, was not inhibited in backing his hunches by the failure of Professor Keynes the economist to provide adequate theoretical justification.

The Liberal Revival

In making the *Nation* a forum for radical economic policies, Keynes found himself at one with Hubert Henderson. Seven years younger than Keynes, Henderson had read Mathematics for Part I and Economics for Part II of the Cambridge Tripos before the War, and had become a teaching Fellow of Clare College. When Keynes became a chairman of the *Nation* in 1923, he insisted on Henderson becoming editor. He struck Virginia Woolf as 'a small, testy, unheroic man',[13] but he and the chairman were to work in close collaboration for the next seven years. Like Keynes, Henderson knew that much economic theory scouted any suggestion that public spending could produce a net increase in employment—a proposition he happily turned against armaments expenditure in 1923, arguing that 'for every "job" which munitions works provide, they take away a "job" somewhere else'.[14] He and Keynes shared a schooling in the Marshallian tradition in economics and in politics an outlook shaped by the New Liberalism of the Edwardian period.

[11] *JMK* xiii. 23 (draft from 1924–5).
[12] *JMK* xix. 450 (*Manchester Guardian Commercial*, 2 Nov. 1925).
[13] Anne Olivier Bell (ed.), *The Diary of Virginia Woolf*, ii (Harmondsworth, 1981), 268 (11 Sept. 1923).
[14] Article by Henderson, *Daily News*, 21 Feb. 1923; cutting in Henderson Papers, Nuffield College, Oxford, box 21.

There are four salient respects in which Keynes can be identified with the New Liberalism. In the first place, he proclaimed the end of *laissez-faire*—'not enthusiastically, not from contempt of that good old doctrine,' he claimed in 1924, 'but because, whether we like it or not, the conditions for its success have disappeared'. A year later he was pointing to the Conservative party as the place 'for those whose hearts are set on old-fashioned individualism and laissez-faire in all their rigour'.[15] This decisive rejection of the economic navigation of the older Liberal tradition cleared the decks for a new agenda in politics.

Secondly, salvation could not be looked for in socialism and class warfare. Keynes therefore rejected, firstly, the theoretical prescription of doctrinaire state socialism, 'because it misses the significance of what is actually happening'. For example, he insisted that there was 'no so-called important political question so really unimportant, so irrelevant to the reorganisation of the economic life of Great Britain, as the nationalisation of the railways'.[16] Secondly, he also rejected the class war as the appointed means of achieving progress. He could 'conceive nothing worse for us all than a see-saw struggle on class lines between the Haves and the Have-Nots'.[17] Moreover, the appearance in the latter guise of trade unionists—'once the oppressed, now the tyrants'—merely masked their 'selfish and sectional pretensions'.[18] Hence the fundamental inadequacy of this whole approach. 'I do not believe', he wrote in 1927, 'that class war or nationalisation is attractive or stimulating in the least degree to modern minds.'[19]

Thirdly, therefore, Keynes envisaged 'a reformed and remodelled Liberalism, which above all, shall *not*, if my ideal is realised be a *class* party'.[20] The experimental use of the state to achieve the ends of social justice did not imply a strategy of catastrophe but rather the application of hard thinking to see how the system could be made to work more acceptably. Keynes concluded 'that capitalism, wisely managed, can probably be made more efficient for attaining

[15] *JMK* xix. 228 ('A drastic remedy; reply to critics', *Nation*, 7 June 1924); *JMK* ix. 300 ('Am I a Liberal?', *Nation*, 8 Aug. 1925).
[16] *JMK* ix. 290 ('The End of Laissez-Faire', 1926).
[17] *JMK* xix. 324 (letter of support to the Liberal candidate in Cambridge, 18 Oct. 1924).
[18] *JMK* ix. 309 ('Liberalism and Labour', *Nation*, 20 Feb. 1926).
[19] *JMK* xix. 640 (speech on 'Liberalism and Industry', 5 Jan. 1927).
[20] *JMK* xix. 441 (lecture on 'The economic transition in England', 15 Sept. 1925).

economic ends than any alternative system yet in sight, but that in itself it is in many ways extremely objectionable'.[21] Even when it functioned well, it was unfair; when it functioned badly, it became intolerable. Keynes was seeking 'the development of new methods and new ideas for effecting the transition from the economic anarchy of the individualistic capitalism which rules in Western Europe towards a regime which will deliberately aim at controlling and directing economic forces in the interests of social justice and social stability'.[22]

Finally, this meant in practice that there was a large amount of common ground between Liberalism and ordinary or moderate Labour. If Liberals were 'inclined to sympathise with Labour about what is just', then their task was 'to guide the aspirations of the masses for social justice along channels which will not be inconsistent with social efficiency'.[23] As things stood in the mid-1920s, there was little immediate likelihood of 'a progressive Government of the Left capable of efficient legislation' unless co-operation with Labour was established,[24] and Lloyd George's efforts in this direction were a major reason why Keynes swung into his orbit, despite the strong pull of old Asquithian loyalties.

These four corner-stones of the New Liberalism were built into the foundations of Keynes's political thinking. He specifically described his aspirations as 'the true destiny of a New Liberalism'[25]—an odd turn of phrase if it was merely a random choice of words. This outlook not only made him a committed Liberal in party terms but also placed him self-consciously on the left of the British political spectrum—'I am sure that I am less conservative in my inclinations that the average Labour voter', he reflected.[26] It does not seem helpful to ignore Keynes's own self-identification in favour of a political taxonomy which would place him as a centrist, or even to

---

[21] *JMK* ix. 294 ('The End of Laissez-Faire').

[22] *JMK* xix. 439 ('The economic transition in England', 15 Sept. 1925).

[23] *JMK* xix. 639–40 ('Liberalism and Industry', 5 Jan. 1927).

[24] *JMK* xix. 327 ('The balance of political power at the elections', *Nation*, 8 Nov. 1924).

[25] *JMK* xix. 439 ('The economic transition in England'); cf. 647 ('Liberalism and Industry') and *JMK* ix. 305 ('Am I a Liberal?'). The balance of historical evidence thus seems to me to invalidate the philosophically plausible view stated by Maurice Cranston, 'Keynes: His political ideas and their influence', in A. P. Thirlwall (ed.), *Keynes and Laissez-Faire* (1978), 111–14.

[26] *JMK* ix. 308–9 ('Liberalism and Labour').

the right of that.[27] When he spoke on politics, he did so as a Liberal of the left, hopeful of co-operation between Labour and a Liberal party which, even in the aftermath of the 1924 election, which reduced it to a remnant of forty MPs, might expect to hold the balance of power 'in one election out of every two'. Keynes argued that, if catastrophe alone made a Labour Government conceivable, it would likewise make its policy inconceivable. Hence the impasse, 'unless Radicals and Labour men stop cutting one another's throats and come to an agreement for joint action from time to time to carry through practical measures about which they agree.'[28]

This sort of Liberalism found its *métier* in the annual Liberal Summer School, at which Keynes gave his highly characteristic talk 'Am I a Liberal?', in Cambridge in August 1925. What revitalized the Liberals as a party, however, was the enlistment of this tatter-demalion army of intellectuals under the generalship of Lloyd George. For Asquithians like Keynes and Henderson, this represented a painfully conclusive break with habitual allegiances. As late as the winter of 1925-6, Lloyd George was accusing the *Nation* of carrying on a vendetta against him. But at the end of May 1926 Henderson wrote a leading article—'against my personal predilections'[29]—which backed Lloyd George's conciliatory line over the General Strike against the lapse into industrial jingoism of the aged Asquith (Lord Oxford). For Keynes, too, this was an ineluctable choice if his hopes for Liberalism were to have a fighting chance. 'Is it too much to hope', asked the *Nation* after this rupture, 'that from the union of the gifts of Mr Lloyd George and the Summer School there may emerge the new radical impulse which we need?'[30]

The Liberal Industrial Inquiry, under the chairmanship of another economist from the Cambridge school, Walter Layton, gave Keynes and Henderson a direct responsibility for the making of Liberal party policy during 1927. Lloyd George pampered his group of intellectuals by hiring Daimlers to drive them down to his country house for a succession of weekend meetings at which he established a relaxed

[27] Cf. Michael Freeden, *Liberalism Divided* (Oxford, 1986), 154–73, esp. 171. My difference from this account stems largely from the definitions employed; see above, ch. 1, n. 11.

[28] *JMK* xix. 327 ('The balance of power at the elections', *Nation*, 8 Nov. 1924).

[29] Henderson to M. Bonham Carter, 4 June 1926, copy, Henderson Papers, box 21; cf. John Campbell, *Lloyd George* (1977), 195.

[30] Freeden, *Liberalism Divided*, 104; ch. 4 comprises a very good treatment of the Summer School.

atmosphere. Keynes, true to his habits, may have spent long hours in bed—'I snuff the candle at both ends', he confessed[31]—but he manifestly left his stamp upon the proceedings. He was responsible for substantial sections of the Inquiry's Report, *Britain's Industrial Future* (1928), notably those dealing with finance and banking. The proposals in the 'Yellow Book' for tackling 'abnormal' unemployment through schemes of national development clearly had Keynes's approval; but there is no record that Book 4, which expounded them, contains any of his own drafting.[32] Keynes obviously hoped that the Yellow Book would help the Liberal party electorally but he recognized too that a *bien-pensant* encyclopaedia of useful knowledge about the British economy—'speaking when it has nothing to say, as well as when it has'[33]—was bound to have a rather discouraging effect upon the reader. According to Thomas Jones, the authors 'seemed rather flat at the reception of the book' when he dined with them at the Tuesday Club on 8 February.[34]

Within a matter of days there was cheering news for partisan Liberals, suggesting that the Yellow Book might have caught a flowing tide. Having won one seat each from Conservatives and Labour in by-elections in 1927, the Liberals made a further gain from the Conservatives at Lancaster on 9 February 1928. This was seen as very much Lloyd George's doing, though the further victory at St Ives in March was tarnished for him by its appearance as a piece of effrontery by old Asquithians. The Liberals remained fairly confident throughout 1928, but further by-elections (like Cheltenham and Tavistock) stubbornly refused to yield to Lloyd George's assaults. It was not until March 1929, after the publication of *We Can Conquer Unemployment*, that the Liberals opportunely enjoyed a further electoral boost, with two gains on successive days from the Conservatives: at Eddisbury in a straight fight and a spectacular upset at Holland-with-Boston in a four-sided contest.[35] These were not, of course, industrial constituencies with high unemployment.

There are grounds for arguing that the Liberals were flattered by their by-election record. 'If God had asked L.G. where he would have

[31] David Hubback, *No Ordinary Press Baron: A Life of Walter Layton* (1985), 77.

[32] For authorship see *JMK* xix. 731, and Harrod, *Life*, 393.

[33] *JMK* xix. 735 (to Lydia, 5 Feb. 1928).

[34] Jones, *Whitehall Diary*, ii. 130.

[35] Campbell, *Lloyd George*, 207, 210–11, 214–16, 227–8; and D. E. Butler, *The Electoral System in Britain, 1918–51* (Oxford, 1953), 181–2, for a statistical comparison with the 1929 General Election results in the same seats.

liked four or five byes, L.G. couldn't have chosen better for himself', Hugh Dalton wrote privately.[36] Yet the raising of expectations may, of course, become self-fulfilling as a bandwagon effect, and it needs hindsight to see that this was not to happen in 1929. The fact that the Conservatives won back so much ground from their opponents between the by-elections and the General Election in 1929 (7.1 per cent from Labour, 4.6 per cent from the Liberals) was not predetermined. To put the matter the other way, had the opposition parties held on to the sort of gains which they registered in the by-elections of February and March 1929 when it came to the General Election at the end of May, the result would have been a much more bruising defeat for the Conservatives. In short, the prospects for the Liberals in a forthcoming General Election were undoubtedly more heartening than they had been for years and Keynes was not self-evidently wrong in supposing that this gave a platform for punching home his own ideas with real electoral muscle. He looked on the Liberal party not as a route to power (in which case, 'I agree that one is probably wasting one's time') but as 'a method of bringing a sensible programme to the notice of the public and of politicians, much of which one party or another will carry out in the next ensuing years'.[37] In 1929 there seemed to be a real chance of remaking the agenda for government, and, as an inveterate political animal, Keynes entered upon the campaign with his blood up.

'A complete volte face'

Although Keynes had manifestly inspired the general approach of *We Can Conquer Unemployment*, it does not follow that he was personally responsible for each and every proposition in the pamphlet. The part of the Yellow Book on national development was one for which he had no direct responsibility. The adaptation of the pamphlet from this source was in the hands of Seebohm Rowntree and the political staff at Liberal headquarters, drawing upon the advice of other financial experts as well as Keynes. Admittedly, the

---

[36] 'End of 1927', Dalton diary, London School of Economics; and see Michael Hart, 'The decline of the Liberal party in Parliament and in the Constituencies, 1914–31', D.Phil. thesis (Oxford, 1982), 346–9; this counters the view in Chris Cook, *The Age of Alignment, 1922–9* (1975), 336–8.

[37] *JMK* xix. 713 (to J. L. Garvin, 9 Feb. 1928).

section entitled 'Some Objections Met' has a Keynesian ring to it. The soundness of the Liberals' theory was defended against (implicitly) the Treasury View that no net increase in employment would result. 'There is no fixed fund of employment,' it was claimed; moreover, it was 'quite wrong to assume that all savings available for investment are always being fully utilised'.[38] How was this rather inchoate assertion justified? The argument was that 'frozen savings' accumulated in a depression, awaiting enterprise to 'thaw' them. Figures were then cited showing an alleged increase in the proportion of time deposits to demand deposits in the banking system over the course of the 1920s. The point had recently been introduced by McKenna in his annual address as chairman of the Midland Bank, with the claim that 'time deposits have more of the character of money awaiting investment and money for which no trading use can be found at the moment'.[39] McKenna, of course, was himself a former Liberal Chancellor of the Exchequer under Asquith, and a bitter opponent of Lloyd George during the years of factionalism. In the search for Liberal unity in 1929, there was more than one reason to propitiate him and to implicate him in the advocacy of the Lloyd George programme.

The argument about 'frozen savings' in *We Can Conquer Unemployment* needed delicate handling. For it was not suggested that time deposits were not used at all by the banks: merely that they were 'used to less advantage from an employment point of view'.[40] Whereas the Treasury View rested on the presumption that private enterprise maximized the return on available resources, this argument really amounted to saying that here it presumed too far. It tacitly accepted that the supply of savings was fixed, but suggested that it was fixed at a rather higher level than was conventionally reckoned. It is also worth noting that there was no direct reference to foreign lending as a source that could be tapped for new investment at home.[41]

The notion that there were idle balances sitting in the banks thus had a lot of work to do in justifying the central claim of *We Can Conquer Unemployment*. Keynes subsequently had a good deal of

[38] The Liberal Party, *We Can Conquer Unemployment* (1929), 54.

[39] *The Times*, 23 Jan. 1929.

[40] *We Can Conquer Unemployment*, 53.

[41] Ibid. 57, is the nearest, with an illustrative allusion to the relative merits of loans for Munich, as against those for Birmingham or Glasgow.

trouble in scotching the idea that it was the crux of his own analysis and admitted that 'when I first began to work on Book III of my *Treatise* I believed something resembling this myself'. But this must refer to his drafts of 1927–8 and it seems unwarranted to conclude that Keynes himself had introduced this argument in March 1929, only to change his mind by the time the *Treatise* was published some eighteen months later.[42]

The direct evidence of his own views appears to indicate the opposite, and this can be supplemented by inference from what he was writing on closely related issues. In a draft of the *Treatise* which he had revised a fortnight before the publication of *We Can Conquer Unemployment*, Keynes examined the proposition that the supply of working capital could be increased if banks replaced their own investments with advances to business. He therefore surveyed the statistics on bank assets, but in a spirit of agnosticism not revelation. He made the point that such diversion of funds as might occur did nothing to increase *aggregate* investment (least of all in a way that would be relevant to public works). 'Our conclusion is, therefore, that when it is desired to increase the production of fixed capital goods, the banks can do nothing to facilitate it by changing the form of their assets.'[43] Whatever bulkheads divided the hull of the banking system, its overall capacity was what really mattered. Yet if Keynes was not pointing to idle balances as a source of finance in 1929, what was his argument?

The galley proofs of the *Treatise*, on which Keynes must have been working during February 1929, show the way his mind was moving. The relevant section is headed 'Methods of increasing (or diminishing) the supply of working capital through the banking system'. Keynes acknowledged that the banks *could* simply aim to maintain price stability. This was the policy he himself had advocated in the *Tract* but, under the influence of Robertson's ideas about credit and the price level, he now deprecated a single-minded concentration on this objective. What was also needed was attention to the wider

---

[42] *JMK* xiii. 246 (*Economica*, Nov. 1931); cf. Jim Tomlinson, *Problems of British Economic Policy, 1870–1945* (1981), 90, endorsed in Alan Booth and Melvyn Pack, *Employment, Capital, and Economic Policy* (Oxford, 1985), 50. The points in both books, however, about the common ground between the theoretical analyses of Keynes and the Treasury are well taken.

[43] *JMK* xiii. 100; cf. 98 and n. There is a reference back to the banking statistics in ch. 13 of the 1929 draft (ch. 14 of the 1928 draft) which occupies the same place in the structure of the argument as ch. 23 of the *Treatise* itself.

objective of 'meeting adequately the demand for credit'.[44] How could the banks do this? Keynes put the alternatives under two heads. One was by 'changing the form of the already available aggregate of real bank credit (i.e. of real savings invested through the banking system)'. Hence the discussion noted above, concluding that juggling with existing items in the balance sheet was irrelevant. The second head subsumed four ways of 'increasing the available aggregate of real bank credit'.[45] In effect, Keynes was confronting within an academic framework the question that was bound to be put in the forthcoming public debate over the Lloyd George scheme: where is the money to come from?

Keynes had long been ready with three answers, which he duly pressed into service. The first was by attracting savings at home. Again, not an awful lot could be expected but, even so, Keynes gave a surprising commendation of higher Bank rate as 'a move in the right direction from this point of view'.[46] It was the second answer which promised 'an important method of escape from these disappointing conclusions', namely 'the possibility of attracting additional working capital *from abroad*'. It was, of course, only a remedy for one country. The relevance of a higher Bank rate was again apparent since it promised 'to make good the temporary shortage of savings at home by attracting them from abroad', and did so by diminishing net foreign lending.[47] Thirdly, Keynes followed Robertson in suggesting that credit inflation could transfer income into the hands of entrepreneurs, thereby enabling additional investment to take place. All these answers presupposed that extra investment depended upon finding extra sources of savings first. These three possibilities were in Keynes's mind in October 1928 when he planned his chapter. By the end of February 1929, another thought had struck him.

This was to argue that resources became available 'by restoring equilibrium between saving and investment'.[48] It seems that this idea first came to him as the obverse of the argument—in effect, Robertson's—that inflation transferred income to entrepreneurs: the validity of which, Keynes now saw, depended on an underlying

---

[44] *JMK* xiii. 91. This section is printed as a variorum; cf. the Table of Contents, p. 81.

[45] *JMK* xiii. 93 n.   [46] *JMK* xiii. 95 n.

[47] *JMK* xiii. 101, 103 (emphasis in original).

[48] *JMK* xiii. 93 n.

assumption. 'We have tacitly assumed above', he noted in tacking on his new section, 'that the savings of the country are being fully invested.' But if these were not so, then some credit expansion might be necessary to *avoid* redistribution of income *away from* entrepreneurs. It was wrong 'to dub an expansion of bank lending as a credit inflation until we have first assured ourselves that it is not merely a necessary corrective for the avoidance of a credit deflation'.[49]

For Keynes, necessity was the mother of invention. He had dreamt up his new argument in the nick of time, and, while revising the *Treatise* with one hand, he ambidextrously supplied the *Nation* with fresh copy. 'The volume of real investment is falling short of the volume of money savings,' he proclaimed. 'Industry is too depressed to absorb all the savings which the public is ready to place at its disposal.' The result was that savings were dissipated in reinforcing the deflationary trend. (No allusion was made, however, to frozen savings, idle balances, or time deposits.) The standard objection to capital spending by government—'crowding-out'—was thus only true under boom conditions. 'A vast amount of deflationary slack has first to be taken up before there can be the smallest danger of a development policy leading to inflation,' the author of the *Nation* article concluded.[50] The author of the *Treatise* subsequently proceeded to chop up his galley proofs and reorder the structure of his argument. The restoration of equilibrium between saving and investment was given pride of place in the page-proofs, which now began: 'The first duty of the banking system is to make sure that there is no deflationary slack available to be taken in.'[51]

Keynes's theoretical analysis of unemployment, and its close application to the situation of Great Britain in the spring of 1929, is thus fairly clear. In so far as unemployment was due to a disequilibrium of saving and investment, the banks could act to correct it, but they also needed a parallel policy by the state in the form of investment. Whether the banks should concentrate on reducing interest rates or increasing the volume of credit was a matter of political judgement. But in the British case, where foreign lending was

---

[49] *JMK* xiii. 108 n., 94.
[50] 'The objections to capital expenditure', *Nation*, 23 Feb. 1929, 710–11. Apart from the strong internal evidence that this is by Keynes, it is also cited as his in the Treasury papers.
[51] *JMK* xiii. 94.

running out of control, it was 'occasionally conceivable that the combination of a higher bank rate with an increased volume of bank credit may be, paradoxically, the right solution'. There was also the possibility of redistributing the flows of investment. Finally, if the problem was that the rate of real efficiency wages was higher than that abroad—a comment made with explicit relevance to Britain in 1929—'there was nothing to be done except to press on with remedies directed to the other factors in the situation', in the hope that they would produce favourable effects.[52]

Though Keynes purported to be writing a formal academic analysis, much of it is a transparent rationalization of immediate policy proposals. There is direct evidence that the Treasury was fully cognizant of his diagnosis because on 7 March 1929 he had a meeting with Hopkins and Leith-Ross, of which the latter left a full record. It shows that Keynes began by stressing the need to restore a harmony between saving and investment, though there is no sign that this idea made much impression upon his hearers. Since wages had not been reduced, he argued, another remedy must be tried which would maintain full employment while efficiency caught up. In the short run, therefore, funds must be attracted away from foreign loans by means of a higher Bank rate. According to Leith-Ross, Keynes 'admitted that our past investment abroad had been of great value and did not deny that in the long run the orthodox theory must operate'.[53]

Clearly, to Leith-Ross this represented an important admission on Keynes's part, and one which he continued to cite against him. But it is equally clear that each understood something different by it. To Leith-Ross the advantage of lending abroad was axiomatic, in that it helped sustain British exports. He did not shut his mind to the possibility that there might have been a speculative lurch into over-lending—'I can't help thinking that there is something in this doctrine'[54]—but even if this were the case, it was also axiomatic that any over-investment would cure itself. To Keynes, however, the process of adjustment itself had come to look like the problem. He subsequently explained himself to Leith-Ross by articulating the process underlying the axiom: 'the struggle to adjust the situation will take the form of restriction of credit, leading to the restriction of

[52] *JMK* xiii. 109, 110 n.
[53] Leith-Ross memorandum, 8 Mar. 1929, T. 172/2095.
[54] Leith-Ross to Sir Henry Strakosch, 16 Mar. 1929, copy, T. 172/2095.

enterprise, resulting in unemployment in the hope that the unemployment will bring down wages, with the result that our exports will increase and so provide for the previous foreign investment.' Keynes did not need to teach the former British Representative on the Finance Board of the Reparation Commission that Britain could no more remit foreign loans *in money* than Germany could remit reparation payments. An allusion was therefore enough: 'That is what I meant by saying that we, too, had an analogy to the transfer problem.'[55]

An article on German reparations in the current issue of the *Economic Journal* illustrated Keynes's line of thought. 'The *transfer* problem consists in reducing the gold rate of efficiency earnings of the German factors of production sufficiently to enable them to increase their exports to an adequate aggregate total,' he wrote. But he confessed his own view that such adjustments in the level of exports were much more difficult to achieve than adjustments in the amount of foreign investment. Since the problem resided in 'trying to fix the volume of foreign remittance and compel the balance of trade to adjust itself thereto,' Keynes drew the conclusion: 'Those who see no difficulty in this—like those who saw no difficulty in Great Britain's return to the gold standard—are applying the theory of liquids to what is, if not solid, at least a sticky mass with strong internal resistances.'[56]

Just as Keynes had queried the 'automatic' process of adjustment implied by the Gold Standard, so he now turned his attention to the conventional claims concerning foreign investment. Leith-Ross records him as saying that 'a temporary embargo on foreign loans would not do any appreciable damage to our export trade for the reason that not more than 20% of the money lent created additional exports'.[57] There is good reason to accept that Keynes said something like this—he used the same figure elsewhere—and Leith-Ross may have thought he had a satisfactory answer in contending that 'the proceeds of every loan we make must ultimately be exported.'[58] But *how* did 20 per cent 'ultimately' climb to 100 per cent? This was the question on Keynes's mind. It was not the 'conclusion that, if we

[55] Keynes to Leith-Ross, 12 Mar. 1929, T. 172/2095.

[56] *JMK* xi. 451–60, at 455, 458 ('The German transfer problem', *Econ. Jnl.*, Mar. 1929).

[57] Memorandum, 8 Mar. 1929, T. 172/2095; cf. *JMK* xix. 800.

[58] Leith-Ross draft for Churchill, 3 Apr. 1929, T. 172/2095.

lend more abroad, this will stimulate our exports', that he sought to deny; it was the reasoning that he wished to elucidate. And he expostulated that, whenever this bland assertion was made, it should always be accompanied by the explication for the unwary: 'because it will make the maintenance of full employment impossible at the present level of wages, so that unemployment will continue until British wages are reduced, which will enhance our competitive power in foreign markets.'[59] In short, Keynes found himself confronting another unargued dogma resting upon the protean assumption of flexible prices.

Was this a reasonable assumption on which to frame policy in the 1920s? On the whole, the Treasury had accepted it, notably over the Gold Standard. But in 1929 significant indications of change appear. Prompted by their discussion, Leith-Ross took up Keynes's contention that, despite the reduction in prices since 1925, there had been no comparable fall in wages. He wrote to Hawtrey that this 'appears to be so surprising that I should be glad if you would go into it'. It could only have been such a surprise to someone who had implicit confidence that the flexibility of relative prices would show through in the long run. The previous summer, Leith-Ross had brushed aside the evidence on this point—'It only shows how fallacious such indices are'—but he now accepted Hawtrey's assurance that wages had indeed, year after year, proved obdurately sticky.[60] Here, it might seem, was an overdue acceptance of Keynes's long-standing contention that the Treasury was wrong to make light of the processes of adjustment. 'They have taken four years to find out this elementary fact,' he was to comment.[61]

But the Treasury had still not caught up with Keynes's reasoning. His analysis was not simply that costs were too high (with the implication that they ought to have been brought down, consistent with cheap money), but that the failure to reduce them should now be accepted as the premiss for a new policy. When Keynes wrote that 'the fundamental blunder of the Treasury and of the Bank of England has been due to their belief that if they looked after the deflation of prices, the deflation of costs would look after itself', it

---

[59] *JMK* xix. 803 (letter to *The Economist*, 26 Mar. 1929).

[60] Compare Leith-Ross to Hawtrey, 13 Mar. 1929, T. 175/26, with Leith-Ross memorandum, 9 Aug. 1928, T. 172/2095.

[61] *JMK* xix. 824 ('The Treasury contribution to the White Paper', *Nation*, 18 May 1929).

was 1928 and the Treasury was not much taken with the point. When Leith-Ross quoted it, adding the moral that 'what we have to do is to reduce costs',[62] it was 1929 and the Treasury was more convinced than ever that the adjustments on which its faith was pinned, having evidently failed to eventuate so far, must now do so. 'If there is money lying idle—and not used to full employment capacity—it is due to our costs of production being above world level,' ran a characteristic jotting, 'therefore Keynes remedy will make things worse instead of better.'[63]

'I have reason to think that, in fact, Keynes is no longer an advocate of inflation,' Leith-Ross reported to Churchill, enclosing a note of their conversation. In advising the Chancellor, Leith-Ross showed that he grasped the case for raising Bank rate to keep money at home, though not its full rationale in bringing under-used resources into production. 'This novel theory', he commented, 'represents a complete volte face from his former doctrine that our troubles are all due to Bank Rate.'[64] In private, then, the Treasury showed that they recognized, even if they did not fully understand, still less accept, the new thrust in Keynes's thinking towards raising interest rates as a means of employing more capital at home. In public, however, both sides had difficulty in pinning the other down as the debate over the Lloyd George pledge and the Treasury View developed during the ten weeks before polling day on 30 May 1929.

Can Lloyd George Do It?

Keynes showed his hand in an article in the *Evening Standard* on 19 March, in the wake of the publication of *We Can Conquer Unemployment*. He accused the Treasury of pigeon-holing desirable schemes 'under the influence of what I can only describe as a mental affliction'. This took the form of the belief that encouraging people to save would achieve the desirable objective of bringing down the rate of interest. Keynes, however, identified a 'leakage' which would prevent this from happening. He argued that 'if we save and can find no outlet for our savings at home, we lend the money abroad on a scale disproportionate to our export surplus at the present level of wages,

---

[62] Leith-Ross, draft for Churchill, 3 Apr. 1929, T. 172/2095; cf. *JMK* xix. 762.

[63] Pencil notes by Leith-Ross, 'Keynes and L.G.', n.d., T. 188/274.

[64] Leith-Ross to Churchill, 12 Mar. 1929, T. 172/2095.

the Bank of England loses gold and raises the Bank rate.' In effect, it was the transfer problem—suggesting that the export surplus set a limit on the amount of capital which could beneficially be transferred overseas rather than that foreign investments automatically guaranteed equivalent exports. Having commended public works as an alternative, Keynes turned to 'the most searching question of all': whether capital would simply be diverted from other productive uses.[65]

Whether his critique of the Treasury View was wasted upon the readers of the *Evening Standard* (trying to digest Keynes in a crowded tube train, perhaps) is a good question. According to Kahn, Keynes made an elementary blunder in giving away his case in these articles. 'Sir Richard Hopkins was warned and the "Treasury view" no longer appeared in the White Paper as fundamental and decisive, taken by itself, as Winston Churchill had made it appear in his Budget statement.'[66] Keynes's first article, of course, appeared nearly four weeks before Churchill spoke, without abashing the Chancellor; but it is clear that the Treasury kept a close eye on the newspaper controversies in which Keynes was engaged, the better to meet his arguments, turn by turn, in the memorandum which they were preparing. Thus when Keynes pointed to overseas lending as a source of funds, he conceded that it would be 'necessary to offer a rate of interest which can compete with foreign borrowers'. Now in print, this admission was quoted in the Treasury Memorandum as showing that the Liberal scheme in fact depended on significantly higher interest rates. For Keynes, however, such an implication could only be drawn by ignoring the fact that 'a large surplus of *unused* productive resources' stood waiting to be utilized. Blazoning across Beaverbrook's newsprint the insight of the latest draft of the *Treatise*, he wrote: 'The orthodox theory *assumes* that everyone is employed.'[67]

Sir Laming Worthington-Evans, the Secretary of State for War, may seem an ill-matched champion to have entered the lists against Keynes, and his reply on 12 April was mainly party political knockabout, larded with time-worn gibes at the Free Traders. Keynes

[65] *JMK* xix. 805, 807.

[66] Richard F. Kahn, *The Making of Keynes's General Theory* (Cambridge, 1984), 81. There is a cutting of Keynes's article in Hawtrey's papers, HTRY 1/41.

[67] *JMK* xix. 807; cf. *Memoranda on certain proposals relating to unemployment*, Cmd. 3331 (1929), 50. This paragraph, like virtually all the Treasury Memorandum, was taken unchanged from the draft of the interdepartmental committee, dated 2 Apr. 1929, CP 104 (29), CAB 24/203.

responded on 19 April by virtually ignoring what Worthington-Evans had written and instead inventing for him a 'credo' which he took to be his real argument. This was, of course, the Treasury View, recently reinforced by Churchill's Budget statement. Keynes now expanded his list of sources for new investment. A reduction in foreign lending was still named but it had been leap-frogged in priority by two other considerations. First came the disequilibrium between saving and investment, meaning that it was currently safe to create more credit without risking inflation. The other source was from savings on maintaining the unemployed, which had long been a favourite argument with advocates of public works. It is worth noting that, although this was a clearly identifiable saving to the Budget, within Keynes's analysis it should really be considered as a special case of excessive saving running to waste in unproductive ways.

It was Keynes's charge against Worthington-Evans that 'he half understands an ancient theory, the premises of which he has forgotten'. The theory posited that all productive resources were normally brought into employment by their willingness to accept a sufficiently low rate of remuneration—and thus began 'by assuming the non-existence of the very phenomenon which is under investigation'.[68] This was deep water for Worthington-Evans but fortunately he was given a helping hand at this stage in struggling back into his depth. For his riposte on 26 April was altogether more coherent than his initial contribution. The Treasury's favourite quotations from Keynes's past writings were marshalled to allege his inconsistency: 'The real trouble, therefore, in the view of Mr Keynes of yesteryear is the excessive costs of production, and, in particular, excessive wage costs.' Leith-Ross could not have put it better. The form of the argument against attracting funds from foreign lending is strikingly close to that of the Treasury Memorandum: 'The damage done to employment by enforcing such high rates would be far greater than any benefit industry could possibly obtain by diverting to home investment the comparatively small proportion of our total national savings which at present goes into foreign investment.'[69]

The form which this controversy took is explained by the Cabinet minutes. The interdepartmental committee of officials examining *We Can Conquer Unemployment* had finished its work, and its draft,

[68] *JMK* xix. 811.
[69] 'Mr Keynes speaks as a politician', *Evening Standard*, 26 Apr. 1929; cf. Treasury Memorandum, Cmd. 3331, 53.

including the Treasury Memorandum, had been circulated to ministers. At the Cabinet meeting on 17 April, Steel-Maitland urged that it should now be revised for publication. It was agreed at this stage that the use of any material from it 'for political purposes must be made on the responsibility of the Minister concerned, who of course in any event would not refer publicly to the document in question'.[70] Hence the use of Worthington-Evans as a stalking-horse.

Ever since *The Economic Consequences of the Peace* Keynes had been a public figure embroiled in continual controversy; but until the General Election of 1929 he had never before been so clearly identified as a party propagandist. There was no dissimulating the fact that the Liberal proposals rested on his ideas. Challenged by Baldwin to name his experts, Lloyd George publicly cited three names: those of Keynes, Layton, and Samuel. When the pamphlet Keynes wrote with Henderson, *Can Lloyd George Do It?*, was published on 10 May, it brought him explicitly into the middle of a controversy which he had already played a considerable part in fomenting. It was in part a scissors-and-paste reworking of polemical articles from the previous weeks. This may have robbed some of the arguments of their freshness; but it also meant that there had been an opportunity to adapt the shape of the argument to criticisms which had arisen.

The pamphlet began by acknowledging that 'the most solid reason for hesitation' about the Liberal programme lay 'not in the difficulty of finding work to do or in the difficulty of financing it, but in the "transfer" problem'—understood as that of moving workers from the derelict industries to new jobs.[71] But it argued that prosperity provided the best conditions for tackling this problem. The priority given to this point is interesting in view of modern criticism of Keynesian economics for ignoring the structural aspect of unemployment. Estimates of the amount of employment to be given, both directly and indirectly, were assessed, and a further consideration was then introduced or, rather, revived. This was 'the cumulative force of trade activity', prompting the modern reader to think of secondary employment. Having conjured up these visions, however, Keynes and

---

[70] Cabinet 17 (29) 7, CAB 23/60. The committee's draft also dealt with the Melchett–Turner report on industrial relations.

[71] *JMK* ix. 89. The term 'transfer problem' was confusingly applied to that of labour mobility as well as that of the international exchanges.

Henderson said no more than that 'in our opinion, these effects are of immense importance'.[72]

The Conservatives' bull point in 1929 was the simple question: where will the money come from? *Can Lloyd George Do It?* provided two sorts of answer. Chapter vii appeared in the *Nation* as 'The cost of the Liberal scheme' and was probably truly collaborative. In it the problem of the Budget was dealt with by juggling various departmental funds and producing 'economies on armaments' as a rabbit out of the hat—with no mention, of course, of consequent unemployment in the arms industries! In chapter ix, however, written by Keynes, a more fundamental issue arose in considering the real resources available. This was where Keynes quoted the Treasury View, as promulgated by Churchill, the better to confute it. He repeated from his *Evening Standard* article of 19 April the three resources which were available: savings on the dole, savings running to waste through inadequate credit, and finally a reduction in net foreign lending. When he concluded by recapitulating these sources, they had mysteriously grown from three to four, for he smuggled into the list the claim that 'something will be provided by the very prosperity which the new policy will foster'.[37] Retrospectively, this may look like a ghostly adumbration of the multiplier concept but at the time it must have looked Panglossian.

On the eve of publication of *Can Lloyd George Do It?*, the Prime Minister answered a planted question in the House of Commons by saying that the Government had decided to publish their own expert appraisal of the Liberal scheme. The Cabinet had, in fact, become dissatisfied with its efforts to leak the expert appraisal and had appointed a ministerial committee, comprising Churchill and Steel-Maitland under Worthington-Evans's chairmanship, to review the possibility of publication. It concluded that much of the draft report could not be published 'without detriment to the Civil Service' but that a White Paper under ministerial responsibility might be extracted from it. Steel-Maitland was charged with this task. The White Paper which was issued on 13 May comprised memoranda from four ministers plus the Treasury Memorandum—a form peculiarly vulnerable to criticism if, as Baldwin claimed, the purpose was to protect the impartial status of the officials. Why Churchill did

---

[72] *JMK* ix. 106–7.
[73] *JMK* ix. 120; cf. 116 and *JMK* xix. 810–11.

not sign it himself is not clear. Even *The Times*, which liked the substance of the White Paper, acknowledged that it 'must be treated as no more and no less than the Conservative party's statement of its case'.[74]

The White Paper drew upon weeks of work in the interdepartmental committee in presenting a cogent critique of the Liberal scheme. A programme of unprecedented scale, locked into an ambitious timetable, it fell foul of many technical objections which were well grounded in administrative experience. In particular, the memorandum by the Minister of Labour Sir Arthur Steel-Maitland, made telling points about schemes which might be good in themselves but, taken together, were 'impracticable on such a scale'.[75] In historical perspective, therefore, there are sound reasons of this kind to suppose that the Liberal programme could not have been implemented on schedule, and that Lloyd George's specific pledge could not therefore have been fulfilled. Keynes and Henderson had chosen to regard this not as a disabling objection but as a friendly doubt: 'Even if it takes more than a year to get going, even if it costs the taxpayer something, even if it brings employment to no more than 400,000 or 500,000 additional men, what does it matter?'[76]

The big issue for economic historians, however, is the extent to which such a programme could 'do it' at all—a question addressed today with a battery of concepts subsequently derived from Keynes. Answers here depend on macro-economic modelling and—crucially—upon the figure that is estimated for the multiplier. The most authoritative modern calculation, based on a low value for the multiplier, suggests that unemployment might have been reduced by 268,000 in 1929 and 300,000 in 1930.[77] Whether this should be seen as a damning verdict upon the proposals depends on what question is being asked. If we are concerned to understand how the argument was conducted in 1929, it is unhelpful and anachronistic to make it hinge upon a dispute over the magnitude of the multiplier—a concept which no one grasped at the time.

[74] *The Times*, leader, 13 May 1929; cf. Cabinets 19 (29) 2 and 20 (29) 2, 1 and 6 May 1929, CAB 23/60.

[75] Cmd. 3331, 14.

[76] *JMK* ix. 88.

[77] See T. Thomas, 'Aggregate demand in the United Kingdom, 1918–45', in Roderick Floud and Donald McCloskey (eds.), *The Economic History of Britain since 1700*, ii (Cambridge, 1981), 337, 345–6; Roger Middleton, *Towards the Managed Economy* (1985), 146–8, 176–8. For the multiplier concept, see appendix to ch. 10 below.

What was claimed in *We Can Conquer Unemployment* was that the specified schemes would give additional employment to 586,000 men in the first year. The pledge was to reduce unemployment to the level normal before the First World War, reckoned as 4.7 per cent of the insured population or about 570,000. The official unemployment figure for 1928 was 1,300,000, leaving nearly 750,000 jobs to be found. The April 1929 figure, as cited in *Can Lloyd George Do It?*, was 1,140,000. This improvement helped the Conservatives argue that things were on the mend; it also helped the Liberals argue that their estimate of new jobs would be enough to get all the way back to normal. In the light of modern research, it looks as though the Liberals were too optimistic by half (almost exactly). There is a compensating irony about the low value of the multiplier, which causes this downward revision. For the other aspect of the argument was over the cost of such a scheme to the Budget. Now the magnitude of the leakages which have been postulated, while they give a smaller multiplier on jobs created, also necessarily imply that public works would have been more largely self-financing, notably through savings on the dole, than Keynes's opponents allowed: so the fewer the jobs, the smaller the Budgetary deficit.[78] Macro-economic models can thus be used to show either that Keynes was unknowingly over-pessimistic about financing the scheme or that he was unknowingly over-optimistic about its impact on unemployment, but not to show both things at once.

On the hustings

It may be true that, even without the twelve pages of the Treasury Memorandum, the other forty-four pages of the 1929 White Paper would have vitiated the Liberal proposals on practical grounds.[79] But the remarks of Steel-Maitland, who had his own reasons for wishing that things were otherwise, give an indication of the priority accorded to Treasury advice by the Government. Steel-Maitland was perfectly ready to acknowledge the demoralizing and unproductive nature of expenditure on maintaining the unemployed. 'On the other hand,' he wrote, 'the ordinary economic and financial objections to

[78] This is the converse of the point about the multiplier made in Middleton, op. cit. 177–8.
[79] Tomlinson, *Problems of British Economic Policy*, 82.

the policy of State-aided work for the unemployed are well known. They are cogently stated in the Memorandum submitted by the Chancellor of the Exchequer.'[80] There is a mordant inwardness to this show of deference, but it acknowledged the rationale of the Conservative case. Other objections to public works could not be ignored but the Treasury View was conclusive.

There was nothing dogmatic or doctrinaire about the manner in which the Treasury View was now stated. The Memorandum examined the proposition that the capital required could 'be raised out of savings which are not now actively employed, or by withdrawing money from foreign investment, and in either case without depriving British industry of its present resources.'[81] A careful statistical appraisal of foreign investments was marred by a crude calculation that they would be wiped out if the whole cost of the Liberal plan were to come from this source. Keynes had good reason to complain of misrepresentation here.[82] Elsewhere, though, the tone was that of sceptical open-mindedness, tempered by the responsibilities of public trust. Claims about the diversion of savings met the response that 'there is no means of saying ... it is a far cry ... it is very doubtful ... appears to be highly improbable ... not the least reason to suppose ... can be no presumption ... such an attempt would certainly prove futile.' Keynes's own essay in scepticism—on whether foreign loans in fact boosted exports—did not, however, strike a chord of sympathy, and he was told that 'this thesis must be regarded as non-proven'.[83] In summing up, therefore, the Memorandum reaffirmed the Treasury View, soberly and discreetly, but emphatically and decisively: 'The large loans involved, if they are not to involve inflation, must draw on existing capital resources. These resources are on the whole utilised at present in varying degrees of active employment ...'.[84] The reason the Treasury was so hard to shift on particular points was because of its general outlook. 'At the very highest, *any* scheme of this kind is but a palliative, which would produce only a temporary improvement,' it observed. 'The ultimate remedy for unemployment is not to be found in such measures.' The real answer lay in the reduction of costs, not only wages but 'in all

---

[80] Cmd. 3331, 13.
[81] Ibid. 45.
[82] *JMK* xix. 821.
[83] Cmd. 3331, 52.
[84] Ibid. 53.

that is implied in the term "rationalisation".'[85] This was to echo the conclusion Hopkins had offered Churchill back in March: 'One of the vices of Mr Keynes' scheme, as it seems to me, is that it invites industry still longer to postpone its reform.'[86]

Published three days apart, there was no direct engagement between the White Paper and *Can Lloyd George Do It?*—ships that passed in the night. In his review of the Treasury Memorandum, Keynes deplored this as the reason why 'their arguments and ours have failed to meet'. If only the Treasury had read his chapter ix, he implied, there would have been no difficulty in seeing where the funds came from! This happy suggestion is not wholly without point, but it is doubly flawed as an accurate statement. In the first place, most of chapter ix had previously appeared in the *Evening Standard*. More significant, when Keynes ostensibly went on to 're-emphasise the main points', he once more recast his argument in a quite striking way. There were now four sources of funds, of which only one— savings on the dole—had figured in the original list in *Can Lloyd George Do It?* There it was part of a list; here it was part of a process. The hint that prosperity itself would generate resources had been expanded into an account of the dynamic impact of an initial act of investment. Keynes now stressed that not all the consumption of the newly employed was additional ('for the poor fellows and their families consume *something* even when they are unemployed'); he identified part of the new expenditure which 'finds its way to business profits, taxation and new saving'; and he enlarged on 'the repercussions of the expenditure of the newly employed out of their wages in increasing employment in other industries'. The weight of the argument had been tipped from international flows of funds to the workings of the domestic economy. In this way Keynes could claim that the Treasury experts 'use an argument which would be correct *if everyone were employed already*, but is only correct *on that assumption*'.[87] As an intellectual *tour de force*, this is dazzling; as an exercise in sticking to the point in a political controversy, it must have been bewildering.

There was admittedly some ambiguity over the appropriate form

[85] Ibid. 52 (my italics).

[86] Comment by Hopkins (15 Mar.) on Leith-Ross's memorandum, 12 Mar. 1929, T. 172/2095.

[87] *JMK* xix. 821–3 ('The Treasury contribution to the White Paper', *Nation*, 18 May 1929); cf. *JMK* ix. 116

and level of debate. Keynes reprimanded the Treasury officials for committing themselves 'in public to opinions, purely scientific and technical in character', which they would regret. In supposing that the Treasury View represented orthodoxy, its authors merely demonstrated their ignorance of modern economic thought.[88] Keynes was able to cite the rejection of the crowding-out postulate not only by his ally McKenna, and by the fiscal expert Sir Josiah Stamp, but also by Pigou. Pigou's refusal to countenance the doctrine was, of course, no secret in the profession and had indeed served as the butt of Hawtrey's academic exposition. Choosing his words with care, so as to exclude Hawtrey, Keynes professed himself unable 'to discover any recent pronouncement to the contrary, outside the ranks of the Treasury, by an economist of weight or reputation'.[89]

While welcoming this exchange 'with my old friends in the Treasury', Keynes claimed that he did 'not expect to debate with them on, as it were, the *hustings*'.[90] As a rebuke for the impropriety of issuing the memorandum as an official publication, this was fair comment; but it was rather late in the day for Keynes to disavow partisan commitments. He must have gone into the 1929 campaign with his eyes open. In linking his own ideas with the political appeal of Lloyd George, he was making a direct challenge to established economic policy through an attempt to mobilize electoral support behind an alternative largely of his own devising. He could not have supposed that a Liberal Government was a likely outcome but the consolation 'that the Conservative Party will be driven out of office' was publicly proclaimed.[91] Once he had appeared in these colours, the role of 'Professor Keynes the economist' was difficult to resume. Already regarded warily in the Treasury, Keynes was now allied with the most widely distrusted political leader of the period. Lloyd George, to be sure, brought a dynamism to the advocacy of the programme which would be much needed if it were to be implemented, and his charismatic presence dominated an otherwise dull election. The pledge he had given at the beginning of March remained the central topic of argument until polling day at the end of May.

In this sense, Keynes may have scented success in dictating the

---

[88] *JMK* xix. 820.
[89] *JMK* ix. 121.
[90] *JMK* xix. 820.
[91] *JMK* ix. 124.

agenda. Temperamentally he usually opted for a high-risk strategy, even if, on this occasion, the risk was to his academic credentials. But the political calculation could only have been vindicated if the Liberals had made a striking electoral advance; and in the event they reaped a disappointing harvest. True, their overall share of the vote went up from 17.8 per cent in 1924 to 23.6 per cent, but this yielded only 59 seats. It was this which impressed contemporaries and limited Lloyd George's potential for manœuvre in the new Parliament, especially since he could not rely upon the loyalty of a united party. Labour almost achieved an overall majority and was determined to slough off Liberal tutelage. From Keynes's perspective, then, the Conservatives were 'driven out of office' in a peculiarly inauspicious way.

Among the defeated Liberal candidates was Hubert Henderson, standing for Cambridge University. Keynes had evidently felt tempted to stand himself and had declined to do so for fear of actually being returned for the University. He claimed that membership of the House of Commons would not leave him sufficient time for the writing on which he was engaged.[92] Finishing the *Treatise* thus remained his first priority and he still hoped that it would be ready for publication in October 1929. The remarkable thing is how much direct interaction there was between Keynes's polemical activities and his academic writing. He may have feared that his immersion in the electoral struggle would distract him from resolving the problems he addressed in the *Treatise*; instead it seems to have sparked an extraordinary burst of creativity in the spring of 1929.

During these months Keynes improvised a series of hand-to-mouth arguments, under pressure from the Conservatives and the Treasury to say where the money could be found to fulfil Lloyd George's pledge. *We Can Conquer Unemployment* had banked on 'frozen savings', a term which could be given a 'Keynesian' twist, though he himself seems never to have used it. The Treasury flushed him out on identifying foreign lending as a hen-roost for Lloyd George to rob, which implied, embarrassingly for an advocate of cheap money, that Bank rate might have to rise. Both in private and in public, this was Keynes's story in March 1929; but he sought to avoid this embarrasing implication by pointing to an excess of saving over investment, and thereby to a condition in which the slack in the

[92] *JMK* xix. 773–4.

economy first had to be taken up. With every recapitulation of the potential sources of funds, a new-minted idea was pushed on to or up Keynes's list: savings on the dole in April and 'prosperity' in May. By the end of the election campaign, Keynes had shifted the argument off 'frozen savings', had made reduction in foreign lending into a residual item, and was glibly reprimanding the Treasury for 'overlooking' entirely the sources of about three-quarters of the funds required.[93]

If Keynes changed horses in mid-stream, however, he changed to better horses. He fastened upon the insights which were to determine the future bearings of his economic analysis, especially the proposition that orthodox theory assumed full use of resources. He saw with a new clarity how the distinction between saving and investment could be put to work, and thus took a large step towards completing the *Treatise*. Finally, he articulated a crude but distinctive multiplier process as his last-minute riposte to the Treasury, almost as though in a race to conceive the *General Theory* before polling day. It was only when he reached this point that he saw a consistent rationale in his past writings which he had rarely glimpsed at the time. He recognized a coherent economic justification for policy initiatives which he had supported through a mixture of political prejudice and sheer intuition.

When he sat down after the General Election to pull the *Treatise* together, Keynes found that it came apart in his hands, because his ideas had moved beyond its provisional framework. 'The rewriting of my book on which I have had to embark turns out to be somewhat drastic, so that there is now no prospect of publication before January,' he told his publisher in August 1929. 'I am, however, clear that the rewriting is worth while and will prove a great improvement.'[94] In the event, he was not entirely disappointed, but not entirely satisfied either. If he regarded the book as an artistic failure, the reason is hardly surprising—'I have changed my mind too much during the course of it for it to be a proper unity.'[95]

[93] *JMK* xix. 823.   [94] *JMK* xiii. 117.
[95] *JMK* xiii. 176 (to his mother, 14 Sept. 1930).

5

The Macmillan Committee:
The exposition of the *Treatise*

The Governor in the dock?

The Committee on Finance and Industry, under the chairmanship of
Lord Macmillan, signed its Report in June 1931, after some eighteen
months' work. During that period, Keynes amply fulfilled his undertaking 'to make it a first charge on my time'.[1] Interlocking with his
writing of the *Treatise* and his activities for the Economic Advisory
Council, his service on the Macmillan Committee was his major
effort to reorientate public policy in accordance with his own
economic theories. The installation of Ramsay MacDonald's Labour
Government, ultimately dependent on Liberal support, promised to
provide a more favourable atmosphere for change, though the
mounting scale of the international slump was now a crucial factor. It
had adverse effects upon exports, upon sterling, upon government
revenue; and made it correspondingly difficult to imagine that
Britain alone could conquer unemployment. The numbers out of
work, as shown in the official figures, had fluctuated around 11 per
cent of insured workers from 1923 to 1929; in 1930 the average rose
to 14.6 per cent and in 1931 to 21.5 per cent. Whatever the frailty of
such statistics, this was the perception of the problem which
influenced the debate on policy. The degree of success which Keynes
enjoyed in pressing for change was partly governed over time by
these brute facts.

The appointment of the Macmillan Committee was in itself an
acknowledgement that monetary policy and state investment had
been thrust on to the political agenda. It had been set up, claimed
Snowden, Labour's Chancellor of the Exchequer, 'largely because of
the impression made on public opinion by Mr Keynes's proposals on
these points as enumerated in the Liberal Yellow Book before the last
election'.[2] This claim may have been disingenuously overstated; but
the terms of reference, as initially drafted in the summer of 1929, to

[1] Keynes to Snowden, 22 Oct. 1929, T. 160/426, file 11548.
[2] Snowden memorandum (drafted by Hopkins), 8 Apr. 1930, copy, T. 175/26.

some extent bear it out, and, although they were subsequently redrafted by Hopkins in a more 'reassuring' sense, the authorities would clearly have preferred no inquiry at all. As Private Secretary to the Chancellor, Grigg was concerned to protect not only the Treasury but also the Bank of England from any imputation of culpability. He advised Snowden that, while they might not be infallible, it had to be said 'that we have had one continuous policy as a guiding principle and a system which is knave-proof', whereas 'the critics, especially Keynes, have changed their ideas and their theories very nearly every year'. The proposed inquiry needed careful handling if it were not to prove unsettling. 'Is there not some danger of giving the impression that the Governor is being put in the dock?' he asked.[3]

The composition of the committee was thus an unusually delicate matter. A barrister specializing in public law, Macmillan was the third choice as chairman, after the diplomat Lord D'Abernon had declined and Lord Blanesburgh, as a Law Lord, had been requested to withdraw by the Lord Chancellor. One reason advanced—that judges should not mingle in semi-political activities—was subsequently given an ironical twist when Macmillan himself was appointed to the bench as a Lord of Appeal in Ordinary while the committee was sitting. The earliest surviving lists of nominations for the committee envisaged the presence of two or three large employers, including Lennox Lee, President of the Federation of British Industries, who actually served. Theodore Gregory, Professor of Banking at the London School of Economics, was mentioned from the outset, plus places for at least one trade unionist and a co-operator, which were filled by Ernest Bevin, General Secretary of the Transport and General Workers' Union, and Sir Thomas Allen, vice-chairman of the Co-operative Wholesale Society. In addition, the Bank of England found the presence of its critic McKenna inescapable and that of Lord Bradbury indispensable as a counterweight, embodying as he did the authority of a former Permanent Secretary to the Treasury. The Bank secured the appointment of one of its Directors, Cecil Lubbock, and of J. Frater Taylor, a 'company doctor' with whom Norman had worked on various rationalization schemes. The merchant banker R. H. Brand, whom Keynes knew as an old colleague at Versailles, was also nominated at this stage. 'An

[3] Grigg to Snowden, 11 Oct. 1929, copy, T. 160/426, file 11548.

economist of the Keynes school—probably Henderson,' had been pencilled in by Grigg, and the name of Layton was mentioned too, before the Treasury took the plunge by settling for Keynes himself.[4]

These were the persons invited to serve on 21 October 1929. To their number were added A. A. G. Tulloch, representing the clearing banks, and J. T. Walton Newbold, a former Communist MP for a Clydeside seat, as the joker in the pack. The final member of the committee was the protectionist Sir Walter Raine, President of the Association of Chambers of Commerce, who was himself included after protesting that the claims of industry and commerce had been overlooked. There was indeed some muttering about the committee having been packed in favour of finance.

It was agreed that Leith-Ross should attend meetings of the committee on behalf of the Treasury, and his colleague George Ismay was to be its secretary. Leith-Ross referred to it as the Bank Committee, and, sharing Grigg's apprehensions on Norman's behalf—'Three of his bitterest critics (McKenna, Keynes, and Bevin) are to be on the Committee, one of them a man (McKenna) who is known to have pursued an intense vendetta against him for years'[5]— made it his business to ensure that the authorities were not caught off guard. In particular, he saw to it that the evidence by the Bank and the Treasury was watertight and that the chairman was primed to ask the right questions. Macmillan later confessed that he 'never learned to move with any ease in the realm of finance. Somehow my mind failed to grasp its principles and its techniques baffled me.'[6] He showed himself ready to learn, however, and made the committee into a forum where complex issues were patiently elucidated by the experts. Its proceedings, reported verbatim, are thus a unique record of how the argument over policy between Keynes and his critics was actually conducted, face to face, in terms accessible to intelligent laymen.

The Bank evidence was given pride of place and Macmillan arranged for the Governor to begin on 28 November. Two days beforehand, Norman's diary tells its own story: 'Bed: seedy.'[7] Unable

[4] List by Grigg, n.d., T. 160/426, file 11548; see also T. 172/1652, which is the basis of the account in R. S. Sayers, *The Bank of England, 1891–1944* (Cambridge, 1976), ch. 16—the best history of the committee.

[5] Grigg to Snowden, 11 Oct. 1929, T. 160/426, file 11548. Leith-Ross's pocket diaries are in T. 188/263.

[6] Lord Macmillan, *A Man of Law's Tale* (1952), 196.

[7] Norman diary, 26 Nov. 1929, Bank of England, ADM 20/18.

to face his critics, Norman passed the task into the capable hands of his deputy, Sir Ernest Harvey. In five days of evidence, Harvey gave a lucid and unprovocative account of the Bank of England's role as a central bank, its constitution and administration, its assets and liabilities, and its relations with the City, the Treasury, and other central banks. The printed version of Harvey's evidence has admittedly been tidied up, chiefly by omission of passages where he had spoken in confidence on highly sensitive matters; but there is no reason to suppose that it seemed any less impressive to the committee than it does on the page. There were one or two moments when future engagements were signalled, notably when McKenna asked whether the Bank's duty to protect the integrity of the currency extended to guarding against an appreciation of sterling. He meant that, with the return to gold, the pound had appreciated by 10 per cent, and warned that he would be exploring the repercussions— 'I wish to put in a proviso that this is the crux of the controversy'.[8] Likewise, Keynes asked whether measures could be taken to insulate Britain from fluctuations abroad in gold movements, and later suggested that 'perhaps the greatest dilemma of the banking system at the present time is that what is the right policy from the internal point of view may be the wrong policy from the external point of view.' At this point the chairman interjected: 'Mr Keynes has formulated a very large issue and I would suggest that it should stand on record until the Governor comes before us.'[9]

Part of the reason for Harvey's easy ride was that major issues, especially over Bank rate, could be shelved in this way. It was expected that Norman would return to deal with them after four or five weeks' absence on a Mediterranean cruise. After his last day in the chair, Harvey wrote a reassuring letter to the Governor. He based this not only on his direct impressions of the proceedings to date but upon 'a very charming letter which I have received from Keynes', and upon conversation with others, including the Chancellor. Harvey told Norman, 'I think you may feel satisfied that whatever the outcome of the Committee may be, we at any rate have nothing to fear.'[10]

By February 1930, the committee had heard nine witnesses, most

---

[8] Committee on Finance and Industry, *Minutes of Evidence* (1931), Q. 334 (hereafter cited as *Macmillan Evidence*).

[9] Ibid., Q. 824; cf. 364.

[10] Harvey to Norman, 19 Dec. 1929, copy, Bank of England, S 44/1.

of them connected with the City and including representatives from each of the Big Five clearing banks, several of whom (Sir Harry Goschen, J. W. Beaumont Pease, John Rae) had been considered for membership of the committee themselves. At this stage, therefore, McKenna, as chairman of the Midland Bank, was in his element, and the tone of the proceedings threatened to become rather technical. The scope of the committee's work, however, underwent a radical transformation when it was decided to convene for a series of meetings in which different members would take the lead in discussing 'the general outlook' of the inquiry. Between 20 February and 21 March there were six such meetings, and at the first five Keynes gave his 'private evidence'. Although not published as part of the committee's official proceedings, these discussions were recorded and circulated in exactly the same way at the time.[11] This record shows that Keynes conducted his evidence like a seminar and seized the opportunity to give his fellow members a privileged foretaste of the main themes of the *Treatise*.

'Not a doctrine peculiar to myself'

The *Treatise* finally took shape as two volumes: Volume One, *The Pure Theory of Money* and Volume Two, *The Applied Theory of Money*. When it was published, it was generally agreed that its most original contribution to economic analysis was the emphasis laid upon the distinction between saving and investment.[12] This was enhanced in late revisions of the book in 1929–30. The notion itself had been 'gradually creeping into economic literature in quite recent years', and Keynes paid tribute to the work of his Cambridge colleague D. H. Robertson here.[13] None the less, the way Keynes put the concept to work opened up a whole new field. In a homely exposition, added at a late stage to Volume Two, he pointed out that it was

[11] The cyclostyled minutes of these private sessions are cited by date and page number from T. 200/4 (21 Mar. 1930), T. 200/5 (23, 24, 30, 31 Oct., 6, 7 Nov. 1930) and T. 200/6 (20, 21 Nov., 4 Dec. 1930). The minutes for 20, 21, 28 Feb., 6, 7 Mar., 27, 28 Nov., 5 Dec. 1930, are printed in *JMK* xx. 38–157, 179–270. Other copies of some of these 'private minutes' have survived in the papers of Bevin, Hawtrey, and Keynes, and in the Bank of England.

[12] See reviews by Norman Angell, *Time and Tide*, 8 Nov. 1930; A. C. Pigou, *Nation*, 24 Jan. 1931; Barbara Wootton, *Listener*, 26 Feb. 1931; anon., *New Statesman*, 31 Jan. 1931.

[13] *JMK* v. 154 n.

usual to think of the world's wealth as having been accumulated by thrift, whereas the truth was that another economic factor—enterprise—was really responsible. 'If enterprise is afoot, wealth accumulates whatever may be happening to thrift; and if enterprise is asleep, wealth decays whatever thrift may be doing.'[14] Saving in itself achieved nothing until investment employed the resources thus made available. Investment depended on entrepreneurs, and their confidence was best generated by cheap credit and inflationary expectations. Keynes's chapter 'Historical Illustrations' is virtually a hymn to inflation. What use could be made of monetary policy to encourage enterprise by facilitating investment? This was the practical question to which Keynes's theory gave rise.

In the *Treatise* Keynes declared that 'the real task' of monetary theory was 'to treat the problem dynamically' in order 'to exhibit the causal process by which the price level is determined, and the method of transition from one position of equilibrium to another'.[15] He considered that here lay the chief failure of the quantity theory (the contention that a rise in the price level was the result of an increase in the money supply). Keynes held that equilibrium supplied the unique condition under which the quantity theory was true. He stated his argument initially for a closed system, where the problem was to balance saving and investment. Since they responded inversely to changes in interest rates, the way was open for the banking system, as 'a free agent acting with design', to control the final outcome. It could *achieve* a balance by throwing the weight of official interest rates to one side or the other. 'Booms and slumps', Keynes maintained 'are simply the expression of the results of an oscillation of the terms of credit about their equilibrium position.'[16] If this was a relatively simple task inside a closed system, it became appallingly difficult when considered within the real world of the international economy. For not only had saving and investment to be kept in equilibrium, so also had the country's international earnings and its foreign lending. Since the banking system had to work with the same instrument on these two different problems, it followed that 'the conditions of international equilibrium may be incompatible for a

---

[14] *JMK* vi. 132. The stages in the composition of the *Treatise* can be followed from material in *JMK* xiii, ch. 2. For a more formal analysis, see below, ch. 10.

[15] *JMK* v. 120.

[16] *JMK* v. 164–5.

time with the conditions of internal equilibrium'.[17] How, then, could it be supposed that a balancing act of such complexity could ever be brought off?

Keynes worked out his answer in chapter 13 of the *Treatise*, 'The *modus operandi* of Bank Rate'. This was a rigorous theoretical account, designed to cover all possibilities. In order to assess where the weight of analysis fell, however, it is necessary to bear in mind the special conditions which were at the forefront of Keynes's own mind. Britain's return to the Gold Standard at an overvalued parity in 1925 set the conditions of the problem. The existing monetary mechanism coped best when it followed the market, up or down, not when it tried to fight the market: in particular, it was 'singularly ill adapted' to impose lower real earnings via high interest rates.[18] Yet the 1925 measures had required credit restriction, 'with the object of producing out of the blue a cold-blooded income deflation'.[19] Bank rate had been given the job of reducing British costs to a level which would restore international competitiveness. Keynes claimed that neither economists nor bankers had been clear enough about the causal process involved, and hence 'apt to contemplate a deflation too light-heartedly'.[20] For the chain of causation here was: first, the deliberate choking of investment by high interest rates; second, its effect in inflicting abnormal losses upon entrepreneurs; third, the consequent withdrawal of offers of work; fourth, the reduction of money earnings as a result of unemployment.

When Keynes gave his 'private evidence' to the Macmillan Committee, he was able to base his policy advice upon a singularly coherent theoretical foundation. The *Treatise* was to appear only a few months later and the effort of composition made him the master—or perhaps the prisoner—of an integrated and consistent theory. There were certainly novel twists in Keynes's exposition, and in stating his case he made it distinctively his own; in particular, he turned the argument from more than one direction towards his favoured policy expedients, with public works to the fore. It should be observed, however, that the *Treatise*, with its sharp distinction between saving and investment, formed the acknowledged framework of this discussion. He was challenged on this point by the

---

[17] *JMK* v. 165.
[18] *JMK* v. 245.
[19] *JMK* vi. 163.
[20] *JMK* v. 244.

banker Brand: 'I suppose you would agree that the whole of your case depends upon whether this relationship that you said existed between savings and investment is actually true, that the losses and profits do occur according to your theory?' Keynes simply answered: 'Yes.'[21] Moreover, he was inclined to stress the innovative force of the *Treatise*'s analysis. 'I think it makes a revolution in the mind,' he told Gregory, 'when you think clearly of the distinction between saving and investment.'

Yet Gregory had reasonable grounds for his sceptical pragmatism at this juncture, commenting: 'Although I have not seen Mr Keynes's full *exposé* there is not a very wide margin of difference between him and myself on some of the analytical points he had raised.'[22] For what Keynes had been expounding was, as he acknowledged, 'the essence of the classical theory' on how Bank rate maintained monetary equilibrium. It was 'not a doctrine peculiar to myself' but 'the historic doctrine of Bank rate policy as it was evolved during the nineteenth century'. Keynes took a delight in his mastery of its inner workings, inviting admiration for its jewelled mechanism. 'I have told you', said the impresario, 'the whole story of how the traditionally sound financier thinks that he can make the adjustments required from time to time in our economic system, and I think—when one sees the way in which one part dovetails into another—there is no need to wonder why two generations, both of theorists and of practical men, should have been entranced by it.' While the rest of the committee piled on the compliments—'An extraordinarily clear exposition', 'An extraordinarily clear exposition, and thoroughly understood by us'—it was left to Gregory to introduce a note of caution. 'I accept everything that Mr Keynes has said,' he interjected, 'but I should like to emphasise that this is not only a beautiful series of assumptions, but assumptions which translated into action have worked.'

It was at this point, and at this point only, that the author of the *Treatise* departed from orthodoxy, proposing next to confront 'the limitations and imperfections of the operation of this method in present-day conditions'.[23] The adjustment mechanism, as he went on to explain, was jammed or hitched—a grave and complex problem so far as policy was concerned, but not one with fundamental implica-

[21] *JMK* xx. 133 (6 Mar. 1930).
[22] *JMK* xx. 87 (21 Feb. 1930).
[23] *JMK* xx. 51–4 (20 Feb. 1930).

tions for economic theory. His orthodox exposition prepared the ground for the more disturbing contention that the return to gold, requiring wage reductions of 10 per cent, had the effect of 'setting Bank rate policy a task it had never been asked to do before in the economic history of this country'.[24] The external constraints had to be met, and could be met; but the price was an interest rate structure inappropriate for the achievement of an internal equilibrium.

When Keynes thereupon broached his own distinction between saving and investment, he was able to produce Bank rate as the key to the position. But it was a key which would not turn in the lock. As Keynes acknowledged, 'if we did not belong to an international system I should have said there was no difficulty whatever; one could simply reduce the Bank rate to that level where savings and investments were equal.'[25] Under those conditions, 'the rate of interest would always tend to fall to the yield of the next thing which was worth doing.'[26] When international conditions dictated higher rates, the mechanics of the system should in theory have produced lower costs and lower prices. 'But if you jam the machine halfway through so that you have a chronic condition in which business men make losses, you also have a chronic condition of unemployment, a chronic condition of waste; and the excess savings are spilled on the ground.'[27] It was when Bank rate was used to regulate income downward that this 'jam' or 'hitch' occurred, preventing the process from working through to its final conclusion, and creating 'the worst possible condition, to be left in this jammed state'.[28]

Keynes had thus begun by investing some of the classical propositions with his own lucidity. Pigou acknowledged that the *Treatise* gave 'an account of the *modus operandi* of bank rate much superior, as it seems to me, to previous discussions'.[29] It was when Keynes used this as a basis on which to build his own distinctive analysis that his efforts found less ready acceptance. As long as saving and investment remained undifferentiated, increased saving seemed a plausible solution to the problem of under-investment; likewise, investors would presumably be attracted once wage costs were cut back to realistic levels. Macmillan's mind, for one, was obviously still working

[24] *JMK* xx. 56 (20 Feb. 1930).
[25] *JMK* xx. 84 (21 Feb. 1930).
[26] *JMK* xx. 79 (21 Feb. 1930).
[27] *JMK* xx. 75 (21 Feb. 1930).
[28] *JMK* xx. 82 (21 Feb. 1930).
[29] Review of the *Treatise*, *Nation*, 24 Jan. 1931.

in this way. Having heard Keynes, it struck him that civilization was not allowing a natural law to operate in preventing the weakest from going to the wall. 'If you impede the action of the law of economics you produce an artificial condition of affairs,' he speculated. Keynes refused to follow this line of thought. 'I do not think it is any more economic law that wages should go down easily than that they should not,' he responded. 'It is a question of facts. Economic law does not lay down the facts, it tells you what the consequences are.'[30] Keynes was now concerned with the consequences in a world where the facts did not correspond with the beautiful series of assumptions which underpinned the theory whose workings he had explained.

For the novelty of the *Treatise* lay in raising the question of *whether*, not *how*, saving and investment were brought into equilibrium. It was orthodox neo-classical doctrine that interest rate was a supply-and-demand mechanism which equilibrated saving and investment; with flexible prices, it argued, full employment of all factors of production would ensue. This role for interest rate is not challenged in the *Treatise*. Indeed, Keynes's contention that saving need not be equal to investment—becaue they are different activities carried out by different people—can be seen as a rhetorical device for showing that the economy is in disequilibrium when they are unequal, so stressing the need to bring them together. The only reason why such a disequilibrium could persist in the real world, leading to waste of resources and unemployment, was that interest rate was thwarted in its assigned role.

Keynes had manifestly carried his hearers with him a good way in his first two days of evidence on 20 and 21 February. The first day settled the *modus operandi* of Bank rate in a form which went straight into the final Report. On the second day, as Keynes told his wife, 'they found my speech much more perplexing as I thought they would.' In challenging accepted notions about saving and investment, he acknowledged that his exposition had been 'unfamiliar and paradoxical, and whilst they couldn't confute me, they did not know whether or not to believe'.[31] But he had succeeded in laying out an analytical framework within which his constructive proposals could be appreciated. 'You are keeping us in suspense; you are a complete dramatist,' Macmillan complimented him. 'At the moment the

---

[30] *JMK* xx. 83–4 (21 Feb. 1930).
[31] *JMK* xx. 73 (to Lydia, 23 Feb. 1930).

remedies have not been unfolded; I suppose they will be on Friday next?'[32]

'The assumptions of Mr Keynes'

What were the main features of Keynes's analysis? The fundamental constraint on Britain's international position was inadequate foreign earnings, in the sense that they were insufficient to finance British investments abroad. The Bank of England therefore stepped in to safeguard the gold reserves, which backed the exchange rate of sterling. Its sole weapon was a high interest rate, which indeed discouraged foreign lending but only at the cost of domestic enterprise. With home investment held back, and foreign lending blocked off, the result was that 'a certain amount of our savings is spilled on the ground' in a wasteful dissipation of potentially useful resources. Savings were eaten up in financing business losses rather than profitable investment. 'Our investment abroad is fixed by the cost of production, our investment at home is fixed by rate of interest, and the two together fall short of our savings, and the difference is accounted for by the loss to the business world.'[33] To what solution did this way of posing the problem point? The logic of the analysis was such that in itself it did not imperatively demand any single remedy, but rather established criteria by which a range of remedies might be judged. This was the technical virtue of formal economic analysis, but it did not foreclose the policy choices that then arose.

At his third session, on 28 February, Keynes spoke blandly of 'classifying the suggested remedies in such a manner as to fit in neatly with this general analysis and diagnosis'. This served to declare his professional credentials, which were accepted by his colleagues with little demur. The chairman, indeed, cut in to supply the right word when Keynes was, for once, momentarily at a loss.[34]

Keynes: I propose as a scientist to be—
Macmillan: Remorseless.

The remorseless method involved a systematic appraisal of the relevance of a variety of proposals, an exercise which spilled over into

[32] *JMK* xx. 84 (21 Feb. 1930).
[33] *JMK* xx. 95 (28 Feb. 1930).
[34] *JMK* xx. 99.

two further sessions the following week. Keynes identified seven classes of remedy, as follows.

1. *Devaluation.* Revaluation of gold (the usual way of putting it) was an obvious possibility in view of Keynes's claim that the return to gold in 1925 lay at the root of Britain's immediate problems. But an opportunity missed was an opportunity lost, so far as Keynes was concerned, and he did not see devaluation as desirable in 1930, because of the consequences for credit and confidence. It was a last resort, if all else failed.

2. *A National Treaty.* This would provide for an agreed reduction of all domestic money incomes. It was really a way of living with the Gold Standard by short-circuiting deflation as the path to a lower level of domestic costs. Keynes had advocated it on these grounds in 1925, but by 1930 he pretty clearly recognized that it was not practicable. 'Its feasibility is almost entirely a matter of psychological and political, and not economic factors,' he commented.[35]

3. *Bounties to Industry.* These, too, constituted a theoretically attractive possibility in that they would use taxation to place the burden of maintaining competitive prices upon the whole community rather than upon certain sections of industry. 'It may be', Keynes argued, 'that our social feelings have caused us to fix wages at a higher level than the economic machine grinds out. If we were to balance that by a bounty that would be the public subscribing to meet the difference out of the common purse.'[36] This was a variant on a plea he had made earlier in the year for seeing the social wage rather than high earnings as the economically viable road to social amelioration.[37]

4. *Rationalization.* This was the vogue word in 1930 for schemes to cut unit costs, especially through economies of scale. Clearly any improvement in efficiency was desirable; the real question was whether this alone could be relied upon to turn the situation round quickly.

5. *Tariffs.* Protection was an old political battle-axe with a new economic cutting edge. New because several of the traditional free-trade arguments now struck Keynes as inverted arguments for tariffs. Would tariffs not increase the profits of entrepreneurs at the

---

[35] *JMK* xx. 102 (28 Feb. 1930).
[36] *JMK* xx. 108 (28 Feb. 1930).
[37] 'The question of high wages', *Political Quarterly*, Jan.–Mar. 1930, in *JMK* xx. 3 ff.

expense of the rest of the community? 'That is precisely what we want ...' Would they not act as 'a surreptitious way of decreasing real wages'? Or induce a rise in prices? Indeed, 'also something we want', said Keynes. Moreover, the classical theory of free trade bore a striking likeness to the *modus operandi* of Bank rate—in fact, it was mere prolegomenon in so far as trade transactions worked through international gold movements to *activate* changes in Bank rate. Thereafter, the precision of the compensating effects depended likewise upon the fluidity of wages and the flexibility of employment. But again, the immediate problem was what to do 'supposing we get jammed at the point of unemployment'? The choice was not between making more suitable or less suitable articles according to a perfect international division of labour, but between making something (albeit unsuitable ideally) and making nothing.[38] Protection was thus helpful even if it was 'not anything like adequate to the situation'.[39]

6. *Home Investment.* Keynes called this 'my favourite remedy' without further ado. He proceeded to justify it by a process of elimination. New employment, he reasoned, might arise from exports (though the snag there was high wages); or from import substitution (the protectionist solution). Alternatively, consumption might rise at home. Although the spending power of the newly employed would create a favourable repercussion, 'you cannot start the ball rolling in this way.' Less saving would also be of some advantage, though it was 'very low in my category of remedies ...'. There remained a fourth possibility: that of creating new capital assets. 'It is the only remedy left, if one holds that the other three remedies are either impracticable in the position today or are inadequate, or are in themselves undesirable.'[40] There were various devices by which private enterprise might be encouraged to invest more at home, but the crux of the case was 'that it must be Government investment which will break the vicious circle'.[41]

7. *International Measures.* High interest rates were choking investment, so reducing them would pave the path to recovery. Cheap money in one country, however, was not much of a slogan—it would put the gold reserves at risk. Concerted action by the central banks was, therefore, in the long term, the most important thing of all.

[38] *JMK* xx. 113–15 (28 Feb. 1930).
[39] *JMK* 125 (6 Mar. 1930).
[40] *JMK* xx. 125–8 (6 Mar. 1930).
[41] *JMK* xx. 146–7 (6 Mar. 1930).

Keynes endorsed all these proposals as having some point. 'While I have my preferences, practically all the remedies seem to have something in them,' he claimed.[42] Rather than argue for one panacea, in season and out, therefore, he suggested that almost any of them might be worth a trial, given particular circumstances. Thus, as far as his Macmillan Committee evidence goes, devaluation was a last resort; a national treaty was a spent hope; bounties were probably impracticable; rationalization was insufficient in itself; tariffs were helpful at the margin; public works remained the favourite emergency measure; and in the long term the international economy needed cheap money. In the *Treatise*, Keynes commended four solutions: rationalization, tariffs, public works, and cheap money. But this was *given* that the Gold Standard obtained (no devaluation), and *given* also that wage reductions were ruled out; so only bounties failed to make both lists.

The close correspondence here is hardly surprising, since Keynes was putting the finishing touches to the *Treatise* while giving his evidence to the Macmillan Committee. But it serves to show that by 1930 there is little reason to charge Keynes with inconsistency on the ground that his polemical advocacy of public works did not match up with his theoretical prescription of cheap money in the *Treatise*. The economic reasoning was the same in both cases, in that both met his criteria for stimulating investment. Thus the *Treatise* insisted that 'the great evil of the moment' lay in 'the unwillingness of the central banks of the world to allow the market rate of interest to fall fast enough', and asserted that 'we cannot hope for a complete or lasting recovery' until such a fall had taken place.[43] But whether to leave a long-term solution in the hands of central bankers—hands tied by national constraints and paralysed by mutual suspicions—was a question of practical judgement. Even in the *Treatise*, therefore, Keynes added that 'there remains in reserve a weapon by which a country can partially rescue itself when its international disequilibrium is involving it in severe unemployment,'[44] and this was, of course, domestic investment promoted by the Government. In short, it was the 'special case'.

The Treasury was in no doubt that Keynes's various policy proposals rested on his analytical premises—premises which they

---

[42] *JMK* xx. 99 (28 Feb. 1930); cf. 125 (6 Mar. 1930).
[43] *JMK* vi. 185, 344.
[44] *JMK* vi. 337.

rejected. Leith-Ross had listened to his first two days of evidence with close attention and drafted a paper entitled, 'The assumptions of Mr Keynes', which he sent to Niemeyer at the Bank for comments. This was accompanied by a full exegesis of the text of Keynes's evidence, revised at the end of March so as to incorporate Niemeyer's comments.[45] Together, these papers give a full indication of the Treasury's response to the analysis of the *Treatise* and to the inferences that could be drawn for policy.

Keynes's diagnosis—'viz. that the normal Bank rate policy has "jammed" owing to the difficulty of reducing wages'—was broadly admitted. This was, after all, only another way of saying that flexibility of prices was absolutely crucial. The Treasury drew the moral that the difficulties were 'capable of being overcome without resort to desperate expedients' and relied on a modified version of Keynes's remedies 2 (national treaty), 3 (bounties), 4 (efficiency), and 7 (international co-operation). It went without saying that numbers 1 (devaluation) and 5 (tariffs) were ruled out. 'The really contentious part of Mr Keynes's programme', the Treasury concluded, 'is his policy of home investment.' The point was taken that his advocacy here was 'based on his theory, that the key to the trade cycle is to be found in the relation between savings and investment'.[46]

Leith-Ross understood Keynes to be assuming that 'there is an amount of savings precisely corresponding to the amount of business losses which fails to be invested and is accordingly wasted.'[47] Both he and Niemeyer made heavy weather of their incomprehension over this remarkable coincidence, without apparently grasping the argument that savings went either to investment (which was *by definition* profitable) or to financing activities which turned out not to be profitable. Thus Leith-Ross worried away at whether 'these business losses must be exactly equivalent to the amount of savings available for investment which do not find an outlet'.[48] Their outlet, in

---

[45] Leith-Ross, 'The assumptions of Mr Keynes', 27 Feb. 1930, with annotations by Niemeyer, and final draft, 28 Mar. 1930 (printed in Jones, *Whitehall Diary*, ii. 288–9); 'Note on Mr Keynes's exposition to the Committee on Finance and Industry', n.d., T. 175/26.

[46] 'Mr Keynes's exposition', 3–4, T. 175/26. Alan Booth and Melvyn Pack suggest that I have exaggerated the importance of public works among Keynes's seven remedies: *Employment, Capital, and Economic Policy* (Oxford, 1985), 174–5. But its salience, as recognized by Keynes and the Treasury alike, seems to me undeniable.

[47] 'Assumptions of Mr Keynes', final draft, par. 2 (par. 3 in 1st draft), T. 175/26; mainly derived from their reading of the evidence in *JMK* xx. 73–5 (21 Feb. 1930).

[48] 'Mr Keynes's exposition', 6, T. 175/26.

Keynes's terms, was *either* to 'materialise in additional wealth' *or* to 'take the form of balancing losses by the business world'.[49] But though Leith-Ross quoted this very passage in an appendix, he insisted on interpreting the theory about a 'surplus of savings' as implying the presence of idle deposits in the banks, and imagined therefore that it could be refuted by a statement—'The fact is that all savings are applied to some sort of investment'—the sense of which Keynes could readily have accepted. Keynes's caveat here would have been over a definition of 'some sort of investment' which included a loss-making application of savings—not an 'investment' at all under his own definition. 'Is it not possible', Leith-Ross therefore concluded, 'that the orthodox theory is correct and that our real trouble is not oversaving but undersaving?'[50]

The Treasury also criticized Keynes for inconsistency. This was their familiar point that since he maintained that British costs of production were too high, the effect of the home investment programme 'would undoubtedly be to accentuate the difficulty from which according to his own diagnosis British industry is at present suffering'.[51] Keynes admitted that his remedies 1 to 5 tackled the problem by increasing *foreign* investment, which meant improving the trade balance, which (unless it meant protection) meant increasing exports, which meant that competitiveness was crucial. 'The sixth remedy', he had warned, 'tackles the problem from the other side.'[52] By acting directly on *home* investment, it was tackling the problem of excess savings in an alternative way which did not therefore demand a reduction in British costs. That this charge of inconsistency was levelled merely shows that the Treasury appraised Keynes's proposals according to their own fixed criteria, of which international competitiveness stood foremost.

Finally, the Treasury dismissed Keynes's public works programme by arguing that 'if, as he alleges, investment is governed primarily by Bank rate, a mere reduction in Bank rate will encourage home investment to whatever extent may be required.' This harked back to Hawtrey's contention that public works could only increase employment if allied with an expansion of credit—in which case they became unnecessary. Keynes's own premiss—the special case where

[49] *JMK* xx. 74 (21 Feb. 1930).
[50] 'Mr Keynes's exposition', 7, T. 175/26.
[51] Ibid. 11.
[52] *JMK* xx. 125 (6 Mar. 1930).

the Gold Standard stood in the way of cheap money—was acknowledged obliquely in a gloss on his motives: 'It looks as if Mr Keynes
was first attracted by the need for an expansion of credit, and then
alarmed at the possible effects of such expansion on our Exchanges
and in order to find a solution which would prevent the creation of
credit increasing our Capital exports, invented the theory of wasted
savings and the scheme of additional Government investments at
home.' The Treasury's central contention was that Keynes's 'argument is novel and ingenious but it can scarcely be said to be so
clearly established as to afford a sound basis for Government
policy'.[53]

'The assumptions of Mr Keynes' comprised a list of the 'theoretic
assumptions' on which his 'remedy for unemployment (which was set
out in the Liberal Yellow Book)' was based. Nine propositions were
articulated, derived from the Treasury's understanding of his
position, with the conclusion that 'none of these assumptions is
indubitably true, and some of them are highly questionable'. Drawing
on Niemeyer's advice, Leith-Ross then gave his alternative analysis,
turning on the structural inadequacies of British industry in the
aftermath of the War, exacerbated by a social policy which fostered
an unrealistic level of consumption. 'The fact is that Keynes, like
other economists, lives in a world of abstractions,' Leith-Ross
concluded. 'He speaks of "Industry", "Profits", "Losses", "Price-
level", as if they were realities.'[54] This was in kilter with Niemeyer's
criticism: 'It is very easy to produce a simple theoretic exposition
which by its very simplicity seems cogent and attractive: but in fact
the economic world is very far from simple and any *single* explanation seems to me to be almost certainly wrong by the very fact that it
is single.'[55] The paper advanced three practical objections against a
programme of public works. First it would entail 'a great extension of
bureaucratic power and considerable waste'. Second, it could not be
guaranteed to reduce foreign lending. Finally, it was 'a pure hypothesis that a permanent revival of prosperity can be secured by large
scale Government expenditure'. The advice Leith-Ross offered was
hardly surprising: 'It is impossible for a responsible government to

---

[53] 'Mr Keynes's exposition', 11–12, 5–6, T. 175/26.
[54] 'Assumptions of Mr Keynes', final draft, T. 175/26; partly based on 'Unemployment—causes and cures', n.d., T. 188/275.
[55] Niemeyer's annotations, 'Assumptions of Mr Keynes', 1st draft, T. 175/26.

embark on such a policy without much clearer evidence that the remedy proposed will be successful.'[56]

The Keynes–McKenna–Bevin Axis

In the Macmillan Committee Keynes had a special status as an expert, though his was not the only kind of expertise relevant to its work. Bankers like Brand, Lubbock, and McKenna spoke with authority on arcane financial matters; Bradbury's administrative pre-eminence could not be brushed aside, nor could the industrial experience of Raine, Frater Taylor, or Bevin. Gregory, however, was the only other economist, and thus technically equipped to stand up to Keynes (though the touchy McKenna also exacted some deference). Keynes held a generally high opinion of his calling and in the summer of 1930 expressly urged the Government to take professional advice within the framework of the Economic Advisory Council. Thus he encouraged the Prime Minister to appoint a committee consisting solely of professional economists, who had 'a language and a method of their own', so that issues could be properly isolated. 'There is no reason', he added, 'why the results should not be expressed in a manner intelligible to everyone.'[57] But how far did he expect economic expertise to settle policy choices?

There is no doubt that Keynes staked great faith in the analysis of the *Treatise*, as expounded to the Macmillan Committee, and equally that the committee was unsure how far to take it at face value. 'We quite realise', the chairman had said, 'we are getting the fruits of your research presented to us in a form in which we can understand it. Behind it there is the technical mind.' Keynes sought to reassure him of its soundness, stating that it had been 'read now by some of the principal economists of Cambridge, who did not all start sympathetic to it, but they are now satisfied, I think, that it is accurate.'[58] If the *Treatise* were to gain general academic acceptance, this would obviously help to change policy. Meanwhile, however, it was no good leaving everything to the experts. 'In a sense there are no experts,' he told a radio audience in 1931.[59] So the fact that public

[56] 'Assumptions of Mr Keynes', final draft, T. 175/26.
[57] *JMK* xx. 386 (Keynes to MacDonald, 10 July 1930).
[58] *JMK* xx. 86 (21 Feb. 1930).
[59] *JMK* xx. 515 (CBS broadcast, 12 Apr. 1931).

works were 'agreeable to common sense'[60] was persistently advanced as a strong recommendation. The main task of *Can Lloyd George Do It?* had been 'to confirm the reader's instinct that what *seems* sensible *is* sensible, and what *seems* nonsense *is* nonsense'.[61] This was a necessary exercise because there were undoubtedly instances 'where uninstructed common sense tends to believe exactly the opposite of the truth'.[62] Expert appraisal might properly be conceived as a filter, separating cogent propositions from plausible fallacies. The real choices could thus be made apparent through professional skill.

What Keynes had won from the committee by March 1930 was not just an acceptance of his credentials on particular points but a willingness to share his perspective on the general problem. They were no longer the uninstructed committee who had sat at Harvey's feet in December but, as Leith-Ross had cause to appreciate, a committee who now needed to be disabused of the assumptions of Mr Keynes. When Norman came to complete the Bank evidence and Hopkins to speak for the Treasury, their task would be correspondingly more difficult. An ominous number of questions was being reserved for their attention. Furthermore, a formidable combination between Keynes, McKenna, and Bevin, as the three most forceful and strong-minded members of the committee, was now dominating its proceedings.

McKenna was an ally of Keynes from the old Asquithian days and a long-standing opponent of deflation. But his name was often coupled with that of Walter Runciman as notorious representatives of business Liberalism, and as such he seemed worlds apart from the uncompromisingly proletarian figure of Bevin. Bevin wanted to broaden the trade unions' concern with economic policy so as to comprehend all the issues which ultimately affected the welfare of his members.[63] In a quite unforced way, he became an apt and able pupil for Keynes, whose strictures on Labour's sectionalism were thus massively confuted in the flesh by a man with whom he could develop an unpatronizing relationship of mutal respect. Keynes, in short, was the pivotal figure in establishing within the committee a powerful axis of dissent from the unargued axioms of the Bank and the Treasury.

[60] *JMK* xx. 129 (6 Mar. 1930).   [61] *JMK* ix. 92.
[62] Committee on Finance and Industry, *Report*, Cmd. 3897 (1931), 206 (hereafter, *Macmillan Report*), Addendum I, also in *JMK* xx. 305.
[63] Alan Bullock, *The Life and Times of Ernest Bevin*, i (1960), 418, 425 ff.

Following Keynes's five sessions of private evidence, the committee heard in the same manner from McKenna on 21 March. He spoke as a leading critic of the deflationary policy pursued by the Bank of England throughout the 1920s; but the authorities, according to Keynes, had possessed over him 'the inestimable advantage of never explaining themselves or having to justify their policies'.[64] The committee provided the opportunity to turn the tables. Keynes had already asked Harvey whether it was 'a practice of the Bank of England never to explain what its policy is'.[65]

Harvey: Well, I think it has been our practice to leave our actions to explain our policy.
Keynes: Or the reasons for its policy?
Harvey: It is a dangerous thing to start to give reasons.

With Keynes, McKenna, and Bevin setting its tone, the committee was in no mood to accept the authorities as oracular.

McKenna's theme was that under current conditions the Bank should have the danger of deflation before it. With a falling price level and a high unemployment rate, its policy should be to increase the quantity of money in the interests of industry. Keynes put this down, not to a neglect of industry as such, but to 'a false view of cause and effect' when restrictive policies were pursued.[66]

Keynes: Equally, when the Chancellor of the Exchequer finds a good reason, or a plausible reason, for turning down some piece of capital expenditure at home it is believed that he is making things easier for both the Bank of England and for industry. Whereas the actual fact is precisely the opposite, and one of the most important things for us to decide is whether what I have just said is true or false.
McKenna: That is right.

Current Treasury policy gave a high priority to converting the War Loan to a lower structure of interest rates. When Keynes demanded whether anyone could give the reason why the Treasury had stepped up its loan conversion operations, it was left to Gregory to prevent this being left as a rhetorical question. 'I do not know that I can give a plausible explanation,' he ventured, 'but I can present alternative hypotheses which would make the thing look a little more reasonable

---

[64] *JMK* xix. 770–1: a review of McKenna, *Post-War Banking Policy* (1928).
[65] *Macmillan Evidence*, Q. 435.
[66] Private session, 21 Mar. 1930, 10.

than you and Mr McKenna seem to think.'[67] His suggestion was basically that the Treasury was hoping to bring forward the date of conversion of the War Loan at lower interest rates. To Keynes it seemed upside down to restrict capital enterprise in this cause—'I think the official authorities have in these respects been standing on their head for quite a long time.'[68] Following this discussion, Leith-Ross was moved to make one of his rare interventions:[69]

I hope the Committee will reserve judgment on 'the wrong-headedness', 'the obvious wrong-headedness', as it has been described, of the recent funding operation until they have had an opportunity of hearing Sir Richard Hopkins, who will be prepared to go into that as into other questions.

McKenna postulated 'that without an increase in the quantity of money you cannot get rid of unemployment'.[70] Gregory took this up as a matter of principle, pointing to the considerable danger of gold losses by the Bank which would cause it to reverse its policy. Keynes had anticipated this point, arguing that 'the Bank of England can very seldom feel that it can expand credit without risking loss of gold except when it has reason to know that there is an unsatisfied home demand for credit waiting to be satisfied.' Since industry was so disheartened at present, the relevance of a deliberate programme of home investment was apparent. 'I think you cannot get more employment unless you increase credit,' he argued. 'I then go on to ask under what conditions is it safe to increase credit?'[71]

The closeness of McKenna and Bevin to Keynes's position can be seen from their subsequent remarks.[72]

McKenna: It is perfectly safe to start the increased expenditure provided the additional expenditure is going to be met by increased production; if it is not going to be met by increased production you will simply have a rise of prices and inflation; you will have more money to spend and no more goods. But my argument is that you have a large number of employable unemployed, unemployed who could be employed at the current rate of wages at a profit; you have the means to get increased production and you will get increased production. Therefore, the primary test to me is: Have you got a falling price level so that there is no inflation, have you got employable unemployment? If you have those two conditions, then increase your volume of credit.

[67] Ibid. 12.   [68] Ibid. 17.
[69] Ibid. 22.   [70] Ibid. 24.
[71] Ibid. 19.   [72] Ibid. 25–6.

Pressed by the chairman to explain how this would result in more employment, McKenna illustrated his contention by talking of how more boots would be bought, more men taken on to make boots, and their wages spent on cotton goods that would create employment in the cotton trade, and so on.

Bevin: I think it is perfectly obvious that Mr McKenna's thesis is right. If you take the minefields of this country and you could by any chance increase the purchasing power of the workers, which is about 42 per cent below the normal standard, just think of the result. The purchasing power in the minefields is about 42 per cent below what it ought to be. It would lead to a greater demand for boots for children, and clothes and furniture and luxuries and things of that kind.

In closing this session, Keynes entered two caveats over McKenna's case, which in general he supported. The first was that 'the effect of all these measures of cheap money *on investment* is more important than anything else.' The second qualification was more substantial:[73]

whether it will be successful without being dangerous. Very much depends upon whether the new investment and new consumption which are brought into existence are divided in the right or wrong proportions between home activities and foreign activities. The essential concomitant is that the home activities should be—not necessarily the whole—but at least the appropriate proportion. If that is not so, if the articles consumed by the people who have the greater purchasing power, or the investments by the new borrower on the new issues market, are too largely of a foreign description, then there will be a danger attaching to the policy. I repeat that any policy of this kind has to be safeguarded by other steps which will make sure that an appropriate proportion of the new credit finds an adequate outlet at home.

This was a circumspect way of saying that McKenna's policy of credit expansion needed to march with more starkly *dirigiste* measures: public works and tariffs. Each of them, moreover, could be justified as a special case under the theory of the *Treatise*.

[73] Private session, 21 Mar. 1930, 29.

6

The Bank under the harrow

'We are not getting the answers over'

The appearance of the Governor of the Bank of England as its chief witness before the Macmillan Committee was bound to be a highlight of its proceedings. Here was the chance for the man of mystery to impose his authority upon his critics and to establish the rationale of official policy. When it came, however, Norman's evidence was a major set-back for the authorities, provoking a real fear that the initiative had slipped out of their hands. This débâcle was not for want of effort or foresight within the Bank. Harvey had prepared a careful brief for the Governor, listing the questions on which he had reserved the Bank's position when giving his own evidence. Moreover, Ismay, as secretary, had made copies of the minutes available, up to date, so that, quite apart from Leith-Ross's communications with Niemeyer, the Bank was fully apprised of the line of questioning to be expected from Keynes, McKenna, and Bevin. Macmillan too had been solicitous in going for lunch at the Bank to prepare the Governor for his appearance. In judging the impression he made, it should also be borne in mind that the evidence as printed for 26 March 1930, while not cooked, was subsequently garnished in such a way as to make its conclusions rather more appetizing to the world beyond Threadneedle Street.[1]

The committee had been tutored to look for the causes of economic depression in the workings of the monetary system. Norman started from a different point altogether. In his opening statement he put it 'in a nutshell' by saying that the salvation of industry lay in the process of rationalization—a process 'which I am not going to attempt to define, which has been defined in many varying ways, but to which I am a strong adherent'.[2] What the

---

[1] Sayers, *Bank of England*, 368–71, authoritatively disposes of the charges about substitution of evidence made in Andrew Boyle, *Montagu Norman* (1967), 255–8, which also misdates Norman's evidence-in-chief to Feb. 1931. The preparation of the Bank's evidence can be seen from its archives in S 44/1 (1 and 2).

[2] *Macmillan Evidence*, Q. 3317.

committee wanted to hear, however, was his answer to the series of deferred questions about the causes and effects of decisions to use the policy instrument over which the Governor had direct control— Bank rate. Norman readily acknowledged that the main factor in deciding on changes was international and, given the weakness of sterling, in this respect 'we have been continuously under the harrow'.[3]

Benefiting from his recent education in economics, the chairman naturally turned the discussion towards the possibly unfortunate internal effects of decisions on Bank rate taken for external reasons. Norman suggested that the 'actual ill effects were greatly exaggerated and that they are more psychological than real'.[4] Still echoing Keynes's analysis, Macmillan pressed on: 'If a machine gets jammed it will not work, and may it not be that some of the troubles at the present moment are due to trying to deal with financial problems with an instrument which was designed to deal with other and more normal conditions?' But Norman would not admit that the financial machine was at fault—it was industry that was jammed. 'I have never been able to see myself', he continued, 'why for the last few years it should have been impossible for industry starting from within to have readjusted its own position.'[5]

It was Bevin who directly raised the connection with the Gold Standard. Norman, of course, defended the return to gold as right and inevitable, though attended by misfortunes. Against Bevin's repeated insistence that the requirement for wage reductions made such misfortunes inevitable, Norman vehemently denied such a link. ('No, I do not think so.' 'I do not think as a necessary consequence.' 'No, I do not, Sir.')[6] It could be agreed, then, that the return to gold, as the chairman put it, was 'not the sole culprit, so to speak, and that other causes have unfortunately aggravated the result'.[7] Norman's specification of the other circumstances, however, was not very happy in so far as it turned on the decisions by France, Belgium, and Germany to return to gold at other parities, which had adversely affected Britain.[8]

---

[3] Q. 3319.
[4] Q. 3328.
[5] QQ. 3338–9.
[6] QQ. 3345–7; cf. 3375.
[7] Q. 3352.
[8] QQ. 3362–3.

Keynes: You mean their stabilising their money at a low level rather than at a high level?
Norman: At a very low level.
Newbold: What do you think induced them to do that at a very low level while we did it at a high level?
Norman: I do not know.

For Norman to concede points in this way to a rank amateur like Newbold, with no animus against the Governor, cannot have impressed confidence in his ability to withstand Keynes's inevitable professional bombardment.

Keynes took up Norman's contention that the effects of Bank rate were largely psychological, which implied that the actual effects on industry of a contraction of credit were not appreciable. To those who, a few weeks previously, had listened to Keynes 'setting forth what I believed to be the orthodox theory of the Bank Rate, the theory that I thought all authorities would accept', this sounded very much like a repudiation of its essential mechanisms. 'I did not mean to repudiate it, as I understand it,' Norman replied.[9] Keynes's lengthy recapitulation of the *modus operandi* of Bank rate hit Norman with an incontrovertible force for which he was clearly ill-prepared. As Harvey learnt from him afterwards, 'much that was said by Keynes he scarcely understood',[10] and his response on the spot was to accept Keynes's account—'I could not dispute it with you'—while shying away from its implications.[11]

Keynes: If that is so, half the point of Bank Rate is that is should have an effect on the internal situation?
Norman: Well, I do not think so necessarily apart from the short money position.

There was one way of reconciling what Norman was saying about the practical effect of a change in Bank rate with what Keynes was saying about its *modus operandi*. This was to see the 'immediate psychological influence' as 'an intelligent anticipation of the market of the result that will flow from Bank Rate in due course'. Keynes held out this interpretation to Norman, only to find it discarded.[12]

---

[9] Q. 3389.
[10] Harvey to Stewart, 11 Apr. 1930, S 44/1 (1).
[11] QQ. 3390–1. Paul Einzig's fanciful supposition that 'he must have thoroughly enjoyed the game' can safely be dismissed; see *Montagu Norman* (1932), 37–8.
[12] Q. 3401.

The Governor thus appeared oblivious of the rationale of his own actions.

The general dissatisfaction with Norman's answers can be sensed from the reactions of other members of the committee, notably Macmillan and Gregory, neither of whom had any reason to make Norman's life difficult. 'I do not think the Governor would suggest that an alteration in the Bank Rate would have no ultimate repercussion in this country,' the chairman pleaded, and coaxed a formal assent out of him.[13] Gregory too found it frustrating that no clear acknowledgement was made of the effect of higher Bank rate in restricting credit. 'I thought that we were working out the theory of how the Bank Rate is supposed to operate under present conditions,' he expostulated, 'but if I am told that it does not work that way I am merely asking for an alternative explanation of how it does work.'[14]

Norman's unwillingness to provide a coherent explanation was manifested time and again. The most he would say was that industry needed rationalization, not credit, in order to meet its difficulties. He agreed with Keynes that this could not be expected to reduce unemployment until 'a late date'.[15]

Keynes: So you look forward to the present level of unemployment remaining for some considerable time to come?
Norman: I would not say that, though I agree that the benefits to be derived from rationalisation would not be immediate.

Bevin asked, did this mean that unemployment would increase? 'It is apt to do so,' was Norman's reply, to which the word 'temporarily' was subsequently added in the printed minutes.[16] When Gregory asked whether the Bank's efforts at international co-operation had shown any favourable results, Norman merely said, 'Directly, no.' In correcting the minutes, Harvey glossed this to read, 'Indirectly yes, though it would be difficult to point to any direct result.'[17] Since liaison with other central banks was Norman's own forte, this made particularly bleak listening. Moreover, the explanation of how such measures might help became internally inconsistent when the man who had denied the proposition that higher Bank rate had the effect

---

[13] QQ. 3397–8.
[14] Q. 3498.
[15] QQ. 3459–60.
[16] Sayers, *Bank of England*, 370 (Q. 3461).
[17] Ibid. (Q. 3470).

of increasing unemployment was now led to advance his own justification for a common monetary policy. It all turned on escaping the international struggle for gold, and thus easing the pressure on sterling.[18]

Keynes: How would it help the internal situation if it were easier to maintain the exchanges?
Norman: I think the internal situation would have been much easier over the last few years if the Rate had been X per cent instead of Y per cent, say 4 per cent instead of 6 per cent.
Keynes: You mean there would have been less unemployment?
Norman: I think there would.

Harvey reported that the Governor 'returned from the Committee in a very depressed state and told me that he felt he had been quite unable to deal satisfactorily with the questions which had been addressed to him'. He particularly resented the aggressive questioning from McKenna, citing banking statistics which he did not have at his fingertips. Harvey was left to do his best with the proofs of the minutes. 'From the original draft,' he admitted, 'it was very easy to understand that, as Keynes said to Stamp, the Committee had been left somewhat bewildered.'[19] Immediate steps were taken to retrieve the situation. The committee was informed that 'the Governor feels that some of his answers were incomplete, and may have led to misunderstanding', and that further evidence should be heard—not, however, from Norman (whose time was 'so fully occupied by the arrangements in connection with the inauguration of the B.I.S.') but from Harvey.[20] The Deputy Governor's further appearance was arranged for July, and he was to be buttressed by two of the Governor's expert advisers, Dr W. W. Stewart and Professor Henry Clay. In the mean time, Stamp, who was a Director of the Bank, had already been booked in for 3 April and was now briefed on points which had been overlooked by Norman the week before.

Stamp had a cordial working relationship with Keynes and was too old a hand to be patronized by him. In a radio broadcast they had done together in February, Keynes had initiated the dialogue ('Well,

[18] QQ. 3492–3.
[19] Harvey to Stewart, 11 Apr. 1930, S 44/1 (1).
[20] Memorandum, 2 Apr. 1930, S 44/1 (1). The reference is to the Bank for International Settlements. Dr Philip Williamson informs me that there is further evidence in Sir Charles Addis's diary that Harvey's rescue operation was a matter for concern at the highest levels in the Bank.

my dear Stamp') and turned it into a popular guide to the *modus operandi* of Bank rate. 'I never can answer you when you are theorising,' Stamp chipped in, ingenuously, 'but is that what happens?' By no means hostile to Keynes's reasoning, Stamp was coyness itself in refusing to be bounced into heretical conclusions. 'Hush, Maynard; I cannot bear it,' he said. 'Remember, I am a Director of the Bank of England.'[21] This urbane, avuncular figure made a far more reassuring impression upon the Macmillan Committee than the aloof and neurotic Governor had done.

Stamp blandly suggested that the return to gold was the most important difficulty, blandly admitted that Bank rate was used mainly to make the Gold Standard work, and blandly accepted that 'having returned to the gold standard you have to play the game according to the rules'.[22] He had meanwhile smuggled in an affirmation ('I suppose it is generally accepted here—I need not go into it') of the effect of Bank rate on domestic prices, which had given Norman just the sort of trouble Stamp was determined to avoid.[23] 'It had been put to us by way of metaphor by one witness,' probed the chairman, 'that the gold standard machine has "jammed" at present.' Stamp simply said 'Yes.'[24] His common-sense account of the difficulties of adjusting real wages to current levels of output was unexceptionable and ingratiating.[25]

Macmillan: If we were all perfect economists and educated by you and Mr Keynes we would then accept all these things with complete equanimity, realising that there was some law of political economy operating?
Stamp: I am afraid the influence of Mr Keynes would be so paramount that the question should be addressed to him.

Stamp's evidence pleased everyone. It flattered Macmillan and his lay colleagues on their grasp of economics, it held the door open to acceptance of much of Keynes's analysis, and it gave the authorities a breathing space, with no further ground lost. Lubbock, a fellow Director of the Bank, was 'quite satisfied' after Stamp's appearance.[26] Having established a better atmosphere, the Bank now needed to deal definitively with the issues that had proved

[21] *JMK* xx. 315, 323.
[22] QQ. 3715, 3747, 3750.
[23] Q. 3735.
[24] Q. 3818.
[25] Q. 3847.
[26] Harvey to Stewart, 11 Apr. 1930, S 44/1 (1).

troublesome in earlier evidence. Niemeyer warned Harvey: 'We are not getting the answers over at present.'[27] It was at this stage that the authorities settled down to prepare a brief capable of meeting the Keynesian challenge. Sir Richard Hopkins, who had sat through Norman's evidence, went back to the Treasury, knowing what was needed. In the Bank, a memorandum headed 'Governor's Questions' was circulated, belatedly seeking the answers which had lamentably failed to come to mind on 26 March.

The Governor's Questions

The Governor's Questions, nine in number, were the work of a devil's advocate. They were sent by the head of the Economic Information Department, J. A. C. Osborne, to Professor O. M. W. Sprague of Harvard University (Stewart's successor as Economic Adviser) who immediately divined their provenance—'I presume an outcome of the Bank Enquiry. The questions themselves seem to have a Keynesian flavour.'[28] Sprague was himself to be examined by the committee when he accompanied the Governor for a final session in February 1931. The questions were also sent to Henry Clay, who had been advising Norman for the past year; and Osborne himself, whose status is indicated by the fact that he was to become Secretary of the Bank in 1934, produced his own comments on them. Together, their responses provide a composite Bank view, articulating what Norman had left unsaid.[29]

The first question concerned the effect of Bank rate upon the volume of credit—the point on which Norman had been unable to satisfy Gregory. It was implicitly conceded that high interest rates curtailed credit, but Sprague quickly added that 'credit policy alone cannot remove all causes of disequilibrium.' To Clay, indeed, this was to raise an issue which he regarded as fundamental: 'Is the origin and basis of commercial and industrial credit to be found in the policies of industry or of the banking system?' He rejected the easy attribution of power here to the banks. 'The truer view seems to me to be,

[27] Niemeyer to Harvey, 22 Apr. 1930, S 44/1 (1).

[28] Sprague to Osborne, 8 May 1930, S 44/1 (1). W. W. Stewart was Adviser, 1928–30; O. M. W. Sprague, 1930–3.

[29] The following six paragraphs draw upon 'Governor's Questions', n.d.; answers by Osborne (15 Apr. 1930), Sprague (n.d.), and Clay, 'Bank Rate, Credit and Employment' (17 May), all in EID 1/2; and Clay to Osborne, 18 May 1930, enclosing 'Remedies', S 44/1 (1).

that, while the conditions of sound banking impose a limit on the extension of credit, the *origin* of credit is to be found in the action of the businessman, who approaches his bank for assistance with a business transaction, and the *basis* of credit in the probability that this transaction can be done at a profit.' A great deal hung on this, notably that while credit restriction might be capable of checking a boom, credit expansion could not guarantee prosperity. 'Taking off the brake is not the same thing as putting on the accelerator,' Clay maintained. 'Bank Rate is an excellent brake; but it will not necessarily serve also, by itself, as an accelerator.' This was very much the opinion of Norman himself, who endorsed it 'good' in the margin.[30]

The second question asked what effect the volume of credit had upon (*a*) employment and (*b*) the price level. Osborne's response was that rising prices stimulated trade and employment. While admitting this, Sprague specified also 'a fairly well balanced situation as a point of departure'. This brought him into close accord with Clay, since the point was that a slide into depression could not be reversed by financial means. Sprague was to argue before the Macmillan Committee that with 'an extreme departure from equilibrium' it was impossible to 'bring about equilibrium by monetary inflation'.[31] The difficulty was too heavily structural to respond to the light touch of monetary regulation. 'Mr Keynes raises very interesting questions supported by much economic analysis as to whether it is possible by means of a sufficiently low rate of interest to induce that additional demand for loans and for investments which will bring about an upward movement in prices,' Sprague concluded. 'I must say I am sceptical about that at a time when there is a very serious disequilibrium about the world.'[32]

Question 3 was the crux: 'Is the internal object of increase in Bank Rate to diminish enterprise, to reduce prices, to cause unemployment?' Thus had Norman been crucified on 26 March. 'The internal *object* of a rise in Bank Rate', Osborne protested, 'is not to diminish enterprise or cause unemployment but to keep the country linked up with other gold standard countries.' He ruefully confessed that this weapon was a blunderbuss, not a rifle, and that 'a *tendency* to a diminution of enterprise and increase in unemployment may be set

---

[30] 'Bank Rate, Credit and Employment'; cf. Clay's statement, *Macmillan Evidence*, 23 July 1930, par. 27.
[31] Q. 9255.
[32] Q. 9230.

up', albeit one that would 'usually be both slight and transitory (as before the War)'. Sprague too preferred to talk of 'the internal effect rather than the internal object', while admitting that 'some diminution in enterprise, accentuation of declining prices and some increase in unemployment' might be unavoidable. To Clay, the question was flawed by its false premiss that Bank rate was the sole and sufficient corrective for an unbalanced situation, whereas in the post-war world it had not in fact been used as the means to force down costs.[33] 'So far as its influence on prices goes, a high Bank Rate, by making credit dear and so restricting its use, does tend to force prices down in this country; and incidentally, and unavoidably, therefore, it may have discouraged enterprise and perpetuated unemployment,' Clay admitted. 'It is, however, a wanton misrepresentation to suggest that this incidental result was its object.' It is interesting to see how much moral indignation was aroused by the importation of this single word into a statement about causal necessity.

The fourth and fifth questions focused on the relative effects of Bank rate upon the exchange rate and upon unemployment. 'If the gold standard is functioning normally and trade is active,' Osborne argued, 'an increase in Bank Rate should have a very small effect in diminishing enterprise and causing unemployment, because the higher Bank Rate should produce the required effect in a very short time, and therefore be again lowered in a short time.' If this was an optimistic assessment, Sprague's was fatalistic. He did not see how the attendant ill effects could be avoided but objected to the assumption 'that if a rise in bank rate is not made, employment will not later be affected unfavorably'. For Clay, likewise, Bank rate acted 'not as a major cause, but as an aggravation of conditions that were due to other causes'.

Questions 6, 7, and 8 turned back to issues of credit, which produced much recapitulation and amplification. The final question, if such it can be called, was the sting in the tail, provocatively asserting that 'we act for advantage of finance and for disadvantage of industry.' Yes, agreed Osborne, 'through being insufficiently ruthless in our deflationary policy'—meaning that the sheltered industries could have been more drastically squeezed in 1925–6. Sprague was more circumspect, reiterating that Britain's 'problems reflect economic or industrial disequilibrium, disequilibrium that requires as remedies industrial reorganization, improvement in

---

[33] See also Henry Clay, *Lord Norman* (1957), 160–7.

management, and additional equipment involving much additional capital'. Until these intractable features had been modified, little could be expected from financial policy—an opinion which he was in due course to relay to the Macmillan Committee. 'Nothing has any effect really, you seem to think?' was Keynes's retort.[34] With the Governor sitting silently beside him, Sprague maintained an impassive detachment in face of such needling.[35]

Keynes: If you were to assume, for the sake of argument, that any large-scale readjustment such as you desire was impossible, what would you then recommend?
Sprague: I should not recommend anything. I should expect a decline of the economic position of this country until it reached a breaking point, and an explosion.

A professor from Manchester, Clay had a less apocalyptic vision than the professor from Harvard; but its general import was the same.

The conclusion I draw is that there is no simple solution of unemployment, and no alternative to the direct attack on the different elements of the problem—on costs, by re-organisation and the reduction of some wages; on interest charges by financial re-organisation; on the burden of taxation by reducing public expenditure; on the shortage of gold for reserves by promoting co-operation between central banks; on stock exchange speculation by a more careful scrutiny by the Banks of the purposes for which advances are asked of them.

This was a view Clay defended effectively before the Macmillan Committee, firmly resisting Keynes's counter-suggestion that the return to gold had been the paramount feature of recent years.[36]

Clay: I should say rather the stabilisation of the internal price level and the maintenance of that in face of a world fall in prices.
Keynes: The stickiness of wages at the high level?
Clay: Stickiness of wages, interest charges, public charges of all sorts.

Clay was perfectly ready to talk about remedies, but always in this context. He argued that British industry was in fact set up to satisfy an international market and that the increase in consumption needed to revive it must therefore come from foreign customers. Hence the

[34] Q. 9252.
[35] Q. 9286.
[36] See par. 33 of his statement, *Macmillan Evidence*, 23 July 1930, and QQ. 8538–9.

importance of competitiveness. But, since the War, British prices had been out of line with those in competing countries—not by the fractional amounts which the Gold Standard mechanism could equilibrate, but by 10 or 20 per cent. Any increase in expenditure, if it were to relieve unemployment rather than add to the dislocation, had to be adapted to the structure of industry as it currently existed. Keynes's remedy of home investment was thus inappropriate to the needs of export industries which had lost their markets. Moreover, Keynes was too optimistic in supposing that cheap money alone could revive the economy, because the structural disparities were now such as to outweigh a marginal new incentive to invest. With his Lancashire experience, Clay did not deny that there were sufficient savings but doubted the investment opportunities. 'The idle capital is largely the property of businesses that would use it if they could do so to earn more than bank deposit rate without the risk of losing it,' he argued; 'that they leave it on time deposit is evidence that the openings for its use do not exist.'[37] This left two available measures, both of which would be necessary. One was to promote suitable investment by means of an institutional restructuring of the capital market. The other was to get costs down so as to open the world market to British goods once more.

'Is anything else wrong with this country?'

By the end of May 1930 the Bank was well briefed to deal with the questions it had found so awkward two months previously. The plan now was for Osborne to prepare a memorandum giving a historical review of the Bank's policy and of the reasoning behind it. Lubbock had privately squared Macmillan, so that such a memorandum could be sent around the committee before it heard verbal evidence from a representative of the Bank. 'We want if possible to secure by arrange-ment with the Chairman that the verbal discussion shall be confined to matters dealt with in the memorandum and will not be allowed to stray into questions of economic theory,' Harvey informed Stewart. 'If the Committee should desire to ask questions under the latter head it is hoped that you might perhaps be willing to deal with such matters.'[38] Stewart was due from America in mid-June. It was settled

[37] Clay, 'Remedies', S 44/1 (1).
[38] Harvey to Stewart, 16 May 1930, copy, S 44/1 (1); cf. QQ. 7509–10.

that Harvey should appear on 2 July, when he put in a characteristically safe performance, and that he should accompany Stewart on 3 and 4 July, with Stewart in practice doing all the talking.

There is no Bank of England memorandum in the official proceedings of the committee. Harvey spoke from a précis, much as Hopkins had done, and Clay submitted a statement under his own name. Osborne's memorandum never got beyond the drafting stage. 'The Bank agree with Professor Clay's diagnosis,' the draft began.[39] It endorsed the view that monetary factors had been exaggerated and criticized Keynes's schemes for home investment as placing further burdens upon the hard-pressed British employer.

Of the remedies proposed, the Bank prefer—

(1) Reduction of real wages in the sheltered industries, and if this is insufficient, in the unsheltered as well.

(2) Reduction of real social service benefits to a point where fear of unemployment is increased and the mobility of labour stimulated.

(3) Redistribution of taxation to bear less heavily on profits and more heavily on sheltered classes of all kinds, and redistribution of social service charges so that they will not be a tax on employment.

(4) Rationalisation.

(5) A Calvinistic outlook.

It is difficult to believe that the tone of this draft would have been left unmodified in a published document. No doubt it served well enough for internal briefing, and Osborne added more in the same vein for Stewart—'what they ought to ask *him*'—the day before he met the committee. This anticipated, or rather indicated, the actual line of questioning fairly closely. Osborne went on to give an unbridled view, not just of what the Bank would have liked to be asked, but of what it would have liked to respond if free to do so.[40]

'Mr McKenna & Committee': Did you not see return to Gold would cause unemployment here?

'The Bank': No, I mean Yes. But if one section of the community decides to impoverish themselves for the benefit of another section, how can the Bk prevent them & why should they complain to the Bk if they repent of their own action. . . .

[39] Osborne, 'Macmillan Committee: Bank of England's Views', n.d. (July 1930), EID 1/2.

[40] Osborne, questions, 2 July 1930, and notes, n.d., EID 1/2; cf. *Macmillan Evidence*, Q. 7611.

'McKenna': Then you think wages are too high?

'Bank': Certainly; so is social service expenditure & the burden is badly distributed, just as world gold, credit granted by your Bank, & labour in this country & elsewhere is badly distributed.

'McKenna': Is anything else wrong with this country?

'Bank': Almost everything. That is why we cannot afford to neglect *anything* that may help.

Before Stewart's appearance, the committee had, in one of Keynes's rare absences, also heard from Niemeyer, speaking as an individual, but incontestably reinforcing the Bank's hard-faced image. He offered an unrepentant account of the return to gold—at a higher rather than a lower parity, and sooner rather than later— which evidently shook Gregory. 'I agree with your analysis, or with 90 per cent of it, at any rate,' he intervened, 'but I cannot see why you should advance the argument that if we had adopted a higher par it would have paid us, as a large importing nation.'[41] Niemeyer was likewise ready to go on to the offensive, obviously with McKenna in his sights, against the joint-stock banks, who had been 'too ready to help industry, I should say, rather than not been ready enough'.[42] This robust treatment prepared the ground for Stewart, who seemed mild by contrast in his defence of both the timing and the parity of the return to gold, as being an outcome where no real alternative was on offer.

Stewart's role was to pick up the pieces. He had just stepped down after two years as one of Norman's closest confidants; he knew the Governor's mind; and as a professional economist he was technically equipped to withstand tough questioning from Keynes, who had no reason to give him quarter. He stuck to the Bank's line in playing down the harmful consequences of the return to gold—in part, on the ground that the underlying position in 1925 'was worse than it looked to most publicists at the time, and they therefore ascribed the subsequent difficulties to the return to gold rather than to the return of the Ruhr to production'.[43] Partly, also, the required adjustments had been exaggerated and had, he maintained, been completed by the end of 1925, at least so far as finance was concerned.[44]

Keynes: But we had not brought costs into line?

[41] Q. 6705.
[42] Q. 6755.
[43] Q. 7635.
[44] Q. 7625.

Stewart: No. I had not regarded that as being primarily a financial question.

There were, of course, other adjustments which were necessary to restore equilibrium in the British economy, but it seemed to Stewart 'rather easy to attribute to the return to gold the entire adjustment which after a lapse of five years appears to be necessary'.[45] In short, it was the industrial not the financial machine that was jammed— just as Norman had said, nearly four months and four thousand questions ago.

Stewart was determined not to be drawn from the ground which he had staked out. When McKenna tackled him on the relation of the money supply to the price level, Stewart adroitly professed himself ready to discuss the quantity theory of money 'on either one of two bases, either of logical necessity, that it must happen, or by an appeal to evidence, that it does happen'.[46] But he refused to be shifted from one to the other and found it 'difficult to reconcile the known facts about credit and trade with the quantity theory'.[47] Indeed, question by question, he progressively reached the point of saying that he saw 'no necessary relation quantitatively between national income and the volume of bank credit'—provoking Keynes to ask, 'Are you not denying a great deal too much?'[48] Stewart's ulterior aim here was to deprecate monetary explanations altogether. 'My feeling is', he ruminated, 'that the monetary theorist is not sufficiently familiar with industrial development to put it in its proper perspective as part of the general economic situation and his dwelling upon monetary factors is frequently the result of lack of familiarity with the industrial conditions.'[49] After a discussion of credit policy with McKenna and Keynes, he made the observation: 'A discussion which turns on logical niceties has the possibility of missing what is, perhaps, the major and essential point of an inquiry into the relations between industry and finance.'[50]

The major and essential point was not the fine equilibration of monetary policy but the structural ossification of British industry, with the danger that any palliative 'would obscure the real situation, and would delay the growth of a state of mind—this is what seems to

45 Q. 7631.
46 Q. 7646.
47 Q. 7656.
48 QQ. 7692–3.
49 Q. 7893.
50 Q. 7879.

me so important—a state of mind which would recognise what are the factors in the situation and how they have to be dealt with.'[51]

Macmillan: It would prevent your facing the music?
Stewart: I think so, and you would be likely to have to face it later in a much weakened condition.

The difference between this and what Keynes was saying turned largely on an assessment of what seemed immediately practicable. On cheap money, Stewart's general opinion was 'that the causal relation between low money rates and business activity was always interesting, frequently important, but seldom decisive'.[52] To Keynes, on the other hand, 'experience showed that the normal situation was that a reasonably abundant supply of credit would do the trick.'[53] Moreover, it had the advantage of being controllable by the authorities, since 'finance is a matter of decision which can be dealt with crisply and at once.'[54]

Keynes: It may be that the weather has much more influence on business than the matter of the Bank Rate; but nevertheless, when one is discussing what should be done, it would not be useful to keep on saying it is the weather which really matters. In a sense it is true it may be the biggest factor?
Stewart: It may be the only thing that the Central Banks can do; but it does not strike me as the only thing that business men can do.

When it came to the practicability of restoring British competitiveness, roles were reversed, as Keynes lapsed into passive scepticism and Stewart became animated into active insistence. Stewart regarded 'wage adjustments as ever so much more important in industry than changes in Bank Rate or anything bankers can do'.[55] He could 'not see how one can approach the problem on the presumption that wages are to be left untouched'.[56] The problem in Britain was that money incomes had been regarded as immutable, whereas he would have thought 'if the worker had the choice he would rather maintain his real income even at some sacrifice of his rate of wages'.[57] Given that readjustments of the price level were implied by the return to gold, Stewart was hopeful—'I thought the community accepted it as being worthwhile'[58]—that the required

[51] QQ. 7722–3.	[52] Q. 7826.
[53] Q. 7835.	[54] QQ. 7842–3.
[55] Q. 7847.	[56] Q. 7736.
[57] Q. 7750.	[58] Q. 7877.

changes would be forthcoming. When Keynes challenged his premiss, by hinting that the difficulty was caused by the return to gold, there was no meeting of minds.[59]

Keynes: If our money had been worth less, all kinds of changes which are necessary if you alter the value of your money are not then necessary?
Stewart: I do not get your question.

The discussion was in this sense inconclusive. When Keynes twisted back to the Gold Standard, rather than remaining confined to industrial problems, Stewart made a final protest:[60]

To interpret this failure as being due to monetary factors, when we had almost reached agreement that all we mean is that monetary factors are important, seems to me to be going back upon the argument and refusing to see the situation as a whole.

At this point, in all essentials, the Bank's case rested. Clay reinforced Stewart's analysis on 23 July, and two days later Harvey returned to his seventh day of testimony—an old friend of the committee, helping to tidy up its left-over business. Stewart and Sprague, it should be noted, had meanwhile picked up a cordial correspondence with Keynes over the *Treatise*, which they read in proof, and Sprague professed himself open to persuasion in a manner which later developments showed to betoken more than politeness.[61]

Whatever Norman's other gifts as Governor, he had never made it his business to see that the Bank's policy was understood. It can be disinterred partly from internal archives and partly from the explication of the Governor's hunches by articulate economists in his confidence, especially Clay. Norman notoriously explained to the committee how he formed his judgements by simply tapping his nose; and he remarked that 'it is a curious thing, the extent to which many of those who inhabit the City of London find difficulty in stating the reasons for the faith that is in them'.[62] The Bank drew on a formidable fund of practical expertise in managing and reading the financial markets. It also held firm views about the dilapidated condition of British industry. But it had no clear understanding of the connections between the two, as its belated exercises in the *modus*

[59] Q. 7888.
[60] Q. 7891.
[61] See *JMK* xiii. 173–5, and below, ch. 12 n. 33.
[62] Q. 3516; Sayers, *Bank of England*, 369.

operandi of Bank rate served to demonstrate. Norman showed that he either did not know or did not want to know the answers here: hence his incoherence.

More fundamentally, the Bank refused to accept a monetary explanation at all—a view expounded with all Stewart's subtlety and sophistication. Whatever expedients were proposed, therefore, the real problem remained the uncompetitiveness of British industry. The well-informed financial journalist, Paul Einzig, provided a sympathetic interpretation of Norman's policy along these lines: 'Devices provided by monetary policy could only have been palliatives, which might have disguised the real situation for some time, but would not have obviated the necessity of facing realities sooner or later.'[63] Keynes may have held out the prospect that, despite 'the enormous anomaly of unemployment in a world full of wants', its existence was really a backhanded tribute to the labour-saving power of technology which meant 'in the long run *that mankind is solving its economic problem*', if only the logistics of abundance could be better organized.[64] Rejecting such easy optimism, the Bank took refuge in 'a Calvinistic outlook'—a moral reinforced after the Wall Street crash. An American banker with whom Norman had a close friendship wrote of the world crisis in 1930: 'The remedy is for people to stop watching the ticker, listening to the radio, drinking bootleg gin, and dancing to jazz; forget the "new economics" and prosperity founded upon spending and gambling, and return to the old economics based upon saving and working.'[65] Likewise, for Norman and his colleagues, the need to face the music presented the same kind of austere challenge as the return to the Gold Standard—the course of realism and rectitude, which had too long been evaded.

[63] *Montagu Norman* (1932), 51.

[64] *JMK* ix. 322, 325 ('Economic possibilities for our grandchildren', 1930).

[65] R. C. Leffingwell to T. W. Lamont, 14 Aug. 1930, quoted in Harold James, *The German Slump* (Oxford, 1986), 16. Both men were partners in J. P. Morgan & Co.

7

The reformulation of the Treasury View, 1929–1930

'The way to conjure outlay out of the fourth dimension'

Within the Labour Government, the main advocate of a radical assault upon unemployment was the Chancellor of the Duchy of Lancaster, Sir Oswald Mosley. His memorandum, outlining the economic and administrative changes he thought necessary, was presented to the Cabinet at the end of January 1930 and was under consideration during the next three months. Keynes had been shown it and offered Mosley general encouragement and specific advice.[1] His own efforts in the Macmillan Committee were now paralleled by the work of the Economic Advisory Council, set up by MacDonald in January, which met thirteen times at 10 Downing Street between 17 February 1930 and 16 April 1931. Keynes was among fifteen non-ministerial members, predominantly industrialists, along with Bevin and Stamp (who were also involved in the Macmillan Committee's hearings) and the socialist intellectuals G. D. H. Cole and R. H. Tawney. Hubert Henderson was persuaded to accept appointment as secretary of the new body, leaving the *Nation* at this point to become a Civil Servant rather than a professor at the London School of Economics. There was a marked overlap in personnel and agenda between the two different bodies set up to review economic policy; indeed Snowden sought to stop the EAC discussing monetary policy or public works on the grounds that the Macmillan Committee was doing this.[2] Keynes was also well placed to play off one against the other by dint of his dual membership, in seeking leverage for his arguments; and in the spring of 1930 he had reason to be pleased at the headway he was making on inside opinion, having failed to enlist outside opinion in 1929.

Shortly after Keynes had finished his private evidence, Macmillan invited Hawtrey to appear before the committee, in his personal capacity rather than as a Treasury official, but plainly to subject

---

[1] *JMK* xx. 312–15; Robert Skidelsky, *Politicians and the Slump* (1967), ch. 8.
[2] Howson and Winch, *EAC* 24–5, 30, 34.

Keynes's analysis to technical scrutiny. Copies of the minutes were therefore made available to him and it was hoped (vainly as it turned out) that proofs of the *Treatise* would also be in his hands before he gave evidence. Keynes's lively sense of affinity with Hawtrey—'One of the writers who seem to me to be most nearly on the right track'[3]—may seem puzzling in the light of Hawtrey's status as, if not the architect, at least the structural engineer of the Treasury View. Yet persuasive claims have also been made on his behalf as an inventor of the multiplier,[4] which seems to remove one puzzle only to create another. How could one man stand on both sides in this argument, at once anti-Keynesian and proto-Keynesian? The paradox can be resolved by looking closely at the way Hawtrey responded to the argument presented in *Can Lloyd George Do It?*

Two weeks after the 1929 General Election Hawtrey composed a Treasury memorandum, 'The Liberal Unemployment Plan'.[5] There were, he argued, two possible means of absorbing unemployment. One was through a reduction in prices and wages, which was fine in theory though in practice likely to 'paralyse initiative and cause a restriction of production'. The second method, then, was to increase the money value of output, that is, to increase demand. Hawtrey assumed that any such increase would be divided in existing proportions between domestic products and internationally competitive goods (what he called 'foreign trade products', whether exports or imports). This was broadly a distinction between sheltered and unsheltered trades. The part of new expenditure which was spent on domestic goods would obviously stimulate home production. But the rest, if it were spent on more imports, would worsen the balance of payments; gold would be lost; credit would accordingly be contracted; and in this way the national income would be 'reduced again to its former level in order to maintain the gold standard'. Suppose, however, that these proportions of expenditure were modified—as indeed the Liberal plan envisaged. If £125 million of loan-financed expenditure were to be found by reducing foreign investment from £150 to £25 million, gold would be imported.

Why did Hawtrey say this? It is important to appreciate his

---

[3] *JMK* xiii. 127 (meeting of the Royal Statistical Society, 17 Dec. 1929). For the arrangements over Hawtrey's appearance see Macmillan to Hawtrey, 14 Mar. 1930, HTRY 11/2, Hawtrey Papers, Churchill College, Cambridge.

[4] See Neville Cain, 'Hawtrey and multiplier theory', *Australian Economic History Review*, 22 (1982), 68–78, from which I have learnt a great deal.

[5] T. 175/26; the original, dated 12 June 1929, is in HTRY 1/41.

implicit reasoning since this was the fork in the road where he left his Treasury colleagues and headed in the same direction as Keynes. Everyone agreed that the means by which foreign lending was transferred across the exchanges was via an export surplus of goods for which Britain waived current payment, hence acquiring a lien on some investment held abroad. Keynes's point was that such a surplus was, in the late 1920s, increasingly difficult to generate, given the uncompetitive level of British prices, and that the outflow of capital therefore prompted deflationary pressures, designed to reduce costs, with adverse consequences at home. He concluded that it might be best to cut back foreign lending in the first place. The ordinary objection was that this would, in the long run, cut British exports by the same amount, since in effect Britain would stop making the loans which had financed them. Trade would balance at a lower level. Hawtrey, however, was looking at the way in which such a balance would immediately be financed in the short run, given that the exports were already in the pipeline. The answer was obvious: Britain's export surplus would be balanced by importing gold.

Under the orthodox Gold Standard mechanism, this would inflate the domestic money supply. 'In order to regain equilibrium,' Hawtrey argued, 'there would have to be an expansion of credit sufficient to attract additional imports to the amount of 125 millions a year.' These imports, by definition, would be 'foreign trade products'. Since these constituted a given proportion of total domestic consumption, simple multiplication showed the total increase in demand that was required, so long as *all* the increase went towards imports. But 'this condition would certainly not be fulfilled', so a deduction must be made for substitution by home-produced goods in the unsheltered industries.

Now all this depended on 'the assumption that the whole of the 125 millions of capital is raised by the diversion of investable savings from export'. This assumption too had to be modified in the light of the case stated in *Can Lloyd George Do It?* In the first place, there were savings on the dole. Clumsily but confidently, Hawtrey showed that this cut both ways: at once alleviating the burden of financing the scheme but simultaneously meaning that 'the beneficial effects of the whole scheme on unemployment is less'. Secondly, Hawtrey imputed to Keynes and Henderson a reliance on idle balances, which he could not countenance—calling it 'a blunder' to suppose that resources could be found 'in any other way than by drawing on the investable savings of the community out of income'. Whatever steps Hawtrey had taken towards the multiplier concept on the expenditure side, his doctrine on the lump of savings, as enshrined in CP 53 (29), held firm, with no acknowledgement of any financial slack to be taken up. Granted this point, 'it will be seen that the whole scheme is nothing more than a very elaborate alternative to raising loans abroad for the strengthening of our gold reserves,' and thus removing 'the one and only obstacle to remedy unemployment by an expansion of credit'.

By following Hawtrey's argument it can be seen how delicately ambiguous his position was. From one viewpoint, he can be seen supporting the Treasury View in arguing that investable funds could only come from existing savings and that a net addition at home must therefore be drawn from foreign lending. From another viewpoint, he seems to be fastidiously if inadvertently inventing the multiplier, albeit in an inverted form, with a mechanism which required finite changes in the national income, given leakages into imports and 'savings on the dole'. In fact, Hawtrey was perfectly consistent throughout in one implied objective: to specify the conditions under which 'crowding-out' takes place. It was not clear that these conditions obtained in Britain at less than full employment. In a book published in 1928 he had written: 'The rise of prices and the increase of production are, to a great extent, *alternatives.*'[6]

When the Treasury View came to be defended before the Macmillan Committee, therefore, Hawtrey's colleagues had some reason to suspect that their economic guru had jumped ship. They were already familiar with his own hybrid plan for tackling unemployment: namely to raise a public loan, *à la* Keynes, and use it to redeem the national debt, *à la* Niemeyer—a strategy which only made sense if the loan were raised from funds that would otherwise flow abroad.[7] The reasoning behind this was that a Government loan from the international investment market produced a favourable effect upon the balance of payments. Credit therefore had to be expanded, with a consequent opportunity to reduce Bank rate. Since it was 'not the Government expenditure, but *the borrowing itself*'

---

[6] Cain, 'Hawtrey and multiplier theory', 70, quoting Hawtrey's revisions in *Currency and Credit* 3rd edn. (1928), 49–50.

[7] Susan Howson, 'Hawtrey and the real world', in G. C. Harcourt (ed.), *Keynes and his Contemporaries* (1985), 166–7. The plan was revived in 'Remedies for unemployment', *Macmillan Evidence*, ii. 315–21, reprinted in R. G. Hawtrey, *The Art of Central Banking* (1933), ch. 8.

which affected the balance of payments and allowed the advantage of cheap money, it followed that the desired end could be reached more directly by dropping public works and using the loan to extinguish the Government's floating debt.[8] Like Keynes, Hawtrey offered an analysis which, on theoretical grounds, allowed the relevance of more than one remedy (including loan-financed public works) while making it clear that he had his own favourite solution. This solution—sometimes referred to as 'Hawtrey's Bill Famine Plan'— found little support either in the Treasury or the Bank, where it was seen as uncritically invoking '(as is usual with Hawtrey) the assumption not only that cheap money is an essential prerequisite to a recovery of industry but that cheap money by itself is sufficient to cause the recovery'.[9]

Hawtrey's Macmillan Committee evidence at the beginning of April confirmed this impression. He called the dear money policy '*the* exceptional cause' of recent unemployment, which he considered 'exclusively due to monetary causes'.[10] In these respects he was much closer to Keynes than to the Bank, whose policy he criticized as timid in its refusal to make full use of the gold reserves in order to reduce interest rates—a stricture which even Keynes thought 'unwarranted'.[11] The committee had been warned in advance by Leith-Ross that Hawtrey 'holds views; not necessarily the Treasury's views'.[12] Hawtrey regarded the position of the Bank of England as having been sufficiently strong to enable it to dictate its own terms albeit at the expense of some depletion of its reserves; in this sense 'it would have been worth getting rid of £100,000,000 of gold to cure unemployment'.[13] The Bank could have bought its way out of trouble, and thus avoided the crucial mistake of high interest rates. For 'the way to conjure outlay out of the fourth dimension is to lower Bank Rate.'[14]

McKenna: Your whole argument is turned upon cheap money?
Hawtrey: Yes.

---

[8] 'Remedies for unemployment', par. 47; *Art of Central Banking*, 443.
[9] Osborne, 'Hawtrey's Bill Famine Plan', EID 1/2.
[10] QQ. 4156, 4162.
[11] Q. 4193. Clay was at one with Keynes here; see his comments on Hopkins's draft, 'Prices and Credit Policy', pars. 6–8, EID 1/2.
[12] Private session, 21 Mar. 1930, 28.
[13] Q. 4257. Keynes thought this would have been right if the reserves had been £100 m. higher: private session, 23 Oct. 1930, 31.
[14] QQ. 4275, 4329–30.

McKenna: For the purpose of reviving trade?
Hawtrey: Yes.

Hawtrey's analytical differences with Keynes were largely ones of definition. Hawtrey provided Hopkins with an exegesis of Keynes's private evidence, with his criticisms on both 'the plan and on the theoretical arguments by which it is supported'. But though he spent several pages arguing whether demand for fixed capital or working capital was more sensitive to changes in interest rates, he admitted that this was a difference 'rather of emphasis than of substance' and that it was 'common ground' that a high Bank rate deterred both classes of borrower. Moreover, Hawtrey scrupulously distinguished what Keynes meant by a contraction of credit from the proposition (commonly imputed to him in the Treasury) that savings exceeded investment because of idle balances in the banks. Hawtrey, for one, was now clear on this point, and he noted that Keynes 'does not mention the possibility of a reluctance of people to put their savings into securities, or suggest any reason why it should occur'.[15] They agreed, therefore, that the whole issue of idle balances simply amounted to 'a diminution of the total velocity of circulation'.[16] Another point on which differences were easily settled was over Keynes's definitions of income and saving, which implied that excessive saving exactly balanced business losses. 'I believe I am to have the privilege of seeing your book in proof presently,' Hawtrey told Keynes, 'and I would like to think it over when I have seen it, but I think in substance I agree with your statement, though I am accustomed to use a different phraseology.'[17]

When it came to Keynes's own remedies, Hawtrey's account of a home investment programme, as sent to Hopkins, was everything that could be hoped for from a sympathetic critic:[18]

Suppose that the Government borrows and spends £1,000,000 a week. This sum is received by those whom it employs and the consumers' income is thereby increased by £1,000,000 a week. The additional income will be spent on commodities of all kinds. A part will be spent on home trade products, giving rise to still more additional income among the producers of those products; a part of the £1,000,000 a week and a part of this other additional income will be spent on foreign trade products and will occasion an

---

[15] Hawtrey, 'Mr Keynes's Theory of Bank Rate', 1 Apr. 1930, HTRY 1/45.
[16] Q. 4227.   [17] Q. 4270.
[18] 'Mr Keynes's Theory of Bank Rate', HTRY 1/45.

unfavourable balance. Moreover, over and above the additional income at the rate of £1,000,000 a week, there is the *cumulative* effect of the steady growth in the total volume of bank credit by that amount.

Hawtrey's chief point here was that, in order to succeed in diverting investment from abroad to domestic uses, it would be necessary to raise the funds from the public rather than through a creation of bank credit. Hawtrey allowed that the policy of expanding credit by diminishing capital exports might be appropriate 'at a time of grave unemployment and depression'. As a matter of practical judgement, to be sure, he did not think Keynes's policy was currently called for; but as regards the framework of analysis, there was a close convergence between them. Keynes told Hawtrey, when he dispatched the proofs of the *Treatise* at the end of April, 'although we always seem to differ on these monetary questions in discussion, I feel that ultimately I am joined in common agreement with you as against most of the rest of the world'.[19]

'Did we say this?'

The official Treasury evidence was given by Hopkins on 16 and 22 May. The committee were obviously expectant and the authorities apprehensive—the more so after the Bank evidence had gone off at half cock. Leith-Ross had done his best to reserve vital matters until Hopkins appeared, and during April and early May the Treasury collected and circulated a series of memoranda which were to serve as Hopkins's brief. There were five main papers, each of which went through several drafts. These covered 'The Liberal Plan', 'Plentiful Credit and Cheap Money', 'Income Tax (contra McKenna)', 'The Currency and Bank Notes Bill', and 'The Conversion Loan and paying-off Treasury Bills'. All of these papers were vetted by Fisher, Hopkins, Leith-Ross, Phillips, Grigg, and Hawtrey. Ismay, the committee's secretary, was sent them, and so was Niemeyer at the Bank of England; indeed the Bank circulated its own set, supplemented by a paper by Hopkins on its relation to the Treasury. This 'bundle of notes' was also sent by Grigg to Snowden as Chancellor of the Exchequer, who had nothing to add.[20] Together, these papers care-

---

[19] *JMK* xx. 131.
[20] The brief, with a circulation list, is in T. 175/46; an earlier draft of 'The Liberal Plan' is in T. 175/26; the Bank's copies, with comments, are in EID 1/2.

fully articulate the skeleton of official policy, which was faithfully fleshed out by Hopkins's testimony.

On some matters, like the availability of credit, Hopkins regarded the brief as 'much more detailed than anything I would propose to say unless questioned closely on the subject'.[21] On others, like management of government borrowing, there was a good deal of arcane technical detail of an uncontroversial kind. The nub of the evidence was bound to be the interlocking issues of Gold Standard, Bank rate, and loan-financed public works. There had been ample warning that the committee would wish for elucidation here. For example, during Stamp's evidence on 4 April, he had referred to 'the alternative between transfer and inflation'.[22]

Keynes: What do you mean by 'transfer'?

Stamp: What has been known, rightly or wrongly, as the Treasury View, namely that if you take money in one way, it is denied to some other source. I do not know whether that is actually the Treasury view?

McKenna: That was the Treasury view, as expressed quite recently. I do not know if it is the Treasury view now. Apparently the view is that there is a fixed quantity of money, and if you transfer any of that fixed quantity from one trade to another, you are not assisting trade at all in general.

Gregory: It is a fixed quantity of savings, rather than a fixed quantity of money—at least I think that is what is meant.

McKenna: I do not know. I thought it was money. I do not think the question of savings for a moment enters into the matter.

Brand: I thought it was a question of investment?

Stamp: Whatever funds are available for investment.

In 1929, under Leith-Ross's influence, the Treasury had had little compunction in promulgating a strong doctrine, as CP 53 (29) testified. Its vestiges rested in the White Paper of May 1929. A year later, however—with a Labour Government in office, with Keynes on the rampage, and with Hawtrey under a cloud—all this made less convincing reading. 'The statement in the Treasury Memorandum,' read the briefing paper, had asserted 'that because money could not be obtained from the sources designated in the first Liberal pamphlet, it seemed to follow that it must come out of funds which would *otherwise soon be taken for British industry...*' In the margin of the copy as circulated was the pencilled query: 'did we say this?' 'Yes, para. (9),' responded Hopkins—a sadder and a wiser man, who

---

[21] Note by Hopkins, EID 1/2.
[22] QQ. 4002–4.

readily agreed that this proposition 'was perhaps rather telescopic'.[23] In fact, he redrafted this section so as to indicate his own line of argument. 'The theory so ably championed by Mr Keynes is based on a number of abstract assumptions which, for my part, I must confess that I regard with a considerable amount of scepticism,' he wrote. 'The question, however, that interests us is the practical application of this theory and I think it will be best if I try to show how the Plan would work in real life.'[24]

Hopkins asserted his authority in reformulating the Treasury position upon this criterion, and ensured that he would not, like Norman, stumble into the lion's den unprepared. It is clear that the chairman was ready to co-operate in ensuring that Hopkins would not be drawn beyond his brief. Pressed by Keynes on the fiduciary issue, Hopkins brought this understanding into force.[25]

Hopkins: This is a point, Mr Chairman, to which I have given no special thought recently, and before I agree to the suggestion made by Mr Keynes I should like to think carefully about it. I confess to feeling rather sceptical.
Macmillan: I think you will have a good many questions on which you would like notice.

And so it turned out. Hopkins's good-natured stonewalling ('I would like time to think it over', 'I should like time to consider this'[26]) set the tone for his first day of evidence. 'I am a layman with regard to control of the Bank Rate and control of the currency,' he said at one point, while expressing sympathy for the Bank's position.[27] This mien was also effective in baffling Keynes's sharp inquiries over the logic of interest rate policy: 'I am sorry; I am afraid I really do not follow. We may, perhaps, be at cross purposes.'[28]

The first day (16 May) disposed of a number of difficult points. It was agreed with the chairman that the position over the fiduciary issue would be better dealt with in a memorandum, which left Hopkins 'to try to draw together the argument after Keynes's

[23] 'The Liberal Plan', T. 175/26; cf. Cmd. 3331, par. 9. The Treasury papers now provide support for K. J. Hancock's hunch that there was a 'great discrepancy' between Hopkins's evidence in 1930 and earlier Treasury advice; 'The reduction of unemployment as a problem of public policy; 1920–9', in Sidney Pollard (ed.), *The Gold Standard and Employment Policies between the Wars* (1970), 113–14.
[24] 'The Liberal Plan', T. 175/46.
[25] Q. 5404.
[26] QQ. 5410, 5413.
[27] Q. 5450.
[28] Q. 5453.

onslaught' with fewer outstanding encumbrances. He busily con-
fabulated with Harvey at the Bank—'I gave you last night Leithers'
suggestion for the points to be made'—to make sure the deferred
questions received proper treatment.[29] Having dealt with these on
22 May, Hopkins was ready to face the issue of whether a development loan would, as Keynes supposed, divert investable money from
foreign to home investment. Hopkins assured the committee that 'if
such a scheme could work in practice as it would work on paper then
I should be in agreement with him'.[80] But here everything depended
upon confidence—a consideration now paramount in Treasury
thinking.

When Keynes had presented the case for loan-financed public
works in his private evidence on 6 March, he identified two
important counter-arguments. The first was the Treasury View, as a
proposition about crowding-out. 'I fancy that the belief that something of this kind is true, or the suspicion that it may be true,' he
surmised, 'has very largely influenced the actual policy, both of the
late Chancellor of the Exchequer [Churchill] and of the present
Chancellor of the Exchequer [Snowden].' He enjoined the committee
to discover whether it was true by putting it as a question to all the
expert economic witnesses—a sure sign that he was confident of
what their verdict would be. Keynes's main objection was that it
followed 'too obediently the teaching of the economics of equilibrium'. It rested on a full-employment assumption—not surprisingly,
he thought, 'because practically all economic treatises do assume in
most of their chapters that unemployment, except of a merely
transitory character of which one need take no serious account, is an
impossibility'. The Treasury View, in this sense, was 'the natural
result of standing half-way between common sense and sound theory;
it is the result of having abandoned the one without having reached
the other'.[31]

The arguments on the other side were those which Keynes had
evolved during the 1929 election campaign, buttressed by the
analysis of the *Treatise*. When Macmillan had reminded him that
'our recommendations are to be designed to be carried into practical
execution', Keynes had given the classic public speaker's riposte:
'That I am coming to. I am only dealing now with the *prima facie*

[29] Hopkins to Harvey, 20 May 1930, S 44/1 (1).
[30] Q. 5553.
[31] *JMK* xx. 129–30 (6 Mar. 1930).

objection that this whole class of remedies, whether feasible or not feasible, is unsound.'[32] When Keynes faced Hopkins ten weeks later, he clearly relished the opportunity to debate this broad proposition. But Hopkins, as we now know, had put the intervening time to good use, not least in familiarizing himself with the minutes of the private evidence.[33] Keynes had thus spread the net in the sight of the bird; but the downy bird, of course, did not let on. Hopkins's strategy relied on diffidence not brilliance.[34]

Hopkins: I think the Treasury view has sometimes been rather compendiously and not very accurately stated.
Macmillan: Now is your chance, Sir Richard?
Hopkins: If I may say so, officials, if their views are published, start a controversy, and they are not able to intervene in its progress, and sometimes the exact form of their view—
Macmillan: Is a little misunderstood?
Hopkins: —is a little misunderstood.

Hopkins began with a statement closely paraphrasing his brief. It was a rehearsal of the administrative difficulties involved in implementing public works—really a 'Whitehall view', the cogency of which can nowadays be fully appreciated.[35] But it needs to be recognized that, while this had long comprised one set of objections to public works, as demonstrated by bulky sections of the 1929 White Paper, it was only in 1930 that the Treasury officials made it the core of their argument. They did so with good reason. The Treasury View, conceived as a dogmatic proposition, may have become vulnerable to intellectual challenge, but, reformulated as a pragmatic proviso, it drew upon a wealth of hard-won practical expertise.

It may have seemed to Lloyd George that, whenever he made a

[32] *JMK* xx. 133.
[33] In Harrod's perceptive and otherwise well-founded account, much is made of Hopkins's presumed unfamiliarity with the *Treatise* analysis; *Life*, 422–3.
[34] QQ. 5562–4. This section of Hopkins's evidence is reprinted in *JMK* xx. 166–79.
[35] See G. C. Peden, 'The "Treasury View" on public works and employment in the interwar period,' *Econ. Hist. Rev.*, 2nd ser., 37 (1984), 167–81; id., 'Sir Richard Hopkins and the "Keynesian Revolution" in employment policy, 1929–45', *Econ. Hist. Rev.*, NS 36 (1983), 281–96; Jim Tomlinson, *Problems of British Economic Policy, 1870–1945* (London, 1981), 76–91; Alan Booth, 'The "Keynesian Revolution" in economic policy-making', *Econ. Hist. Rev.*, 2nd ser., 36 (1983), 103–23, and his exchange with J. D. Tomlinson, ibid. 38 (1984), 258–67; Roger Middleton, 'The Treasury in the 1930s: Political and administrative constraints to acceptance of the "new" economics', *Oxford Econ. Papers*, NS 34 (1982), 48–77, and *Towards the Managed Economy* (1985), chs. 5 and 8.

suggestion, 'up jumped some scrubby-faced civil servant and said it couldn't be done. And that was always final!'[36] But able Labour ministers like Herbert Morrison, who faced the reality of the problems Hopkins outlined, had 'no complaint against (the) Treasury', and dismissed the charge of 'undue delay'.[37] After all, expenditure on public works was rising under the Labour Government, albeit not on a Lloyd Georgian scale. By June 1930, schemes costing over a hundred million pounds had been approved, even though only forty per cent of this money had been spent. This was one of the few occasions between the Wars when policy was 'correct' in stabilizing the investment cycle, and the apparent effect was to create nearly 200,000 new jobs at this stage. To put these results in proportion, however, it should be recalled that unemployment had now reached a total of two million.[38]

The notion that a big scheme of road-building could swiftly be put in hand looked somewhat ingenuous when tempered with Hopkins's seasoned advice on the inevitably lengthy process of clearing the ground in the localities. Moreover, he was apprehensive about public opinion, which might regard the whole business as extravagant and feckless. 'Whether the view would be a right one, that this would be wasteful and uneconomical,' Hopkins deftly added, 'is really apart from what I have in mind.' But without a feeling of 'buoyancy and confidence', any additional employment 'would be to some extent offset by diminished employment in other directions'.[39]

In Keynes's private evidence, two distinct counter-arguments were identified. He had distinguished the prima-facie objections to public works from the quite separate proposition (which did 'not base itself on any high theoretical ground') that productive schemes were difficult to find.[40] It was the first proposition on which Keynes had concentrated his attention, thinking he had a good hand to play. But Hopkins, not unnaturally, now refused to follow suit, and countered Keynes's court-cards of economic theory with the low trumps of administrative pragmatism. Keynes was thrown back upon speaking of his 'misunderstanding' of the Treasury View, which he had

[36] Dalton diary, 9 July 1930 (Pimlott, 116).
[37] Jones, *Whitehall Diary*, ii. 257 (19 May 1930); and see Bernard Donoughue and G. W. Jones, *Herbert Morrison* (1973), 155–9.
[38] Roger Middleton, 'The Treasury and public investment: A perspective on inter-war economic management', *Public Admin.*, 61 (1983), 351–70, esp. 353, 361.
[39] QQ. 5565, 5573.
[40] *JMK* xx. 137.

conceived as 'a theoretical view, that the objection to these schemes was that they caused diversion on theoretical grounds'.[41] Hopkins kept blandly maintaining that everything turned upon practical criteria.[42]

Keynes: It bends so much that I find difficulty in getting hold of it?
Hopkins: Yes; I do not think these views are capable of being put in the rigid form of a theoretical doctrine.

It would surely be naïve to take these exchanges at face value, as indicating not only Hopkins's pragmatism but also Keynes's acceptance 'that the Treasury View has been gravely misjudged'.[43] It is true that Keynes could not afford to dismiss administrative difficulties, acknowledging their reality if not their centrality. But he hardly seems to have been convinced by Hopkins's criteria for discriminating between good schemes and bad.

It has recently been argued that the Treasury View should not be construed as a Ricardian postulate about public investment crowding out an equivalent sum of private investment, but rather as a sophisticated appraisal of the distortions involved and of the disruptive effect upon confidence. In economic terms, this makes for a more coherent account of the conditions under which crowding-out becomes relevant—not necessarily those of full employment. In historical terms, however, this reading is vulnerably dependent upon inference and speculation.[44] It is the sort of thing Hawtrey might well have seized upon, but there is not much evidence that Hopkins maintained such a view. His nearest approach was when he suggested to Keynes that the unpopularity of a scheme 'immediately alters its dynamic effect'. But he was unable to follow this up.[45]

Keynes: So the issue between those who are in favour of these schemes and those who are against them is not whether they cure unemployment ... ?
Hopkins: Do you wish me to agree?

---

[41] QQ. 5603, 5624. [42] Q. 5625.

[43] Q. 5689. In his well-researched account, Peden seems to me to accept this comment too literally, with insufficient sensitivity to the kind of game Hopkins and Keynes had been playing; 'Treasury View', 169.

[44] Middleton, *Towards the Managed Economy*, 149, 153–65, 171, makes out an impressive case but admits (155) that 'the textual evidence is far from conclusive'— and not through lack of assiduity on his part in seeking it. My hesitation in accepting his interpretation is partly on this score and partly on whether the view argued in 1930 can be read back into the arguments of 1929.

[45] QQ. 5606–8; suspension marks below in the original text.

Macmillan: I do not think you must take it that Sir Richard agrees.
Keynes: What is the point where we differ?
Hopkins: The capital for these schemes has got to come from somewhere.

On the sources of investment, Hopkins showed himself accommodating towards much of Keynes's analysis; but he still supposed that idle balances were part of the answer. In this he was probably influenced by the briefing he had been given by A. W. Flux and S. J. Chapman, the chief economists at the Board of Trade. Flux's point was a simple one. 'The saving of an individual is here not the appropriate conception, but the saving of the community as a whole,' he wrote; and in this sense 'no reserving of resources to provide "idle" savings is possible.'[46] Keynes's own response—'I would have said that savings cannot keep'—was, of course, in complete agreement.[47] Chapman, however, had mounted a different argument. It was better to refrain from forcing uninvested savings into public works so as to ensure that 'the £100,000,000 is there, to be put into the industries of the country when confidence recovers and there is sufficient enterprise to absorb it'. When Hopkins tried this line on Keynes, he was answered: 'You cannot keep it there and use it for rationalisation schemes two years hence.'[48] The spectre of idle savings, however, continued intermittently to haunt Whitehall.

When Hopkins agreed that a scheme which yielded five per cent was a good scheme, Keynes naturally progressed to four per cent, and then inexorably to three per cent. It thus became a question of how to justify the loss to the taxpayer of abating the rate of return. Keynes thereupon suggested making 'a list of the sources from which that justification might be found'. There would, he mused, be an increment from increased employment; something from saving on the dole; also a gain from increased tax revenue.[49]

Keynes: ... the right criteria would be reached by summing up all those elements?
Hopkins: Supposing it were possible to sum them up.

The question to which Kahn's multiplier was to be addressed was thus posed across the table in the Macmillan Committee.

---

[46] Flux, '"Idle" Savings', with note from Chapman to Hopkins, 16 Apr. 1930, T. 200/1; cf. Q. 5613.
[47] Q. 5679.
[48] Chapman, 'The enforced spending of savings', T. 200/1; Q. 5680.
[49] QQ. 5663, 5667.

'I think we may characterise it as a drawn battle!' the chairman concluded when Keynes had finished his cross-examination.[50] Hopkins had undoubtedly succeeded in shifting the terms of debate on to ground of his own choosing and he himself made a notably emollient impression. The contrast in personality and emphasis with his predecessor at the Treasury was apparent two weeks later in Niemeyer's evidence (given in Keynes's absence). Niemeyer was constitutionally incapable of sustaining the air of open-minded pragmatism which now befitted the Treasury. As to a large loan for roads, 'I should think that was a pretty bad loan on its merits'; and though the question of whether it was economic or productive would be considered, 'having said that I must go on to say that my inclination would be hostile to it.' It would raise not only interest rates for industry but also awkward questions about 'spendthrift works'. ('That might not be a just criticism, but I think that criticism would be made.') The psychological effects of 'a flaming programme' might well intensify the depression instead of alleviating it. 'I cannot get away—I know Mr Keynes has held different views,' he said, 'from the conviction that, at any rate, the vast majority of such a loan, inflation being ruled out, must come out of savings which otherwise might go to other things.'[51] As a deductive precept the Treasury View may have been abandoned by 1930, but as an inductive generalization it proved more resilient. It would not have surprised that connoisseur of mandarin tactics, Sir Arthur Steel-Maitland: *Expellas furca, tamen usque recurret.*

'The Lord & Giver of Inflation'

At the beginning of 1930 the official unemployment figures stood at virtually the same level as at the beginning of 1929 (12.2 per cent in January 1929; 12.4 per cent in 1930). But whereas in the first half of 1929 the proportion dropped steadily, so that it was under 10 per cent during the General Election campaign, in 1930 it mounted throughout the year. By May it had reached 15 per cent (and in December was to touch 20 per cent). The collapse of the American boom brought with it other effects, notably on British interest rates. Bank rate, which had stood at over 5 per cent for twelve months, was

---

[50] Q. 5690.　　[51] QQ. 6850–1.

reduced in February 1930 and by stages it reached 3 per cent on 1 May. 'The country has entered upon a period of cheap money,' Hawtrey enthused, 'and as the cheap money extends also to foreign countries the resulting expansion of credit may be expected to occur in all simultaneously.' Hopkins, too, apparently foresaw 'a big fall in unemployment'.[52] Since, like Hawtrey, Keynes had blamed dear money for British unemployment, ought he not likewise to have let events take their beneficent course, now that salvation was at hand? Admittedly, the formation of more sanguine expectations was crucial. 'Taking a long view,' wrote Henderson in April, 'the possibility that cheap money rates may prevail at home and abroad for a considerable time opens out a more hopeful prospect than a mere recovery from the recent trade set-back.'[53]

Yet Keynes himself remained at this juncture an advocate of more drastic remedies. On the Economic Advisory Council, he joined with Cole in putting teeth into the report of the Committee on Economic Outlook. Henderson had written a memorandum offering an exhaustive catalogue of remedies, rather in the manner of Keynes's private evidence, which he had doubtless seen. Unable to agree with Sir Arthur Balfour and Sir John Cadman, the two businessmen on the committee, Keynes and Cole identified the practical remedies as measures of protection and schemes of home development, between which they expressed no preference. 'But we see no third alternative,' they insisted, 'so far as the near future is concerned, except a policy of inactivity in the hope of some favourable development turning up in the outside world.'[54] Faced with a growing world slump, in short, the urgency of seeking an insular solution was greater than ever. In a letter to the Governor of the Bank of England on 22 May, Keynes acknowledged the international difficulties with which Norman was faced. 'But that is why', Keynes countered, 'I twist and turn about trying to find some aid to the situation, even if only temporary, on the home front, which *is* much more in our own control.'[55]

---

[52] Hawtrey, 'Mr Keynes's Theory of Bank Rate', 1 Apr. 1930, HTRY 1/45; Hopkins reported in Dalton diary, 1 May 1930 (Pimlott, 104).

[53] 'The Economic Outlook', in Howson and Winch, *EAC* 167. The interest rate structure was, of course, a good deal more complex; see Susan Howson, *Domestic Monetary Management in Britain, 1919–38* (Cambridge, 1975), 47–54, 104–8. Keynes took the view that expectations were still of a high Bank rate: Macmillan private session, 7 Nov. 1930, 8.

[54] Report by Cole and Keynes; Howson and Winch, *EAC* 175; cf. 34 for the drafting.   [55] *JMK* xx. 350.

It is not surprising, therefore, that at this stage Keynes found a natural ally in Mosley—like Lloyd George in 1929, a potential executive force complementing Keynes's professional advocacy of radical policies. It was Mosley who promised to 'master the actual hard details of the administrative problem'.[56] If Keynes's essential object was a revolution in macro-economic strategy, Mosley's was a revolution in the machinery of government itself. Each needed the other. When, at a meeting of ministers on 19 May, J. H. Thomas, the Lord Privy Seal, said, 'Business men riddle Keynes', Mosley responded, 'I consider Keynes wipes the floor with them.'[57] The danger in this alliance was obviously that it all seemed too clever by half. The Treasury critique of Mosley's memorandum was co-ordinated by Leith-Ross and followed the same line as Hopkins's evidence over what was economic and productive. 'However much we may be criticised,' it affirmed, 'we must not be rushed into shovelling out public money merely for the purpose of taking people off the unemployed register to do work which is no more remunerative and much more expensive than unemployment.'[58] Despite the Prime Minister's private qualms about his Chancellor—'Snowden's hard dogmatism expressed in words & tones as hard as the ideas'[59]— he was as sceptical as the Treasury about any alternative.

Mosley's resignation on 20 May—occurring between Hopkins's two days of evidence—was not averted by MacDonald's efforts to shelve the issue further. 'Credit questions were for the Macmillan Committee,' the Prime Minister had pleaded, but Mosley had retorted that he 'could not wait for the Macmillan decision on loans'.[60] Rumours of Mosley's future plans—'Touch to be kept with Keynes & McKenna, etc.'—at once chased around Westminster, their drift conveyed by a Labour back-bencher's parody of the creed of the economic radicals. 'I believe in one Lloyd George, the Father Almighty, the giver of political wisdom, & in all his promises, possible & impossible,' it began, its blasé tone manifested in every canticle. 'And I believe in one J. M. Keynes, the Lord & Giver of Inflation,

---

[56] *5 Hansard* (Commons) ccxxxix, 1347 (28 May 1930); cf. 1366–9.

[57] Jones, *Whitehall Diary*, ii. 258 (19 May 1930).

[58] Leith-Ross to Grigg, 8 Mar. 1930, T. 175/42; the final draft is quoted from CAB 24/211 in Robert Skidelsky, *Oswald Mosley* (1975), 205; and see ch. 10 *passim* for a full account.

[59] MacDonald diary, 29 Apr. 1930, in David Marquand, *Ramsay MacDonald* (1977), 538.

[60] Jones, *Whitehall Diary*, ii. 259 (20 May 1930).

who with Lloyd George & Sir Oswald together is worshipped & glorified; who spake through the *Nation*.'[61]

This distinctly jaundiced perception of Keynes's professional integrity and ideological bearings was now shared, perhaps more surprisingly, by the *Nation*'s former editor. At the end of May, Henderson sent Hopkins a memorandum which highlighted the cumulative repercussions of rising unemployment via the unemployment fund, taxation, and confidence. It was a plea to consider, 'freely and without regard to the limitations set by preconceived doctrines, whether it is not possible to do something to break through the vicious circle of reactions'.[62] Essentially, its emergency proposals amounted to financing both the dole and rationalization from a revenue tariff. In one of his last leaders in the *Nation*, Henderson had advocated a pragmatic approach to import duties. He would not have been impressed by Hugh Dalton's judgement that, 'This piece of folly is neither Free Trade, nor Liberalism, nor practical politics.'[63] Henderson's whole case rested on 'the belief that the economic situation is likely to develop very badly indeed, and that no one can tell what may or may not be practical politics quite soon'.[64] Henderson's change of perspective was now unmistakable. His conviction that little could be expected from public works struck Thomas Jones as 'an interesting observation from one of the two authors of *We Can Conquer Unemployment*, and of the policy of the famous Yellow Book'.[65]

'My first shifting of opinion from my position a year or so ago,' Henderson explained to his erstwhile collaborator, 'is that I am less disposed to regard (I don't say our 2 million unemployment) but our 1,200,000 unemployment as a short-period transitional problem, yielding to the treatment of a purely temporary stimulus.' His first point, therefore, was that Keynes now laid less emphasis on the jolt of a transitional programme: in which case, a permanent deadweight of debt was the real prospect. Secondly, Henderson had become an

[61] Dalton diary, 20 May, 9 July, 1 Aug. 1930, transcribing the 'creed' by M. Philips Price (Pimlott, 111, 120).

[62] Henderson, 'Industrial Reconstruction Scheme', T. 175/50. There are obvious parallels with the contemporary problem in Germany; see Harold James, *The German Slump* (Oxford, 1986), esp. 108–9.

[63] Dalton diary, 1 June 1930 (Pimlott, 115); cf. H. D. Henderson, *The Inter-War Years* (1955), 39–48.

[64] Henderson to Hopkins, 30 May 1930, T. 175/50.

[65] *Whitehall Diary*, ii. 262 (3 June 1930). He meant, of course, *Can Lloyd George Do It?*

apt pupil of the reformulated Treasury View on the importance of psychology in a deteriorating financial position. Loss of confidence 'might quite easily serve to counteract fully the employment benefits of the programme', with an escalating Budget crisis leading ultimately to a flight out of sterling. Finally, Henderson thought that Keynes should now realize that a watershed had been passed; the current standard of living was no longer one that the British economy could support, and he told Keynes that 'in making light of dangers of that kind, you're over-moved by a sense that it's inconsistent with your self-respect to accept anything savouring of a conservative conclusion'.[66] Keynes's provocative remark at a meeting of the EAC, that he was 'the only socialist present',[67] was the sort of thing that simultaneously alienated the businessmen, hurt the Prime Minister's feelings, and irritated Henderson, who now claimed to have outgrown party political name-calling. 'What are your answers,' he asked Keynes, 'other than that Balfour and Cadman would agree with me?'

Keynes met the last point first, by denying that his public works scheme was 'a solution of our difficulties which *competes* with a solution by means of wage reductions'. Secondly, he looked to the actual profits businessmen would make as the means of instilling confidence. On the rationale of the whole plan, however, he virtually conceded Henderson's claim that their case for a temporary programme in *Can Lloyd George Do It?* had been overtaken by events. If home development could really turn business losses into capital goods which yielded even half the current interest rate, it was 'not obvious that this would not pay *as a permanency*', as compared with the losses and the unemployment it replaced.[68]

This startling change of front did nothing to reassure Henderson, now as worried as any Treasury mandarin by the Budget difficulties. By ignoring them, he warned Keynes, 'you are in great danger . . . of going down to history as the man who persuaded the British people to ruin themselves by gambling on a greater illusion than any of those which he had shattered'.[69] Licensed by old friendship, Henderson used intemperate language in signalling his current pre-

---

[66] *JMK* xx. 358, 359–60 (Henderson to Keynes, 30 May 1930); and see Howson and Winch, *EAC* 66–8.

[67] Dalton diary, 1 June 1930 (Pimlott, 115).

[68] *JMK* xx. 360, 362 (Keynes to Henderson, 4 June 1930).

[69] *JMK* xx. 364 (Henderson to Keynes, 5 June 1930).

occupations. His new colleague Hopkins, by contrast, had equally professed himself amenable to persuasion—'I do not know but what I would be prepared to give you that argument'[70]—when he re-examined the contention of *Can Lloyd George Do It?* that the Treasury View was fallacious because it had not allowed for the availability of sources of finance. Who had converted whom was an open question.

The Government's rejection of the Mosley memorandum was a political act of the first magnitude, bringing into play the ambitions and strategies of competing sections of the Labour leadership. Though Mosley himself generated intense hostility among his various opponents, the case he presented in his resignation speech received full and fair official scrutiny. Indeed Mosley's appraisal of the poor prospects for a revival of the export trade evoked a surprisingly sympathetic response in a paper from the Board of Trade, which Hopkins duly relayed to the Chancellor of the Exchequer. The subsequent decision to suppress the document—'P.M. has been refused a copy'—was Snowden's alone.[71]

The events of May showed that radical proposals on unemployment faced considerable obstacles and objections—economic, administrative, and political, as well as theoretical. After a shaky start, moreover, the authorities were now making a more effective job of explaining their nature and force. Although modest steps were sanctioned by MacDonald to increase the Government's existing public works programme, especially the allocation for trunk roads, there was little sense of conviction. When he left home on 4 June to listen to Niemeyer's evidence to the Macmillan Committee, the MacDonaldite Newbold had in his pocket a personal letter from the Prime Minister denouncing 'this humbug of curing unemployment by Exchequer grants'.[72] If the Treasury View no longer stood as a conclusive reason against adopting a Keynesian policy, a persuasive case in favour had not displaced it.

[70] Q. 5613.
[71] Skidelsky, *Mosley*, 218–20.
[72] MacDonald to Newbold, 2 June 1930, in Marquand, *MacDonald*, 538.

8

Rigid prices and flexible doctrines, I:
Public works

'I am in favour of practically all the remedies'

The Macmillan Committee had, in effect, been presented with the analysis of the *Treatise* to justify Keynes's seven practical schemes for tackling unemployment. 'The assumptions of Mr Keynes' were recognized by the Treasury officials as constituting the rationale of his case, and they had had adequate opportunity to study it before reformulating the Treasury View. In identifying the seven appropriate remedies, and in singling out home investment as his own preference, Keynes was constrained by his commitment to the postulate that '*if* our total investment (home *plus* foreign) is less than the amount of our current savings (i.e. that part of their incomes which individuals do not spend on consumption), then—in my opinion—it is absolutely certain that business losses and unemployment *must* ensue.' This was, he told the Governor of the Bank of England, 'a difficult theoretical proposition' and it was 'very important that a competent decision should be reached whether it is true or false'. But the author of the *Treatise* had no qualms. 'I can only say that I am ready to have my head chopped off if it is false!'[1]

At the time of the *Treatise*'s final revision and publication, Keynes's consistency of approach stemmed from this confidence. His hope that 'a competent decision' would come down in his favour can similarly be seen in his successful effort to persuade MacDonald that a committee of economists should be appointed within the EAC. It was to be a committee of specialists, reflecting Keynes's current view that the economic problem 'should be a matter for specialists—like dentistry',[2] and it was set up under his own chairmanship in July 1930. The preparation of its report took up much of his time in September to October, during a lull in the Macmillan Committee's proceedings. The other members of the committee of economists were Henderson and Stamp, who were already involved with the

---

[1] *JMK* xx. 350–1 (Keynes to Norman, 22 May 1930); cf. *JMK* v. 161–2.
[2] *JMK* ix. 332 ('Economic possiblities for our grandchildren').

1. Lloyd George (*left*) and Keynes (*right*) at the 1927 Liberal Summer School in Cambridge (with the Vice-Chancellor Revd G. A. Weekes and Mrs Weekes)

2. Keynes and Bernard Shaw leaving the Fitzwilliam Museum, Cambridge, June 1936

3. (*Left*) Keynes in 1936

4. (*Below*) Maynard and Lydia Keynes. From an oil painting by William Roberts, 1932

5. 'The Lifeboat That Stayed Ashore', by David Low, 1929

work of the EAC, together with Pigou, the doyen of the profession, and Lionel Robbins, its *enfant terrible*. Keynes unsuccessfully canvassed the names of D. H. Robertson and Henry Clay; he had better luck in recruiting Richard Kahn, a young Research Fellow of King's College, Cambridge, as joint secretary of the committee. Among the preliminary papers circulated to the committee in September were three sets of minutes from the Macmillan Committee—the evidence of Stamp (3, 4, and 10 April), Robertson (8 and 9 May), and Pigou (28 and 29 May).[3] By following the arguments among his fellow dentists, it should be possible to see how far Keynes's own analysis was consistent, how far it was distinctive, and how far it succeeded in winning professional approbation.

Keynes made four systematic attempts to state his views on economic policy, in slightly different contexts, six months either side of the *Treatise*'s publication in October 1930. Two of these involved committee work—the economists' report in October 1930 and the Macmillan Report, especially Addendum I, published in July 1931. Before looking at Keynes's role in drafting these, it is interesting to observe what he was writing under his own name in two formal statements in the summer of 1930.

The first was his letter to the Governor of the Bank of England, quoted above, with its crucial dependence upon the *Treatise*'s proposition about an excess of saving over investment. In that case, only an increase of investment, at home or abroad, was a real solution. Increased foreign investment implied higher exports (which implied lower costs); or lower imports (which implied lower costs or tariffs); or more loans to countries which took British exports. Any of these were compatible also with increased home investment; but this would not materialize unaided. A further alternative—'a counsel of despair'—was to decrease saving. Thus *given* the Gold Standard, and *given* the international difficulties of reducing interest rates, which eliminated two of the seven remedies Keynes had indicated to the Macmillan Committee, the remaining options were variations on the other five. It was no use talking to Norman about a national treaty on incomes, or about bounties whatever their relevance to making exports competitive. Instead Keynes flattered him—'this is where your rationalisation schemes come in'—by indicating other means of

---

[3] Howson and Winch, *EAC*, 40–1, 47–8. The papers of the committee are in the PRO, CAB 58/150–1. For a pioneer analysis of the Macmillan Committee evidence see A. J. Youngson, *The British Economy, 1920–1957* (1960), 235–50.

reducing costs. The alternatives were to resort to protection or to stimulate home investment.[4]

Two months later Keynes tried again, this time in response to the set of questions which the Prime Minister posed to the EAC. Keynes's scheme remained the same. 'Our dilemma in recent years, as I see it, is that if we raise the rate of interest sufficiently to keep our foreign lending down to the amount of our favourable balance, we raise it too high for domestic enterprise.' The touchstone in appraising remedies was therefore whether they increased either the foreign balance or the outlet for savings at home. Under the first head came five methods, of which the most significant were a reduction in the costs of production (by rationalization, tax cuts, or wage cuts) and protection, which was the quickest, easiest method. This was basically what Keynes had told Norman; but to this cluster of measures he appended some refinements, like import boards or arrangements with the Dominions. All of this would work on the foreign balance; the alternative was to concentrate on the problem of home investment.

An organized programme of development by the state obviously came first. ('I attach the greatest possible importance to this.') The same general objective could conceivably be reached by other means, like subsidies to private enterprise. At this point, Keynes's taxonomy of measures became somewhat involuted. For another method was 'by making it possible for home enterprises to afford a higher rate of interest'. On examination, this meant restating the case for a reduction of costs and for protection—so the only new consideration was the desirability of promoting confidence. The final method of encouraging home investment was 'by making lenders willing to accept a lower rate of interest', which, on closer inspection, meant a tax or embargo on foreign loans, or an international reduction of interest rates. The residual means of influencing lenders again turned on confidence, which had already been adumbrated as a factor influencing borrowers.[5]

It is clear from Keynes's answers to the Prime Minister's questions that he had not shifted from the seven remedies he had outlined earlier. True, a national treaty and bounties both went unmentioned, and devaluation was unmentionable. But international measures

---

[4] *JMK* xx. 350–6 (Keynes to Norman, 22 May 1930). This letter was sent to Henry Clay for comments and discussed with Keynes at the Bank on 23 June.

[5] *JMK* xx. 370–84 (Keynes's answers, 21 July 1930).

remained at the top of the list as a theoretically sound long-term solution, even if, from a local point of view, they were at the bottom of the list as a likely source of relief. If rationalization meant increased efficiency, it was, of course, desirable. This left tariffs and home investment as the real options. As to which of the relevant policies should be tried, Keynes told MacDonald that 'the peculiarity of my position lies, perhaps, in the fact that I am in favour of practically all the remedies which have been suggested in any quarter'. It was the negative attitude that was unforgivable—'the repelling of each of these remedies in turn'.[6]

There is one striking difference between what Keynes was telling Norman in May and what he was telling MacDonald in July—the new salience of the confidence factor. This can be seen as Keynes's response to the reformulation of the Treasury View, which had been impressed upon him in the mean time by Hopkins's evidence of 22 May (the same date as his letter to Norman), by Henderson in correspondence, and, perhaps, by the discussions at the Bank on 23 June with Norman, Stewart, and Sprague, of which there is no record. When Henderson had confided his worries at the beginning of June, Keynes had been very airy—'After all, the budgetary problem is largely a by-product of unemployment'—in playing them down.[7] By July, like a good magpie, he had appropriated the point himself and was lecturing the Prime Minister about confidence being 'very much tied up with the Budget'. Keynes now proposed to restore it by means of a three-pronged plan, which was presented as a necessary auxiliary to home investment. First, new social service expenditure should be postponed. Second, 'the abuses of the dole' should be scrutinized for economies. Third, tariffs were now 'essential to a sound Budget in present circumstances'. After Mosley's resignation, Keynes may have thought that the opening to the left had closed and that a more consensual approach was needed. 'We shall do well to advance on a broad front,' was his conclusion.[8]

There was, however, one remedy which Keynes still refused to embrace with any warmth, even though he was bound to acknowledge that it was relevant to the diagnosis of Britain's problems. This was, of course, a cut in existing money wages. To be sure, his own plan for a national treaty had addressed this problem; and the

---

[6] *JMK* xx. 375, 384; cf. 99, 125 (private evidence, 28 Feb., 6 Mar. 1930).

[7] *JMK* xx. 364–5 (Keynes to Henderson, 6 June 1930).

[8] *JMK* xx. 383–4.

necessity of reducing labour costs by one means or another could be covered by the expansive term 'rationalization', which was another of Keynes's seven approved remedies. In the *Treatise* his analysis showed that an equilibrium rate of interest, appropriate to the needs of home investment and the foreign balance, was only feasible if 'the money rate of efficiency earnings of the factors of production' were flexible.[9] Since every other means of achieving this flexibility had been covered under other heads, the remedy of income reduction was inescapably an option every time Keynes had to produce an exhaustive list.

Keynes did not deny that the economic position would be improved by wage cutting. In November 1928, the fact that 'the resistance to it has been tenacious and on the whole successful' was cited to explain 'why the phase of unemployment has been so exceedingly prolonged'.[10] In August 1929 Keynes wrote that 'there are only two means open to us to get our national economy into better equilibrium. One is an all-round reduction of real efficiency wages; the other is an increase of home investment.' He admitted, moreover, that 'the former expedient, if it were practicable, would operate with the greater efficiency and certainty.'[11]

There is thus no doubt that Keynes recognized the need to cut costs and that some of his proposals were indirectly designed to reduce real wages; but it is surely also true that he consistently rejected a policy of wage cuts on political and social grounds.[12] In offering advice, in short, he regarded the theoretical premiss of flexible prices as inappropriate to the real world. 'The idea of the Conservatives,' he said in 1925, 'that you can, for example, alter the value of money and then leave the consequential adjustments to be brought about by the forces of supply and demand, belongs to the days of fifty or a hundred years ago when trade unions were powerless, and when the economic juggernaut was allowed to crash along the highway of progress without obstruction and even with applause.'[13] The course of beating down wages, therefore, was not one which he approved, even if the opportunity to implement it were offered. After the General Strike, when such a policy might have

[9] *JMK* v. 165.   [10] *JMK* xix. 772 (*Britannia*, 2 Nov. 1928).

[11] *JMK* xix. 833 (*The Times*, 15 Aug. 1929).

[12] Alan Booth and Melvyn Pack, *Employment, Capital, and Economic Policy* (1985), 176–7, question my interpretation on this point.

[13] *JMK* xix. 439–40 ('The economic transition in England').

been feasible, 'Mr Baldwin decided—quite rightly—that it would be socially and politically inexpedient to take advantage of the situation in this way.'[14] In the *Treatise* he described an attempt to cut wages as 'a dangerous enterprise in a society which is both capitalist and democratic'.[15] In his private evidence he said that 'for centuries there has existed an intense social resistance to any matters of reduction in the level of money incomes.'[16] Listening to the employers' evidence to the committee, he found their unwillingness to recommend this solution 'truly remarkable', even when they had been pressed to fall back upon it.[17]

Once Keynes had, to his own satisfaction, closed this avenue, he could blandly suggest that 'if we are to avoid putting wages lower we must look around for some other method.'[18] In theory, as in the *Treatise*, price flexibility would tend to restore equilibrium. In practice, however, policy might have to be framed in terms of a special case governed by immediate circumstances—rigidities of an intractable kind which pragmatists could hardly ignore. It was one thing to acknowledge that high wages were a contributory cause of Britain's economic difficulties; it was another to conclude that it was desirable or practicable to seek a remedy through wage cuts. The author of the *Treatise* had no quarrel with the first but every objection to the second. He was, moreover, fortified in his judgement by the opinions of many of his fellow economists.

'The gluttability of wants'

The EAC's committee of economists had before it the evidence given by two of its members (Stamp and Pigou) to the Macmillan Committee, as already noticed, together with that given by Dennis Robertson. Robertson's evidence is of peculiar interest because of its searching exploration of a number of analytical issues, common to himself and Keynes, notably the role of saving and investment. When Keynes later repudiated what he called 'classical' economics, he meant by it a self-equilibrating system in which the rate of interest was 'determined by the interaction of the demand for new capital

[14] *JMK* xix. 763 ('How to organise a wave of prosperity'); cf. 833.
[15] *JMK* vi. 346.
[16] *JMK* xx. 64 (20 Feb. 1930).
[17] *JMK* xx. 377 (answers to the Prime Minister).
[18] *JMK* xx. 322 (*Listener*, 26 Feb. 1930).

with the supply of saving'. Given that all prices were flexible, all markets would clear, with the optimum utilization of resources, including full employment of available labour. 'Before the war we were all classical economists,' he recalled. 'I taught it myself to Robertson, undoubting and unrebuked.'[19] Yet it was Robertson to whom Keynes subsequently expressed gratitude for his 'emancipation' from this system, initially through their discussions of Robertson's *Banking and the Price Level* (1925); so that, in the eleven years between then and the *General Theory*, 'both our minds have been changing continuously and enormously, though on parallel lines that all but, yet don't quite, meet ...'.[20] Their encounter before the Macmillan Committee, right in the middle of this period, brings this out well.

Robertson's evidence took the form of a substantial statement, which the committee found heavy going. He was accordingly asked to explicate it in his testimony. The first section was built around his concept of the 'gluttability of wants', by which he meant either a temporary saturation of the market for consumer goods or a faltering and uneven expansion of capital projects—'in lumps and by jumps'.[21] What he said about the difficulties in expanding consumption rang a bell with the Co-operator Sir Thomas Allen, who remarked that in his home district of Lancashire 'it has been a question of under-consumption for very many years', through low wages and unemployment.[22] Allen doubtless recalled that, only a week previously, the committee had heard the opinion of Major Douglas, the pioneer of social credit, that the real difficulty 'is simply lack of effective demand'.[23] Robertson claimed no panacea for deficient consumption, though it might be met in the long term by the 'rather unattractive' remedy of 'the perpetual stimulation of new wants' and in the short term possibly alleviated by stockpiling.[24]

The stimulation of demand on the capital side was another matter. It went to the root of Robertson's analysis. For there was 'no preordained harmony' between saving and investment, and the current

---

[19] *JMK* xxix. 270 (Keynes to Haberler, 3. Apr. 1938), and see J. R. Presley, 'D. H. Robertson', in D. P. O'Brien and J. R. Presley (eds.), *Pioneers of Modern Economics in Britain* (1981), 175–98.

[20] *JMK* xiv. 94 (Keynes to Robertson, 13 Dec. 1936).

[21] Robertson statement, *Macmillan Evidence*, i. 321–6, par. 11.

[22] Q. 4950.

[23] Q. 4511 (1 May 1930).

[24] Statement, par. 12.

failure of investment to keep pace with saving meant that excess saving was 'being dissipated in consumption at unexpectedly low prices or checked by the curtailment of production . . .'.[25] This was very close to Keynes's position, but Robertson's own emphasis was on the role of the banks. Now the quantity theory held that the price level was determined jointly by the amount of money in circulation (which was controlled by the banking system) and its velocity of circulation (which was controlled by the public). The public's wish to save more meant a lower velocity of circulation—idle deposits in the banks—which would result in prices falling, with harmful consequences for investment, unless it was offset by an increase in the money supply. Hence the need for the banks to increase credit so that real investment took place.[26]

Tulloch: It is necessary, then, if the banks are to give effect to the desire to save on the part of depositors, that they should create loans?
Robertson: That is the point.
Tulloch: That is the whole basis?
Robertson: Yes.

It can be seen that Robertson's analysis of under-investment could be translated, via a low velocity of circulation, into a proposition about idle balances. He said in one answer that 'the evidence seems to be that there are these bank deposits piling up and not knowing what to do with themselves.'[27] But his point, of course, was that the bank should take remedial action by creating credit, which 'for the purposes of the present situation would be simply a means for placing at the disposal of industry the saving which is being done by the bank depositors'.[28] Indeed he insisted that it was 'one of the paradoxes of economics that saving is the one thing that cannot be saved: saving that is allowed to go to waste today cannot be utilised tomorrow.' When asked to expand on this, he repeated that savings had to be embodied in actual industrial capital: otherwise, 'they all get sucked away in falling prices and extravagance on the part of the consumer.'[29] Such 'extravagance', presumably, was a result of consumers cashing in on the lower prices when business men had to off-load unwanted stocks at a loss. 'During deflation you are making

[25] Ibid., pars. 15, 3.
[26] QQ. 4717–18.
[27] Q. 4781.
[28] Q. 4779.
[29] Statement, par. 12; Q. 4922.

a present to the consumer all the time,' was how Keynes later put it.[30] So although Robertson had been non-committal—'I do not feel sure of that'[31]—when Keynes had suggested to him that business losses represented the fall in prices, there was plainly a broad measure of agreement between them.

The urgency of taking action was demonstrated by the existence of idle balances, which were a symptom of excessive savings, which was only another way of describing under-investment. On Robertson's theory, surely an increase of credit ought to have provided the effective way out? 'No, not altogether,' he responded, 'because a mere increase in the volume of credit without organising the uses to which it is put may simply lead to the result of the money lying idle on deposit, and then it is no good.' To Keynes this seemed 'very unlikely', but to Robertson it was a crucial reason for advocating 'schemes of public works, as they are usually called, of development of the capital resources of the country by the Government'.[32] His concept of temporary gluttability, which underpinned this proposal, was thus 'in direct conflict not only with the so-called "Treasury View" that such a policy of promoting public works absorbs resources which would otherwise anyhow be employed by private enterprise, but also with the doctrine, which has been maintained, for instance, by Mr Hawtrey, that the public works are "a mere piece of ritual"...'. The Treasury View was fallacious because public works could turn unused savings into capital goods of value to the community; Hawtrey was wrong because, 'when the spirit of investment is really costive unto death', cheap money could not be relied upon to do the trick.[33]

This was clearly a more radical position than that of Keynes, who, closer to Hawtrey, described Robertson as 'more pessimistic than I should be as to whether you could stimulate investment by lowering the rate of interest'.[34] The analysis of the *Treatise* postulated equilibrium if only interest rates were sufficiently flexible; the special case covered a situation where they were not, for international reasons—thus justifying public works in order to rectify disequilib-

[30]   Private session, 31 Oct. 1930, 11.
[31]   Q. 4722.
[32]   QQ. 4803–4, 4873.
[33]   Statement, par. 13. For Robertson's long-standing criticism of Hawtrey over the Treasury View see J. C. Gilbert, *Keynes's Impact on Monetary Economics* (1982), 244, esp. n. 73.
[34]   Q. 4877.

rium. Keynes naturally pursued this line, pressing Robertson on whether a cut in interest rates could not be expected to bring in further investment. 'One hopes it would,' Robertson replied, 'but again I feel the situation may arise where people have so little confidence in anything that the bond rate is not effective.'[35]

In retrospect, he admitted to having been somewhat muddled over the sense in which Keynes was using the term investment and he was unsure how far the minutes were faithful to his argument. After subsequent discussion with Gregory, Robertson appended a note clarifying his meaning: 'that under conditions of lack of confidence and saturation of demand, it may require an extremely *low* rate of interest on long period investments to attract industrial borrowers, while it requires a relatively *high* one to induce the holders of balances to part with them for long period investments: hence equilibrium may not be reached.'[36] Robertson thus agreed with Keynes that a reduction of interest rates would encourage *borrowers* to come forward. 'But I still think there is a difficulty of the lenders coming forward,' he argued; 'you may get such a lack of confidence that people may prefer to go on getting 1 per cent on their deposits with the bank rather than invest in bonds which are yielding 3 or 4 or even 5 per cent.'[37]

In the light of the *General Theory*'s concept of liquidity preference, such an explanation seems highly suggestive; but in 1930, as Robertson later reproached Keynes, 'this train of thought woke no response in you whatever'.[38] Instead, true to the *Treatise*, Keynes kept hammering away at the deleterious effects of the international factors which prevented interest rates from returning to the pre-war level:[39]

I should have thought the reason why the bond rate was so high in London was that there were rows and rows of foreigners who were very willing to pay extremely high rates for the money. We cannot accommodate them owing to the deficiency in our balance of trade. If we were to let the rate down we should lose gold, because the foreign borrowers would be so eager; on the other hand, the effect of keeping it up to these levels, which in pre-war days were unprecedented, chokes off home borrowers.

[35] Q. 4832.
[36] Macmillan Evidence, i. 334 n.; cf. *JMK* xxix. 167 (Robertson to Keynes, 1 Jan. 1938).
[37] Q. 4834.   [38] *JMK* xxix. 167.   [39] Q. 4841.

Robertson, conversely, stuck to his view that the psychology of savers themselves was a significant part of the problem, with increased balances as 'an indication that perhaps people want to keep their money unspent rather than spend it'—probably 'because they have ingrained habits of thrift'.[40]

According to Robertson, then, public works might well be needed as a cure for unemployment irrespective of difficulties brought on by the Gold Standard; and they might be needed for an appreciable period. When asked how far he would be prepared to go, in terms of quantity and time, he would not put a figure on it, but affirmed, 'I should like to go a very considerable way.' His goal was 'the disappearance of abnormal unemployment'.[41]

Brand: You would regard this as a temporary expedient, would you; that at some moment when you arrived at some sort of equilibrium this Government enterprise should diminish?
Robertson: Yes, I would, but I think 'temporary' may mean fairly long, for the reason I give later, that if you are at the same time rationalising private industry I do not see how that is to result in anything but a temporary decline in employment, and therefore the need for supplementing private demand by public demand may continue for a long time.

Robertson was naturally pressed on this point, not least by Keynes, who put it to him that 'this satiation of demand' need not prove permanent and that 'in the ordinary course private enterprise would some day revive'. While Robertson was prepared to assent, he insisted that any tiding-over operation would prove protracted.[42]

This admission, however, was not disabling to the case for public works, any more than the admission that they would necessarily bring a rate of return less remunerative than that on private enterprise, thus requiring subsidy from taxation.[43]

Macmillan: Our attitude is, we are all desperately hard up; let us spend more money?
Robertson: We are not desperately hard up, but we are wasting a good deal of our resources, both of labour and fixed capital, through under-use, and that makes certain people very hard up.

Here was the justification for public works '*as a permanency*'—the

---

[40] QQ. 4976–7.
[41] QQ. 4879, 4881–2.
[42] QQ. 4908–9.
[43] QQ. 4883–4, 4888.

suggestion Keynes tried on Henderson the month after Robertson's evidence.[44] What it amounted to was an acceptance that economic recovery would not come through international trade but through home development, by making 'a special effort to absorb in useful occupations at home the productive resources which are being rendered superfluous in the export trades'.[45] Robertson candidly avowed—'I think my view in that respect is more socialistic than some people's'[46]—that public works were not simply emergency measures and that the state should become permanently involved in such activities as house-building. Although such measures had an emergency aspect, therefore, they were to be regarded, not so much as a drug to cure a disease, but 'rather in the nature of a diet'.[47] The main constraint on such activity would be the need to watch for inflationary tendencies once the level of demand had been raised and then to 'be ready to damp down the policy somewhat'.[48]

Gregory: That might involve renewed instability in construction?
Robertson: Unless you could use it as a balancing factor to remove instability arising from other causes. That is the purpose of it.

It followed from Robertson's analysis that he did not think wage cuts were the real answer. If demand were inelastic at home, because of gluttability, even considerable reductions in wages would not turn the market round. He would therefore 'expect smaller results on employment from a successful drive against wages, unaccompanied by any other change, than some people would'.[49] His scepticism had a different ground from that of Keynes, who was chiefly sceptical whether such a drive would be successful. Nor did Robertson accept that British costs were crucially out of line with world prices as a result of the parity established under the Gold Standard. In casting doubt on 'the whole theory of a 10 per cent crime in 1924–5', he was implicitly removing the premiss for the special case under the *Treatise* (despite his substantial agreement with its general thrust). Robertson thus dismissed 'the scheme for a concerted reduction of British money incomes by 10 per cent'—Keynes's national treaty idea—as 'based upon a quicksand'. In fact, by deprecating the export

---

[44] See above, ch. 7 n. 68.
[45] Q. 4916.
[46] Q. 4932.
[47] Q. 4983.
[48] QQ. 4905–6.
[49] Statement, pars. 19–20.

market as the governing criterion on costs and wages, and proposing to boost home consumption instead, he suggested that the level of wages in the sheltered industries might not be 'too high' at all but a reasonable norm. Such a shift to increased national self-sufficiency, of course, depended upon a reduction in net foreign lending in order to finance home investment.[50]

The alternative was to look for a revival of the export trade, but again Robertson judged that demand was inelastic.[51]

Gregory: ... even if wages were reduced, or costs reduced in some other direction, it would not make much difference?
Robertson: Yes, I think it would not, on the whole.
Keynes: I am sympathetic to that view, but it is very much opposed to what we have been told.

The chairman put it to Robertson that the upshot of his case was that it was no use looking to reduction of costs for salvation. 'Not for salvation of employment, if employment is what we care about,' Robertson agreed.[52] But he stopped short of dismissing the relevance of wage reductions altogether, on the hypothesis that they could be achieved without any political or economic friction.[53]

Keynes: I should be willing to accept the theory of inelasticity in the present condition of world-wide depression, but supposing the present world-wide depression came to an end and we could then reduce our costs by 5 or 10 per cent by some method which did not apply to the rest of the world, could we not expand our exports?
Robertson: Yes, I think we could, so far as we were in competition.

In principle, then, even for Robertson, wage cuts were a possible remedy, but under conditions which he thought unlikely to be realized. He had, to this extent, disappointed Gregory's startled anticipations—'Are you not advancing rather a novel theory?'—that his general line of argument would lead him to say, 'For Heaven's sake do not reduce wages, because this is one way of creating a demand for things which we cannot otherwise get rid of.'[54]

'The extreme importance of what Mr Robertson has been saying to us is not rebutted because it is contrary to what other witnesses

---

[50] Statement, pars. 28–9, 33.
[51] QQ. 4955–6.
[52] Q. 5000.
[53] Q. 5003.
[54] QQ. 4972, 5007.

have been telling us,' Keynes concluded[55]—which is no doubt why Robertson's evidence was later circulated to the committee of economists. Accustomed to adopting an 'unsound' stance among his professional colleagues, Keynes may have found it useful to point to one whose diagnosis and methods were more radical than his own. Although there was a substantial measure of agreement on both theory and policy between himself and Robertson, it was by no means clear in 1930 which of them might be more likely to make a decisive break with the Marshallian tradition. The clever money might well have been on Robertson, rather than the author of the *Treatise*, going on to write the *General Theory*. At any rate, there is abundant justification for Keynes's later remark to Robertson: 'The last thing I should accuse you of is being classical or orthodox.'[56]

Pin-and-tuck Marshallians

What had Stamp and Pigou told the Macmillan Committee? So far as Stamp was concerned, there was no difficulty in agreeing that the Gold Standard machine was jammed: 'Yes, I have said that myself even before this committee had invented the term.'[57] What, then, could be done about it? Three things might be tried ('if any of them were politically possible'): first, a better adjustment of wages between industries; second, to get 'a reasonable resiliency in wages'; and third, to work on the international gold problem; 'but all those things are politically impossible.' In talking about wages, therefore, he would 'not use the words "too high" because that is liable to be read in an invidious sense'.[58] He had not dissented when Keynes put it to him in an earlier discussion that 'I do not think, any more than you do, that it is practicable to reduce wages, whether they are too high or not.'[59] Stamp was, above all, a man of the world, only prepared to lend his advocacy to what seemed feasible, and ready to settle for second-best solutions. Thus he was prepared to consider measures to restrict foreign investment, on 'the basic assumption that probably a closed

---

[55] Q. 5009.
[56] *JMK* xiv. 94 (Keynes to Robertson, 13 Dec. 1936). On subsequent developments see M. K. Anyadike-Danes, 'Dennis Robertson and Keynes's General Theory', in G. C. Harcourt (ed.), *Keynes and His Contemporaries* (1985), 105–40.
[57] Q. 3824.
[58] QQ. 3826–7.
[59] *JMK* xx. 322 (Keynes–Stamp broadcast, Feb. 1930).

system would give you a lower standard of life but a more stable one: because what is the good of having a higher standard of life if you are ever-lastingly falling short of it'.[60]

What worried Stamp about foreign lending was that it required an export surplus which might not in practice be forthcoming, given the lack of competitiveness of British industry. Otherwise gold would be exported. This would set off a Gold Standard adjustment process via a higher Bank rate, and 'the danger is that by putting the rate up you have savings that are "spilled" by deflation and you make it difficult to develop things at home'.[61] With this measure of acceptance of Keynes's analysis and terminology, it is not surprising that Stamp was also prepared to countenance public works—'I am only on the principle'—provided suitable schemes could be found. It was not financially unsound, therefore, to use savings on the dole to finance a pump-priming programme. 'It is quite possible to spend money which has no profit in itself, or even has a loss, in such a way as will bridge over from one state of equilibrium to another.'[62]

Brand: Your idea is to have an expenditure of Government money so that the circulation of that in the form of wages, and so on, would bring profits back to certain industries; having reached that equilibrium, we should stop there? *Stamp:* Yes, once you have quickened the thing up.

Hence Stamp was 'not afraid of a little anti-deflation' in order to get the wheels turning again.[63] He was even prepared to follow Keynes into further speculation on the cycle of prosperity, given that profits could be expected to rise *pari passu* with new investment.[64]

Keynes: That would be one example of how the mere fact of there being more investment might bring into existence more profit? *Stamp:* Yes. *Keynes:* Which might go part of the way towards financing it? *Stamp:* I agree.

Pigou's two days of evidence at the end of May displayed an altogether more tortured and convoluted approach to the whole problem. The workings of his mind remained a puzzle to Keynes, and not only because of intellectual differences. It might be supposed

[60] Q. 3927.
[61] Q. 3942.
[62] QQ. 3969, 3972, 3975.
[63] Q. 3979.
[64] QQ. 3997–8.

that, as colleagues in the Cambridge Economics Faculty, they would have been able to thrash out the main issues informally. It was Austin Robinson's experience, as a young lecturer, however, that whatever else Pigou regarded as a suitable topic of conversation—'We talked climbing. We talked cricket.'—economics was always taboo.[65] It may not have been a waste of public money, therefore, to put Keynes and Pigou on the train to London for a discussion which they could otherwise have had on the King's high table. Instead, this was a rare opportunity for Keynes to get to grips with 'the Prof.', whose elusiveness he often found so frustrating.

Pigou based his evidence upon a memorandum, not intended for publication, which was subsequently circulated to the committee of economists. He attributed the current level of unemployment to the superimposition of a normal cyclical depression upon a structural shift in the 'centre of gravity' from an unemployment level of about 4 per cent to one of about 10 per cent. The cause of this shift was a maladjustment which could be described in two different ways. 'Given the state of demand, excessive real wage-rates is the cause; given the state of real wage-rates, the inadequacy of demand is the cause.'[66] It is apparent that this impressed Keynes, for within a fortnight he had appropriated as his own the idea of 'two lines of diagnosis, both of which are sure to be partly right'.[67]

Given the state of demand, Pigou argued, abnormal unemployment would be less if there were wage cuts in the trades that were not depressed and if a transfer of labour took place out of the trades that were. The two things interacted, since transfer of labour would help push down wages elsewhere. Because this had not happened, 'rates of real wages in the non-depressed industries are too high to allow of full employment'—a contention which Pigou constantly reiterated with his proviso, 'in the existing state of demand'.[68] If the real wage were lower, it would clearly pay employers to take on extra workers. 'Simply as a general thing,' he repeated, 'it is obvious that if you reduce real wages you are likely to get more employment.'[69]

[65] Don Patinkin and J. Clark Leith, *Keynes, Cambridge and the General Theory* (1977), 30.

[66] EAC (E) 6, par. III, 2; Heads of evidence, circulated 6 Sept. 1930, CAB 58/150; also in Keynes papers, EA/4. This is actually the *same* memorandum quoted in Robert Skidelsky, *Politicians and the Slump* (1967), 207–9. See also Q. 5949.

[67] *JMK* xx. 365 (Keynes to Henderson, 5 June 1930).

[68] EAC (E) 6. par. V, 2; cf. QQ. 6035, 6042.

[69] Q. 6054.

Moreover, this was a practical point since, even if Robertson were right about the inelastic demand for British exports, the argument still held for the sheltered industries. Since these were not currently depressed, however, it was presumably not 'obvious' to the employers or workers in these trades that their level of wages was too high, and, 'simply as a general thing', one might have expected the market to get this right.

Members of the committee were premature, however, if they jumped to the conclusion that Pigou was recommending a policy of wage cuts.[70]

Newbold: What method would you put forward as the best to enable us to reduce real wages?
Pigou: I come to that later. I am not advocating a reduction in real wages.

His prime task was to analyse the reasons for maladjustment, not to draw hasty inferences for policy. Wages had become unduly high because there was insufficient mobility of labour, because of the effects of the dole, and because of a general sentiment after the War that people ought to get a decent wage. Pigou also acknowledged that 'the return to gold caused prices to fall while money wages were held rigid through various frictions'; so although he was 'not particularly inclined to sit in a white sheet' over the advice he had given in 1925, the requisite flexibility of prices had clearly not been forthcoming.[71] Indeed, the resistance to reducing money wages was fully explicable by genuine fears that in practice workers would not themselves recoup any ultimate advantage. 'All these are reasons for what you may call stickiness in money rates of wages,' Pigou concluded.[72] Yet he was also 'clear that if this diagnosis is in any way right there will be three possible lines of remedy'—of which the first was a reduction of wages in the non-depressed industries.[73]

A second possibility was to alter the conditions of demand and productivity so as to afford existing wage rates. Thirdly, Pigou was ready to consider what he called 'devices', which, accepting the rigidity of prices and the inelasticity of demand, sought to promote

---

[70] Q. 6044; cf. 5984.
[71] QQ 6071, 6074.
[72] Q. 6552.
[73] Q. 6129. In the otherwise useful study by Mark Casson, *Economics of Unemployment* (Oxford, 1983), Pigou is represented as arguing, like Clay, that wages were too high, especially in *depressed* industries (50–2, 55–9, 248–9). The opposite is nearer the truth.

employment more directly. Of these three kinds of remedy, Pigou regarded the second as 'the best way of all of enabling more men to be employed at a given real wage'.[74] Everything really turned upon what seemed practicable and efficacious. Pigou spent a good deal of time explaining how a cut in real wages would help, without conveying the impression that much help could actually be expected—at least if it were to be achieved openly by a cut in money wages. Devaluation and inflation were, of course, indirect means of reducing real wages, but they could 'only succeed where direct action fails in so far as wage-earners allow themselves to be bamboozled'.[75]

It was left to the chairman to direct attention to what was effectively the hinge of Pigou's case in the memorandum:[76]

If my diagnosis is right, our bad situation is due to the presence of an obstruction to the free working of economic forces. It may in these conditions be true that forms of State interference which, if there were no such obstruction, would do harm, will in fact do good. A man ordered to walk a tightrope carrying a bag in one hand would be better off if he were allowed to carry a second in his other hand, though of course if he started bagless, to add a bag would handicap him. This is a very important principle.

Faced with the rigidity of prices, in short, some flexibility in doctrine was required to determine when the best was the enemy of the good. In one of his infrequent interventions, Lord Bradbury spoke up uncompromisingly in favour of getting rid of the first bag. 'If you could,' Pigou conceded; 'but sometimes you cannot.' Being Pigou, he characteristically shied away from the practical implications which were in everyone's minds, the day after Mosley's resignation speech.[77]

Brand: Judging by recent debates in the House of Commons, one may assume that the other bag is going to be terribly big and heavy?
Pigou: As a matter of fact, I think Governments are always certain to give them a very bad bag.

With much hesitancy and prevarication, Pigou was led to endorse the main steps in Keynes's practical argument, starting with the responsibility of the Gold Standard for keeping Bank rate too high.[78]

[74] EAC (E) 6, par. VIII, 8.
[75] Ibid., par. VIII, 4; Q. 6151.
[76] Ibid., par. VIII, 13; cf. QQ. 6480–1.
[77] QQ. 6482, 6484.
[78] QQ. 6622–3.

Pigou: That is one thing. I would not say that is the only thing.
Keynes: Is not that very important?
Pigou: I should say it is very important.

Since Pigou also agreed that the Bank rate mechanism was obviously failing to equilibrate saving and investment satisfactorily, the conditions required in theory for its successful operation received only a wistful mention.[79]

Brand: Rigid wage rates make it very difficult to work the gold standard?
Pigou: If wage rates vary absolutely freely, it would not much matter what happened with money.

When asked for his own recommendations on remedies, Pigou admitted that he had 'been thinking of my function rather as trying to make an analysis', but managed to make clear his support for a number of 'devices' or 'gadgets' for an emergency, including 'large Government expenditure on really useful public works'.[80] This case was valid, as he later explained, 'even though they are likely to yield a return substantially below current rates, and even though guarantees of interest involving a cost to the Treasury are necessary'.[81]

Pigou's support for public works was reaffirmed the week after his testimony, in a letter to *The Times*, allowing that the Treasury View was a good reason against state action, 'provided that there were no unemployment to reduce!' In equilibrium, then, the crowding-out effects might obtain, but what was important in conditions of unemployment was 'to be sure that our presuppositions are adjusted not to imaginary but to actual conditions'.[82] Whatever the subsequent myths, there is little historical reason to reproach Pigou as a doctrinaire advocate of market forces; but neither is it right to depict him as an incipient Keynesian because he was ready to endorse measures to counter the slump. Pigou was a pin-and-tuck Marshallian coping with an anomaly. In this respect, perhaps, he was not very different from the author of the *Treatise*.

At a theoretical level, it is significant that it was Pigou who had pointed out to Keynes that the 'fundamental equations' of the

[79] Q. 6644.
[80] QQ. 6648, 6658.
[81] Note, *Macmillan Evidence*, ii. 93, par. II, 3.
[82] *The Times*, 6 June 1930; cited in T. W. Hutchison, *Economics and Economic Policy in Britain, 1946–66* (1968), 285, which makes a strong defence of Pigou's 'thoroughly sound and relevant policy advice, in broad agreement, of course, with Keynes' (301).

Treatise implied that, whatever happened to saving and investment, output was unaffected.[83] As his letter to *The Times* demonstrates at a practical level, Pigou was not guilty of a tacit full-employment assumption, and it was not inconsistent with neo-classical analysis to allow for output fluctuating below its optimum level so long as disequilibrium persisted. The crucial point was that interest rate tended to bring saving and investment into equilibrium at full employment. Though the *Treatise* dwelt on the persistence of disequilibrium, it was singing the same tune with different words. Thus, when Pigou presented his theoretical analysis to the Macmillan Committee, there was an immanent consensus on most substantive points.[84]

Pigou: I do not know whether Mr Keynes would agree with this—that in general there is much difference between his way of putting the thing and the way with which I myself am more familiar . . .
It is easier to talk in my own language. I think your language comes to much the same as mine, but I do not want to change my language in the middle.

Resisting Keynes's gadfly efforts to distract him otherwise—'May I go on? Is it better to do it in your order or take my own first?'[85]— Pigou told his own story. It explained a cyclical depression, such as that which was superimposed upon Britain's structural maladjustment, by a contraction in the money income stream. This contraction occurred when people withdrew money into a hoard, thus reducing the velocity of circulation. 'It is the same thing as Mr Keynes means when he speaks of people saving more than they invest,' Pigou explained. Keynes reciprocated on this use of terminology: 'Provided that hoarding means the difference between saving and investment, I am quite willing to use the word hoarding.'[86] Such hoarding did not depend on what individuals did with their bank balances, leaving them idle on deposit or otherwise: the real effect was upon prices, which would fall through lack of demand for goods, unless the banks put the money to work in other ways. If this did not happen, Pigou told Macmillan, 'then your saving, though it is very meritorious of you, reacts on the general price level—your saving is spilt'.[87] Keynes

---

[83] *JMK* xxix. 5; the significance of this as brought out by Murray Milgate, 'Keynes and Pigou on the Gold Standard and monetary theory', *Contribs. to Pol. Econ.*, 2 (1983), 46–7.
[84] QQ. 6551, 6226.
[85] Q. 6478.
[86] QQ. 6563, 6627.
[87] Q. 6594.

stressed the significance of a high interest rate, which might prevent the banks from acting, and yet could not, for international reasons, be reduced so as to enable hoarding to be offset. Pigou, however, envisaged 'a general state of stagnancy', where the banks were powerless.[88]

Keynes: Does this not depend on the rate of interest?
Pigou: Undoubtedly, in part.
Keynes: Is not that fundamental?
Pigou: There is the state of mind of the business man. The business man might be in such a state that he would not borrow money or use money at 0 per cent.
Keynes: That is an extremely abnormal state of things?
Pigou: It is the two things—interest and his state of mind.

Keynes was thus, if anything, more firmly attached than Pigou to the neo-classical postulate that interest rate was what restored equilibrium between saving and investment, and that disequilibrium only arose when it was thwarted or obstructed in its assigned role. In private Keynes continued to expostulate about his 'attempt to explain to Pigou and Robertson the difference between excess hoarding and excess saving, about which they have been making obstinate misunderstandings'—which, it may be noted, did not augur well for future concord. In front of the committee, however, Pigou expressed agreement with Keynes on the general effect of 'hoarding' or 'excessive saving' in inducing the slump.[89]

Pigou: That is the fundamental thing. It is the fundamental thing behind the fall in the money income stream which in turn has been associated with the diminution of employment in consequence of the rigidity of the money wage rate.

Given the rigidity of the price of labour, Keynes could count on the support of Stamp and Pigou in sanctioning a flexible response by government to the problems of the real world.

The dentists

As its chairman, Keynes circulated a questionnaire to the committee of economists in September 1930. It did not mention public works

---

[88] QQ. 6613–16.
[89] Compare *JMK* xiii. 135 (Keynes to Hawtrey, 18 July 1930) with Q. 6633 (Pigou's evidence, 29 May 1930).

directly but concentrated on the effects of an increase in investment or a tariff or a reduction in wages upon the British economy, and directed attention to the level of wages. Keynes doubtless intended to make the other dentists specify exactly what treatment they considered necessary. The effect on Pigou, whose answers Keynes carefully annotated, was to throw him back upon wage reductions as the real key to the position. Each cut in money wages of 10 per cent should lead to a cut in real wages of 5 per cent in Britain, and 'a 10% reduction in the real wage rate should lead to not less than (roughly) a 10% increase in employment'.[90] Keynes defined the 'main difference of bias' between them as being Pigou's confidence that 'although we belong to an international system, the facts are such that things work out much the same as if we were in a closed system', whereas he himself found 'the main explanation of the vagaries of recent years in the fact of our belonging to an international system'.[91]

In a closed system, Keynes agreed, a reduction in real wages would increase employment because goods would become cheaper and, provided demand were elastic, this would increase consumption and therefore output. But in a closed system it would not be easy to bring about a reduction in real wages through cuts in money wages, because prices too would tend to fall. 'If we were, in fact, a closed system,' he argued, 'then in my view employment could be mainly restored not by a fall in money wages, but by a fall in the rate of interest—a fall which is impracticable in existing circumstances because the rate of interest has to conform to world conditions.'[92] Since Britain was not a closed system, she could in principle cut money wages unilaterally while the general price level, determined by international factors, would not fall commensurately. For this reason, real wages would be reduced and the obvious immediate gain to employment would come from cornering a bigger share of world trade. Pigou thus maintained the general proposition that a reduction in *real* wages would have a beneficial effect on employment, without seeing that such a reduction could only be achieved if Britain were not a closed system; but in that case the real benefit to Britain came from a reduction in *money* wages in a way that could not be

---

[90] EAC (E) 12, par. IV, 7; Pigou answers, 22 Sept. 1930, CAB 58/150; also in Keynes papers, EA/4. Keynes's questionnaire is in *JMK* xx. 405. The whole of this section leans on the account in Howson and Winch, *EAC* 50–72.

[91] *JMK* xx. 414 (EAC (E) 23, Keynes's notes on EAC (E) 12).

[92] Ibid. 415.

universally valid in a closed system. In short, the theoretical consistency of this reasoning troubled Keynes as much as its practical pertinence.

'Real wages seem to me to come in as a by-product of the remedies which we adopt to restore equilibrium,' Keynes declared. 'They come in at the end of the argument rather than at the beginning.' In answering his own questionnaire, the most he would say was 'that if we cut ourselves off from all other remedies, this is the only remedy which is left'.[93] Moreover, in so far as it was necessary to reduce real wages, he maintained that it was better to do so by raising prices than by cutting money wages. Keynes's own answer—'the lines along which I should analyse the problem of unemployment, if I had only myself to please'—was now different. It was to distinguish between 'primary' employment, brought about through increased investment, and 'secondary' employment, resulting from the consequent increase of consumption. 'Mr Kahn has produced an argument, which seems to me convincing,' Keynes wrote, 'for supposing that in present conditions in Great Britain a given amount of primary employment gives rise to an approximately equal amount of secondary employment.'[94]

Kahn's 'multiplier'—to use the name which Keynes was to give it in 1933—introduced a new argument in support of public works. The paper circulated to the committee of economists from its joint secretary, 'The Relation between Primary and Secondary Employment', ran to a sparse four pages of typescript and was largely mathematical; it was no more than 'a primitive draft' of one part of the article he was to publish in the *Economic Journal* the following year.[95] On his own account, he was inspired by *Can Lloyd George Do It?* (though in fact Keynes had gone further in the direction of the multiplier in his subsequent reply to the 1929 Treasury Memorandum).[96]

Kahn was concerned with the repercussions of public works. The significance of his multiplier, however, does not reside in an expansive wave of the hand towards the infinite possibilities of

[93] *JMK* xiii. 179–81 (EAC (E) 15, Keynes's answers).

[94] Ibid. 187–8.

[95] This was not an official EAC paper, although it was circulated to the committee, and it survives (undated) only in the Keynes papers, EA/4, with one extra page giving illustrative figures on expenditure. Kahn's own account of its inception is in *The Making of Keynes's General Theory* (1984), 91–7.

[96] See above, ch. 4 n. 87.

cumulative prosperity but in specifying the finite limits to such an impact. It was an exercise in arithmetic, addressed to the sort of effects—'Supposing it were possible to sum them up'—which Hopkins, for one, had been politely sceptical of yielding to such techniques.[97] The statistician Colin Clark, who helped Kahn, had already, with A. W. Flux of the Board of Trade, prepared a paper for the EAC on the effects of a rise in exports on unemployment—the same sort of problem Hawtrey had addressed. Clark referred to 'an infinite series of beneficial repercussions'. With no leakages, indeed, the multiplier would be infinity. Did Clark mean this? Or did he, as a trained physical scientist, appreciate that the sum of an infinite series may well be finite?[98] Hints about the repercussions of cumulative prosperity were commonplace, but Kahn's achievement in the summer of 1930 was to show that it was indeed 'possible to sum them'. As Keynes later put it to Clark, there was all the difference between 'some sort of formal statement', like Kahn's and 'the general notion of there being such a thing as secondary employment'.[99]

Kahn's formula specified 'the secondary employment that directly results from the increased expenditure of the newly employed and of their employers'. The net effect upon employment would be limited by any rise in prices—'by an amount that depends on the elasticities of supply and demand for production as a whole'. Rises in output and in prices were thus alternatives. Moreover, in a pregnant couple of sentences, Kahn estimated the saving to the Unemployment Fund and added the reduction in foreign lending plus the increase in the amount of savings not spent, thus showing that 'we arrive at a sum that is exactly equal to ... the cost of the primary employment'. It was a more rigorous version of the sort of list which Keynes had improvised for Hopkins, to indicate the offsetting gains of a capital programme even if its market rate of return were low. 'In such a case,' Kahn concluded, after doing the sum, 'it pays the State to

[97] See above, ch. 7 n. 49.

[98] See Howson and Winch, *EAC* 36 n. and Don Patinkin 'Keynes and the multiplier, *Manc. Sch.*, 46 (1978), 216–17. Patinkin noted (217 n.)—but was not convinced by—the interesting suggestion which had been put to him by John Flemming, that Clark may have had in mind a finite magnitude. Four years later, in the revised version of Patinkin's article, he added that he had since asked Clark which interpretation, 'mine or Flemming's, was correct—and he unhesitatingly replied that Flemming's was'; *Anticipations of the General Theory?* (1982), 197, addendum to n. 10. Kahn has now claimed: 'I cannot recall any doubt on his (Clark's) part that the sum of an infinite convergent series is finite'; *Making*, 96. Patinkin's scepticism still seems justified.

[99] *JMK* xii. 806 (Keynes to Clark, 31 May 1938).

undertake primary employment and pay the whole expense, even though the product is almost valueless'.[100]

The immediate use to which Keynes put Kahn's argument was in showing the extent of secondary employment. It was not well received by the committee of economists at its weekend meeting at Stamp's house at the end of September. Pigou obviously resented having it sprung upon him and passed round a note of criticism, which he subsequently corrected—'it is quite likely that there is a mistake in this note also, as everything has to be done in a hurry'—without, however, conceding Kahn's point. Pigou supposed that 'in the limit, according to this method', unemployment of two million could be absorbed through secondary employment if primary employment were found for one man.[101] Kahn responded that this was only true on Pigou's own assumption that, in effect, there were no leakages.[102] Keynes built the multiplier into his first draft of the economists' report, only to find that Henderson also objected to it—clearly not feeling that it was an extension of his own contribution to *Can Lloyd George Do It?* Since the multiplier was standing in the way of agreement, it was thrown to the wolves at this stage.[103]

These exchanges left no mark upon agreed policy advice, therefore, but they give an interesting indication of the way Keynes's own mind was working. Pigou had sought to show how a rise in employment could be explained by an increase in the velocity of circulation without any talk of 'secondary employment'. His more fertile intervention, however, had been to question Keynes's contention that excess savings of £1,000 led to £1,000 of business losses. This might be true, Pigou conceded, if prices fell immediately, meaning that the same volume of output was then sold for £1,000 less. Keynes's response showed that he had been led to examine his own implicit assumption that changes in price rather than output were the key to the position; whereas he now saw that the elasticity of supply was crucial. It made all the difference whether an increase in demand pushed up prices or whether—'when there is unemployment and surplus capacity at home'—output and employment would increase

[100]   Kahn, 'Primary and Secondary Employment', EA/4.

[101]   EAC (E) 26, Pigou, 'Primary and Secondary Employment', 4 Oct. 1930; copies in CAB 58/151 and Keynes papers, EA/4.

[102]   EAC (E) 30, Kahn, 'Primary and Secondary Employment', 6 Oct. 1930, CAB 58/151.

[103]   See *JMK* xx. 437–43 (draft of 'Remedies of Class C', 6 Oct. 1930). Howson and Winch, *EAC* 69, is surely correct in saying that the multiplier disappeared from the final draft, despite the contention in Kahn, *Making*, 96–7.

instead. This point, Keynes reflected, 'ought to have occurred to me, thinking along my own lines'; and he glossed it in *Treatise* terms by saying that 'the excess of saving over investment causes a determinate loss of entrepreneurs but not a determinate amount of unemployment'.[104] His real answer to Pigou, then, was that £1,000 of losses were inescapable but that they might take the form of loss of profits on a fixed output at lower prices—or loss of sales at fixed prices, with lower output and employment. This line of thinking, however, was not developed within the committee of economists.

Keynes's influence upon the report was considerable, but in its drafting he was in the hands of formidable professional colleagues, of whom only Stamp was fully amenable to his suggestions. That Keynes managed to carry Pigou and Henderson with him in the final report, and Robbins for a good part of the way, is evidence of his adroitness in committee work rather than an unruffled unanimity among the experts. This is shown in the way that Keynes bought support for his favoured proposals by accepting his colleagues' way of approaching the problem. Thus his draft defined the remedies at the outset as confronting the problem of a disparity between wages and prices. Starting from here, Keynes proceeded to classify the options in terms of their relevance to it.

The initial class of remedies were those which permitted present wages to be paid: by tackling restrictive practices, conditions for the dole, and productivity. Next came those which involved raising prices. This might be achieved through a rise in world gold prices or by sterling devaluation. An intermediate category followed, which gave Keynes plenty of elbow room. It became, in the first place, a means of justifying measures to promote home investment—the 'confidence' package for the Budget, including tariffs, fiscal incentives to favour domestic projects, and, of course, public works. It also turned into an advocacy of ways of increasing investment abroad, one method again comprising tariffs. Finally, it ushered in, naked and explicit, the tariff-bounty proposal which Keynes had been working out. The last group of remedies was for wage cuts. It can be seen that all of this was within the framework of Keynes's Macmillan Committee evidence, and in his original scheme he remained faithful to it also in giving practically every other remedy a higher priority than wage cuts.[105]

---

[104] *JMK* xx. 422–3 ('An additional way of increasing employment: note on Professor Pigou's argument', 27 Sept. 1930); cf. 420–1 for Pigou's notes of 26 and 27 Sept. 1930.
[105] *JMK* xx. 423–50.

In the final report, as endorsed by Pigou, Henderson, and Stamp, however, although sections IX, X, and XI elaborated the variants under Keynes's umbrella of remedies, in section VII the case for wage cuts became prominent.[106] This was a concession to Pigou and, above all, Henderson, who forcefully criticized the 'practical gist and tenor' of Keynes's draft. 'It seems to me to run away, under cover of complex sophistication, from the plain moral of the situation which it diagnoses', Henderson stated. Under current conditions—falling world prices, structural maladjustment, Budget worries—there was 'no alternative now but to face up to the disagreeable reactionary necessity of cutting costs (including wages) in industry and cutting expenditure in public affairs' and the fact that this was 'the moral drawn by the ordinary, conservative, unintellectual businessman' was no longer a sufficient reason for rejecting it. He did not pretend it would be easy, and the ultimate alternative was devaluation. But he had come to the conclusion that 'the really important issues which divide the committee are of a broad and almost temperamental nature and are merely obscured by disputes about investment and secondary employment'. The trouble was that Keynes's draft, 'after half-recognising the truth of the foregoing, runs right away from it, and proceeds to twist and wriggle and turn in a desperate attempt to evade the logic of the situation'.[107]

This is virtually what Keynes would have admitted himself—'I twist and turn about trying to find some aid to the situation'[108]—because his acceptance of the theoretical conclusion that lower labour costs were the ideal remedy did not persuade him that wage cuts were the best policy. So although the economists' report made a recommendation for income reductions, Keynes managed a final twist by adding his own summary to section VII, in which it was stated that 'every other remedy with any serious balance of argument in its favour should be tried first'. Since this paragraph alone appeared at the end of the report, in its overall summary of conclusions, busy ministers might well have been misled by this piece of sharp practice into supposing that it represented the conclusion of all except Robbins rather than, in effect, Keynes alone.[109]

Although Kahn's multiplier was removed from the report, a

---

[106] The Economists' Report is printed in Howson and Winch, *EAC* 180–227, which gives (71–2) an authoritative account of its composition.

[107] *JMK* xx. 452–6 (Henderson, 'The drift of the draft report', 13 Oct. 1930).

[108] *JMK* xx. 350 (Keynes to Norman, 22 May 1930).

[109] Economists' Report, par. 51; Howson and Winch, *EAC* 195, 219.

rudimentary reference to the 'beneficial repercussions upon trade in general' appeared in the section on public works—a policy which was commended as a sound principle under conditions of extensive unemployment. 'We do not accept the view that the undertaking of such work must necessarily cause a mere diversion from other employment,' the report stated, in line with the Macmillan Committee evidence of Stamp and Pigou as well as the case argued by the erstwhile authors of *Can Lloyd George Do It?*[110] The Treasury View, as a doctrine about crowding-out, was thus rejected; but, as reformulated by Hopkins, it substantially reappeared in three paragraphs appended by Henderson stating the conditions which had to be satisfied by public works. 'A hastily improvised programme of dubious projects,' he wrote, 'which was widely regarded as wasteful and profligate, and raised doubts as to the general soundness of public finances, might have serious reactions, for example, on the rate of interest at which the Government could borrow.'[111] Even Robbins, who had more far-reaching doubts about whether a public works programme would do good, subscribed to these criteria. It was on another issue—tariffs—that he was to break ranks completely.

Most of the dentists were agreed, therefore, in conceding the relevance of public works under conditions of high unemployment. Whereas they tended to accept the rigidity of wage rates with manifest reluctance, Keynes seemed to do so with unbecoming alacrity and proceeded to argue from there. He may have been more radical than his colleagues—if Robertson is excluded—in advocating public works, but he did not fundamentally dissent from them on matters of theory. Such differences as arose between Keynes, Pigou, Stamp, and Henderson were matters of judgement about what was prudent and realistic; it was Robbins, not Keynes, who challenged the analytical consensus.

'If the doctors were all of one mind . . .'

Upon resuming its labours in late October, the Macmillan Committee achieved a fair measure of agreement in the course of twelve

---

[110] Ibid., par. 63; the summary of this paragraph (Howson and Winch, *EAC* 221) is quoted in support of Kahn's claim that it implicitly embodies the multiplier; Kahn, *Making*, 96–7.

[111] Economists' Report, par. 66; for the drafting of pars. 65–7 see Howson and Winch, *EAC* 72.

private sessions. When Keynes insisted that its report should focus on the deflation since 1924—'I think it was the fall of prices that brought us into existence'[112]—he received immediate support not only from McKenna but also from Brand. Brand had spent part of the summer studying Keynes's theory of savings and investment. 'Its main argument seems, as Mr Keynes says, to be acceptable to common sense,' he wrote.[113] He was prepared to assume that it was right and to accept that home investment could in principle boost the national income. His reasons for scepticism were therefore practical—whether useful schemes employing the appropriate kind of labour could be found and whether they were adequate to the deteriorating economic situation.

Gregory, too, accepted much of Keynes's analysis, which pointed to a monetary explanation of Britain's difficulties rather than to a structural industrial maladjustment. On this reading, unemployment was 'not due to national decline but to some muddle, and it is to disentangle that muddle which is our task'.[114] This was in line with Keynes's published views on the world slump: that it meant 'we have involved ourselves in a colossal muddle, having blundered in the control of a delicate machine, the working of which we do not fully understand'.[115] He told the committee that it was 'a misapprehension of the facts' to suppose that 'these troubles are due to very deep-seated causes, that our productivity is not increasing at the same rate as other countries, that labour is greedy, and is asking for a larger and larger share of a smaller product, and that we are getting nearer and nearer to the abyss.' So much for the despondent croakings of the Bank of England! What is more surprising is that Gregory added: 'I think I should agree with practically everything that Mr Keynes has said; in fact, I have been saying it myself . . .'.[116]

What was now of most interest to the committee was not how the self-equilibrating economic and financial machine was supposed to work but how it had failed to do so. Bradbury, as a defender of the Gold Standard mechanism, did not maintain that the dear money policy had proved successful. When pursued for a long period, its

[112] Private session, 23 Oct. 1930, 11; cf. ch. 8 of the *Report*, Cmd. 3897 (1931), 69–78.

[113] Paper No. 55 (Memorandum by Brand, 14 Aug. 1930), Keynes papers, MC/3.

[114] Private session, 23 Oct. 1930, 16.

[115] *JMK* ix. 126 ('The great slump of 1930', *Nation*, 20 and 27 Dec. 1930).

[116] Private session, 23 Oct. 1930, 16–17.

effect had been, not to administer a 'short and sharp' squeeze on excess demand, but to cut back supply as well.

Macmillan: It has lost its curative power.
Bradbury: Its curative power is very largely inhibited unless it is exercised very rapidly. I do not know if Mr Keynes would agree with that.
Keynes: Yes, I should.

Bradbury reflected that 'according to the orthodox pre-War theory the effect of the price fall ought to be to reduce costs; that is to say, if wages were elastic the fact that there is a certain amount of unemployment would bring down the rate of wages'. But since the War a degree of rigidity in all prices had supervened which obviously 'inhibited the application of this theory'.[117]

A major issue was how the Bank of England had responded to the new conditions and how flexibly it had adapted its policy; and a major difficulty, it was agreed, was that nobody seemed to know exactly what was in the Governor's mind. 'He is not only irresponsible in fact,' said McKenna, 'but there is no occasion and no opportunity given to him to explain his policy or make his views clear to the World at large.'[118] His phrase about 'a mute and irresponsible despotism' was picked up by Keynes: 'I think the despotism largely depends on the muteness.'[119]

Keynes: If at every stage in the last ten years the Governor of the Bank of England had stated publicly what his object was and what he thought the things he was doing were likely to result in and how he assessed the advantages and disadvantages of his policy, if he told us what he was aiming at and what his method was and what he thought his method would cost in order to gain the advantages he was seeking, then it would be possible for public opinion of an informal kind to be crystallised on the point whether his policy was wise and successful.

Was this a matter for public opinion or for the experts? 'In the domain of the expert,' the chairman mused, 'it is not possible even for such a democracy as we are hoping to see to form opinions that are almost infallible.'[120] Keynes's view was that 'if you could convince

---

[117] Ibid. 24 Oct. 1930, 3–4.
[118] Ibid. 30 Oct. 1930, 14.
[119] Ibid. 26, 16; Keynes returned to this theme on 5 Dec., *JMK* xx. 262–3. The private sessions of 27 and 28 Nov., 5 Dec. 1930, are printed in *JMK* xx. 179–270.
[120] Private session, 30 Oct. 1930, 17.

a comparatively small number of people in key positions, I think you would have advanced a long way.' Challenged by Newbold on this apparently élitist remark, Keynes elaborated his meaning: 'I do not think the opposition has come from the great public,' he said; 'rather the position is that while the great public has had a suspicion of where the truth lay, it has not been able to express it clearly. It is as though those responsible for policy have had certain ideas which they have believed in and what has been happening has been largely in pursuance of those ideas.'[121] Here was a further kind of rigidity in the system—the obdurate refusal of the financial system, and the Bank in particular, to adapt to new circumstances.[122]

Keynes: Industry has no orthodoxies; industry is changing all the time, industry is not governed by wise sayings and traditions, it is all the time experimenting; it is opportunist, it is always trying new things; but the extraordinary character of finance is the extent to which it is governed by orthodoxy, it is kept back by maxims and orthodoxies and things handed down and things that were established as being sound a long time ago.

If the authorities could only be persuaded, a revolution in policy might be engineered; but their preconceptions were such that they were unlikely to be persuaded unless outside influences were brought to bear upon them. The political situation, however, meant that remedial action was also likely to be impeded by the party dogfight, which was largely irrelevant to the real issues. Bevin, for one, was close to Keynes in wishing to remove the problem 'into the non-party sphere', and to use the committee for this end, if it were possible.[123]

Tulloch: Whatever we say, if we say anything, nobody is going to suspect us of any bias whatever. We should be regarded as non-political and entirely unprejudiced.
Keynes: I think it is important if we could say something of that sort, because, as Mr Bevin says, all the possible ways out are unpopular and open to objection.
Bevin: I think that is right.

---

[121] Private session, 30 Oct. 1930, 7.
[122] Ibid. 9.
[123] Ibid. 7 Nov. 1930, 28. Churchill's Romanes lecture showed that he was currently of the same view: 'It might well be that the measures which in the course of several years would vastly improve our economic position actually and relatively, and open broadly to us the high roads of the future, would be extremely unpopular, and that no single party, even if they possessed the secret, would be able to carry their policy in the face of opposition by the others.' *Thoughts and Adventures* (1932), 176.

Keynes: Therefore, they are things which it is very difficult to carry forward, except in the absence of contentious opposition.
Bradbury: The main difficulty is in ourselves. If the doctors were all of one mind, it is possible that the patient might be treated non-politically.

Were the doctors more likely to be of one mind than the dentists? Clearly the Macmillan Committee did not attach the same weight to theoretical analysis as the committee of economists, but it was no less vital for Keynes to have persuaded it of the essential soundness of his case. He was manifestly on top form during these autumn meetings, reasserting the mastery over the committee which he had first exerted in February. Leith-Ross recollected that the Greeks had a word for it: *epideixis* (display).[124] What is notable is how many members of the committee showed themselves receptive to his general message.[125]

Macmillan: It is very desirable that we should express it in different language, or it might be said the Committee had swallowed Mr Keynes's arguments whole!

As the other economist on the committee, Gregory was in a pivotal position. Although he differed from Keynes on the relevance of wage cuts, Gregory was not entirely the 'bankers' (tame) orthodox economist' he was sometimes painted.[126] He had indeed taken the committee by storm on 21 November with his scheme to amalgamate the Issue and Banking Departments of the Bank of England—a highly abstruse business but one which, broached in this way, ruffled the authorities. 'Professor Gregory's proposals were naturally supported with vigour by Keynes and McKenna,' Leith-Ross reported, 'and rather surprisingly also by some of the conservative members of the Committee like Mr Tulloch'.[127] Only Bradbury and Lubbock proved reliable in resisting this bright idea. 'I doubt whether the Political Economists have the remotest glimmering of the technical difficulties involved,' commented Phillips of the Treasury.[128]

When Keynes had been pressed by Gregory on 23 October over the relation of investment to the interest rate, his answer was: 'I must really refer you to my book, which will be out in a week, where I deal

[124] Leith-Ross, note, 27–8 Nov. 1930, T. 200/3.
[125] Private session, 30 Oct. 1930, 26.
[126] e.g. John Hargrave, *Professor Skinner alias Montagu Norman*, n.d. (?1939), 148.
[127] Leith-Ross to Phillips, 24 Nov. 1930, T. 200/3; cf. Report, Cmd. 3897, pars. 330–45.
[128] Phillips to Leith-Ross and Hopkins, 26 Nov. 1930, T. 200/3.

with that question.' On 20 November, when Gregory led the discussion, he admitted that he had not yet read the *Treatise*, but he was seized of its gist, if only from Keynes's recent recapitulation.[129] According to Keynes, the long-term swings of the business cycle could be explained by the rate of interest being above or below the equilibrium level for a number of years. When it was too low, the result was a rising price level; when it was too high, depression. 'I am quite familiar with the kind of theory which underlies Mr. Keynes's remarks,' Gregory commented, meaning that it was similar to Wicksell's concept of the natural rate of interest; and he accepted that this constituted 'a very large part of the explanation'.[130] He was, as he later put it, 'prepared to accept the distinction between saving and investment as an important conceptual contribution to the elucidation of the trade cycle'. But he parted company with Keynes on the cause of the divergences between the two.

Rather like Robertson, Gregory was inclined to regard 'hoarding' as manifesting a lack of confidence which might not be amenable to changes in the rate of interest. Keynes's position was in this sense more purely neo-classical in its confident assumption that cheap money could itself be relied upon to restore equilibrium. Gregory's sensitivity to the psychology of savers made him apprehensive that 'large-scale government intervention may deter as much or more investment directly as it produced directly'.[131] While more pessimistic than Keynes about the putative impact of state action, he was more optimistic about the trend of market forces since he took the view that the general rate of interest was now heading down after being held above the equilibrium level since the War.[132]

Macmillan: When we use the expression 'rigidity', do we mean that modern political theory prevents the operation of the natural laws of Political Economy?
Gregory: I should say simply that the way in which the economic system works, under the present accepted standards of what to do, is different from the way in which it would work if you did not accept the present standard. I do not like using the words 'natural laws', because it is question-begging in these matters.

[129] Private session, 23 Oct. 1930, 20; 20 Nov. 1930, 4.
[130] Ibid. 20 Nov. 1930, 11–12; cf. 7 Nov., 10.
[131] *JMK* xx. 275 (Gregory memorandum, 17 Apr. 1931).
[132] Private session, 20 Nov. 1930, 13. This was, of course, close to Hawtrey's opinion.

Gregory's essential differences with Keynes lay not in theory but in disposition—because he was in the end prepared to sit out the slump and wait for the upswing of the trade cycle, even though the process now worked much more slowly because of the inelasticity of the system. Like Brand, he was not necessarily hostile to the analysis of the *Treatise*; and even Bradbury, who was, as he put it, 'a little more "stick-in-the-mud" perhaps', showed an impressive capacity to grasp Keynes's central insights.[133]

Keynes: The demand for savings coming on to the market is always equal to the enterprise, the question is how far that is made up of really new investment or how far it is made up of replacement of losses. Or it may be the opposite. It may be excessive profits.

Bradbury: I hope I am not parodying your theory, but it occurs to me like this, that saving has nothing at all to do with individuals, or anything of that kind, but saving is the mere outcome of the course of industry.

Keynes: I should put it this way, that the increment of capital wealth in the world each year depends on the entrepreneurs—how much capital wealth they produce. The bearing of thrift on the matter does not affect that; it only affects prices. If thrift falls behind the enterprise, then prices will rise.

Bradbury: If thrift is in excess of the production of capital goods then there is so much thrift wasted.

Keynes: Yes.

Bradbury: If, on the other hand, the production of capital goods is in excess of the amount of thrift, that in itself will create the necessary amount of investable capital through the increased profit of the entrepreneur?

Keynes: What thrift determines is how much new enterprise you can have without inflation.

It should not, of course, be assumed that 'the doctrine of the new school of economists that the profits resulting from capital expenditure will themselves provide the savings to finance it' had made a convert; Bradbury was later to compare it to the maxim, 'let us eat and drink for to-morrow we die'.[134] But he clearly understood what he firmly rejected.

Keynes gave his opinion at the committee's final meeting 'that in the near future economics will become increasingly technical and difficult for the outsider, because the economists will be settling a number of matters among themselves and will have to discuss them in their own way', and that meanwhile 'the difficulty is that parts of

---

[133] Ibid. 7 Nov. 1930, 10–11; cf. 23 Oct., 31.
[134] *Macmillan Report*, Cmd. 3897, 280 n. (memorandum of dissent by Bradbury).

the subject which one feels ought to be elementary are still in this disputed condition'.[135] His hopes for the *Treatise* obviously shaped this utterance. But he probably staked too much upon it, for better or for worse, so far as the policy argument was concerned. To be sure, it provided him with an analytical framework which he found helpful; it gave him a terminology about saving and investment in relation to equilibrium which was rhetorically persuasive; and it offered a consistent set of criteria for all the policy advice he tendered in 1930. Yet the *Treatise* did not in itself make the case for his 'favourite remedy', although it licensed it. If, by 1930, Keynes could produce a knock-down refutation of the Treasury View of 1929, on the grounds that it illicitly assumed full employment or optimum output, this owed little to the *Treatise*, which arguably harboured the same illicit assumption.

Conversely, few other economists had much trouble in translating the propositions of the *Treatise* into their own preferred language, for the good reason that they shared the same fundamental neo-classical postulates. Though the *Treatise* seemed novel in defining saving and investment so that they need not be equal, it still postulated a tendency for the interest rate to bring them into equilibrium. The disequilibrium which obtained in Britain was attributed by Keynes to the fact that interest rates were insufficiently flexible; but he could not deny that flexibility of real wages was also intrinsic to the process. Most economists told a similar story—in their own words, of course. If there was no happy ending in the real world, it was because of some rigidity, inelasticity, obstruction, or other imperfection, which meant that prices (including wages and interest rates) were jammed or hitched or otherwise impeded in their assigned task. Many economists joined Keynes in seeking gadgets or devices to tackle unemployment, given that prices exhibited an unwonted rigidity—while not overlooking the relevance of wage cuts, if only they were practicable. Such arguments allowed for public works as a special case in the conditions of 1930; and much the same could be said for tariffs.

[135] *JMK* xx. 269 (5 Dec. 1930).

9

Rigid prices and flexible doctrines, II: Free Trade

'Essentially the same story'

Among the official papers of the committee of economists, the most surprising document to find is EAC (E) 3, circulated to all members by the chairman at the outset of its deliberations. It is a copy of a letter by him to the *Manchester Guardian*, the most venerable organ of incorruptible Liberalism, entitled 'Buying a British Car'. The issue was in the air because E. D. Simon, at the Liberal Summer School, had asked whether buying a British rather than an American car would not increase employment in Britain. Keynes's approach to the question shows that, by the middle of August 1930, the multiplier was already in his mind. For if £200 spent on a car employed an extra man in the motor trade, this man, 'having an increased income, would spend and consume more, and thus produce a favourable repercussion on employment in other industries; and so on'. There would at each stage be leakages into imports of food and raw materials—say £50. The net effects would therefore be a relative improvement of £150 on the balance of trade and hence foreign investment, plus more than £200 of increased home output, with attendant benefits to employment, profits, the dole, and tax revenue. Keynes noted that 'the whole argument depends on there being unused productive resources in this country suitable for making a car and not likely to be used for the present in making anything else.'[1]

This proviso was not only very important in itself: it was also very important that Keynes, as a good Liberal and Free Trader, should make it. 'The classic Free Trade argument', as Pigou had put it, 'tacitly assumes that labour is mobile and that wages are not artificially high. If those assumptions disappear, the argument in its classic form breaks down; and, so far as that argument goes, the case for Free Trade collapses.'[2] This was the arid logic of the case; but in the real world certain economic propositions, which were dependent

---

[1] *JMK* xx. 385–7 (*Manchester Guardian*, 14 Aug. 1930).
[2] *Macmillan Evidence*, Q. 6482.

upon special assumptions, had been treated as truisms, and the truisms had become slogans charged with inescapable party connotations. Keynes had broadly succeeded, without undue resistance, in attaching Liberal support to public works; but any suggestion of tariffs, as he knew, needed to be broached with more care. 'The liberal programme of organised capital development', he suggested, 'is, in effect, a method of subsidising home investment; tariffs, in so far as they allow us to employ home productive resources of men and plant which would otherwise be unemployed, are in effect (in present circumstances), a method of subsidising foreign investment. The principle is the same in both cases, and the immediate effect on employment and on wealth is the same.'[3]

Keynes had first made out the case for protection as one of the seven remedies outlined in his private evidence to the Macmillan Committee in February 1930. There was a perceptible *frisson* of excitement or alarm as soon as the subject was mentioned. 'It would be a surprising result if our Report were a Report in favour of tariff reform,' the chairman commented; later observing that it had been 'mixed up with political considerations and then people indulge in gibes about inconsistency'. Indeed he raised the question of how far it fell within the terms of reference. 'I am frankly rather concerned about that,' he explained, 'because I think one of the results of our appointment may be a report dealing with tariff reform.' If that happened, 'our Report might become a document of first-rate political importance'.[4] This would no doubt have pleased a committed protectionist like Sir Walter Raine—'I certainly expect the draft Report to be on those lines'[5]—but it raised delicate problems for the others.

'It is extremely difficult', Keynes said, 'for anyone of free trade origin, so to speak, at this juncture to speak in a way that he himself believes to be quite truthful and candid without laying himself open to misrepresentation and to being supposed to advocate very much more than he really does.'[6] McKenna, too ('I speak as a life-long free trader'), was concerned that any protectionist noises in their Report should be accompanied by 'a clear statement of the free trade case,

---

[3] *JMK* xx. 386; for the ideological context see Michael Freeden, *Liberalism Divided* (Oxford, 1986), 121–4.
[4] *JMK* xx. 116, 121, 123, 125.
[5] Ibid. 116
[6] Ibid. 120

which I still uphold, and I would like it to be stated that the theory breaks down here and there because of particular conditions'.[7]

What were these conditions? The *modus operandi* of Bank rate was again crucial to the analysis, since an outflow of gold would be the immediate result of an excess of imports over exports, thus setting off a chain reaction of compensating adjustments. 'Just like the Bank rate argument, it works beautifully in a fluid system', Keynes explained. 'But supposing we get jammed at the point of unemployment, the alternative for a time may be between producing motor cars or producing nothing.'[8] The reason why the machine was jammed could be put in different ways. Given the structure of domestic costs, it was because of the defence of sterling. Given the uncompetitiveness of British exports, it was because of excessive foreign lending. Given the existing level of foreign investment, it was because of excessive costs, especially wages, at home.[9]

Keynes: We shall have to say a great deal about the failure of wages to adjust themselves easily as a prime factor in the situation—I think everybody agrees about that. That fact reacts on the validity of a good many orthodox maxims—it reacts on the validity of Bank rate policy and also on the free trade argument. It is essentially the same story that I am telling in both cases.

The trouble with free trade, therefore, was the assumption 'that if you throw men out of work in one direction you re-employ them in another. As soon as that link in the chain is broken the whole of the free trade argument breaks down.' The essence of the choice was 'that with protection we should have lower real wages but less unemployment'.[10] It was in this sense a better means of reducing real incomes in Britain than seeking the same effect through wage cuts. The virtue of free trade was that in theory it maintained real wages, and thus living standards, even though money wages might be reduced. 'But the virtue of protection is that is does the trick,' Keynes maintained, 'whereas in present conditions free trade does not.'[11]

It would not be fair to call Keynes a protectionist on the strength of these remarks in February and March 1930. His attachment to free trade was more than a pious disclaimer, though he was now determined to reassess the balance of advantage under changed

[7] Ibid. 116.
[8] Ibid. 114.
[9] Ibid. 124.
[10] Ibid. 117.
[11] Ibid. 115.

conditions. It was still his view that protection was 'radically unsound, if you take a long enough view', whatever its short-term efficacy: so 'the question, in my opinion, is how far I am prepared to risk long-period disadvantages in order to get some help to the immediate position'. He therefore resisted the invitation from Raine—who had been 'hoping that Mr Keynes would tell us quite seriously what his views were'—to commit himself explicitly; and continued to profess himself 'afraid of the general protectionist atmosphere'.[12] The view which Grigg later expressed about the alleged effect of Keynes's 'conversion' at this stage is evidence, if anything, of the valetudinarian hypersensitivity of the dyed-in-the-wool Free Traders.[13] Keynes's talk to the Tuesday Club in April, 'Are the Presuppositions of Free Trade Satisfied Today?', was posing the same awkward dilemma. Likewise his report, with Cole, for the Committee on Economic Outlook stressed the pertinence of protection without formally advocating it.

It was the confidence issue which finally tipped the scales. Since Henderson was more troubled by this, it is not surprising that he anticipated Keynes in declaring himself. Henderson's 'Industrial Reconstruction Scheme' at the end of May conceived a revenue tariff as the means of squaring the circle—permitting capital expenditure at home while encouraging rationalization and promoting the recovery of business confidence.[14]

I venture to doubt whether a single competent economist in the country would dispute that, under conditions such as now obtain, the effects of a 10% tariff on manufactured imports would be beneficial to employment; and I also doubt whether many businessmen, whose general position is that of Free Traders, would dispute that such a tariff would have a materially beneficial effect upon business psychology.

This was an argument which Keynes had made his own by the time he wrote to the Prime Minister in July 1930, when he stated that he had 'become reluctantly convinced that some protectionist measures should be introduced'. Considerations of confidence clearly played a large part in bringing him to this conclusion, and in this respect a revenue tariff had the advantage of being 'the only form of taxation which will positively cheer people up!'[15]

---

[12] *JMK* xx. 120–1.

[13] P. J. Grigg, *Prejudice and Judgement* (1948), 232, 242–3. Maybe he confused 1930 with 1931, though in general his dating is notably accurate.

[14] 'Industrial Reconstruction Scheme', 30 May 1930, T. 175/50.

[15] *JMK* xx. 378–9.

Free Trade and the economists

The ground swell of opinion in favour of tariffs during 1930—as illustrated by the TUC's shift away from Free Trade, by the 'bankers' manifesto' (signed by McKenna) in July, and the Conservative party's adoption of a protectionist platform in October—shifted the balance of proof on the issue. The economic benefit of a tariff might not have been sufficient to outweigh a political objection against it; but once the political advantage had tipped in its favour, a tariff might be justifiable provided that it did not actually bring economic loss. Keynes's advocacy of tariffs from the summer of 1930 undoubtedly had this political dimension. They were to be part of a 'confidence package' which was not only necessary in itself but also a potential means of buying support across the political spectrum for measures, like public works, which conservative opinion might otherwise have stymied. For Keynes, always the temperamental activist, the principle might plausibly have seemed 'the same in both cases'; conversely, those who were more sceptical about public works tended also to look askance at protection.

Pigou was no doctrinaire and was well aware of the vulnerability of 'the classic Free Trade argument' to changes in circumstances. In view of his principle that two bags were better than one, he was asked by Lord Macmillan whether, when wages were stuck at an artificially high level, he ought not to resort to the artificial remedy of protection. 'I agree', Pigou responded, 'that in that artificial condition there may be cases in which particular tariffs will be advantageous to the nation where they would not otherwise.'[16] As with other devices or gadgets, Pigou really thought that in practice governments would always choose 'the wrong bag' and that the political argument against tariffs was decisive. But he was prepared to discuss the economic conditions under which they were appropriate with such open-mindedness as to lull some members of the committee (yet again) into undue inferences.[17]

Bradbury: Would you try a tariff tentatively until you have just absorbed unemployment?
Pigou: I would not try a tariff at all.
Bradbury: I thought you said that in certain cases a tariff would be in the national interest?

[16] Q. 6496.
[17] QQ. 6512–14.

Pigou: It may be, but I think the indirect disadvantage would be so great for political reasons.
Bradbury: But economically?
Pigou: Economically, I would make a case.

So far as Stamp was concerned, the same line of reasoning led to a different practical conclusion. He called himself a Free Trader because, although confident that he could invent an ideal tariff which would increase total productivity, he was also 'quite certain it would not be properly handled politically'. For Stamp, however, this was only a staging post in the argument rather than, as for Pigou, its terminus. He chose to claim that 'while theoretically a Protectionist, I am practically a Free Trader, contrary to most people, who say they are theoretically Free Traders, but practically Protectionists'. Even as a practical matter, though, he was now ready to contemplate whether to 'risk political doubts'.[18] Keynes tried to interest him in thinking of domestic wages as being 90 per cent economic costs of production and 10 per cent subscription towards working-class well-being for social reasons—on the analogy of an excise duty.[19]

Keynes: If you argued that imports ought also to pay the same subscription, would you be infringing the orthodox Free Trade doctine?
Stamp: You would be camouflaging it all right, I think.

Keynes's ingenious efforts at camouflage were to be renewed in the committee of economists in the autumn of 1930. He was now convinced of the 'simply enormous' benefit of a tariff, on the lines of 'Buying a British Car'. In reaching this conclusion, he confessed, 'I have moved away somewhat from what I used to believe.' It was a feeling, not only that the advantages of industrial specialization were overrated in the modern world, but also that they were outweighed by the disadvantages in instability now that other countries had opted for self-sufficiency. It followed that, if a tariff could prevent the crippling of major industries, 'I should regard that as a *conclusive* argument for giving them a tariff.' Moreover, agriculture was an example of a fundamental industry that should be preserved in Britain—as a luxury if need be. 'I would rather see', Keynes proclaimed, 'a prosperous agriculture *plus* tariff log-rolling at Westminster to the extent prevailing (say) in Germany than the rural population driven to live in Birmingham making screws (and the like)

---

[18] Q. 4014.   [19] Q. 4029.

with the purity at Westminster at its present level.'[20] This conjures up nothing so vividly as the Chamberlainite vision of 'national economy' which Keynes had trailed the country deriding in his youth. 'When I want not to be too Free Trade,' he was to confess, 'I read my own writings on the subject at the time when I was a Free Trader.'[21]

Perhaps Keynes had some sense of confronting his younger self in the fierce dispute which ensued with Robbins over the economists' report. With Stamp, there was no difficulty; with Henderson—if anything a more ardent advocate of tariffs—only a difference of opinion over the feasibility of bounties; with Pigou, a series of qualms about the practical wisdom of protective measures, in particular whether a temporary tariff for revenue would, in fact, be removed when good times returned. All of this was negotiable among men with a common Free Trade pedigree, a long-standing familiarity with each others' foibles, and an overriding desire to stake out the widest measure of consensus in the report. Pigou was given his four paragraphs of dissent, in one of which Henderson joined with him to deprecate bounties.[22] Keynes too had given ground in this manner; but his efforts either to cajole or to browbeat Robbins foundered on the rock of principle.

Robbins was unable to accept Keynes's entire analysis, with or without translation into his own vocabulary. Rather than looking for the explanation of the slump in excessive savings, Robbins was, as he subsequently wrote, much influenced by the tradition which blamed 'the excessive conversion of circulating capital into fixed, or, as Cassel was to put much the same thing later on, a position in which the supply of saving is inadequate to take over at profitable prices the real capital goods currently produced'.[23] Fundamentally at odds with the *Treatise*, Robbins was unconvinced by the remedial policies which stemmed from it. The subsidizing of public works thus carried 'grave danger of waste and maldistribution';[24] and on tariffs, Robbins fought a lonely battle to submit a minority report. 'One never does that,' Pigou is reported as saying. 'One tries to reach the greatest possible measure of agreement and then, if necessary, adds a

[20] *JMK* xiii. 191–4 (Memorandum for the committee of economists, 21 Sept. 1930).
[21] Macmillan Committee, private session, 7 Nov. 1930, 30.
[22] See pars. 74, 92, 97, 106 of the Report, printed in Howson and Winch, *EAC* 180–227; and their account of these disputes, 57–8, 61–3.
[23] Lionel Robbins, *Autobiography of an Economist* (1971), 153.
[24] Report by Robbins in Howson and Winch, *EAC* 227–31, at 228.

minute of dissent on particular points.'[25] Unsupported by his closest ally, Robbins none the less ultimately defeated all Keynes's wiles as chairman in order to record his disagreement.

The tariff–bounty proposal, which was an initial stumbling block, had been framed by Keynes for the committee's weekend meeting at Stamp's house at the end of September. It made no bones about being a functional alternative to devaluation, and one that would cut real wages. Keynes concluded that 'a great advantage of this method is that it is capable of being put into force by legislative enactment, whereas a reduction of money wages cannot be enforced in this way, but only as a result of a sort of civil war or guerilla warfare carried on, industry by industry, all over the country, which would be a hideous and disastrous prospect'.[26] Though its macro-economic effect was the same, the scheme thus differed from devaluation on political grounds, and from wage cuts on social grounds too. Failing the full scheme, which was endorsed only by Stamp, Henderson was ready to join Keynes and Stamp in advocating a simple revenue tariff.

Section XI, 'Tariffs', is the heart of the economists' report. It was drafted by men who accepted 'the validity of the traditional Free Trade argument', but who asked whether it had been invalidated by changed conditions. First among these stood chronic large-scale unemployment which, it was claimed, had not been central to the pre-war fiscal controversy. But now they agreed that aggregate employment in Britain would be increased by appropriate duties— 'though one of us (Professor Pigou) thinks that in practice it might not be easy to devise them.' Pigou's chief reservation, however, was not over the direct effect of a tariff but its indirect effect upon exports, which he thought would quickly contract in readjustment to the reduced level of imports. This was the traditional Free Trade view; but Keynes, Henderson, and Stamp now thought that 'in present conditions' exports would be maintained.[27] Underlying this was a pragmatic scepticism about the flexibility of the overseas market in adjusting to a new equilibrium position; and a good part of the case for protection was an opportunistic effort to exploit such rigidities and inelasticities to Britain's immediate advantage.

The potent arguments against tariffs, which Section XI

[25] Dalton diary, 23 Oct. 1930 (Pimlott, 122).

[26] *JMK* xx. 419 ('A proposal for tariffs plus bounties', 25 Sept. 1930); this was substantially incorporated into the Report as par. 104.

[27] Economist' Report, pars. 71–3.

acknowledged as remaining 'with undiminished force', were ones which spurned such gains as 'a means of snatching, at the expense of other countries, an advantage for ourselves which is not so great as the damage done to them', and foresaw that, with the surrender of universal welfare to national self-interest, the surrender of national welfare to sectional self-interest would be only a matter of time. This was, indeed, the thrust of Robbin's own report, which declared, with emphasis, that 'I do not believe that the form of the discussion adequately represents the balance of the arguments involved.' He objected to the whole tone of his colleague's dispassionate enumeration of the arguments—as though the immense weight of the historic presumption in favour of free trade, which was built into the thinking of the economics profession as a whole, could so lightly be set aside. Since a tariff was 'an affirmation of separatism, a refusal to co-operate', even to discuss such measures was 'a sad reminder, not only that some men lose faith in a great ideal when it is not realised quickly, but that most are totally blind even to the most obvious considerations of material interest'. But even where these material considerations had been assessed in a clear-eyed way, as with the proposal for a duty on Danish bacon, which might indeed produce revenue without hurting the English consumer, the argument—'which some might think to be in *favour* of the taxation of Danish pig-products'—was open to the more opprobrious imputation of being 'mean and despicable'.[28]

'Some economists in this country,' Robbins wrote, 'despairing of the rigidity of money wages, may have turned to Protection as a desperate expedient, but, in my opinion, it is questionable whether their verdict will be generally accepted.' With untarnished scorn for such backsliding, Robbins was divorced from the pragmatic outlook adopted by his older colleagues. In discussing tariffs with MacDonald, Keynes had written, 'I am afraid of "principle". Ever since 1918 we, alone among the nations of the world, have been the slaves of "sound" general principles regardless of particular circumstances.'[29] On the main charges which Robbins levelled, Keynes was manifestly guilty and the incriminating evidence was shamelessly unconcealed.

When Hugh Dalton heard Robbins's account of the wrangles in the committee of economists, he was full of admiration for his stand

---

[28] Ibid., par. 86; Robbins in Howson and Winch, *EAC* 229–31.
[29] Ibid. 229 (Robbins); *JMK* xx. 379 (Keynes for MacDonald, 21 July 1930).

against the 'pitiable' proposals on tariffs. 'I was brought up to despise Protectionists at Cambridge,' Dalton wrote. 'I do so still.'[30] There were other ministers who had the same gut feeling—especially since Mosley represented the other side of the argument. The failure of the economists to produce a unanimous report critically weakened its impact; grounded on tariffs, it failed to catch the tide with its cargo of public works. Although there was no reference to these dissensions during the EAC's discussions of the report in the winter of 1930–1, they were mentioned in Cabinet; and the leak in the *Manchester Guardian* (9 December 1930) contained the revelation that the committee was divided.[31] Since MacDonald was not prepared to use the EAC to challenge the primacy of Snowden and the Treasury, the ammunition supplied by the economists was never fired in anger. If the report remained officially 'on the agenda' it was only in the specialized sense of something that would not be acted upon.

'The field of pure hypothesis'

By the autumn of 1930, the Macmillan Committee had to view Britain's problems within an entirely different context from that in which it had first been appointed. Keynes publicly reminded Baldwin in August that 'in the last year there had developed one of the greatest international slumps in prices, trade and employment which has ever occurred in modern economic history'.[32] The super-imposition of this world slump upon Britain's own economic *malaise* meant that the export market had contracted and that the gap between British costs and international prices had widened. Was it feasible, Keynes asked, to expect exports to recover?

If we want to have the old amount of exports in this new environment we shall have to cut our wages. But it may be that there are other ways of bringing about national equilibrium. The savings which used to be embodied in the surplus and which used to employ the labour which created that surplus have not found an alternative outlet. That, I think, is the kernel of the muddle.

Granted that the old export staples were lethargic, it was still the job

---

[30] Dalton diary, 23 Oct. 1930 (Pimlott, 122).
[31] Howson and Winch, *EAC* 74 n., 76–7.
[32] *JMK* xx. 385 (letter, *Nation*, 2 Aug. 1930).

of the monetary machine to find a productive outlet for the savings of the community.[33]

Keynes: I should almost be inclined to define the purpose of the banking and financial system to act as a conduit between the savings of the public and the enterprise of the business man.
Lubbock: How can money do that if the business man will not ask for it?
Keynes: He will on terms, and the banking and financial system depends on what terms the business man is asking.

The clear implication was that, at a sufficiently low interest rate, all sorts of new paying propositions would open up. What worried Gregory, however, was whether cutting foreign lending would in fact improve the position at home. Keynes did not dispute the inherent desirability of foreign investment but questioned the current practicability of finding enough exports to transfer it abroad.

I think if we can we ought to increase our exports, but I am awfully sceptical as to how far we can do that without a very large cut in money wages. If reducing our prices 10 per cent enables us to sell 10 per cent more in volume, we are no further forward. We have to increase our volume much faster than we cut our prices. I think a cut in prices would increase the volume several times over, but in the near future—or perhaps for several years to come—in many of the staple industries I believe that cuts made by ourselves would be met by cuts made by our rivals.

This was a wholly pragmatic argument, addressed to the immediate position. It was the part of Mosley's case which the Board of Trade had found most convincing: the assessment that, in the world of 1930, gains in competitiveness capable or reviving the British export trade were inconceivable. When Macmillan suggested that 'we should try to recapture it by reducing our costs,' Keynes answered: 'We should, but I feel so pessimistic about it.'[34]

If cutting costs no longer seemed a promising way out for Britain, however, because of falling international prices, for the same reason it might now be impossible to avoid cutting wages at home, simply to stop things getting worse. It was left to Gregory to pose the question of 'whether we are really subject to an absolutely inelastic wage standard', especially in the sheltered industries. 'Personally I cannot help expressing my own view for the first time on this particular point,' he said. 'I believe the rise of real wages in the last few years

---

[33] Private session, 23 Oct. 1930, 18–19.
[34] Ibid. 20–1.

has been too high.'[35] As a Free Trader, his considered view was that 'to embark upon a regime of tariffs and to refuse obstinately to face the question of costs are both undesirable'.[36] He stuck to his guns despite facing a double-barrelled attack from Keynes and Bevin. Keynes's point was 'that our social and contractual system is not adapted to violent changes in the value of money'. Bevin simply contended that no informed body with the facts of the matter before them would recommend a reduction.[37]

Gregory: That depends purely on the premises with which we start. As at present constituted, the central bank is not in a position to bring pressure on the wage level.
Bevin: It can create unemployment.
Keynes: It does help to create unemployment by damping down enterprise.
Gregory: May I leave that on one side. If we want to restore equilibrium in the economic system one has either to face a reduction of wages or say that wage reductions are not necessary and try and provide some alternative—my own feeling being that wage reductions are probably necessary but that a greater elasticity of wages is most undoubtedly necessary.

Gregory knew that he was treading on dangerous ground, but he knew, too, that his analysis was bound to win a measure of assent. Whatever Bevin might say, Brand, for one, saw that Keynes of all people could hardly disagree that the level of unemployment in 1929 was a result of British costs failing to adjust to Gold Standard prices.[38]

Gregory: I want to investigate the question as to whether part of the existing volume of unemployment is not due to the maintenance of a level of money wages at a rise of real wages over ten per cent.
Bevin: I do not admit the rise of real wages.
Brand: You and Mr Keynes too part company on this subject.
Macmillan: I do not see why the subject of the reduction of wages should not be discussed as dispassionately as the question of fixed charges.
Gregory: It is very difficult to avoid the implication that one is a monster in human form if you suggest the wage level is too high.

Keynes's position was to acknowledge that in theory real wage cuts would increase employment. In a closed economy, this would be because of the elasticity of demand—increasing consumption with

[35] Private session, 20 Nov. 1930, 25.
[36] *Macmillan Report*, Cmd. 3897 (1931), 218 (Addendum III by Gregory).
[37] Private session, 20 Nov. 1930, 30–1.
[38] Ibid. 34.

every fall in prices. But in the closed economy it would be difficult to bring about real wage cuts because every cut in money wages would also bring prices spiralling down. In the actual open economy, however, real wages would indeed be reduced by cuts in money wages, because the general price level for a country like Britain was fixed by international factors and it would not, *ceteris paribus*, fall by as much as British wages. Hence the true advantage of wage reductions—not the theoretical response of the closed economy but the improved competitiveness of British exports in world markets. If Keynes rejected the course of relying on cuts in money wages, as he always had, it was not because the economic reasoning was faulty but because of political and social considerations.

By 1930, however, the assumption that cheaper British exports would find an elastic world demand had itself come into question. Competitiveness now meant a competitive scramble between countries which were anxious to secure their share of a contracting world market, thus forcing prices down further. The net effect was to render the whole argument over wage cuts less pertinent. Those who wanted to 'face up' to the problem did not promise a panacea; those who wanted to 'run away' had a fatalistic foreboding that the game was up anyway.[39]

Keynes: I think a fall in wages might easily happen both in the United States and Germany without its happening here; but if it did happen there, in the long run I do not see what we are going to do. It is a race against time.
McKenna: I think so. We must postpone the day as long as we can without a fight.

All of this added up to a strong case against wage cuts as a likely means of increasing British exports; but if it were desirable to strengthen the trade balance, the alternative means of doing this was obviously by decreasing imports. With a strong pound, imports were presumably too cheap just as exports were arguably too dear.[40]

Keynes: In history every country has adopted a tariff, often to a ridiculous extent, in those circumstances. When they have found this maladjustment of Home prices and foreign prices, every country has flown to a tariff to meet the situation.

The tariff–bounty scheme, of course, was explicitly directed to this

---

[39] Ibid. 7 Nov., 27.
[40] Ibid. 40.

problem of adjusting relative prices. It avoided the sort of objection Bevin made against wage cuts by reducing the real value of all British incomes, not just those of vulnerable sections of the working class. But, as Bevin himself persistently reminded the committee, there was an even quicker and more direct remedy for the disparity in prices—devaluation. He protested against Bradbury's proposal 'to take the Gold Standard as more or less *chose jugée*' and insisted that it be regarded as a real issue—with the effect of revealing his colleagues' ultimate priorities.[41]

Bradbury: I am afraid of tampering with Free Trade, and I am also afraid of tampering with the gold standard. If I had to choose between tampering with the gold standard as a remedy and Protection, I should be solid for tampering with the gold standard. I should much prefer it to Protection.
Bevin: I agree.
Lubbock: I should be very sorry to think that the choice of one of those was the dilemma.
Bradbury: So should I.
Bevin: I think it is bound to be one of two things.

The economists on the committee, however, took the other view. Gregory, 'speaking as one of those economists who was in favour of devaluation', did not wish to disturb the settled parity: which was not very different from what Keynes argued.[42]

Keynes: I should like to try these other remedies first. They seem to me much more promising. I agree it is very doubtful how far going off the gold standard on balance would help the situation. It might. It would be a way of bringing money incomes generally in this country into a better equilibrium with the outside world.

In view of the significance which Keynes attached to the initial adoption of an inappropriate parity, his lukewarmness about changing it, even in the course of confidential discussions, may seem surprising. It is surely a powerful if indirect testimony to his mounting conviction that tariffs were necessary. For tariffs not only served the same macro-economic function as devaluation: they promised to meet the Government's exigencies in the winter of 1930–1 in other ways. Whereas going off gold would be seen as a

---

[41] Private session, 29; cf. 7 Nov., 20 and 23 Oct., 23.

[42] Ibid. 23 Oct. 1930, 24; 7 Nov. 1930, 15; cf. Bevin's subsequent charge that 'the Chairman, even Mr Keynes, refused to look at an alternative' (Alan Bullock, *The Life and Times of Ernest Bevin*, i (1960), 496).

political defeat, protection had a potential appeal as a patriotic policy—achieving the same ends not with a whimper but a bang of the drum. When Keynes looked across the table at the bluff figure of Sir Walter Raine, did he see in him the 'ordinary, conservative, unintellectual businessman' of Henderson's imagination? Could such single-minded advocates of tariffs ('whatever may be our Party Political colour'), who prided themselves on 'looking at questions from the business standpoint only', now be brought to accept that a more thorough-going renunciation of *laissez-faire* was requisite?[43] In this sense, Keynes's dream—or pipe-dream—was to give public works the ideological and financial cover of tariffs. 'For the bad effects of the former on business confidence and on the foreign exchanges', he explained early in 1931, 'would be offset by the good effects of the latter; whilst both would increase employment.'[44]

Keynes made public his support for a revenue tariff in the recently amalgamated *New Statesman and Nation* in March 1931. It was a plea to make expansion safe by buttressing confidence. 'Two years ago there was no need to be frightened,' he explained. 'Today it is a different matter.' Having 'thought twice', as the situation demanded, he commended the sort of 'confidence package' he had put to MacDonald the previous summer—essentially a welfare standstill plus a revenue tariff. 'Free traders may, consistently with their faith,' Keynes suggested, 'regard a revenue tariff as our iron ration, which can be used once only in an emergency.'[45] If Keynes hoped that the debate would thus be shifted on the issue of whether the emergency had arrived, rather than whether the traditional Free Trade case had been misconceived, he was to be grievously disappointed. The controversy which his article provoked merely showed that his old political allies—Liberal and Labour alike—had learnt nothing and forgotten nothing. He concluded that 'new paths of thought have no appeal to the fundamentalists of free trade', who had forced him 'to chew over again a lot of stale mutton, dragging me along a route I have known all about as long as I have known anything', and which

---

[43] Raine's remarks as President of the British Chambers of Commerce, deputation to the Chancellor of the Exchequer, 17 Feb. 1931, T. 172/1516. For Henderson see above, ch. 8 n. 107; and for the growth of protectionist pressure, Forrest Capie, *Depression and Protectionism: Britain between the Wars* (1983), chs. 4 and 5, and Philip Williamson, 'Financiers, the Gold Standard and British politics, 1925–31', in John Turner (ed.), *Businessmen and Politics* (1984), 119–20.

[44] *JMK* xx. 488 (foreword to Rupert Trouton, *Unemployment: Its Causes and their Remedies*). [45] *JMK* ix. 235, 238 ('Proposals for a revenue tariff', 7 Mar. 1931).

was nothing but 'a peregrination of the catacombs with a guttering candle'.[46] To Keynes, for whom the appeal of the Liberal party lay in its intellectual vitality and its freedom from vested interests, it was disillusioning to discover the deadweight of its intellectual vested interest.

Among the economists who wrote in criticism of Keynes at this juncture were Gregory and Robbins, who rehearsed in public arguments which they had unavailingly pressed in private. It was Robbins who best isolated the point at issue; and in response Keynes conceded that 'free trade, combined with great mobility of wage rates, is a tenable intellectual position'—one which the author of the *Treatise* might have claimed it expounded. 'The practical reason against it,' Keynes explained, 'which must suffice for the moment, whether we like it or not, is that it is not one of the alternatives between which we are in a position to choose. We are not offered it. It does not exist outside the field of pure hypothesis.'[47]

There was one further point upon which Robbins hit home, by accusing Keynes of resorting to 'the mean and petty devices of economic nationalism'. Keynes could well meet such a charge by pointing out that, just as tariffs were like devaluation and wage cuts in addressing Britain's lack of international competitiveness, so each of these three remedies shared a common limitation. If tariffs were said to snatch a purely national advantage, how different in practice was a competitive wage scramble? In advocating tariffs, Keynes was meeting an immediate difficulty with the weapons that lay to hand; but, as he told the Macmillan Committee, the dimensions of the problem were wider:[48]

My view is that industry, in the world at large, cannot make a profit until there is more enterprise; all we can do is just to undercut our neighbours and get a little more of the profit that is going. We cannot increase the total pool of profit; the only way that one can increase the total pool of profit is by increasing the field of investment in the world at large.

The Macmillan Report

Following its last meeting on 5 December 1930, the Macmillan Committee delegated the drafting of its Report to a group com-

---

[46] *JMK* xx. 505 (comment, *New Statesmen and Nation*, 11 Apr. 1931).
[47] *JMK* xx. 496–7 (Letter, *New Statesmen and Nation*, 21 Mar. 1931).
[48] Private session, 7 Nov. 1930, 7.

prising Keynes, Gregory, Lubbock, Brand, and the chairman. Of these, Keynes was the most active, drawing up a scheme for the Report which was substantially adopted, and drafting the text of most of its original chapters himself. But he was not given a free hand. Lubbock was the Bank of England's watch-dog; Gregory was the conscience of the economics profession; Brand was a constructive but far from compliant critic.

Macmillan himself seemed to be losing interest, possibly because of the conflicting claims of his new legal responsibilities. After chairing the committee with a good lawyer's astuteness in picking up a complex new brief, he displayed a lawyer's propensity to cleanse his mind of it almost immediately. The paragraphs he drafted as a suggested conclusion show that almost none of his recent economic education had stuck permanently. He admitted wearily that 'no revelation has been vouchsafed to us'. He referred disparagingly to the gadgets and devices which had been proposed for temporarily dodging unpleasant facts. 'To live beyond one's means, to dissipate one's capital, to prefer extravagance to thrift, to cultivate dependence rather than independence, pleasure rather than work—such courses for a nation no less than for an individual can have only one end, which financial devices may postpone but which no financial devices can avert.' A timely reminder 'that the word "sterling" which is applied to our currency has acquired a secondary meaning and stands for what is upright and reliable' was his idea of a peroration.[49]

If Keynes achieved nothing else, he ensured that none of Macmillan's homilies survived in the eponymous Report. Keynes's draft began by identifying a disequilibrium between prices and costs, which was attributed chiefly to the return to gold: in which case, the problem was one of adjusting incomes to changes in the value of money. Keynes made his familiar point that modern Britain—with its load of fixed debt, its social conscience, and its democratic government—was 'extremely ill-adapted to violent upward changes in the value of money'.[50] Keynes then included sections on the adequacy of the supply of gold and credit, followed by his account of the functions of Bank rate—an analysis which had remained essentially unchallenged since he presented it in his private evidence. In a

[49] Undated draft by Macmillan in Keynes papers, MC/3; cf. Macmillan, *A Man of Law's Tale* (1952), 196–7.

[50] Draft of 20 Jan. 1931, MC/1; for the scheme of the draft see *JMK* xx. 270–1.

passage omitted in the final Report, the reliance on Bank rate alone to effect the necessary adjustments after the return to gold was singled out for criticism. Keynes next asked how far the fall in prices was due to monetary causes. He answered that it was 'a monetary phenomenon which has occurred as the result of the monetary system failing to solve successfully a problem of unprecedented difficulty and complexity set it by a conjunction of highly intractable non-monetary phenomena'.[51] By and large, all this survived into the Report with only verbal amendment.

Keynes then turned to proposals. On the Gold Standard, his draft of 2 February 1931 was unequivocal that, since there was no risk of being *forced* off, a virtue should be made of the necessity to stay on, by working towards a world monetary system. 'This country is marked out by its traditions and its aptitudes to take up the leadership in this endeavour', proclaimed the financial jingoist. The monetary system should be frankly recognized as a managed system, enjoined the financial radical; and the charge of exercising 'knowledge, judgement and authority' should rest with the Bank of England, averred the financial traditionalist.[52] Keynes's protean and eclectic opportunism in putting this view was considerably dampened and diluted by his more sober colleagues. They were assisted, over measures affecting the Bank, by the discreet efforts of Leith-Ross behind the scenes. 'Ismay feels that there may be considerable difficulties in getting Keynes's proposals turned down,' he warned the Bank at one point, with the purpose of bringing Lubbock into play.[53] Niemeyer might cluck to 'Leithers' over 'recent deliveries of your friend Master Keynes';[54] but Nanny was on hand to prevent any real mischief.

Pushing ahead with his chapter on proposals relating to domestic monetary action, Keynes struck out boldly in a section on the measures relevant to the present emergency. Here he attempted to specify all the possible sources of an increase in output and employment:

   (1) by an increased output of capital goods for use at home;
   (2) by subsidies to exports and tariffs on imports;

[51] Draft of Section III, 2 Feb. 1931, MC/5; cf. *Macmillan Report*, par. 209.
[52] Draft of Pt. II, Section I, MC/5; cf. *Report*, pars. 243 ff.
[53] Leith-Ross to Harvey, 18 Mar. 1931, Bank of England S 44/1 (2); Harvey to Leith-Ross, 20 Mar. 1931, T. 188/275.
[54] Niemeyer to Leith-Ross, 13 Jan. 1931, T. 200/3.

(3) by diminishing savings;
(4) by a reduction of salaries and wages (relatively to similar costs abroad).

What he stressed was that all of these might be relevant but that none was the wholly sufficient and exclusive solution—'in every case it is a question of *balance* of advantage'. Though it might be useful to examine each line of policy in turn—capital development, protection, and wage cuts—his draft suggested that 'the issues are of such a wide character, involving political and social, as well as financial and economic, issues, that a committee, such as ourselves, can scarcely be expected to give a clear-cut adjudication upon them in an agreed document'.[55]

Even this qualified prospectus, however, had gone too far. In a succession of contributions from Brand, Keynes was pulled up in April 1931, forcing him to reconsider the entire strategy of the Report. Keynes attributed the trouble to his failure to emphasize his own fundamental analysis sufficiently—which was, of course, that the interest rate was too high, as it had been during comparably depressed periods of history. 'This time we should probably abolish our existing economic system if present conditions looked like lasting indefinitely,' he wrote. 'More probably still (that is, if I am right), we shall find the solution before things have got quite intolerable.'[56] But the qualms of the other members of the drafting committee were not so easily allayed. Gregory warned Keynes that they could not be expected to swallow the *Treatise* whole and that the absence of scholarly dissent in the six months since its publication was 'simply due to the fact that no one with a sense of responsibility will commit himself in print on so vast a subject without adequate and intensive study'. It was clear that his prospective colleague Hayek, for one, was merely biding his time. Gregory's point was that '*we* have no right, as it seems to me', to make the assumption that the *Treatise* was correct before the academic issue had been settled; and he therefore protested against 'the unnecessary aggravation of the task through the importation into it of J. M. K.'s main thesis'.[57]

These exchanges, though cordial in manner, marked the end of Keynes's attempt to make the *Treatise* into the spine of the

[55] Draft, Pt. II, Section IIIB, 31 Mar. 1931, MC/5.
[56] *JMK* xx. 273–4 (comments on Brand, 7 Apr. 1931); Brand's memoranda are in MC/3.
[57] *JMK* xx. 274–6 (Gregory comment, 17 Apr. 1931).

Macmillan Report. His own draft, he felt, was *Hamlet* without the Prince; but his colleagues had no stomach for all those long soliloquies. The practical upshot was an agreement to differ, with a largely descriptive Report that was consistent with much of Keynes's analysis, but one that stopped short of making recommendations on immediate policy measures. These were supplied instead in a series of addenda, of which the first and most substantial was, not surprisingly, drafted by Keynes.

There were five other signatories of Addendum I. McKenna's support was axiomatic. The Lancashire banker Tulloch had belied his conservative reputation several times during the committees proceedings and had declared his support for tariffs. Frater Taylor was another dark horse—out of the Bank of England stable, and as taciturn as the Governor, but plainly more open to suggestion. Keynes had the support of these three for his draft, which he then showed to Bevin, who also signed, subject to some modification; and the Co-operator Allen joined them. On Bevin's suggestion, Keynes approached the industrialist Lee—'My own feeling is that there is not really much between us'—and also wrote to Raine, having baited the hook with a nice fat tariff. Although neither of them signed Addendum I, they were obviously within touching distance.[58] Brand entered his reservations about public works (on Hopkins–Henderson lines) in Addendum II. Gregory, too, was sceptical about public works and frankly opposed to a tariff, as Addendum III made clear. The hard core of resistance to Keynesian ideas thus comprised Lubbock, a loyal Director of the Bank; Newbold, part MacDonaldite and part crank; and the two unreconstructed individualist peers—the ingenuous Smilesian Macmillan and the sophisticated Gladstonian Bradbury. Bradbury alone refused to sign the Report itself, submitting instead his own memorandum of dissent.

The case made in Addendum I rested on the view that there were only three ways to stimulate employment: by increasing exports, or by substituting home goods for imports, or by increasing home investment. There were thus three practical courses: wage cuts or tariffs or public works. If there had to be cuts in British real incomes,

---

[58] See *JMK* xx. 280–2, for the correspondence. Raine's note of reservation to the *Report*, while disapproving of local authority expenditure, urged the merits of railway electrification and drainage schemes on a large scale, arguing in support that 'it is common knowledge that for every man in ordinary employment another man finds employment to produce the necessities of life for the first-named and his family' (261).

it was argued, they should not be confined to wage-earners. Only Bevin and Allen spoke up for devaluation as a means to this end; the rest followed Keynes in preferring a tariff–bounty scheme, and the theoretical beauty of a national treaty got a mention. (The seven appropriate remedies which Keynes had outlined in his private evidence still constituted the framework of choice.) On tariffs as such, the existence of disequilibrium was held to invalidate the free trade case, meaning that British output could actually be increased; protection would boost confidence and would facilitate the adoption of a programme of capital development. Public works, finally, remained the crux of the Keynsian policy agenda. In favour, the multiplier effect upon secondary employment was now invoked. Against, the Treasury View was cited from the 1927 Government statement to the ILO, and from the 1929 White Paper which 'was also capable of interpretation' as a proposition about crowding-out. 'We gathered, however,' Keynes commented, 'from the evidence of Sir R. Hopkins that it would be a mistake to attribute this view to the Treasury at the present time.'[59]

What, then, was the argument now about? The point that crowding-out only held good at full capacity was conceded on all sides. 'So long as capital equipment and labour-power are out of employment, and current savings are hoarded because of lack of confidence, it is, *of course*, true that national works are not impossible because they cannot be financed except at the expense of withdrawing resources from other possible avenues of employment.' The signatories of Addendum I all accepted this; but so—of course—did Gregory, from whose Addendum III it is quoted.[60] It was the reformulated Treasury View, that there would be an offset to the value of public works through loss of confidence, to which Addendum I now turned, arguing that 'if "official" investment is successful in restoring the volume of output and of profits, this may help to restore the business optimism which is a necessary condition of expansion'. Likewise, the Budget burdens were put in the context of a prospective restoration of prosperity which would itself help to spring the trap. 'The main obstacle in the way of remedying unemployment, by means of organised schemes of investment,' it was stated, 'is probably to be found, not so much in any of these arguments, as in the practical difficulties of initiative and

[59] Addendum I, par. 47 (i); reprinted in *JMK* xx. 283–309.
[60] *Report*, 229 (emphasis supplied).

organisation'. While these were real enough, the point was to surmount and master them through longer-term planning of public investment.[61]

Having said all this, the Addendum suggested that 'the fundamental objection' of the critics was 'on a different plane of thought'. This was the view 'that all these devices are merely temporary shifts to enable us to postpone facing the problem, which sooner or later we shall be compelled to face, namely, that our money costs of production are too high compared with those elsewhere.' No one who had listened to the evidence given on behalf of the authorities would have doubted the percipience of this assessment. 'The ultimate differences between those who feel this and those who think that it is worth while to gain a breathing space,' Keynes concluded, 'are not so much matters of theory as of the practical judgement of probabilities and of what is most prudent.'[62]

Crisis

There was no need for a new theory to justify either public works or tariffs. Both were easily accommodated as special cases within the analysis of the *Treatise*. 'It may be that the attainment of equilibrium in accordance with our traditional principles would be the best solution—if we could get it,' Keynes had written. 'But if social and political forces stand in the way of our getting it, then it will be better to reach equilibrium by such a device as differential terms for home investment relatively to foreign investment, and even, perhaps, such a falling off from grace as differential terms for home-produced goods relatively to foreign-produced goods, than to suffer indefinitely the business losses and unemployment which disequilibrium means.' This case for a tariff, of course, rested on 'the assumption that the remedy of reducing money wages, fluidity of which is essential to the free-trade position, was not available'.[63] It was a matter of practical judgement to decide whether it was in fact available. What the *Treatise* stated was, in this respect, only the application of orthodox neo-classical economics to the real-world difficulties of rigid prices—

---

[61] Addendum I, pars. 47 (ii), 48.
[62] Ibid., par. 52.
[63] *JMK* vi. 169, 167.

when 'human nature makes it impossible for some things to find their proper levels quick enough'.[64]

Keynes had already succeeded, by the time the Macmillan Committee was appointed, in rendering the Treasury View, as a general principle about displacement, an untenable doctrine. Of course Archimedes could have a bath, without spilling any water, *if the bath were half-empty in the first place.* Gregory, Pigou, Clay, Henderson, Stamp, Robertson—none of them dissented from this proposition; nor did that prudent and practical layman, Sir Richard Hopkins. By August 1930, moreover, the elasticity of supply for output was salient in Keynes's thinking—an egg which Hawtrey may have been sitting on but which Kahn succeeded in hatching. When the May Committee later demanded an actual reversal of capital expenditure plans, Keynes could reasonably accuse them of 'flying in the face of a considerable weight of opinion. For the main opposition to the public works remedy is based on the practical difficulties of devising a reasonable programme, not on the principle.'[65] The real arguments about both public works and free trade, then, partly turned on judgement and prudence, but partly involved also the importation on both sides of moral and political considerations. The authorities fell back upon a Gladstonian language of probity and morality which eschewed mere party politics but gave them a deep affinity with Snowden—their favourite Chancellor. Keynes, conversely, took to mocking Snowden's attachment to 'principles' and could be more overt in his political objectives.

In the late 1920s Keynes had not been shy about declaring his Liberal allegiance and clearly hoped to use the Liberal party as a vehicle for his own ideas, which were indeed evolved under the pressure of political contingencies. In the second part of 1930, serious negotiations continued between Lloyd George and the Labour Government about unemployment policy; but Keynes was not directly involved in these. The recasting of the Liberal proposals in *How to Tackle Unemployment*, published in October 1930, took a step back from public works and kept its distance from tariffs. Lloyd George had decided to propitiate 'confidence' by talking economy rather than protection; whereas the programme on which Mosley was currently campaigning was closer to Keynes's approach. The Liberals found that their schemes, notably for road-building,

---

[64] *JMK* xx. 490 (*Daily Mail*, 13 Mar. 1931).
[65] *JMK* ix. 143 ('The Economy Report', 15 Aug. 1931).

encountered formidable technical objections from the Ministry of Transport; and in any case the political will to clinch a Liberal–Labour accommodation was lacking at this stage. The task of preparing a White Paper which would effectively counter the Liberal proposals—practically an annual exercise for the Treasury—fell to the veteran gamekeeper Hopkins, now assisted by the veteran poacher Henderson; and its measured scepticism is a tribute to their close collaboration.[66]

Keynes's disenchantment was less with his erstwhile proposals than with his old party, in so far as it was inconstant in its support of them. On the same day that he finished work on the Macmillan Report, he wrote to a Liberal official that he was 'keener than ever on schemes of home development, and indeed on much of the Yellow Book'. But the party's current 'concentration on the cries of the past, such as free trade, quite regardless of circumstances', made him feel 'that life has gone out of it—which I did not at all feel when the ideas of the Yellow Book were in the forefront'. Nor was the Labour party, with its equally hidebound dogmas, any better in this respect. He could sympathize with Churchill's dread of 'a General Election in which eight million voters were taught to sing in chorus, "Make the foreigner pay", and eight million more to chant in unison, "give the rich man's money to the poor, and so increase the consuming power"; and five other millions to intone, "Your food will cost you more."'[67]

The real differences over economic policy, Keynes believed, were not properly expressed through the existing party system. Snowden's policy, in which he was supported by Liberals like Herbert Samuel, rested on trust that the invisible hand would in the long run restore equilibrium. 'The first Socialist Chancellor is also the last adherent of true blue *laissez-faire*,' was how Keynes put it.[68] But the Government flinched from enforcing the policy of wage cuts which would have made these natural tendencies effective. The real alternative, then, was some kind of planning. The political problem was that 'party organisation and personal loyalties cut across the fundamental

[66] 'Statement of the principal measures taken by H. M. Government in connection with Unemployment', Cmd. 3746 (1930). The Treasury's draft is in T. 172/1734, and the Hopkins–Henderson correspondence (Dec. 1930) in T. 175/43. See also Robert Skidelsky, *Politicians and the Slump* (1967), 222–7, and David Marquand, *Ramsay MacDonald* (1977), 552–4.

[67] *JMK* xx. 528 (Keynes to Aubrey Herbert, 29 May 1931); W. S. Churchill, *Thoughts and Adventures* (1932), 179 (Romanes lecture).

[68] *JMK* xx. 523 ('Mr Snowden's Budget', 28 Apr. 1931).

differences of opinion', obscuring the logic of the choices that had to be made. The three parties, as they appeared at the end of 1930, ought to comprise: first, the Snowden–Samuel position, which Keynes now called Liberal; second, the position of Beaverbrook and the archetypal Labourist J. H. Thomas, which was essentially Conservative; and finally, a 'Socialist' party enlisting Lloyd George, MacDonald, Bevin, and Mosley.[69] Clearly this was Keynes's own preference.

Keynes thus expressed support for Mosley in December 1930, when he published his Manifesto, broadly along the lines of his earlier Memorandum, calling for protection and planning. With the Liberal and Labour parties clinging to free trade, Mosley represented the sort of fresh thinking in economic policy which Keynes thought necessary, and he saw the attractions of the New Party which Mosley formed on leaving the Labour party in February 1931. Yet Harold Nicolson, who was heavily implicated in this venture, makes it clear that Keynes had reservations, if only because it was 'almost impossible, with these vast constituencies of today, to get across an economic programme when the only arguments the electorate can understand are the simple political slogans'.[70]

Keynes efforts to bring about a revolution in economic policy did not strike him as successful. 'During the last 12 years,' he told MPs in 1931, 'I have had very little influence, if any, on policy.'[71] The assault on public opinion via the Liberal party had not produced the desired results in 1929. The EAC and its committee of economists did not loosen the grip of the Treasury over economic strategy. Through the Macmillan Committee, Keynes had for a while seized the initiative in 1930; but by the time its Report appeared in July 1931 there was little likelihood that it would herald immediate changes.

The mounting economic crisis of 1930–1 made unemployment a bigger problem than ever, but one which seemed less susceptible to reformist tinkering. The proposals of the Yellow Book in 1928–9 had envisaged cutting the dole queue in half when it stood at around a million. It was a call to go on the offensive against unemployment. By the time of the Macmillan Report, Keynes had won many of the arguments which would have justified this plan; but by then the unemployment figures had more than doubled. Fears of economic

[69] *JMK* xx. 474 ('Sir Oswald Mosley's Manifesto', *Nation*, 13 Dec. 1930).
[70] Harold Nicolson, *Diaries and Letters, 1930–1939* (1966), 74 (6 May 1931).
[71] *JMK* xx. 611 (notes for speech to MPs, 16 Sept. 1931).

collapse could no longer reasonably be dismissed and hopes of conquering unemployment could no longer reasonably be entertained. There were still economic choices to be made, but within an essentially defensive context.

The defence of sterling lay at the root of the problem, both in theory and in practice. Addendum I of the Macmillan Report indicated three practical courses: wage cuts, tariffs, and public works. Given the existing interest rates, one or other of these was necessary to relieve unemployment. In theory, of course, as the *Treatise* reiterated, a fall in Bank rate could itself restore domestic equilibrium—but it remained jammed at a higher level because of the Gold Standard. In the real world the maintenance of the existing parity became the overriding issue within a month of the Macmillan Report's publication.

Although the Treasury officials were inclined to blame 'the political agitation against the gold standard carried on here by Keynes, Bevin, Mosley and Co.' for part of the trouble, in fact they knew that the Macmillan Committee would not countenance devaluation.[72] It was the publication of another official report—that of the May Committee on National Expenditure—which precipitated the British political crisis in the first days of August 1931. The May Report presented an alarmist estimate of the scale of the prospective Budget deficit but one which, as Hopkins recognized, would be 'flashed around the world'.[73] The Government was thus faced with a true crisis of confidence; it was now largely in the hands of the Bank of England in taking steps which were adjusted to the psychology of the international financial market. McKenna, for example, as chairman of the Midland Bank, ultimately fell into line in supporting deflationary measures to hold the position.

Ever since his private evidence in February 1930, Keynes had consistently presented his professional advice under two heads: what was appropriate and what he himself preferred. However elaborate his taxonomy of remedies, his 'peculiarity' had always been to find something in favour of each of them—as compared with the 'unforgivable' attitude of negation. By opting to drift, with the

---

[72] Memo for Snowden, n.d., T. 188/275 (?Leith-Ross, amended by Hopkins).

[73] Quoted in Philip Williamson, 'The formation of the National Government, 1929–31', Ph.D. thesis (Cambridge, 1987), 330; and id., 'A "bankers' ramp"? Financiers and the British political crisis of August 1931', *EHR* 99 (1984), 770–806, for an excellent account of the crisis.

rudder jammed, the Government was merely prolonging the misery of unemployment and exacerbating the inevitable reckoning. Drift and deflation were not alternatives but foreseeable stages—the longer the drift, the harsher the deflation—and it takes hindsight to discern in this a policy of masterly inactivity. By August 1931 the choice was simple: between the orthodoxy of deflation and some form of planning. The effect of the May Report, Keynes told MacDonald on 5 August, was to bring him 'hard up against a prompt and definite decision whether I am in favour of making deflation effective, or whether I prefer to seek another exit'. Since his advice was 'that we do *not* attempt to make the deflation effective', he had a double criticism of the May Report. Not only did it seek the wrong ends (which was admittedly a matter of opinion) but it proposed inappropriate means, and would therefore prove 'futile and disastrous'.[74] Keynes explained himself in print by specifying the negative multiplier effects of a cut in government spending upon employment, savings, profits, and output—thus eroding the net reduction in the Budget deficit. 'There is nothing rational to dispute about,' he claimed, 'except the size of the various items entering into this equation.'[75]

To MacDonald, moreover, Keynes cited 'the new fact' that it was 'now nearly *certain* that we shall go off the existing gold parity at no distant date'. Hence his striking suggestion that, in effect, the Prime Minister supersede the Bank of England and 'consult a Committee of all living ex-Chancellors of the Exchequer, whether they believe that deflation *à outrance* is possible and are in favour of attempting it, or whether we should not at once suspend gold convertibility and then take collective thought as to the next step'.[76] This proposal seems at first sight distinctly bizarre if the logistics of summoning an actual committee are envisaged. It may, however, be explained figuratively and by *ad hominem* considerations—as a notional appeal to the judgement of these particular ex-Chancellors, none of whom was so impermeable to Keynes's influence as the current incumbent, Snowden. The old Coalitionists, Horne and Austen Chamberlain,

---

[74] *JMK* xx. 590–3 (Keynes to MacDonald, 5 Aug. 1931). My interpretation thus differs from that in the challenging article by Ross McKibbin, 'The economic policy of the second Labour Government, 1929–31', *Past and Present*, 68 (Aug. 1975), 95–123, esp. 114.

[75] *JMK* ix. 141–5 ('The Economy Report', *New Statesman and Nation*, 15 Aug. 1931).

[76] *JMK* xx. 591.

were comparatively amenable, and Baldwin too, though Neville Chamberlain was another matter. On the other hand, Lloyd George and McKenna were both included; and so was Churchill, now ruefully apprehensive that a financial crisis might break. 'I hope we shall hang Montagu Norman if it does,' he wrote. 'I will certainly turn King's evidence against him.'[77]

Needless to say, there was no such committee; Norman had collapsed of his own accord; the Government became locked into negotiations on the conditions for support of sterling; the option of devaluation was not seriously explored. Keynes's advice did not shift. He reaffirmed on 12 August that, while it was 'still possible for us to keep on the gold standard if we deliberately decide to do so', some kind of 'drastic and sensational action' was called for. He told the Prime Minister that he would 'support for the time being whichever policy was made, provided the decision was accompanied by action sufficiently drastic to make it effective'.[78] It was the policy of drift which, as so often before, he most feared and despised. Bevin's belated effort to use the TUC to put devaluation on the agenda was, however, already doomed; and MacDonald was left to meet the political consequences of the logic of Snowden's economic policy. The Labour Government in fact fell before sterling did so; but the National Government which MacDonald formed in its place, amid a welter of recrimination, proved incapable of avoiding devaluation. In September 1931 Britain went off the Gold Standard.

Having drifted into devaluation, however, it could be said that Britain avoided the odium of a calculated decision to default. 'As events have turned out,' Keynes wrote the following week, 'we have got the relief we needed and, at the same time, the claims of honour have been, in the judgement of the whole world, satisfied to the utmost.'[79] What was this relief? It surely meant that Bank rate no longer had the task of maintaining an artificially high parity for sterling. With a lower exchange rate, British exports would no longer be uncompetitive and the need to reduce wages would disappear. Moreover, Keynes would, presumably, be bound to withdraw his

[77] Churchill to E. Marsh, 7 Aug. 1931, in Martin Gilbert, *Winston S. Churchill*, v, Companion Pt. 2 (1981), 339; McKibbin calls the idea of a committee 'preposterous', op. cit. 111 n.

[78] *JMK* xx. 594 (Keynes to MacDonald, 12 Aug. 1931). Williamson suggests Keynes had changed his ground (thesis, 350); cf. Skidelsky, *Politicians and the Slump*, ch. 13, Marquand, *MacDonald*, ch. 25.

[79] *JMK* ix. 245 (*Sunday Express*, 27 Sept. 1931).

support for tariffs. Indeed he did so, immediately after devaluation, on the ground that 'the events of the last week have made a great difference'[80] (though not, for him, a lasting difference). Furthermore, with Bank rate unhitched and unjammed, the special case for public works was no longer applicable. Instead, however, of abandoning his advocacy of public works, now that its theoretical premiss had disappeared, Keynes was, within little more than a year, ready to argue this case on the basis of an entirely new theory. Why?

---

[80] *JMK* ix. 243 (letter to *The Times*, 29 Sept. 1931).

PART IV

A Revolution in Economic Theory?

PROLOGUE TO PART IV

If tactical commitments and opportunism fuelled Keynes's progress towards the position of the *Treatise*, can the origins of the *General Theory* be explained along similar lines? Was it simply 'a tract for the times'? Keynes's abandonment of the *Treatise*, so soon after publication, is remarkable, given the forceful way in which he deployed its rhetoric about a gap between savings and investment. But this appealing rhetoric concealed difficulties in the formal logic of the theory. Did it mean, asked critics, that the excess savings took the form of hoarding? Keynes was forced to explain himself. And how could excess savings exactly equal business losses? Hawtrey played a significant part here in exposing anomalies in the definitions used in the *Treatise*. Moreover, the 'circus' of younger economists at Cambridge—notably Richard Kahn and James Meade—worked out a line of analysis which reorientated the whole argument. Instead of a dog called savings wagging his tail labelled investment, they suggested the tail was in fact wagging the dog. This was the doctrine seized on as the 'multiplier'—the wider implications of which are perhaps better appreciated if its original formulation as 'Mr Meade's Relation' is kept in mind. These developments (examined in Chapter 10) were inescapably somewhat technical in form, but their gist was such as to make the author of the *Treatise* see that he would have to 'work it out all over again'.

Keynes subsequently regarded his progress towards the theory of effective demand as the outcome of a series of 'moments of transition'. It is an account which stands up to historical scrutiny, and it suggests that there were four chronological stages, of which the principle of effective demand constituted the second. Since the third stage (the explanation of interest in terms of liquidity preference) had demonstrably been reached by November 1932, it seems that the crucial breakthrough must have come earlier than has generally been supposed. If this is so, the nature of the theory of effective demand must be essentially as Keynes understood and explained it by the end of 1932. He himself constantly reiterated that 'the simple basic ideas' were more important than the forms in which they were expressed. Looking both at his students' lecture notes and at the architecture of the *General Theory*, it is apparent that Keynes continually stressed the distinction between actions which were possible for *one* and for *all* simultaneously. This can be called the fallacy of composition; it is the methodological foundation of macro-economics; and it became the unifying conception in Keynes's work.

The *General Theory* was thus a fundamental challenge to the theoretical basis of neo-classical economics. No longer did Keynes join with Pigou in identifying the rigidities which allowed disequilibrium to persist in the real world. Instead, he joined issue with Pigou, arguing that an equilibrium at less than full employment was possible—indeed, in the real world, normal. For equilibrium described not an optimal state towards which market forces tended, but a position of rest which no market forces would budge. Savings and investment, in short, were equilibrated not through a flexible level of interest rates but through a flexible level of output and employment. Here was the revolution in economic theory of which Keynes now spoke.

While the writing of the *Treatise* can, in important respects, be explained along 'externalist' lines, by invoking the political context in which it was conceived, the composition of the *General Theory* must, in essentials, be understood in 'internalist' terms. It was the outcome of a process of intellectual discovery rather than of political invention. Keynes's own lack of party affiliations needs to be emphasized. Moreover, his essays in policy in this period—notably *The Means to Prosperity* (1933)—while drawing upon the theory of effective demand, stand apart from it. The *General Theory* itself contains almost nothing by way of immediate practical guidance. Nor did Keynes place so much faith in 'the presuppositions of Harvey Road' as to imagine that it would achieve a bloodless triumph on a purely intellectual plane. In fact he acknowledged without rancour that his ideas would be picked up by different people in different ways—among academics, who argued over 'expectations' as against a more determinate approach, just as among a wider public whose ulterior passions would inevitably be enlisted. Knowing all this, Keynes none the less confidently proposed his revolution in 'the way the world thinks about economic problems'.

10

The *Treatise* under the harrow

At the time of its publication, Keynes set a high value on the *Treatise*, as can be seen from the confidence of his references to it before the Macmillan Committee. It is safe to dismiss the idea that he was simply struggling to get it off his hands 'in order to clear the way for the *General Theory*'.[1] Yet if anyone supposed that this would be Keynes's last word, he was to be disillusioned. F. A. Hayek, Tooke Professor of Economics at the LSE from 1931, has recalled that, when he was asked to review the *Treatise*, he 'put a great deal of work into two long articles on it', which appeared in *Economica* in August 1931 and February 1932. Here was a sustained critique of Keynes's *magnum opus* from an eminent economist schooled in continental analysis. 'Great was my disappointment,' claimed Hayek, 'when all this effort seemed wasted because after the appearance of the second part of my article he told me that he had in the mean time changed his mind and no longer believed what he had said in that work.' To Hayek the subsequent moral was clear; that the *General Theory* belied its name by being 'a tract for the times' and in this respect characteristic of a man who was 'more of an artist and politician than a scholar or student'.[2]

This raises a question put even more sharply by Harry Johnson. Was Keynes 'an opportunist and an operator', whose brilliance as an applied theorist only meant that 'the theory was applied when it was useful in supporting a proposal that might win current political acceptance, and dropped along with the proposal when the immediate purpose had been served or had failed'? There is nothing inherently implausible in this view, which partly reflects a gibe already in circulation by 1931: 'Where five economists are gathered together there will be six conflicting opinions and two of them will be

---

[1] Elizabeth S. Johnson and Harry G. Johnson, 'The social and intellectual origins of the *General Theory*', reprinted in their book *The Shadow of Keynes* (Oxford, 1978), 65–83, at 69, from *Hist. of Pol. Econ.*, vi (1974), 261–77.

[2] F. A. Hayek, *A Tiger by the Tail*, ed. Sudha R. Shenoy (Institute of Economic Affairs, 1972), 100, 103–4.

held by Keynes!'[3] The charge of intellectual inconsistency, as has been seen, is often misconceived, arising from a confusion of theory with policy, ideal solutions with second-best remedies, and rational strategies with Keynes's own preferences.

Yet in the 1920s it is true that Keynes's policy intuitions, fuelled by his political commitments, had often outrun the justifying theory, which was dragged along behind until ultimately they were reconciled in the exposition of the *Treatise* to the Macmillan Committee. The *General Theory* has likewise been depicted as 'the apotheosis of opportunism', on the grounds that 'a new theory' would be 'virtually certain to sell', if it satisfied the proviso that 'to be a new theory it had to set up and knock down an orthodox theory'.[4] If Johnson's hypothesis were valid, one would expect the shift from the *Treatise* position to be signalled by some more obvious external ideological purchase available to the *General Theory*. Conversely, one would not expect to find the process inaugurated by a fundamental transformation in the internal structure of its logic. The making of the theory of effective demand is the theme of this chapter and the next, and it will be examined with these implications in mind.

'The propensity to hoard'

The *Treatise* was, as Keynes had fully expected, 'exposed to the hostile criticism of the world for an appreciable time',[5] but he was less happy in arguing out its propositions than he had anticipated. A major difficulty was the ambiguity which developed over the role of hoarding. This controversy was joined not only by Hayek, whom Keynes privately identified as lacking 'that measure of "good will" which an author is entitled to expect of a reader',[6] but by Robertson, who was broadly in sympathy with Keynes's endeavour. Both attributed to Keynes the view that the excess of saving over investment could be measured by inactive deposits in banks.

[3] 'Keynes and British economics', in Milo Keynes (ed.), *Essays on John Maynard Keynes* (1975), 115, reprinted in Johnson, *Shadow of Keynes*, 211; Thomas Jones, *A Diary with Letters, 1931–50* (1954), 19 (20 Oct. 1931).

[4] M. Keynes (ed.), *Essays*, 116; Johnson, *Shadow of Keynes*, 212; cf. 27 for Elizabeth Johnson's apparently dissident view that the *General Theory* was required by Keynes's 'intellectual honesty and concern for economic science'.

[5] *JMK* xx. 87 (Macmillan evidence, 21 Feb. 1930).

[6] Keynes's comment was noted on his copy of *Economica*, *JMK* xiii. 243.

As Robertson's testimony to the Macmillan Committee had shown, he was close to Keynes position in identifying a gap between saving and investment, but insisted on citing the existence of idle balances as prime evidence of this. It is not therefore surprising that, in his review of the *Treatise*, Robertson, despite other cavils, professed 'no doubt that Mr Keynes is right in laying stress on "hoarding" as a dominant feature of trade depression'. But neither is it surprising that Keynes gave the teeth of this gift horse a gracelessly close inspection.[7]

By 'hoarding' does he here mean (1) 'an increase in inactive deposits', or (2) 'an increased propensity to hoard', or (3) 'an excess of saving over investment'? Only in cases (2) and (3) is he giving my meaning correctly.

For if Robertson construed the *Treatise* in the first sense, he was falling into the same error for which Keynes privately castigated Pigou.[8]

A. C. P.'s interpretation of my theory seems to be this. An excess of saving is only another way of talking about an increase of inactive deposits; an increase of inactive deposits means a decrease in the velocity of circulation; thus, when I say that an excess of saving leads to a fall in the price of consumption goods, I am only repeating in a very complicated way the old story that a fall in the velocity of circulation must bring prices down, other things being equal. But, truly, this is not what I am saying.

Keynes should, perhaps, have reflected that if friends and colleagues like Robertson and Pigou none the less took him to be saying this, he was himself largely to blame. In particular, he was paying the price for his silver-tongued facility in finding a formula to which they could all subscribe in the evidence heard by the Macmillan Committee. His *sotto voce* reservations at the time—'I was using Professor Pigou's word for convenience'[9]—had not been enough to allay the impression that Keynes's own analysis could be couched in terms of hoarding.

In order to clarify his meaning, Keynes put forward in May 1931 a new elucidation of how the prices of liquid and non-liquid assets were

---

[7] Robertson, 'Mr Keynes's theory of money', *Econ. Jnl.*, 41 (1931), 395–411, at 409; Keynes, 'A rejoinder', ibid. 423, reprinted in *JMK* xiii. 235. See also Gilbert, *Keynes's Impact on Monetary Economics*, 70–2.

[8] Variorum of Keynes to Robertson, 5 May 1931, and 'A rejoinder', *JMK* xiii. 226 and n. 2.

[9] *Macmillan Evidence*, Q. 6625; see above, ch. 8 n. 85.

determined. His object was to show that 'hoarding' was important in his system not as an actual *process* but as a psychological *motive* which price changes had to offset. He told Robertson that when there was extra demand for investment, the price of all existing investment goods would 'have to rise sufficiently to induce the existing holders, given their degree of bearishness, to part with non-liquid assets ... Presumably this will mean some increase in the price of non-liquid assets, how much depending on the shape of the curve.' In redrafting this passage for publication, he described this sort of reluctance to hold non-liquid assets not as 'bearishness' (the *Treatise* term) but as the 'propensity to hoard'. Keynes also summarized the argument afresh: 'What the state of mind of the public towards holding money, and the changes in this state of mind, determine is the price of non-liquid assets'—it depended on 'the propensity to hoard'.[10] In defending and explicating the *Treatise*, Keynes had been pushed into saying more than is to be found there in its discussion of the bearishness of the public.[11] It would, however, be wrong to jog his elbow at this point and simply write 'liquidity preference', which, as will be seen, did not emerge as a proper concept until there was a proper job of work for it to do.

When he replied to Hayek's criticisms on 'hoarding', therefore, Keynes acknowledged that since Hayek was not alone 'in falling into this misapprehension (or into some more subtle variant of it) it must be my own fault at least in part'.[12] In writing to a research student in Hayek's department at the LSE in December 1931, Keynes was already saying, 'I must be more lucid next time'.[13] One of his publications had been entitled *A Revision of the Treaty*; would the next be *A Revision of the Treatise?*

Keynes's difficulty was that he did not have concepts that were at once formally rigorous and rhetorically persuasive. The distinction between saving and investment was a splendid means of conveying that they were different activities, that they need not be equal, and that their economic roles needed to be distinguished. In the fine passage on thrift and enterprise in the *Treatise*, Keynes could claim that 'mere abstinence is not enough by itself to build cities or to

---

[10] *JMK* xiii. 228–9, 230–1.
[11] *JMK* v. 128–31.
[12] *JMK* xiii. 246 ('The pure theory of money: a reply to Dr Hayek', *Economica*, Nov. 1931).
[13] *JMK* xiii. 243 (to Nicholas Kaldor, 9 Dec. 1931).

drain fens', and that it was 'enterprise which builds and improves the world's possessions'. Thus, though 'thrift may be the handmaid and nurse of enterprise', the felicity of this relationship could not be presumed.[14] Its problematic nature, in short, was thrown into relief by the rhetoric. In this sense, Keynes had found a striking way of formulating his insight that the dynamics of the economy stem from the extent to which the expectations (of entrepreneurs) are cheated or enhanced (in outcome).

In order to maintain that saving and investment might be unequal, however, the 'fundamental equations' of the *Treatise* had to employ a formal definition of income which excluded 'windfall' gains or losses. If expectations were realized, there would, of course, be no such windfalls (and equilibrium would persist).[15] In that case, savings could unambiguously be defined as income *minus* consumption. Now the value of output is by definition the same as total income, which represents the money available to purchase it. Since income can only be spent on consumption goods *or* investment goods, it follows that investment can be defined as income *minus* consumption—the same definition as that for savings. Thus savings are equal to investment, *provided that expectations are realized*. But if not, not.

This was the story the *Treatise* told. Its novelty, of course, lay not in the equilibrium case, when saving and investment were equal, but in the disequilibrium case when they were unequal. Here, everything depended upon saying that it was the *expected* profit for entrepreneurs which defined income. But, under conditions of over-saving, consumption was necessarily cut back. If demand for consumption goods were reduced, without a compensating increase in that for investment goods, the value of output as a whole necessarily fell. That part of income, therefore, which entrepreneurs had expected to constitute their normal profit margin had simply gone missing. It was fairy gold which never materialized. But the *Treatise* definition of income comprised the expected, not the realized, level of receipts.

By doing so, it made its 'fundamental equations' add up in the same way as its rhetoric implied. Investment was defined as equal to actual remuneration minus consumption. Robertson's difficulty really

[14] *JMK* vi. 132.
[15] Fausto Vicarelli's lucid account of the fundamental equations leaves itself open to misapprehension in saying: 'Hence the only condition for equilibrium—in the sense of nil pressure for change—is when *profits* are zero.' *Keynes: The instability of capitalism* (Milan, 1977; London, 1984), 65–71, at 69. By *profits* (my italics) throughout this paragraph, *windfall* profits must be understood.

stemmed from the fact that the definition of saving was not symmetrical with this. As Kahn told Keynes, 'surely Dennis is merely adopting a perfectly simple-minded and natural definition of saving—receipts minus expenditure'[16]—in which case it would indeed have been the same as investment. But the *Treatise* treated saving as the residual, not from 'receipts' but from 'income', defined to include the fairy gold. It can be seen that the excess of saving over investment is equal to this unexpected loss (a 'windfall'). Robertson thus had a point when he cautioned readers about this 'extremely confusing terminology':[17]

How many of those who have taken up the cry that a slump is due to excess of Savings over Investment, and a boom to be an excess of Investment over Savings, realise that the savings which are so deplorably abundant during a slump consist largely of entrepreneurs' incomes which are not being spent, for the simple reason that they have not been earned?

According to the *Treatise*, excess savings exactly counterbalanced unexpected or windfall losses, being a product, indeed, of the difference between the anticipated income level and that actually realized. Excess savings were thus spilt upon the ground in covering business losses, meaning that only part of the desired savings were actually manifested in productive investments. The windfall thus measured the extent by which actual incomes had been reduced. Now another way of putting all this would be to say that savings and investment, though necessarily equal, were only brought into equality by changes in the level of income—but this is to jump ahead to the theory of effective demand. As long as Keynes remained faithful to the *Treatise* formulation, there was an ambiguity over what happened to excess savings (which, going to finance losses, did not constitute part of net savings at all). This is surely why Keynes was so persistently misunderstood to maintain that 'hoarding' was the explanation.

'Working it out all over again'

Keynes had no more conscientious nor rigorous nor persistent critic than Ralph Hawtrey. Hawtrey began reading the *Treatise* from the

---

[16] *JMK* xiii. 238 (Kahn comments, 15 Aug. 1931). For Keynes's subsequent (1934) discussion of the two definitions of income see *JMK* xiii. 424–5.

[17] *Econ. Jnl.*, 41 (1931), 407.

proof-sheets Keynes sent him in April 1930, interlocking with the work of the Macmillan Committee. He prepared a lengthy critique during the summer of 1930 and sent the corrected draft to Keynes at the end of October, having checked his references with the final published text of the *Treatise*. This draft was then revised for the Macmillan Committee, with the benefit of Keynes's own comments, as an official paper, which was completed by the end of 1930, but not published at the time. It was this text which Hawtrey amended and expanded in 1932 for publication in *The Art of Central Banking*. 'You have taken amazing pains about my book,' Keynes told him; and assured him that, whatever their disagreements, he had 'no complaints of misrepresentation or misunderstanding'.[18]

Hawtrey's approach was highly characteristic, beginning in the summer of 1930 with issues of definition which his exact scholarship was well suited to resolve. 'Since "savings" are the difference between earnings and expenditure on consumption,' he wrote, 'and "investment" is the difference between the value of output and expenditure on consumption, it follows that the difference between "savings" and "investment" is equal to the difference between earnings and the value of output.'[19] In fact, they were only different to the extent that actual remuneration differed from the *Treatise* definition of 'income'—that is, by excluding 'what in ordinary usage is called profit'. The much-vaunted difference between saving and investment, Hawtrey maintained, 'is simply another name for the windfall gains or losses or for the difference between prices and costs of output', and depended therefore on 'movements of the price level relative to

---

[18] *JMK* xiii. 172 (to Hawtrey, 1 June 1932). It is useful to discriminate between six versions of the text of 'Mr Keynes's *Treatise on Money*', which will be cited subsequently by capital letter only:

A: MS, summer 1930, Hawtrey Papers, HTRY 11/3;

B: TS, pp. 1–67, Oct. 1930, Keynes Papers, TM/12; as referred to in Keynes to Hawtrey, 28 Nov. 1930, *JMK* xiii. 139–49, with excerpts from B printed, ibid. 150–64;

C: MS of first part of Macmillan Committee draft, ?early Dec. 1930, incorporating pp. 2–5, 14–16, 17, 22–5, from B (namely, pars. 31–8, 41–4, 46, 75–83, from E), in HTRY 11/4;

D: TS of C, with MS par. nos., ?30 Dec. 1930, +pp. 40–67 of B (namely, pars. 108–213 of E), in HTRY 11/4;

E: Macmillan Committee, Paper No. 66, Jan. 1931, pars. 1–213, in HTRY 11/3 and PRO T. 200/3;

F: published text in R. G. Hawtrey, *The Art of Central Banking* (1933), 332–411, following E on 332–4 (pars. 3–16), 336–44 (pars. 20–52), 365–71 (pars. 71–85), 379–84 (pars. 86–102), and 384–411 (pars. 108–213, omitting 150 and 193).

[19] B, 5.

costs'.[20] Hawtrey thought that fluctuation in the level of stocks was crucial—'It is mainly on this point that I find it necessary to differ from Mr Keynes's analysis'—since it disclosed that the *Treatise* only recorded a disturbance from equilibrium to the extent that prices rather than output changed.[21]

In a highly influential study, Leijonhufvud identified the main innovation of the *General Theory* as its 'systematic analysis of the behaviour of a system that reacts to disturbances through *quantity adjustments*, rather than through price-level or wage-rate adjustments'. The Marshallian analysis, by contrast, was taken to postulate an infinitely adjustable price mechanism. On this reading, therefore, the essence of the Keynesian revolution in economic theory was to *reverse* the Marshallian ranking order for speed of adjustment as between *price* and *output*. And why a revolution was necessary 'becomes understandable only when one realizes the full extent to which the Marshallian dynamics was entrenched in the thinking of Keynes's contemporaries'.[22] Among such contemporaries, however, Hawtrey is clearly not to be numbered. In 1930, it was Hawtrey who (in Leijonhufvud's terms) took up the 'Keynesian' position, and the *Treatise* which he convicted of holding a 'Marshallian' assumption.

Keynes's immediate response was to concede that changes in stocks were 'an *earlier* indication of what price falls are going to occur' and to seek Hawtrey's agreement that 'what matters is the *anticipated* price fall at the end of the production period.' There is no recognition here than an accumulation of stocks was significant except in that 'it temporarily retards and disguises the ultimate effect on prices'.[23]

Did Hawtrey himself mean more than this? He certainly presented Keynes with a numerical example which encourages the supposition that he did. In it he imagined the public to increase their saving by £5,000,000 a month. On the hypothesis that prices of consumption goods fell commensurately, the fundamental equations held good—at least in the sense that producers, facing windfall losses, were 'deemed to "save" the £5,000,000 of their "earnings" which they do not receive'. (This was the same point as that made by Robertson.)

[20] E, par. 20; F, 336.

[21] B, 7, printed in *JMK* xiii. 151; cf. F, 337.

[22] Axel Leijonhufvud, *On Keynesian Economics and the Economics of Keynes* (1968), 24, 51–3. The distinction is interesting even if its original doctrine-historical pertinence is doubted; see above, Prologue to Part I, n. 6.

[23] *JMK* xiii. 142.

Hawtrey's distinctive criticism was to ask what happened on the alternative hypothesis. For if prices did not fall in the first instance, the fundamental equations 'would record no disturbance of equilibrium'. Moreover, if reduced orders led to a cut in output, incomes would be cut. So although eventually some reduction in prices would ensue, a cut in output caused directly by a contraction in demand would have supervened. 'And incidentally,' Hawtrey added, 'it may be pointed out that this progressive contraction in the consumers' income could not fail to cause some falling off of savings.'[24]

Keynes himself specified the 'normal order of events' as (1) a decline in investment, (2) a fall in prices, though less than necessary for adjustment, (3) a fall in output, and (4) a more severe fall in prices than necessary for adjustment.[25] Again, there is no sign that Hawtrey's example struck him as more than an elaboration of how the higgling of the market worked through to bring about price changes. He can perhaps be forgiven for overlooking Hawtrey's casual mention—'incidentally'—of a possible link between savings and the level of economic activity.[26] It needs to be borne in mind that Hawtrey's main concern at the time was with changes in stocks and with the incapacity of the fundamental equations to allow for them. Even so, these exchanges are illuminating in view of Keynes's comment after the *General Theory* that 'in recent times, I have never regarded Hawtrey, Robertson or Ohlin, for example, as classical economists', and that 'I regard Mr Hawtrey as my grandparent and Mr Robertson as my parent in the paths of errancy, and I have been greatly influenced by them.'[27]

In his 1930 illustration of the process by which a decline in consumption could curtail output before it had a significant impact upon prices, Hawtrey extracted a revealing amplification from Keynes. 'The greater the contraction of output,' Hawtrey insisted, 'the less is the windfall loss.'[28] Keynes responded in November 1930

[24] B, 7–9, printed in *JMK* xiii. 151–2; this is broadly repeated in E, pars. 25–7, and 28 verbatim, reprinted in F, 337–8.

[25] *JMK* xiii. 143–4.

[26] This link is emphasized in E. G. Davis, 'The correspondence between R. G. Hawtrey and J. M. Keynes on the *Treatise*: The genesis of output adjustment models', *Can. Jnl. of Econ.*, 13 (1980), 716–24, at 719.

[27] *JMK* xxix. 270 (Keynes to Haberler, 3 Apr. 1938); *JMK* xiv. 202 n. ('Alternative theories of the rate of interest', *Econ. Jnl.*, June 1937).

[28] B, 12, in *JMK* xiii. 152.

by seeking to clear up any ambiguity over what was meant by 'departure from equilibrium', and defined it as primarily 'equilibrium of prices and costs'. He also held 'that there is not likely to be more than a transitory departure from the optimum level of output unless there is an actual or anticipated profit disequilibrium'. There could hardly be a more unequivocal affirmation that when the *Treatise* spoke of equilibrium it meant an equilibrium at optimal output or full employment.[29]

Hawtrey's logic was impeccable when he showed that, on an ordinary definition of income, saving must be equal to investment. But Keynes's message, of course, was that such equality could not simply be presumed and that productive investment did not automatically result from the availability of funds. Thus when Hawtrey wrote that it was 'approximately true that bank credit is created for purposes of investment',[30] Keynes responded that this made him 'feel, in spite of the exact understanding of many of my detailed points shown in the preceding pages, that our minds have not yet really met'.[31] The whole point of the definition employed in the *Treatise* was to proclaim that there was a problem in accounting for the equilibration of savings and investment. Hawtrey suggested that, when new issues exceeded the investable funds available, the market would find expedients to meet this call. Keynes noted that the balance was as likely to be struck 'through an increased tendency to divest as through an increased tendency to invest'.[32] Perhaps influenced by Robertson, he seems to have taken a pessimistic view of the market's propensity to bearishness, which might lock it into a position of under-investment. He merely added the parenthetical remark: 'There is here, I think, the germ of an important difference of opinion.'[33]

Hawtrey's understanding of the market mechanism is clearly illustrated by his account of what happened when saving increased. If new issues proved insufficient to take up the excess of funds avail-

[29] *JMK* xiii. 145; cf. the *General Theory*: 'I had not then understood that, in certain conditions, the system could be in equilibrium with less than full employment' (*JMK* vii. 242–3).

[30] B, 20, in *JMK* xiii. 154; E, par. 54. The underlying assumption was one which Hawtrey subsequently acknowledged that he 'took for granted too readily' in this period; see R. D. C. Black, 'R. G. Hawtrey', *Proc. Brit. Acad.*, 63 (1977), 377.

[31] *JMK* xiii. 146.

[32] Keynes's marginal comment on B, 27.

[33] *JMK* xiii. 147; cf. E, pars. 95–6 and F, 382.

able, the banks would find their advances curtailed and would lower their interest rates. This would have a stimulative effect which would reinforce the revival of investment. 'The causal chain runs from cheap money to increased consumers' income and outlay, increased sales of consumption goods, and increased capital outlay to extend productive capacity.' The alternative was that the market might be able to bring about 'an activity among producers of capital goods just equivalent to the loss of activity among the producers of consumption goods'.[34] In that case, the effects were simply those of displacement, whereas only a relaxation of credit could permit a net expansion. The filiation of this argument with the Treasury View is unmistakable.

The version of 'Mr Keynes's *Treatise on Money*' which Hawtrey prepared for the Macmillan Committee as Paper No. 66 expounds his criticisms with force and precision. Keynes, he maintained, 'is mistaken in treating the discrepancy between investment and saving, when it does occur, as the *cause* of the divergence between prices and costs; it *is* the divergence between prices and costs. When saving differs from investment, this presents not a change in the *behaviour* of the public in regard to the accumulation of unspent sums, but a change in the classification of the sums they receive as between earnings and windfalls.'[35]

In Paper No. 66, which was finished by the end of December 1930, Hawtrey added a new section on the role of investment which Davis has rightly brought to attention as an important theoretical advance. Hawtrey here presented a further numerical model showing how, if investment changed, income would change until saving and investment were once more brought into equilibrium. His example supposed investment to increase by £5,000,000 a month, thus increasing consumers' income by the same amount. 'Consumers have to decide what to do with the additional £5,000,000 a month,' he argued. 'They might save it all or spend it all, but they are more likely to spend part and save the rest.' Depending on the proportion which was passed on in consumption—say, £3,000,000—total output and incomes would again rise to this extent. Thus, provided there were no rise in prices, a progressive increase of output could continue to work itself out—'the limit will be reached when the consumers'

[34] B, 36.
[35] E, par. 48; F, 343.

income has been increased by £12,500,000 a month, and consumption by £7,500,000; leaving £5,000,000 saved to balance the £5,000,000 of additional investment.'[36]

The process which Hawtrey outlined here can easily be understood as a multiplier mechanism, focusing on what might be called secondary consumption, just as Kahn had focused on secondary employment in his EAC paper, circulated two months previously. In view of Hawtrey's earlier adumbration of such a process of income expansion, there is no need to postulate a direct influence from Kahn.[37] Indeed, the fact that this way of thinking was generally in the air among Keynes's circle during the winter of 1930–1 is the really significant point.

Hawtrey refined his model at this point by relaxing the assumption that an expansion of income would raise output not prices. He showed that a rise in prices at any stage, by bidding up the price of existing stocks rather than inducing them to be replaced from production, would 'interfere with the tendency towards increased output'. Income would be expanded to the same extent but the increment of increased output would be proportionately eroded by the extent of the rise in prices.[38] Hawtrey did not add—perhaps he thought it implicit—that the extent to which this happened depended on the elasticity of the supply curve.

That Hawtrey's model embodies the multiplier is, in retrospect, incontrovertible. That it proved suggestive to Keynes is imperscriptible. That Hawtrey himself fully realized what he had done, however, is improbable. Whereas most of Paper No. 66 was a direct reworking of the drafts he had submitted to Keynes in the autumn of 1930, Section VI, dealing with his 'multiplier', was a last-minute addition in December 1930, comprising paragraphs 53–63. Moreover, when Hawtrey revised the paper for publication in the summer of 1932—a year after Kahn's seminal article had appeared in the *Economic Journal*—he reprinted all but twenty of its 213 paragraphs. The only sizeable omission, in fact, consisted of paragraphs 53–70, including the whole of Section VI. The self-effacing Hawtrey may, as Davis claims, deserve a more prominent place in the literature on the coming of the multiplier[39]—but notably as the man who, having

---

[36] E, pars. 60–1; cited to support the claim by Davis, 'Hawtrey and Keynes', 720.

[37] See above, ch. 7 n. 6 and ch. 8 nn. 95–6.

[38] E, par. 62.

[39] Davis, 'Hawtrey and Keynes', 721 and n. 18; reiterated in Davis, 'R. G. Hawtrey', in D. P. O'Brien and John R. Presley (eds.), *Pioneers of Modern Economics in Britain* (1981), 203–33, at 216–17.

stumbled upon it, painstakingly suppressed news of its discovery in his subsequent publications.

When Keynes, as a member of the Macmillan Committee, received Paper No. 66, he told Hawtrey that he 'felt enormously honoured' to get criticism 'so tremendously useful' as this, especially in the first seven sections, where 'there is comparatively little from which I dissent'.[40] With the significant exception noted above, therefore, Hawtrey subsequently published the paper much as it stood, albeit supplemented by an additional reinforcement of its central argument. Quoting Keynes's statement that the fundamental equations were 'mere identities; truisms which tell us nothing in themselves', Hawtrey maintained that it was 'essential that savings and investment, as defined by Mr Keynes, and employed in the fundamental equations, should be *the same things* as are determined by the "decisions" in which he finds their causation'. What, then, of the 'windfall' elements in entrepreneurs' remuneration which were not included in the definition of their 'income'? If there were a windfall gain, the recipients had a decision to make over what to do with it. But a windfall loss was deemed, by the definitions of the *Treatise*, to be saved—even though it was never received by the 'saver'. What manner of 'decision' was this?[41] Hawtrey was surely right to contend 'that in the minds of many of Mr Keynes's readers, and sometimes in the mind of Mr Keynes himself', the formal definitions were, in effect, subordinated to the persuasive rhetoric of a common-sense assertion that saving exceeded investment.[42] And in commenting on Keynes's recent exchanges with Robertson, Hawtrey remarked that the definitions really made 'nonsense of the whole controversy'. Of course the *Treatise* was necessarily correct in claiming that 'entrepreneurs as a whole must be making losses exactly equal to the difference', when saving exceeded investment. 'For the excess savings *are* the losses made by the entrepreneurs and have no other existence whatever.'[43]

After studying Hawtrey's revised copy, Keynes wrote to him on 1 June 1932 that 'I really have nothing material to say'. He went on to explain his unwonted docility:

As I mentioned to you, I am working it out all over again. Whilst in some respects my new version will please you no more than the old, in some

[40] *JMK* xxix. 10 (16 Feb. 1931).
[41] F, 345; cf. E, pars. 65–6.
[42] F, 349.
[43] F, 374, commenting on *JMK* v. 131 and on *Econ. Jnl.*, 41 (1931), 395–423.

respects I shall, I think, be meeting some of your points. The main respect in which you may find the exposition easier is that I now put less fundamental reliance on my conception of savings and substitute for it the conception of expenditure.

Increments of expenditure were 'so to speak the inverse of saving'; but, as he feelingly acknowledged, 'since there are two senses in which income can be used, it is much preferable to use a term about which everyone agrees'.[44]

'Mr Meade's Relation'

There was a third and even more subversive line of attack on the *Treatise*—more subversive because it came from quarters whose approval of Keynes's objectives was unquestionable. This arose from the discussions of the *Treatise* by the younger economists at Cambridge ('the Circus'). Joan and Austin Robinson, Piero Sraffa, Richard Kahn, and James Meade were the members of this group, which met chiefly in the early months of 1931. There are virtually no contemporary records of the thinking of the Circus, because of its closely informal operation, and the chief sources are subsequent recollections, with their attendant frailties. The most obvious hazard is that memory may have telescoped and antedated what took place. The position of Meade, however, who was visiting for the year from Oxford, offers some external control in that he was physically extracted at a known moment. Meade, moreover, makes the surprising statement that, when he returned for the new academic year in the autumn of 1931, he 'is cautiously confident that he took with him back to Oxford most of the essential ingredients of the subsequent system of the *General Theory*'.[45]

Meade's understanding of the 'essential ingredients' can be gauged from a striking apophthegm in one of his essays, which has been widely quoted since its publication in 1975: 'Keynes's intellectual

[44] *JMK* xiii. 172.

[45] *JMK* xiii. 337–42, at 342; other first-hand accounts of the Circus, mainly from Austin Robinson, are in his 'J. M. Keynes', esp. 39–40; Paul Lambert, 'The evolution of Keynes's thought from the *Treatise on Money* to the *General Theory*', *Annals of Pub. and Coop. Econ.*, 40 (1969), 243–63; Don Patinkin and J. Clark Leith (eds.), *Keynes, Cambridge and the General Theory* (1977), 33–7, 146–8; Richard Kahn, *The Making of Keynes's General Theory* (Cambridge, 1984), 105–11; G. C. Harcourt (ed.), *Keynes and his Contemporaries* (1985), 42–63.

revolution was to shift economists from thinking normally in terms of a model of economic reality in which a dog called *savings* wagged his tail labelled *investment* to thinking in terms of a model in which a dog called *investment* wagged his tail labelled *savings*.'[46] Unknown to Meade, he was in fact repeating a metaphor employed by Keynes himself, which adds further authority to the phrase and may, through a subconscious echo, be the origin of it.

It is important to appreciate the senses in which Keynes was thinking of saving and investment after the publication of the *Treatise*, with its emphasis upon their potential disparity. 'In the past,' Keynes proclaimed in June 1931, 'it has been usual to believe that there was some preordained harmony by which saving and investment were necessarily equal...'[47] It was the *presumption* that they were the same which led both him and Robertson to look for definitions which made the matter problematic, even if they disagreed about the form of these definitions—a quest which their correspondence illustrates:[48]

The old 'common-sense' view not only held that savings and investment are necessarily equal (as—we have seen—*in a sense* they are), but inferred from this that therefore one need not bother. (Keynes to Robertson, Mar. 1932)

But the Savings $\left\{ \begin{array}{l} \text{exceeding} \\ \text{falling short of} \end{array} \right\}$ Investment phrase is so attractive for expressing what we both want to convey that one longs to find some definition of the words which will enable one to use it without straining the meaning of either word unbearably. (Robertson to Keynes, 19 May 1933)

What common sense said was that realized savings and investment must be the same. What Keynes was contending was that this outcome need not correspond with what had been intended. Contemporary Swedish economists, notably Gunnar Myrdal, introduced a distinction between *ex ante* (the viewpoint of intention) and *ex post* (the viewpoint of accomplishment) which could have cut through much of this ambiguity. Shackle calls Myrdal's concept 'a suggestion of utter simplicity yet of transforming power'.[49] When Keynes later became aware of it, he told Bertil Ohlin: 'This is in fact almost precisely on the lines that I was thinking and lecturing somewhere about 1931 and 1932, and subsequently abandoned.' Even in 1937 he

---

[46] James Meade, 'The Keynesian Revolution', in M. Keynes (ed.), *Essays*, p. 82.

[47] *JMK* xiii. 355 (Harris Lectures, June 1931).

[48] *JMK* xiii. 278; *JMK* xxix. 25.

[49] G. L. S. Shackle, *The Years of High Theory* (Cambridge, 1967), 94.

acknowledged that 'from the point of view of exposition, there is a great deal to be said for it'.[50]

It is only a trivial anachronism, therefore, to interpret the 'Notes on the definition of saving' which Keynes submitted to Robertson in March 1932 in these terms. The argument was presented largely in symbolic notation. Thus adding E (cost of production) to Q (net profits of the entrepreneurs) gave E'—'which is total income in Hawtrey's, Hayek's and D.H.R.'s sense, and in the sense to which I have now bowed the knee.' Keynes, in short, was ready to abandon his peculiar definition of income as excluding 'windfalls'. What implication did this have for the sense in which saving should be understood? It provided 'two alternative definitions of savings'—by subtracting consumption from income as defined *either* in the *Treatise* (anticipated return) *or* in the knee-bowing sense (realized earnings). The first gave S, which can be taken as saving *ex ante*; the second S', which can be taken as saving *ex post*.

It was S' which provided 'the justification for the old-fashioned "common-sense" view that savings and investment are, necessarily and at all times, equal ...' Keynes continued (using I for investment):[51]

On the other hand the implications of this use of language are decidedly different from what 'common sense' supposes. For S' always and necessarily accommodates itself to I. Whether I consists in housing schemes or in war finance, there need be nothing to hold us back, because I always drags S' along with it at an equal pace. S' is not the voluntary result of virtuous decisions. In fact S' is no longer the dog, which common sense believes it to be, but the tail.

The influence of the Circus can hardly be ignored in explaining why Keynes was thinking in this way as early as March 1932. The most notable monument left by the Circus is the article which Kahn published in the *Economic Journal* in June 1931 on 'The relation of home investment to unemployment'. Its central message was that public investment could create not only an initial amount of employment but also secondary employment through its repercussions on spending. Keynes publicized this conclusion in 1933 under the irresistible title 'The Multiplier', but this name may give a misleading

---

[50] *JMK* xiv. 184 (Keynes to Ohlin, 27 Jan. 1937).
[51] *JMK* xiii. 276 ('Notes on the definition of saving', sent to Robertson, 22 Mar. 1932).

impression of the concept in the original article which, as Kahn has observed, 'is often cited but apparently little read'.[52]

The importance of the multiplier (in Kahn's formulation) stems from the questions it was designed to answer; and to some extent its implications were for the time being restricted by those questions. It was obviously an outgrowth of an argument over policy not theory. Thus Kahn at the outset twice referred to the 'beneficial repercussions' which were notoriously invoked by the (unnamed) advocates of public works. His purpose was to evaluate them in concrete arithmetical terms. The article, originating in Kahn's paper for the committee of economists in September 1930, was preoccupied with two questions. First, as clearly shown in the EAC draft, what are the net effects on unemployment of a public works programme? Second—equally inescapable for anyone challenging the Treasury View—how to pay for it?

Kahn's mathematics had an elegant simplicity. His essential reasoning was that secondary employment depended on the *proportion* of *extra* expenditure generated by new investment. This proportion was calculated by adding the amounts spent on consumption out of increased profits and, above all, out of the increased income of the newly employed men (as compared with their previous dole). The amount of extra consumption would thus form the income of a further number of men brought into employment. In order to simplify the analysis, however, it rested on the 'sweeping assumption' that supply was elastic (prices would not rise).[53]

What Kahn incorporated into the final draft of his article, as a result of the Circus, was 'Mr Meade's Relation'. This showed that his multiplier was 'merely a particular case of a general relation, due to Mr J. E. Meade, that covers the case when supply is not perfectly elastic, so that prices rise when employment increases'.[54] Meade focused on the cost of investment and showed that it necessarily comprised the sum of three items: saving on the dole *plus* increased net import costs *plus* the increase in unspent profits—from which

[52] Richard Kahn, *Selected Essays in Employment and Growth* (Cambridge, 1972), vii, reprinting 'The relation of home investment to unemployment', 1–27, from *Econ. Jnl.*, 41 (1931), 173–98; parallel citations to both sources are supplied below.

[53] *Econ. Jnl.*, 183; Kahn, *Essays*, 11. Thus far the reasoning and equations were simply an expansion of his EAC draft, 'The relation between primary and secondary employment', Keynes Papers, EA/4. For a non-technical account see the appendix at the end of this chapter.

[54] *Econ. Jnl.*, 188; Kahn, *Essays*, 17.

total must be *subtracted* any diminution in savings due to a rise in prices. What Meade was doing was adding up all the parts of the initial investment which were *not* passed on via consumption and must therefore have lodged in some pocket of savings. Savings on the dole, primarily to the national Budget but also to household budgets which had helped support unemployed members, were obviously the first item. The second identified increased costs of imports under 'savings', in the sense that a reduction in foreign lending would liberate resources at home. The final item—unspent profits—spoke for itself. The offset against this sum was any effect higher prices might have in increasing expenditure at the expense of savings.

The net increase in savings was necessarily exactly equal to the original outlay because 'money paid out by the Government to the builders of roads continues to be passed on from hand to hand until it reaches one of the *culs de sac . . .*'. Here was the answer 'to those who are worried about the monetary sources that are available to meet the cost of the roads', since these turned out to be 'available to precisely the right extent'.[55] While Kahn demonstrated the leverage of the multiplier via its consumption effects, the article was, as he has affirmed, 'far more important for a quite different contribution'.[56] For Mr Meade's Relation showed that the *unconsumed* fractions necessarily summed to unity.

Kahn comments: 'Of course what we had done—but failed completely to realise—was, by a very roundabout method, to establish the identity of saving and investment—if saving is defined on commonsense lines rather than those of the *Treatise*.'[57] There is some disagreement over whether the multiplier formula is logically equivalent to the theory of effective demand (defined as the 'formal proposition that *saving and investment are brought into equality by variations in the level of income (output)*'). Milgate contends that Kahn's multiplier argument fell short of the *General Theory*'s contention that an increase in expenditure on investment *generates* savings of exactly the required amount.[58] But this is surely the point established by Mr Meade's Relation. Patinkin, by contrast, accepts that there is a logical but not a chronological equivalence: 'the fact

---

[55] *Econ. Jnl.*, 188–9; Kahn, *Essays*, 18.

[56] Kahn, *Making of General Theory*, p. 98, reinforcing what Kahn wrote at the time of Keynes's death: 'John Maynard Keynes', *Proc. Brit. Acad.*, 32 (1946), 409.

[57] Kahn, *Making of General Theory*, 99; he might better have said the 'equality' not the 'identity'.

[58] Murray Milgate, *Capital and Employment* (1982), 78–82.

that A implies B does not in turn imply that at the time scholars understood A they also understood B.'[59] As a general caution, this point is well taken, but in this respect too it may be proper to distinguish between Kahn and Meade. It is not unnatural that Mr Meade's Relation should have bulked largest in the mind of its begetter.

It should not be forgotten that, as befits a seminal article, we are dealing with a seed,[60] not a flower. Its present importance is as an indication of the thinking of the Circus in their undocumented discussions of the *Treatise* during the period from November 1930 to March 1931. Keynes's own commitments at this juncture were extraordinarily heavy. Having finished the *Treatise*, he turned, 'without a day's rest', to the work of the committee of economists,[61] from which he successively moved on to the final stages of the Macmillan Committee. True, he spent part of each week during term in Cambridge, but he was an immensely busy and distinguished man of affairs, not simply another don. Meade, by contrast, not yet twenty-five and with all the advantages of a man on academic leave, was, according to Austin Robinson, 'more active than any of us' in the deliberations of the Circus.[62] But it was not a forum in which the great man normally met his young colleagues face to face, and it is recalled that Keynes, puzzled, looked around the room for 'Mr Meade's Relation' on first acquaintance.

The proceedings of the Circus were usually transmitted through Kahn, Keynes's protégé as a Fellow of King's and joint secretary to the economists' committee, who acted as 'angel messenger' (to the God of a miracle play, dominating the action though never appearing).[63] Kahn's role has provoked intermittent speculation, notably from Schumpeter, that his share in the making of the *General Theory* 'cannot have fallen very far short of co-authorship'. Schumpeter's contemporary contacts (only with members of the Circus rather than Keynes himself) have been mentioned by Austin Robinson as a possible source of misapprehension, and Kahn himself

[59] Don Patinkin, *Anticipations of the General Theory?* (Chicago, 1982), 30–1.
[60] Or an egg, as Lawrence Klein called it in his early statement of the view that it was Kahn who took 'the necessary step': *The Keynesian Revolution* (New York, 1947; London, 1952), 38.
[61] Keynes to Hawtrey, 8 Oct. 1930, HTRY 11/4.
[62] Austin Robinson, 'Keynes and his Cambridge colleagues', in Patinkin and Leith (eds.), *Keynes*, 33.
[63] This image derived (somewhat later) from Mrs Meade, *JMK* xiii. 338–9.

has consistently resisted any such suggestion.[64] It is more plausible to say that he was an excellent conduit for the ideas which became the common property of the group—they seem to have had little sense of intellectual copyright—as well as the perfect foil for Keynes, almighty, invisible.

If there is a theme to the activities of the Circus it is surely the insistence on identifying fixed output as a special assumption. As Austin Robinson has put it, 'we learned to distinguish very clearly in those months between those propositions that are universally true and those propositions that are only true in conditions of full employment'.[65] The Treasury View was a clear target here, and the immediate butt of the multiplier article. It would be a mistake to imagine that the young iconoclasts of the Circus were original in establishing a point which even the Prof. had already noticed.[66] But its salience in their own thinking should not therefore be ignored. In particular, they seized on the passage in the *Treatise* referring to the widow's cruse (1 Kings 17: 12–16). Here Keynes had maintained that however much of their profit entrepreneurs spent, profits as a whole would not be depleted because the effect would be to increase the profits on consumption goods by the same amount. But this was only true if the whole adjustment were made through a rise in prices rather than a rise in output. Only with full employment of resources would this be true; and the elasticity of supply, in determining the extent to which either output or prices would rise, had not been taken into account in the *Treatise*.[67]

There is no doubt that Keynes was much attached to the widow's cruse at the time of the *Treatise*'s publication. In the same week, he spoke in these terms to the Macmillan Committee, first dealing with the case when production of investment goods exceeded savings.[68]

Keynes: If the entrepreneurs are producing more capital goods than there is

---

[64] J. A. Schumpeter, *History of Economic Analysis* (New York, 1954), 1172; Patinkin and Leith (eds.), *Keynes*, 79–81; Lambert, 'Evolution of Keynes's thought', 245; Kahn, *Making of General Theory*, 223–4, 240.

[65] Harcourt (ed.), *Keynes and his Contemporaries*, 55.

[66] See above, ch. 8 n. 83, for Milgate's demonstration that Pigou was alive to the significance of the full-output assumption.

[67] *JMK* xiii. 339–40, discussing *JMK* v. 125; cf. Harcourt (ed.), *Keynes and his Contemporaries*, 47–9. Nor had the *Treatise*'s glib remarks about profits remaining undepleted, 'however much of them may be devoted to riotous living', taken account of the redistribution of income from riotous to frugal entrepreneurs.

[68] Private session, 7 Nov. 1930, 11; cf. *JMK* v. 126.

thrift, then prices will rise, and that inflation will put profits into the pockets of the entrepreneur, and that will finance the difference between the capital goods they have created and the thrift.

In this way inflation redistributed income via profits to entrepreneurs, whose income, as a class, varied directly with the level of economic activity. The contrary process would be set up if, under deflationary conditions, the class of consumers on fixed incomes sought to save more.[69]

Keynes: ... prices will fall still further, so that they can both save and consume as much as before, and however much they save they can always consume as much as before. It is the widow's cruse.
McKenna: Will not their investment be less remunerative; will they not save less?
Keynes: No, because the more they save the more the other class, the business men, will lose, and the more the assets of the business men will change hands, so that if the business men refrain from enterprise gradually the whole wealth of the community will pass into the hands of those savers, and those savers can go on consuming all the time just as much as they did before.

But of course this is only true if output remains unchanged and businessmen carry on producing at lower and lower prices, with greater and greater losses. This is what the widow's cruse implies; and this is why the Circus decided it was a fallacy. Yet the *Treatise* also contains a famous passage which tells another story altogether— the banana parable, which had made its first appearance in Keynes's private evidence on 21 February 1930.

In the banana republic, bananas are the only item of production and of consumption. 'Into this Eden there enters a thrift campaign urging the members of the public to abate their improvident practice of spending nearly all their current incomes on buying bananas for food.' What happens when saving is thus increased? The same quantity of bananas is produced and sold (for they do not keep) but at lower prices, with windfall losses to the entrepreneurs as a result. 'The only effect,' Keynes said at this point, 'has been to transfer the wealth of the entrepreneurs out of their pockets into the pockets of the public'—or even into their cruses perhaps. 'But that is not the end of the story,' Keynes added, as he went on to 'disclose the full

[69] Ibid. 13.

horror of the situation'. For what else would ensue but a concatena-
tion of falling profits, unemployment, wage cuts—all with cumulative
effects in reducing output.[70]

In some ways the banana parable, rather than illustrating the
fundamental equations, would serve better as an example of a multiplier process working through reduced consumption to contract
incomes, output, and employment. Yet, as a multiplier, it is flawed by
the implicit assumption that if income were reduced, spending would
be reduced by the whole amount. Under these conditions—the
limiting case of the multiplier—repercussions are infinite rather than
finite and no equilibrium position is reached.[71] In short, a reduction
in *savings* too out of reduced income is not envisaged. Keynes was
evidently not thinking in terms of a crucial gap between changes in
income and changes in consumption.

There was a subsequent refinement of the multiplier doctrine,
following Kahn's article, to which attention has recently been drawn.
In June 1932, Jens Warming, a Danish economist, published a
sympathetic comment which sought to add one point to Kahn's
analysis. He questioned the supposition 'that the new income (or
rather the profit) is devoted to consumption in its entirety', and
maintained that 'the saving from this income is a very important by-
product to the secondary employment, and is just as capable of
financing the activity'.[72] In short, Warming pointed to the lack of a
general savings function—except in so far as it was indicated by
reference to 'unspent profits', as Kahn did not fail to point out.[73]
Since Keynes was the editor of the *Economic Journal*, it would be
interesting to know when he saw Warming's submission and what he
made of it; but unfortunately there is nothing in the relevant files in

[70] *JMK* xx. 76–8: cf. *JMK* v. 158–60.

[71] Patinkin elucidates this point in *Anticipations*, 15–16.

[72] Jens Warming, 'International difficulties arising out of the financing of public
works during depression', *Econ. Jnl.*, 42 (1932), 211–24, at 214. Moggridge carved out
a small niche for Warming in the second edition of *Keynes* (1980), 94 and n. 4 on 182;
and Kahn has paid tribute to his breakthrough, *Making of General Theory*, 100–1. But
the credit for rediscovering Warming belongs to the important article by Neville Cain,
'Cambridge and its revolution: A perspective on the multiplier and effective demand',
Econ. Record (1979), 108–17, which also has some pregnant observations on Meade
and the multiplier.

[73] Patinkin made no reference to Warming in 'Keynes and the multiplier', *Manc.
Sch.*, 45 (1978), 209–23, but in reprinting the article in an amended form he claims
that Cain's point about Kahn's lack of general savings function is 'unwarranted'
(*Anticipations*, 198 n. 17). Kahn's lack of attention to personal savings, however, in his
concentration on unspent profits, surely provides the necessary warrant.

the Keynes papers bearing upon this point. Kahn's short riposte took up Warming's theme as his own—'When people's incomes are increased, the amount that they save will increase.' It is difficult to know exactly how this should be construed. Kahn now recognizes the significance of Warming's contribution; but if he—and Keynes as his protective editor—fully appreciated the point at the time, the acknowledgement is admittedly rather cursory. Kahn's further assertion that, since Warming was not defining 'savings' as in the *Treatise*, 'in this simple-minded sense of the term, savings are *always and necessarily* equal to investment', was doubly barbed.[74] Ostensibly patronizing towards Warming, it concealed an unflattering appraisal of the adequacy of the *Treatise*. Kahn has since offered the gloss: 'Dennis Robertson deduced from my use of the adjective "simple-minded" that I was opposed to these sensible definitions rather than strongly in favour.'[75]

The substantive point about personal savings was quickly assimilated—at any rate by Meade, whose work with the New Fabian Research Bureau was carrying Keynes's ideas into a new context in 1932. The New Fabians, under the patronage of Dalton, for the most part regarded the *Treatise* with scepticism—not least Evan Durbin, a young economist in Hayek's department at the LSE. But Durbin confided in the early part of 1932 that Meade's writings had 'driven me back' to Volume One of the *Treatise*:[76]

Although you would be the first to admit your indebtedness to him, and although much of what you say is in him, yet you are an immense advance on him in lucidity and precision. Why don't *you* write the Second Edition?

Instead, Meade wrote *Public Works in their International Aspect* for the New Fabians. It introduced 'individual savings' as the first of the ways in which additional expenditure was 'held up' in explaining how additional investment generated an equal amount of savings.[77] This pamphlet, indeed, appearing in January 1933, can be seen as the first published adumbration of the theory of effective demand.

[74] R. F. Kahn, 'The financing of public works: A note', *Econ. Jnl.*, 42 (1932), 492–5, at 494. I read Kahn's response as more accommodating than does Cain, 'Cambridge and its revolution', 114.

[75] Kahn, *Making of General Theory*, 101.

[76] Durbin to Meade, 6 Feb. (1932), Meade Papers, LSE 2/3. I initially owe this reference to Elizabeth Durbin, *New Jerusalems* (1985), 139–40, which quotes part and is an excellent guide to the work of the NFRB.

[77] J. E. Meade, *Public Works in their International Aspect* (1933), 14–15.

By this time, in preparing *The Means to Prosperity*, Keynes had likewise made personal savings into the prime form of what he now called 'leakages' in explaining 'the multiplier'—thus, at a stroke, establishing the conventional terminology. Kahn, who was in the USA, told Keynes that he 'had been grappling for something of the sort ... even going so far as to use the word "leakage" '.[78] But here at least, the great plagiarist was only plagiarizing his younger self, not his younger colleagues. Keynes had, in fact, used the term leakage in a somewhat analogous sense in defending Lloyd George's pledge in March 1929.[79] Keynes was now well on the way to finding a stylish new rhetoric in which to clothe his ideas, allowing him to dispose discreetly of the old clothes of the *Treatise*, which had come to fit so badly. Thus, in October 1933, his reference to 'what I call saving in my queer sense', in a letter to Robertson, was almost embarrassed;[80] and two months later the *Economic Journal* printed Keynes's final contribution in the protracted controversy over saving and hoarding:[81]

Perhaps I should add that my own use of terms today is not the same as it was when I wrote my *Treatise on Money*, and that I do not now consider my analysis in that book to be as clear or as logical as I can make it. But the question of what uses of language and modes of expression are best does not alter the essential character of the fundamental ideas which Mr Robertson and I are both trying to elucidate.

APPENDIX: THE MULTIPLIER

Primary employment was provided by an initial investment ('unity'). The expenditure of men in primary employment provided incomes for a number of men (k) in secondary employment. For one man put into primary employment, the extra consumption that was generated, as *a determinate proportion of unity* (say, two-thirds), defined k. If this specified the first repercussion of

[78] *JMK* xiii. 414 (Kahn to Keynes, 30 Mar. 1933); cf. *JMK* ix. 340.
[79] *JMK* xix. 805 (*Evening Standard*, 19 Mar. 1929); cf. ch. 4 n. 65.
[80] *JMK* xiii. 315.
[81] *JMK* xiii. 330 ('Mr Robertson on "Saving and Hoarding" ').

cumulative prosperity, the same calculation held good for the second repercussion, which would be *a determinate proportion of a determinate proportion—* in short, it would be squared. Further repercussions simply extended the series, e.g.

$$\frac{2}{3} + \frac{4}{9} + \frac{8}{27} + \ldots$$

This equation $(k + k^2 + k^3 + \ldots)$, which gave the ratio of secondary employment to primary employment, could be written in the simpler form

$$\frac{k}{1-k}.$$

Say, if $k = \frac{2}{3}$,

$$\frac{k}{1-k} = \frac{2/3}{1/3} = \frac{2}{1} = 2.$$

Whatever the value of k (the proportion of extra consumption from a given investment), Kahn's equation would specify the total secondary employment from increased expenditure and income.

Kahn's multiplier postulated that a specified fraction of income (k) from an increment of investment was passed on successively in expenditure, thus increasing final income in determinate proportion. If half is spent $(k = \frac{1}{2})$, final income works out at 2; if $k = \frac{2}{3}$, it works out at 3; if $k = \frac{3}{4}$, at 4. The multiplier is determined always by the denominator of the residually *unspent* fraction $(1 - k)$. Now Mr Meade's Relation showed that, irrespective of any rise in prices, this residual fraction of saving would necessarily accumulate in proportion until the sum reached unity. If the multiplier were low, large fractions of savings were obviously there at the outset; if high, smaller fractions of a larger final income successively accumulated. Whether final income were two, three, or four times unity (the initial increment of investment), although the amount of secondary employment would vary, the savings generated always summed to unity. So far as the Budget is concerned, if there are large savings on the dole, the multiplier will be low and the impact on employment correspondingly disappointing. But, conversely, if the multiplier is low, because of these savings, there will be a smaller Budget deficit to finance.

11

The making of the theory of effective demand

Stages

A prominent member of the Circus, Joan Robinson was a young left-wing Fellow of Newnham College, Cambridge: a woman who developed firm views about the nature of the Keynesian revolution—and what became of it. For her, it was all summed up in the article, 'The general theory of employment', which Keynes published in the *Quarterly Journal of Economics* in 1937, emphasizing uncertainty; and other 'fundamentalists' have taken this as 'Keynes's ultimate meaning'.[1] Joan Robinson's notorious remark, that 'there were moments when we had some trouble in getting Maynard to see what the point of his revolution really was',[2] may actually have some pertinence at an earlier stage. For in the summer of 1931, when the Circus disbanded, it was by no means clear how far they had shifted Keynes's own position. It is hardly surprising that he stood by the *Treatise*, less than a year from its publication, with reviews still coming in. He cancelled the university lectures which he was due to give in May 1931, maybe because he needed more time for reappraisal, or, more likely, because he simply needed more time. He sailed for the USA on 30 May 1931 to give the Harris Lectures in Chicago. The previous day he had written to Kahn: 'By a miracle I finished the work of the Macmillan Committee by 2 p.m. today, after going at it practically continuously since I left Cambridge.'[3] Drafting the Report and its Addendum had pressed hard upon him throughout April and May—hardly the ideal conditions for reflection.

---

[1] Shackle, *Years of High Theory*, ch. 11 on the *QJE* article is subtitled 'Keynes's ultimate meaning'; the article is reprinted in *JMK* xiv. 109–23. The term 'fundamentalists' is part of Coddington's taxonomy, comprising not so much a reverence for 'the texts' as a rejection of the whole notion of a determinate equilibrium position. See Alan Coddington, *Keynesian Economics: The search for first principles* (1983), esp. 92–114.

[2] Joan Robinson, 'What has become of the Keynesian revolution?', in Milo Keynes (ed.), *Essays*, 125.

[3] *JMK* xx. 310. Kahn has suggested that the Easter Term lectures were cancelled 'because under Circus influence he wanted to do some rethinking': Harcourt (ed.), *Keynes and his Contemporaries*, 49.

The Harris Lectures in June 1931 give rise to conflicting interpretation. Kahn has written that 'the members of the Circus could
claim that their influence was beginning to be revealed'.[4] It is true
that Keynes spoke—as he had sixteen months previously to the
Macmillan Committee—of the possibility of 'a kind of spurious
equilibrium' at less than full employment, and made references to
adjustments of output as well as prices. But Patinkin's judgement
that the lectures were 'first and foremost a song of praise to his
Treatise' seems well-founded.[5] As in the *Treatise*, Keynes vehemently
rejected the notion that saving and investment were necessarily
equal, saying, 'this is not so. I venture to say with certainty that it is
not so.'[6] The Harris Lectures, in fact, marked the finale of the
euphoric period in which he was ready to have his head chopped off
in defence of the *Treatise*. There ought to be no puzzle over Keynes's
apparent imperviousness to the arguments of the Circus up to this
point. It was only after he returned to England in July 1931 that he
had, even by his standards, adequate time to consider criticisms
which, after all, went to the root of his proclaimed doctrines. The
remarkable thing is not that this process took so long but that
Keynes was ready to enter into it at all.

The fundamental equations of the *Treatise* were themselves a
barrier to fresh thinking. It is notable that Kahn became handi-
capped in his multiplier article precisely at the point where he loyally
attempted to formulate it in terms of the *Treatise*. Keynes likewise
often felt encumbered by his own formal apparatus, especially when
it became mathematical. Even after the *General Theory* was
published, Keynes wrote of one passage: 'I have got bogged in an
attempt to bring my own terms into rather closer conformity with
the algebra of others than the case really permits.'[7] He had considerable respect for the discipline and rigour of formal argument. But he
maintained that 'theoretical economics often has a formal apparatus
where the reality is not strictly formal. It is not, and is not meant to

---

[4] *Making of General Theory*, 109–10; Donald Moggridge is much more tentative
than this, 'From the *Treatise* to the *General Theory*: An exercise in chronology', *Hist. of
Pol. Econ.*, v (1973), 79. Vicarelli, while noting new elements, points to the unhelpful
inhibition of the *Treatise* schema; *Keynes: The instability of capitalism*, 104–6.

[5] Patinkin, *Anticipations*, 23–6; cf. *JMK* xiii. 343–67, at 356, and *JMK* xx. 63–4
(private evidence, 20 Feb. 1930).

[6] *JMK* xiii. 355.

[7] *JMK* xxix. 246 (Keynes to H. Townshend, 23 Apr. 1936).

be, logically watertight in the sense in which mathematics is.'[8] His insights were not translations into words of what he glimpsed in the equations: he implied the reverse in the way he spoke of equations in his lectures:[9]

These equations are mere truisms arising out of the analysis. Hence the dilemma that things must be either truisms or unimportant. Whole of mathematics is a truism. But truisms help to clear up one's mind. (24 Oct. 1932)

These equations are merely a means of exposition, and not a productive tool. The real tool is thought, and they are not a substitute for it, but at most a guide, or embodiment. (4 Dec. 1933)

All who knew Keynes speak of his mind jumping ahead intuitively to conclusions which he could only later fully substantiate. It follows that there are two reputable schemes on which the chronology of the making of the *General Theory* can be founded. One is to set rigorous criteria for the consistent exposition of the doctrine in a form accessible to a professional readership.[10] The other is that adopted here: to look for indications of developments in his thinking which represented his initial insights, even if they were disjointed flashes of illumination. Keynes's statement in March 1932 that saving was no longer the dog but the tail is surely just such an indication rather than a chance verbal curiosity. It is all of a piece with the response which he was by then prepared to make to the contributions offered by the members of the Circus. In April 1932 he told Joan Robinson that 'of course my treatment is obscure and sometimes inaccurate, and always incomplete, since I was tackling completely unfamiliar ground, and had not got my mind by any means clear on all sorts of points. But the real point is not whether all this is so, as of course it is, but whether this sort of thinking and arguing about the subject is right.'[11]

---

[8] *JMK* xxix. 37–8 (lecture notes, 25 Apr. 1932); and see *JMK* vii. 297–8 (*General Theory*).

[9] Lecture notes by R. B. Bryce (24 Oct. 1932) and Marvin Fallgatter (4 Dec. 1933); transcripts in the Keynes Papers. Professor T. K. Rymes has made the transcript of Bryce's notes, 1932–4, from the originals at Carleton University, Ottawa; as from the parallel set by Lorie Tarshis, 1932–5, now in the Keynes Papers. I have relied upon Rymes's exemplary editorial work throughout. The economist James S. Earley's transcript of the notes by his friend Marvin Fallgatter for 1933 only are in the Keynes Papers. Citations below to any of these notes are broadly corroborated in the other sets for the same date unless indicated to the contrary.

[10] Essentially the methodology specified by Patinkin, *Anticipations*, esp. 11, 16, 85.

[11] *JMK* xiii. 270 (Keynes to J. Robinson, 14 Apr. 1932); cf. Keynes's comments on intuition and proof in Newton, *JMK* x. 365 (*Essays in Biography*).

Keynes gave at least three retrospective accounts of the stages by which he reached the *General Theory*.[12] All three are mutually consistent, but the clearest chronology is in the letter he wrote to Harrod in August 1936, when his future biographer was preparing his paper 'Mr Keynes and traditional theory'. The documentary status which this letter has acquired can be gauged by the fact that it has been so often quoted in recent years and never challenged. Patinkin, for example, leans heavily on 'that most revealing letter to Roy Harrod'.[13] It is fair to say that it has been analysed primarily in terms of its conceptual coherence; and the first section graphically conveys Keynes's sense of moving from one world-view to another:[14]

I have been much pre-occupied with the causation, so to speak, of my own progress of mind from the classical position to my present views,—with the order in which the problem developed in my mind. What some people treat as an unnecessarily controversial tone is really due to the importance in my own mind of what I used to believe, and of the moments of transition which were for me personally moments of illumination. You don't feel the weight of the past as I do. One cannot shake off a pack one has never properly worn. And probably your ignoring all this is a better plan than mine. For experience seems to show that people are divided between the old ones whom nothing will shift and are merely annoyed by my attempts to underline the points of transition so vital in my own progress, and the young ones who have not been properly brought up and believe nothing in particular. The particles of light seen in escaping from a tunnel are interesting neither to those who mean to stay there nor to those who have never been there! I have no companions, it seems, in my own generation, either of earliest teachers or of earliest pupils; I cannot in thought help being somewhat bound to them,—which they find exceedingly irritating!

If the second section, which was composed with some care, is scrutinized more closely as a historical record, it can be broken down into four distinct chronological stages, as indicated below by the roman numerals (of which the first two are actually mentioned in reverse order).

---

[12] Keynes to A. P. Lerner, 16 June 1936 (*JMK* xxix. 214–16); Keynes to Harrod, 30 Aug. 1936 (*JMK* xiv. 84–6); 'The general theory of employment', published in the *QJE* in Feb. 1937, but drafted late 1936 (*JMK* xiv. 109–23, esp. 119–23).

[13] *Keynes's Monetary Thought*, 66, 80.

[14] The text of the main sections of Keynes's letter to Harrod is taken from the original pencil draft, dated 27 Aug. 1936, in the Keynes Papers. There are a few variant readings compared with the version dated 30 Aug. 1936 in *JMK* xiv. 84–6 (corrected *JMK* xxix. 298). The letter as dispatched is now in the Harrod Papers, Chiba University of Commerce, Japan.

You don't mention *effective demand* or, more precisely, the demand schedule for output as a whole, except in so far as it is implicit in the multiplier. To me, regarded historically, the most extraordinary thing is the complete disappearance of the theory of the demand and supply for output as a whole, i.e. the theory of employment, *after* it had been for a quarter of a century the most discussed thing in economics. One of the most important transitions for me, after my *Treatise on Money* had been published, was [ii] suddenly realising this. It only came after I had enunciated to myself the psychological law that, when income increases, the gap between income and consumption will increase,—[i] a conclusion of vast importance to my own thinking but not apparently, expressed just like that, to anyone else's. Then, appreciably later, came [iii] the notion of interest as being the measure of liquidity-preference, which became quite clear in my mind the moment I thought of it. And last of all, after an immense lot of muddling and many drafts, [iv] the proper definition of the marginal efficiency of capital linked up one thing with another.

The first stage thus came 'after I had enunciated to myself the psychological law that, when income increases, the gap between income and consumption will increase,—a conclusion of vast importance to my own thinking but not apparently, expressed just like that, to anyone else's'. Expressed *just* like that, the formula does not appear before the second proof of the *General Theory* in the summer of 1935.[15] The nub of it, however, is surely there in the notes from which Keynes gave his first university lectures for three years in the Easter Term of 1932.

These lectures, entitled 'The Pure Theory of Money', as in the *Treatise,* were attended not only by undergraduates and research students but also by Kahn, Sraffa, and the Robinsons. What Keynes appears to have said in his second lecture is that 'whenever there is a change in income, there will be a change in expenditure the same in direction but less in amount'.[16] Why did he come to attach such importance to this mere piece of common sense? Because if an increase in income were not wholly absorbed by consumption, some part would be saved. Hence a possible deficiency in demand for consumption goods. It was thus demand for investment goods which

[15] Compare *JMK* xiv. 446, with the *General Theory, JMK* vii. 96. This passage was a reworking of the mid-1934 draft of the chapter on 'The propensity to spend', *JMK* xiii. 445. Keynes's university lecture of 20 Nov. 1933 began with the 'psychological law', as noted by Bryce, Tarshis, and Fallgatter.

[16] *JMK* xxix. 39. Keynes would certainly have been aware by this time of Warming's contribution to the *Econ. Jnl.,* which must have been in the press.

was crucial in determining the total size of income—essentially a multiplier process. And if this were the case, then 'the volume of output and the volume of investment go up and down together; or, in more familiar language, the volume of employment directly depends on the amount of investment.' By arguing in this way, Keynes claimed to show how, 'if we introduce a few simple assumptions based on our general knowledge of the outside world, we can galvanise our truisms into being generalisations of far-reaching practical importance'.[17]

The whole argument strongly suggests that Keynes reached stage (i) during the early months of 1932. Admittedly, he was unsure how to handle this insight and reverted to the terms of the *Treatise* in his mid-1932 drafts, which has been interpreted as evidence that he had not apprehended the 'fundamental pyschological law'. It is also true that his lectures in May had not satisfied everyone and led to a series of criticisms in a manifesto from Kahn and the Robinsons. Keynes responded, however, that their objections were insufficient 'to induce me to scrap all my present half-forged weapons'.[18]

It can be agreed that at this stage Keynes simply did not have the tools to do the job. He had stepped out of the *Treatise*—but only with one foot. Milgate writes of a 'half-way house' and Patinkin similarly characterizes the drafts which survive from 1932: 'The voice is that of the *General Theory*: but the analytical framework is still largely that of the *Treatise*.'[19] The controversial point comes with Keynes's university lectures for 1932–3, given during the Michaelmas Term. Keynes's own fragmentary notes for two of these lectures only came to light when a laundry basket full of additional papers was discovered at Tilton in 1976; but these are now complemented and elaborated in the available sets of lecture notes taken by his students, notably R. B. Bryce and Lorie Tarshis. They were both Canadian graduates—Tarshis in economics but Bryce in engineering—who came to Cambridge in 1932 as affiliated students, took the BA in 1934, and worked as graduate students thereafter.

---

[17] *JMK* xxix. 39–40 (lecture notes, 2 May 1932); cf. 215 (Keynes to Lerner, 16 June 1936). For a helpful exegesis see T. K. Rymes, 'Keynes's lectures, 1932–5: Notes of a representative student. A prelude: Notes for the Easter Term, 1932', *Eastern Econ. Jnl.*, 12 (1986), 397–412, esp. 401 for a demonstration that Keynes's exposition was premised on the multiplier.

[18] *JMK* xiii. 378 (Keynes to J. Robinson, 9 May 1932) on the memorandum, *JMK* xxix. 42–7. For Patinkin's arguments against accepting this as stage (i) see *Anticipations*, 19–20.

[19] Milgate, *Capital and Employment*, 81; Patinkin, *Keynes's Monetary Theory*, 72.

In an impressive exegesis of the 'laundry-basket' notes, Milgate demonstrates that Keynes was unable to make his assertions theoretically watertight. True, Keynes now claimed that 'there is no reason to suppose that positions of long-period equilibrium have an inherent tendency or likelihood to be positions of optimum output'.[20] But Milgate's point is that 'this conclusion does not follow from the *Treatise*-type analysis Keynes had presented in the same lecture', because by that analysis an 'equilibrium' always implied full employment. Milgate may well be correct in thinking that his extension of Keynes's argument, so as to reveal its inconsistency, 'follows from the *Treatise* framework'.[21] But surely it *only* follows if the *Treatise* framework is explicitly worked through with more rigour than Keynes himself supplied. In which case, one might conclude that Keynes seriously intended to maintain his proposition about sub-optimal equilibrium and lapsed from consistency in simultaneously invoking the *Treatise*.

Patinkin drew upon Bryce's notes, before the discovery of the laundry basket, to argue that implicit *Treatise* definitions vitiate Keynes's analysis. He goes on to cite what he identifies as 'further evidence that Keynes formulated his theory of effective demand after 1932'.[22] This evidence comprises the rough notes for Keynes's university lectures in the Easter Term of 1937, surveying his own ideas. 'I reached the conception of effective demand comparatively late on,' he then confessed. 'Those who are old enough and attended in 1931–1932 may remember a contraption of formulas of process of all sorts of lengths depending on technical factors with income emerging at a given date corresponding to input at an earlier date.' This was the time when the *ex ante* and *ex post* concepts would have been useful, as also in the correspondence of March 1932. But it should be remarked that Keynes deliberately restricts his statement to the 1931–2 academic year.[23] The obvious implication is surely that

[20] *JMK* xxix. 55 (Keynes's notes for 14 Nov. 1932); this part of the fragment is corroborated in both Bryce's and Tarshis's notes of that date.

[21] Milgate, 'The "new" Keynes papers', in John Eatwell and Murray Milgate (eds.), *Keynes's Economics and the Theory of Value and Distribution* (1983), 187–99, at 194. It is quite possible that the *Treatise*-like part of this fragment was not actually delivered; see n. 37 below.

[22] See *Keynes's Monetary Thought*, 72–3, for Patinkin's pioneering use of an early transcript of Bryce's notes; citation at 73 n. 11.

[23] *JMK* xiii. 180 (notes, 'Ex Post and Ex Ante'). In Cambridge the Michaelmas Term is Oct.–Dec., the Lent Term Jan.–Mar., and the Easter Term Apr.–June. The reference cannot be to the calendar years (hence including the Michaelmas Term of 1932) because, as has been seen above, Keynes did not lecture in 1931. The 1931–2 lectures were those of the Easter Term, 1932.

things had changed by the time Keynes began the following year's lectures in October 1932.

Given that stage (i) of the Harrod letter had been reached by May 1932, when therefore did stage (ii) come? To anticipate slightly, it can be shown that stage (iii), which came 'appreciably later', had been reached by October 1932. It seems overwhelmingly likely, therefore, that it was in the summer of 1932 that Keynes believed himself to have grasped the principle of effective demand. His long-standing concern with the relation between saving and investment thereby found new expression. As he put it later: 'The novelty in my treatment of saving and investment consists, not in my maintaining their necessary aggregate equality, but in the proposition that it is, not the rate of interest, but the level of incomes which (in conjunction with certain other factors) ensures their equality.'[24] Thus output had to be envisaged not as fixed or unique or optimal but as an equilibrator with many different possible positions.

Having experienced this revelation, Keynes recalled, 'the result of it was to leave the rate of interest in the air. If the rate of interest is not determined by saving and investment in the same way in which price is determined by supply and demand, how is it determined?'[25] In his letter to Harrod, Keynes described how the answer struck him: 'Then, appreciably later, came the notion of interest as being the measure of liquidity-preference, which became quite clear in my mind the moment I thought of it.' It was like a ripe apple falling off the tree—the fruit of his stale controversy with Robertson over hoarding and bearishness. Keynes acknowledged that the concept was 'somewhat analogous to the state of bearishness' but now simplified it into the public's 'preference for holding money and holding debts'. This idea now fell into place with a wholly new importance. In Keynes's university lecture of 31 October 1932 the new theory of interest was unveiled. As Bryce recorded it, Keynes's exposition led up to a triumphant conclusion: 'in itself the rate of interest is *an expression of liquidity preference.*'[26]

It is easy to find earlier adumbrations of the notion of liquidity preference—once one knows what to look for. Virtually any precautionary motive for holding money which an exhaustive treatment of the quantity theory might mention may seem to point in this direction. Here too 'everything is to be found in Marshall'; and

---

[24] *JMK* xiv. 211 ('Alternative theories of the rate of interest', *Econ. Jnl.*, Dec. 1937).
[25] Ibid. 212.
[26] Bryce notes, 31 Oct., 1932 (emphasis in original).

the *Treatises*'s reflections on bearishness can be read in the same way.[27] Yet at the time—as his exchanges with Robertson before the Macmillan Committee show—Keynes did not make the connection which later struck him as so obvious. The significance of liquidity preference was *as a theory of interest*, once the theory of interest was no longer conceived as equilibrating saving and investment.

This story has a bearing upon two contested points in Keynesian scholarship. The first is that it reinforces Milgate's convincing argument for seeing liquidity preference as a positive new suggestion rather than part of a negative critique of the classical theory of the rate of interest. Neither Keynes's rejection of the classical theory, therefore, nor his advocacy of the new theory of effective demand, depended crucially upon liquidity preference being true.[28] Secondly, however, there is an anomaly in Patinkin's contention that the theory of effective demand cannot be found in the Michaelmas 1932 lectures. His reading of the Bryce and Tarshis notes has led him to conclude that in October and November 1932 'Keynes's thinking was still largely in the mould of the *Treatise*'.[29] As has been acknowledged, from a doctrine–historical point of view the exposition of effective demand may still leave something to be desired at this point. But whatever the arguable shortcomings in this respect, the unambiguous proclamation of the liquidity preference concept surely clinches the chronology which Keynes outlined to Harrod. And since this new theory of interest constitutes stage (iii) of 'that most revealing letter', it can hardly be denied that stage (ii)—effective demand—must already have been reached.

'The Monetary Theory of Production'

When Tarshis arrived in Cambridge as an affiliated student he had already received a thorough drilling in the *Treatise*, in which he had become a devout believer; Bryce, on the other hand, as a refugee

---

[27] See Patinkin, *Keynes's Monetary Thought*, 37–40; reaffirmed in *Anticipations*, 9; also Kahn, *Making of General Theory*, 42–3.

[28] 'Keynes on the "classical" theory of interest', in Eatwell and Milgate (eds.), *Keynes's Economics*, 79–89, and Milgate, *Capital and Employment*, 111–22. It is interesting that Joan Robinson latterly showed no love for the liquidity preference concept; see her essay with Frank Wilkinson, 'Ideology and logic', in Fausto Vicarelli (ed.), *Keynes's Relevance Today* (1985), 88.

[29] Patinkin, *Anticipations*, 21–3, at 21; cf. *Keynes's Monetary Theory*, 79.

engineer, started with an open mind. Tarshis has testified that when he 'heard Keynes's first lecture in the autumn of 1932, along lines that seemed to differ from the *Treatise*, I wondered what he was talking about'.[30] The notes which he and Bryce took show why.

Keynes's lectures—like the early drafts of his new book—were now called 'The Monetary Theory of Production' and he began by pointing out that the change of title from 'The Pure Theory of Money' indicated a change of attitude concerning 'the influence of monetary manipulation on production rather than on prices'.[31] A monetary economy, he claimed, was different from Marshall's 'neutral economy', where money was simply treated as another commodity. Keynes now argued that 'so long as there is a deficiency [of] disbursement, entrepreneurs as a body will incur a loss whatever fluidity of adjustment and hence will throw men out of work.'[32] What, then, determined the volume of output in a monetary economy? The 'supply curve of output as a whole', Tarshis noted, was conceived 'as being a function of profit rather than of cost'. Profit in turn depended on aggregate demand. Changes in volume of output were how adjustments took place, and since income was equal to spending on current output, any curtailment of disbursement must be reflected in a contraction of income.[33]

This is really Keynes's first consistent exposition of 'the theory of the demand and supply for output as a whole' (as in stage (ii) of the Harrod letter). He was attempting to give an academic justification for his vernacular comment that 'one man's expenditure is another man's income'.[34] He had assured Hawtrey in advance: 'The whole thing comes out just as conveniently in terms of expenditure.'[35] But in the effort to make good this claim, his propositions about 'disbursement' were still rather cumbersome.

It was when he came to define savings that Keynes looked back to the *Treatise* rather than forward to the *General Theory*. In writing, '$S' = I$ under all circumstances', he was defining S' as 'Surplus'.[36] It

---

[30] Tarshis, 'Keynes as seen by his students in the 1930s', in Patinkin and Leith (eds.), *Keynes*, 49.

[31] Tarshis notes, 10 Oct. 1932.

[32] Bryce notes, 10 Oct. 1932; cf. *JMK* xxix. 51–2 (Keynes's notes for 10 Oct. 1932).

[33] Tarshis notes, 17 Oct. 1932.

[34] *JMK* xxi. 53 (Halley-Stewart lectures, Feb. 1932). The phrase was still in Keynes's mind in the winter of 1932–3. He repeated it in a letter to his mother, 11 Dec. 1932 (Keynes Papers); and in a radio broadcast, 4 Jan. 1933 (*JMK* xxi. 145).

[35] *JMK* xiii. 172 (Keynes to Hawtrey, 1 June 1932).

[36] Bryce notes, 24 Oct. 1932.

was still possible in this scheme for saving to be in excess of invest-ment, albeit with no reference to a full-employment equilibrium.[37] For Keynes explicitly challenged the orthodox notion of a unique position of equilibrium. 'If this is right, it is true that there is no long-period tendency to an optimum position, i.e. to destroy unemploy-ment.'[38] It followed that traditional theory was dealing with a special assumption—that of full employment—rather than a general case. In attempting to summarize the parameters of his new theory, Keynes suggested: 'Difficulty with all this is particularly in the language rather than the ideas.' He advised that the 'way to get all this is not to try to learn "the Russian"—the language but struggle through it and after that get the ideas then put them and use them in your own language'.[39]

In his final lecture (28 November 1932), Keynes offered a historical commentary on his conclusion that the volume of output was dependent upon the volume of investment, pointing out that it was only in the past century that this view had come to be regarded as eccentric. No sooner had he stumbled upon his new theory than he sought to establish a distinguished if unsuspected ancestry for it. The significant conjuncture is with the work which Piero Sraffa had been doing for his great edition of the works of Ricardo, notably the discovery of Malthus's side of the correspondence between them. Keynes had written a paper on Malthus in 1922, partly based on a pre-war draft, which he was currently revising for publication in *Essays in Biography*. He had started work on it by the end of October and it is highly likely that his copy was ready for the printers at the end of November 1932—certainly the proofs were sent out in mid-December. There are two major interpolations into the 1922 text, which cannot be later than November 1932 (with a further short emendation in page proof a few weeks later).[40]

---

[37] This is suggested in the fragment reproduced in *JMK* xxix. 55–6—an argument which Kahn now finds 'disconcerting'; *Making of General Theory* 113. Patinkin, however, has pointed out that the absence of such a passage in either Bryce's or Tarshis's notes means that there is no direct evidence that this passage was actually delivered; *Anticipations*, 21 n. 18.

[38] Bryce notes, 14 Nov. 1932.

[39] Bryce notes, 21 Nov. 1932. Tarshis has nothing on these concluding comments in the lecture.

[40] The stages of emendation can be dated from the manuscript and correspondence in file B/1, and from the letters to Lydia, in the Keynes Papers. Much of this is summarized by Moggridge in *JMK* x. 71 n (esp. pb. edn., 1985), and I am most grateful for his assistance. The misleading impression may have been created, however, that it is the major changes which date from early 1933, instead of just the short passage on 101–3. Everything quoted in the text below must have been written before the end of Keynes's lecture course on 28 Nov. 1932.

It was a new Malthus who emerged, one whose major discovery was 'something which might be described, though none too clearly, as "effective demand"'.[41] Compared with Ricardo, Malthus was found to have 'a firmer hold on what may be expected to happen in the real world'. It was Ricardo, by contrast, who had fathered the quantity theory of money. 'When one has painfully escaped from the intellectual domination of these pseudo-arithmetical doctrines', Keynes wrote, 'one is able, perhaps for the first time in a hundred years, to comprehend the real significance of the vaguer intuitions of Malthus.'[42] Keynes used the correspondence which Sraffa made available to him to draw his own picture of Ricardo as 'investigating the theory of the distribution of the product in conditions of equilibrium', while Malthus was 'concerned with what determines the *volume* of output day by day in the real world'. At this point Keynes added an afterthought: 'Malthus is dealing with the monetary economy in which we happen to live: Ricardo with the abstraction of a neutral money economy.'[43] These were, of course, exactly the lines along which he had been lecturing that term.

Keynes suddenly discovered in Malthus just what he was looking for. The retrieval of the lost correspondence by Sraffa ('from whom nothing is hid') enabled Keynes 'to show Malthus's complete comprehension of the effects of excessive saving on output *via* its effects on profits'. But the crucial letter, in which Malthus explained 'that the effective demand is diminished',[44] had not in fact remained hid until unearthed by Sraffa. It had been published in the *Economic Journal* in 1907, but was ignored by Keynes in preparing his 1922 paper. Only ten years later did it speak to his concerns and give him a name for his new concept—effective demand.

The evidence thus suggests that the inception of the *General Theory* must be placed firmly in 1932. Keynes's subsequent toils were chiefly in making its exposition fit for his professional colleagues. In this, as in other ways, what he wrote of Malthus—'The words and the ideas are simple'[45]—had application to himself. When Keynes gave a lecture in Stockholm after the publication of the *General Theory* he began (according to his notes):[46]

---

[41] When Keynes corrected the proofs, he changed 'might be described' to 'he described'; *JMK* x. 88 (*Essays in Biography*).

[42] *JMK* x. 88.

[43] Ink insertion into the text, printed in *JMK* x. 97.

[44] *JMK* x. 99; cf. 97.

[45] *JMK* x. 89.

[46] *JMK* xiv. 124

What I have to say intrinsically easy
Difficulty lies in its running against our habitual modes of thought
It is only to an audience of economists that it is difficult

This was, of course, precisely the audience ('my fellow econo-mists') he chose to address in the *General Theory*, which, he assured R. H. Brand, would be 'on extremely academic lines'.[47] Likewise, he responded to Robertson's comment that a large part of the theoretical structure was to him 'almost complete mumbo-jumbo' by stating that 'this book is a purely theoretical work, *not* a collection of wise-cracks'.[48]

By his own conception of economics as a branch of logic, he was committed to a rigorous formal presentation. In this respect his university lecture course in the Michaelmas Term of 1933 gave a more cogent account of the theory of effective demand according to the criteria of professional economists. It is easy to see why it was this account which reconciled Tarshis at the time and which has sub-sequently persuaded others to place the formulation of the theory in 1933.[49] Yet Keynes also paused to reflect in his lecture of 6 November upon a distinction between original thought, on the one hand, and what he called scholasticism on the other (rather akin to Schumpeter's distinction between the 'vision' and the rules of procedure). Keynes saw these as two necessary stages. His remarks made a considerable impression upon both Bryce and Tarshis; but the fullest version is given by a newcomer (Marvin Fallgatter):[50]

Even in mathematics, when it is a matter of original work, you do not think always in precise terms. The precise use of language comes at a late stage in the development of one's thoughts. You can think accurately and effectively long before you can so to speak photograph your thought. A not quite perfect epitome of this would be to say that when you adopt perfectly precise language you are trying to express yourself for the benefit of those who are incapable of thought.

Though he put the point somewhat differently on different occasions, Keynes continually adverted to a distinction of this kind. He thought that 'economics is a branch of logic, a way of thinking', but that attempts 'to turn it into a pseudo-science' should be

---

[47] *JMK* xxi. 344 (Keynes to Brand, 29 Nov. 1934).
[48] *JMK* xiii. 520 (Keynes to Robertson, 20 Feb. 1935).
[49] Tarshis in Patinkin and Leith (eds.), *Keynes*, 49.
[50] For Bryce's reaction see his notes and his recollections in Patinkin and Leith (ed.), *Keynes*, 41.

resisted.[51] The claims Keynes made for the *General Theory* were accordingly at once immodest and humble. 'If the simple basic ideas can become familiar and acceptable,' he wrote in 1937, 'time and experience and the collaboration of a number of minds will discover the best way of expressing them.'[52]

There has been no lack of economists ready to take up this invitation in elaborating widely differing versions of Keynesian economics. But Keynes's remark also poses a problem for historians, not in projecting his work forwards in time but in tracing it backwards. The task here is to identify the essential paradigm or message as Keynes apprehended it—the general theory behind the *General Theory*. What simple basic conception impressed itself upon Keynes's mind during 1932, allowing him to make sense in a new way of the relation between income and expenditure and between saving and investment?

The structure of his lecture course in the Michaelmas Term of 1932 points to the answer. After preparing the ground in his first lecture, Keynes stated his theme in the second. It was the distinction between what was true for the individual and what was true for the community as a whole which constituted that linchpin of the analysis. 'For [the] community as a whole disbursements must equal income, but this is not necessary for an individual. How are these compatible [?]—this is what people find difficult.'[53] Keynes was posing a basic issue which economists tend to take for granted. How could individual liberty in decision-making be reconciled with the necessity for an aggregate equality? Keynes's answer was that aggregate income would change so as to bring about this reconciliation. In the third lecture he introduced his variations in the form of 'two fundamental propositions'. One was familiar: that the harmony between individual choice in holding money and the necessity for total holdings to be what the banks create was brought about by changes in prices and income. The other he claimed as less familiar: 'while every individual has liberty to settle his own dispersals, the aggregate disbursements must be equal to total income.'[54]

It is generally understood that Keynesian economics shifted attention to aggregates and established a macro-economic approach

[51] *JMK* xiv. 296 (Keynes to Harrod, 4 July 1938).
[52] *JMK* xiv. 111 ('The general theory of employment').
[53] Bryce notes, 17 Oct. 1932
[54] Ibid. 24 Oct. 1932

to the analysis of the system as a whole. In doing so it identified as fallacious the claim, for example, that because individuals might benefit from cutting wages, everyone could beneficially do so at once: or that because any individual could achieve liquidity of investment, it was possible for the community as a whole. This 'fallacy of composition', however, plays a larger part than has been recognized in the structure of the *General Theory*. It is built into the architecture of the work as a whole. Book I, 'Introduction', concludes with a rejection of the direction taken by classical theory since Malthus. The last words of Book II, 'Definitions and Ideas', point to 'the vital difference between the theory of the economic behaviour of the aggregate and the theory of the behaviour of the individual unit, in which we assume that changes in the individual's own demand do not affect his income'.[55] Book III, 'The Propensity to Consume', likewise concludes with the sentence identifying unemployment as 'an inevitable result of applying to the conduct of the State the maxims which are best calculated to "enrich" an individual by enabling him to pile up claims to enjoyment which he does not intend to exercise at any definite time'.[56]

The first time the idea is introduced it is a *paradox*: 'It is natural to suppose that the act of an individual, by which he enriches himself without apparently taking anything from anyone else, must also enrich the community as a whole.' This ultimately forms the basis for a *distinction* between 'the theory of the individual industry or firm and of the rewards and the distribution between different uses of a *given* quality of resources on the one hand, and the theory of output and employment *as a whole* on the other hand'.[57] Keynes's master-stroke, however, was to provide an *explanation*. The reconciliation of aggregate saving and investment depended 'on saving being, like spending, a two-sided affair', with consequences for the incomes of others. 'The mere act of saving by one individual, being *two-sided* as we have shown above, forces some other individual to transfer to him some article of wealth, old or new.'[58]

---

[55] *JMK* xii. 85. In identifying Keynes's paradigm, Josef Steindl hammers home the general point I am stressing here; 'J. M. Keynes: Society and the economist', in Vicarelli (ed.), *Keynes's Relevance Today*, 99 ff. Harcourt and Shaughnessy also bring out the salience of the fallacy of composition in Harcourt (ed.), *Keynes and his Contemporaries*, 34–5.

[56] *JMK* vii. 131

[57] Ibid. 20, 293.

[58] Ibid. 84, 212.

In the *Treatise*, Keynes had emphasized the potential aggregate disparity between saving and investment from the point of view of the individual decision-makers. In the *General Theory* he insisted on their aggregate equality and showed how the double aspect of every transaction accounted for this identity, requiring changes in prices, output, and employment in the process. This followed 'merely from the fact that there cannot be a buyer without a seller or a seller without a buyer'.[59] This conception informed all his thinking by the end of 1932. 'The course of exchange, as we all know, moves round a closed circle,' he wrote in the *New Statesman*. 'When we transmit the tension, which is beyond our own endurance, to our neighbour, it is only a question of a little time before it reaches ourselves again travelling round the circle.'[60]

What prompted Keynes to take up this idea? At a formal level the fallacy of composition must have been familiar to him. The standard modern treatment was in Book III of J. S. Mill's *System of Logic*, which he had utilized for his own purposes in his work on probability. Admittedly, Keynes wrote in his *Treatise on Probability*: 'The treatment of this topic in the *System of Logic* is exceedingly bad.'[61] The work of J. A. Hobson, to whom the *General Theory* paid a belated but generous tribute, ought to have proved suggestive to Keynes, but there is little evidence that it actually did so.[62]

The general notion, in fact, enters prominently into Keynes's writings from the end of 1930. In 'The Great Slump of 1930', he gave several examples of the way 'individual producers base illusory hopes on courses of action which would benefit an individual producer or class of producers so long as they were alone in pursuing them, but which benefit no one if every one pursues them'.[63] In February 1931 he suggested that 'each individual is impelled by his paper losses or profits to do precisely the opposite of what is desirable in the general interest'.[64] When advocating a tariff in the next month, he cited the advantage each employer saw in wage cuts when he ignored the consequent reduction in his customers' incomes. This point was

---

[59] Ibid. 84.
[60] *JMK* x.xi. 213 (*New Statesman and Nation*, 24 Dec. 1932).
[61] *JMK* viii. 298 n.
[62] For Hobson's work and its relation to that of Keynes see Peter Clarke, *Liberals and Social Democrats* (1978), esp. 46–54, 125–7, 226–42, 268–74. I shall shortly publish a further essay on this topic.
[63] *JMK* ix. 128 (*Nation*, 20 Dec. 1930).
[64] *JMK* xx. 480 (Royal Institution lecture, Feb. 1931).

reiterated in the summer in the Addendum to the Macmillan Report, which also stressed the 'false analogy between the position of a particular firm and that of the community as a whole' in another respect, namely that each, but not all, could increase liquid resources. Almost an identical proposition was to reappear in the *General Theory*.[65]

By 1932 he was speaking of 'the *disharmony* of general and particular interest', and citing in illustration the remedies now popularly advocated: 'Competitive wage reductions, competitive tariffs, competitive liquidation of foreign assets, competitive currency deflations, competitive economy campaigns, competitive contractions of new development ...'.[66] It seems fair to conclude that, at this juncture, Keynes was continually prompted by the experience of the world slump to ask whether strategies which were advantageous for one firm or one country—on the paradigm of 'competitiveness'— offered a universally valid solution; and that he progressively came to generalize this distinction.

The General Theory of Employment

In the discussions which took place in 1930 under the auspices of the Macmillan Committee and the EAC's committee of economists, Keynes tried to apply the analysis of the *Treatise* to Britain's current economic difficulties. He succeeded in establishing a fair measure of rapport with such economists as Pigou, Robertson, and Hawtrey, basically because he shared with them a fundamentally neo-classical outlook which they were all prepared to adapt to unpropitious circumstances. Only when he subsequently evolved the theory of effective demand did Keynes really break with this tradition. If he must bear the main responsibility for breaching this consensus, it would be a misleadingly static view to suppose his the sole responsibility. Just as the face-to-face arguments of 1930 helped set Keynes's mind working in new directions, so were Hawtrey and Robertson, those astoundingly assiduous students of his *œuvre*,

---

[65] *Macmillan Report*, Addendum I, par. 15, reprinted in *JMK* xx. 289; cf. *JMK* ix. 235 (*New Statesman and Nation*), 7 Mar. 1931; *JMK* vii. 160. See also his Columbia address, *New York Times*, 6 June 1934, quoted in Winch, *Economics and Policy*, 246.

[66] *JMK* xxi. 52–3 (Halley-Stewart lecture, Feb. 1932).

prompted to reformulate their own critical exposition. Above all, Pigou, who deplored that fact that 'Dennis has been spending years meticulously examining and criticising Mr Keynes on this and that',[67] published his own major study of unemployment. Lionel Robbins, too, who had resisted the move towards an interventionist consensus on policy, now subjected it to a full critique. It would be ludicrous to suppose that Keynes's *General Theory* was produced in a vacuum, while his professional colleagues laid down their pens, awestruck, waiting for him to finish it and convert them.

This was not at all Pigou's frame of mind. He was, after all, the Professor of Political Economy at Cambridge, and not inclined to submit to the intellectual hegemony of a turbulent junior colleague, returned like the prodigal son from the flesh-pots of Whitehall. If Keynes was treated at all deferentially, it was by the impressionable young who thronged his lectures. 'It was as if we were listening to Charles Darwin or Isaac Newton,' one student recalled. 'The audience sat hushed as Keynes spoke.'[68] While Pigou conceded that it was 'natural and right in the present deplorable state of the world's affairs that many economists should seek to play a part in guiding conduct,' he insisted that they were essentially 'engineers, not engine drivers'. He considered, moreover, that economists who had concentrated on monetary explanations of depression had tended 'to overstress somewhat the role that money plays in more normal times'.[69] (Keynes's lectures for two years had been called 'The Monetary Theory of Production'.) Pigou called his own study *The Theory of Unemployment* and began his preface: 'This book is addressed to students of economics.' By December 1933 Keynes had upstaged him by changing the title of his forthcoming study to *The General Theory of Employment* and was to begin his preface: 'This book is chiefly addressed to my fellow economists.' Keynes's choice of Pigou as his prime target of criticism has often occasioned surprise throughout the world of economics; in its own parochial setting it is readily comprehensible.

In front of the Macmillan Committee, Pigou had often spoken in a way which seems to anticipate Keynes's later ideas. Thus, while it was generally agreed that, at least in theory, unemployment could be attributed to the fact that real wages were too high, Pigou insisted

[67] *JMK* xxix. 177 (Pigou to Keynes, July 1938).
[68] Michael Straight, *After Long Silence* (1983), 57.
[69] A. C. Pigou, *The Theory of Unemployment* (1933), v.

that one could alternatively explain unemployment by saying 'that the real rate of wages is all right, but there is not enough demand'.[70]

If a ship is overloaded you can either say there is too much cargo, or you can say that the ship is too small. It is really a matter of adjustment.

By 1933, Keynes was quite clear that the size of the ship was determined by total investment, thereby adjusting so as to accommodate the requisite cargo of output (or employment). This was the theory of effective demand. It was not, however, what Pigou had in mind in reproducing 'the parable of the overloaded ship' in his book. For he now juxtaposed it with the assertion that 'from a long-period point of view, the real wage-rates for which people stipulate, so far from being independent of the demand function, are a function of that function in a very special way'. The tendency was thus for real wages to adjust to demand. Hence, with free competition and perfect mobility of labour, there would 'always be at work a strong tendency for wage-rates to be so related to demand that everybody is employed'. Unemployment was due to the fact that 'frictional resistances prevent the appropriate wage adjustments from being made instantaneously' when demand changed.[71] Saying that demand was deficient was thus only a way of saying that prices were— temporarily or exceptionally, albeit for understandable reasons— insufficiently flexible to restore full employment.

'Have you read the Prof's book carefully?' Keynes demanded of Robertson in September 1933. The reason Keynes thought that 'it's simply nonsense from beginning to end' was essentially that its propositions about real wages rested on a concealed assumption that prices were constant.[72] In short, as Keynes put it in his lectures, it rested on the 'supposition that reduction in real wages is [the] same thing as reductions of money wages'.[73] But if prices and wages simply chased each other down a spiral—since 'one man's expenditure is another man's income'—then in theory there was no means of

---

[70] *Macmillan Evidence*, Q. 5949.

[71] *Theory of Unemployment*, 252–3; cf. 27. It should be said that Michael Stewart, in the first edition of *Keynes and After* (Harmondsworth, 1967), 68, conveyed a fair impression of the thrust of this passage; his treatment was in this respect the butt of special pleading from T. W. Hutchinson, *Economics and Economic Policy in Britain* (1968), 289–90. There was actually no need for Stewart to withdraw these particular remarks in his 2nd edn. (Harmondsworth, 1972), 73–4.

[72] *JMK* xiii. 310.

[73] Tarshis notes, 16 Oct. 1933.

effecting the necessary cut in real wages. One firm might do it; one country might do it; but in *aggregate* it could not be done. Here was Keynes, Robertson reflected, 'saying wage reductions are no good, and Pigou saying they are a lot of good', splitting the Faculty wide open—'How I wish we could form a Cambridge front again!'[74]

Keynes's lectures in the Michaelmans Term of 1933 illustrate the breadth of his disagreement with Pigou. Keynes began by surveying the different forms in which he had sought to express his underlying ideas over the years and identified a general analytical trend towards 'what determines output', and hence the level of employment.[75] Pigou's theory was in this sense the latest expression of the 'classical' approach, resting on two postulates: first, that the wage was equal to the marginal product of labour and, second, that the utility of the marginal wage was equal to the disutility of that amount of work. The first postulate explained the demand for labour—it was worth while for an employer to pay an extra man just as much as the value he produced—and Keynes accepted it. The second postulate explained the supply of labour in terms of decisions by workers to set their real wages at the going rate that was compatible with them all getting the jobs they wanted. This formed the gist of the lecture of 16 October 1933, just as it later formed the gist of chapter 2 of the *General Theory*. What the 'classical' theory implied was that unemployment of a frictional nature could perfectly well exist, as could unemployment that was 'voluntary' in the sense that workers, individually or collectively, preferred it to settling for a realistic wage.

According to Keynes, the classical theory assumed that the reward of labour was set in real not money terms, whereas in a money economy such barter conceptions were inapplicable. The existence of money thus crucially impaired labour's ability to set its own real wage, since the prices of the goods to be purchased with a given money wage—which gave it its real value—were themselves set in an interdependent way. This, rather than any generalizations about uncertainty, was the significance of the money economy. For there was no saying how much of current money income would be spent and, as Malthus had discerned, a deficiency of effective demand was a possibility. 'Ricardo foisted on economics the idea that supply creates its own demand,' Keynes explained; but he preferred to say

---

[74] *JMK* xiii. 313–14 (Robertson to Keynes, 15 Sept. 1933).
[75] Bryce notes, 16 Oct. 1933.

that 'expenditure creates its own income'.[76] It followed that 'firms taken as a whole cannot protect themselves as a whole'—either by switching production, which was simply a game of musical chairs, or by cutting money wages, which in aggregate would not reduce real wages.[77]

There was enough matter here for four lectures. In the fifth Keynes repeated much of what he had initially advanced a year previously as his resolution of the paradox: that individuals were free to make their own decisions about saving and spending, yet, in aggregate, demand was necessarily equal to income, and saving to investment. Bryce and Tarshis had heard all this before, but to Marvin Fallgatter it was doubly novel; for Fallgatter was not only a new arrival but was himself a physicist, sitting in on Keynes's lectures for an economist friend back in Wisconsin. With his combination of an innocent ear and a facility in shorthand, Fallgatter gives the most mimetically faithful impression of how the lectures of November 1933 actually sounded. (At one point, for example, it sounded to him as though Keynes were talking about 'Mr Carns' and his multiplier.)[78]

In this equality of aggregate Disbursements equalling aggregate Income, there is widespread confusion, which is really quite a simple-minded paradox. It arises from the supposition in that one is free to spend what he chooses, apart from his income (within limits), and to earn what he may, apart from his expenditures. But your decision to disburse is not yours only, any more than marriage is. You must find a vendor to agree, if you wish to disburse.

Though savings and investment might be distinct for each individual, they were reconciled in aggregate because of the double-sided nature of each transaction. What did not follow, however, was the 'common-sense' conclusion that an increased propensity to save thereby produced the same increment of investment. Keynes introduced the illustration that a decision not to have dinner today merely dampens down expectations rather than, as in the classical theory, transferring entrepreneurs' efforts to the provision of dinner next week. Since savings are still equal to investment, the net effect is that[79]

---

[76] Bryce notes, 23 Oct. 1933.
[77] Ibid. 30 Oct. 1933.
[78] Fallgatter notes, 13 Nov., 1933; cf. above, n. 9. The sense of 'apart from' in this passage is 'irrespective of'.
[79] Ibid. 20 Nov. 1933.

income will settle down at such a level that people in the aggregate will choose to save an amount $S=I$. Although the act of saving seems to be a matter of individual free will, it is actually determined for society at large in this manner.

Keynes naturally gave a forceful account of his new theory of interest, based on liquidity preference, which was an alternative to the classical theory, based on the demand for saving and investment. But he also acknowledged that Marshall had been groping for a more subtle and complex conception, based on the marginal efficiency of capital. In a revealing passage, Keynes characterized Marshall's efforts to allow for the interactions here:[80]

in effect he says to himself, Good Lord, I am in danger of becoming circular! and to the reader he passes on the warning not to pay too much attention to what has just been said, and the argument vanishes in smoke. This is characteristic of Marshall. You can't find much truth in him, and yet you cannot convict him of error. He always seems to sense the difficulties and to shun them. He skates about most beautifully, and seems to have a keen sense of the nearness of thin ice, and he never crosses it or lingers too near it. So you don't realize that he has never met the problem and solved it, for he has kept on going all the time, and he has travelled a considerable distance.

Keynes's decision in the *General Theory* to take issue explicitly with Pigou was offensive in a double or triple sense. 'The two teachers under whom I was first brought up in the subject, Marshall and Prof. Pigou,' Keynes wrote in a draft, 'have both held that controversy in our subject is unsatisfactory and distasteful and should be strongly deprecated.'[81] Pigou not only agreed with Marshall: he was chauvinistically protective of his memory. Keynes not only departed from their precepts: he did so by betraying an unfilial disrespect for Marshall—out loud, in front of the under-graduates—and by subjecting Pigou's own work to a frontal assault. Keynes's basic rationale in doing so was his sense that, however sophisticated the refinements made to it, the orthodox analysis was generically different from his own, and that this needed to be brought out.

It was not that the Prof. was to be chastised for falling down on the job—'Professor Pigou's *Theory of Unemployment* seems to me to get out of the classical theory all that can be got out of it'[82]—but that

---

[80] Ibid. 27 Nov. 1933; cf. *JMK* vii. 186–90.
[81] *JMK* xiii. 469.   [82] *JMK* vii. 82.

he was flogging a dead horse. Keynes eventually decided to devote an appendix to a detailed critique of Pigou's work which, he told Kahn, 'has a dreadful fascination for me, and I cannot leave it alone'.[83] Pigou, claimed Keynes, was not really presenting a theory of *unemployment* but rather 'a discussion of how much employment there will be, given the supply function of labour, when the conditions for full employment are satisfied'.[84] Keynes thus began his lectures in the Michaelmas Term of 1934 (as Tarshis boldly set out):[85]

The *General* Theory of Unemployment (in contrast to 'the *classical* theory of unemployment')
—the postulates of classical theory relevant to particular limited case
—the special case assumed by classical theory is not a picture of actual society.

When Keynes gave a radio broadcast in November 1934 which presented his current thinking alongside what a number of other economists were saying, he spoke of a gulf between two groups: 'On the one side are those who believe that the existing economic system is, in the long run, a self-adjusting system, though with creaks and groans and jerks, and interrupted by time lags, outside interference and mistakes.' Among other contributors to the series, Henderson, Brand, and Robbins were examples. This was a formidable position, buttressed by a century of economic analysis. But Keynes now chose to range himself, by contrast, with the heretics, like Hobson, believing that 'their flair and their instinct move them towards the right conclusions'.[86]

As in the economists' committee in 1930, the young Robbins resisted the insidious trend of Keynes's thinking with trenchant lucidity fortified by singular intellectual courage. *The Great Depression* (1934) conceded that 'the majority of the leaders of public opinion seem to have drawn from the events of the last few years the conclusion that more intervention is necessary.'[87] With Roosevelt's New Deal under way, Robbins echoed an old aphorism of one of its prominent British supporters, saying that 'it has been easier to bamboozle a President than to debamboozle him'. In other comments

[83] *JMK* xiii. 525.
[84] *JMK* vii. 275.
[85] Tarshis notes, 22 Oct. 1934; cf. *JMK* xiv. 106 ('The theory of the rate of interest', 1937).
[86] *JMK* xiii. 486–7, 489 ('Poverty in Plenty', Nov. 1934).
[87] *Great Depression*, 197.

on 'the dilettante economists of wealthy universities', too, Keynes was surely an unidentified target, as he was for the rebuke that 'it is not really very clever to pretend that the bulk of expert opinion in the past has always been actuated by ignorant prejudice'.[88] Although Robbins fully appreciated that *laissez-faire* was now a tainted philosophy, he thought it one which was misunderstood, and, as a prospectus of economic freedom, that it constituted a guide to real recovery. For his case was that, since the First World War, the economy had been hampered in its free workings by manifestations of institutional inelasticity—'The post-war rigidity of wages is a by-product of Unemployment Insurance'[89]—which had entrenched restriction and maladjustment. 'If the obstacles to cost adjustment in Great Britain had been less formidable,' Robbins insisted, 'the whole history of the last ten years would have been different.' Misplaced philanthropy, muddled policy, and electoral pusillanimity had combined to *prevent* the economy returning to health. 'We eschew the sharp purge,' he commented. 'We prefer the lingering disease.'[90]

In speaking of a gulf, therefore, Keynes was not exaggerating. Although given to a popular audience, his talk focused on differences of fundamental theory rather than immediate policy, and he explicitly rejected any postulate that the market tended towards a full-employment equilibrium, even a postulate qualified in practice by imperfections which inhibited this tendency.[91] This marked the distance he had moved since the *Treatise*, where the analysis is basically imperfectionist. It may also account for a striking difference which has often been observed between the *Treatise*, with its concern for international considerations, and the *General Theory*, with its model of a closed economy. The theory of the *Treatise* was premised upon equilibrium, with market forces tending towards it; but the policies appropriate for Britain at the time of its composition were those which would tackle an actual disequilibrium. If wages or interest rates displayed a rigidity inappropriate for domestic harmony, it could all be blamed upon the Gold Standard—in short, the special case.

---

[88] Ibid. 124, 142, 168.

[89] Ibid. 61.

[90] Ibid. 186, 73.

[91] Eatwell and Milgate have established the useful term 'imperfectionist' and identify the possible reasons in a string of frictions, rigidities, and misapprehensions—'any factor which causes the market to work *imperfectly* will do'; *Keynes's Economics*, 3.

After September 1931, however, there was no such external constraint. Nor does the *General Theory* depend upon any assumption about the rigidity of wages. On the contrary, it was the 'classical' theory which was 'accustomed to rest the supposedly self-adjusting character of the economic system on an assumed fluidity of money-wages; and, when there is rigidity, to lay on this rigidity the blame of maladjustment'.[92] As for the interest rate, where Keynes of the *Treatise* had supplemented 'creaks and groans and jerks' with deleterious 'outside interference' in keeping Bank rate too high, its significance was now conceived quite differently. Though important, it was no longer the crucial mechanism whose *modus operandi* equilibrated saving and investment. As Keynes put it, 'interest rates are determined by the demand and supply for money, not by the demand and supply for durable goods'.[93] The interest rate might well be higher than the rate of return (on marginal investments) needed to sustain full employment; but since the one was primarily determined by liquidity preference and the other by effective demand, the whole process of equilibration must be understood in a new way.

The theory of effective demand maintains that an equilibrium between savings and investment is achieved through changes in total income, in overall output, and in aggregate employment. Keynes therefore wrote that 'the weight of my criticism is directed against the inadequacy of the *theoretical* foundations of the laissez-faire doctrine upon which I was brought up and which for many years I taught ...'.[94] The lack of self-adjusting forces was the real meaning of the new emphasis upon the possibility of a sub-optimal equilibrium. His initial exposition in 1932–3, however, did not rest upon any general propositions about the role of uncertainty; at least in the making of the theory of effective demand, Keynes was no fundamentalist.

Now equilibrium is a concept which economists have refined since Keynes wrote. Patinkin has identified 'the rigorous sense that nothing in the economy tends to change', and in this sense it remains true that the *General Theory* can be seen as 'a dynamic theory of unemployment *dis*equilibrium'.[95] But the salient point for Keynes

[92] *JMK* vii. 257.

[93] Keynes to Henderson, 28 May 1936, Henderson Papers, Box 10; cf. the formulation by Bryce (approved by Keynes), *JMK* xxix. 142.

[94] *JMK* vii. 339.

[95] *Anticipations*, 14; *Keynes's Monetary Thought*, 113. Patinkin stresses the consistency between these two propositions. See also Gilbert, *Keynes's Impact on Monetary Economics*, 46, 178–9.

was that nothing would tend to change *the level of employment*. He once expostulated to Hawtrey: 'heavens, my doctrine of full employment is what the whole of my book is about!'[96]

Bryce records that when Keynes first advanced the argument that there was 'no long-period tendency to an optimum position' in his lectures of October and November 1932, he distinguished two senses of 'long period':[97]

(A)—one towards which short period moves (1) if no other forces arise (2) the stable position it would arrive at

(B)—or is it the period when the optimum disposition of production would be achieved.

This reads in a somewhat ragged way, but the first sense focuses on the notion of the economy reaching a position of rest, whereas the second focuses on the extent to which the market has satisfied all agents. When Keynes used the term equilibrium in the *Treatise*, its rhetorical overtones were benign, but in the *General Theory* the connotation was minatory. The author of the *Treatise* recognized unemployment as a symptom of disequilibrium, because the economy was not *in balance*. The author of the *General Theory* disclosed the enormity of unemployment at equilibrium, because the economy was *at rest*.

In writing the *General Theory*, Keynes sought to grapple with economic theory in a fundamental way. Admittedly, certain directions were set by his long-standing concerns. But Schumpeter is misleading in suggesting that the 'vision' of the *General Theory* is to be found as far back as 1919, in *The Economic Consequences of the Peace*.[98] It was to be another decade before Keynes, almost against his inclinations, became progressively drawn into a reappraisal of everything he had taught and been taught. Little wonder that he wrote of it as 'a struggle of escape from habitual modes of thought and expression'.[99] His project must be understood as a rigorous inquiry, the course of which became crucially determined by the unfolding of an immanent logic of discovery. Joan Robinson recalled of this period:[100]

---

[96] *JMK* xiv. 24. The salience of *employment* is nicely brought out by A. Asimakopulos's review of Patinkin, 'Anticipations of Keynes's General Theory', *Can. Jnl. of Econ.*, 16 (1983), 517–30, at 518–19; the same author's 'Keynes, Patinkin, historical time, and equilibrium analysis', ibid. 6 (1973), 179–88, is also very much to the point, esp. 184–7.   [97] Bryce notes, 14 Nov. 1932.

[98] Joseph A. Schumpeter, *Ten Great Economists* (1952), esp. 267–8; *History of Economic Analysis*, 42.

[99] *JMK* vii, p. xxiii (preface to *General Theory*).

[100] Quoted in Lambert, 'The evolution of Keynes's thought', 256.

I don't really agree with the idea of who influenced whom. Logic is the same for everybody. Keynes opened up a whole subject—we helped to clear up some connections which we saw—discovered—not invented.

The move away from the *Treatise* was determined in this way. The searching critique from the Circus pointed towards new concepts; their significance took time to sink in; at least one fruitful contribution fed in from outside Cambridge; and the sharp minds of Robertson, Hawtrey, Harrod, and others helped shape the book in draft. It may not be perfect in exposition but it can fairly be taken as a considered expression of its author's central convictions.

Those convictions, as he recognized, had been formed in his own mind in several stages. What organized them was a view of market transactions in which the random disparities of individual behaviour were contained by the requirement that all such transactions were double-sided. So in aggregate they were reconciled—not through a unique market-clearing adjustment of prices but through output and income changes. In equilibrium the economy was 'at rest' but might well not be 'in balance'. It followed that economic theory could not postulate market tendencies of a self-righting nature. To do so was to lapse into the fallacy that what one could do, all could do. Such were the relatively simple ideas, linked by a strong sense of logical necessity, which, by the close of the year 1932, guided Keynes's thinking.

12

The impact of the theory of effective demand

Policy and politics

In the years 1928–31, surrounding the publication of the *Treatise*, Keynes had wallowed up to his neck in public affairs—not only as an expert who uniquely combined membership of both the Macmillan Committee and the committee of economists of the EAC, but also as a partisan whose polemics against Baldwin or Snowden and in favour of Lloyd George or Mosley were as often considered unforgivable as unforgettable. Yet October 1931 saw a General Election in which 'Mr Keynes the politician' took no active part, while it marked the beginning of an academic year in which 'Professor Keynes the economist' resumed his scholarly duties in a more single-minded way than at any time since the Great War. Whereas the *Treatise* could be seen as a *tour de force* in squaring the current policy of the Liberal party with neo-classical economic analysis, there is a striking absence of similarly explicit political influences upon the making of the theory of effective demand. It was not until the beginning of 1933— after those 'moments of transition which were for me personally moments of illumination' had led from 'what I *used* to believe' to 'my present views'—that Keynes again intervened decisively in the debate on economic policy. If his proposals for loan-financed public works sounded familiar, his arguments in support had now been recast.

Keynes had not, of course, kept himself in purdah. In March 1932, for example, he made a broadcast in which he sought to appropriate the new catch-phrase 'state planning' for his own macro-economic strategy. 'Let us mean by planning, or national economy,' he proposed, 'the problem of the *general* organization of resources as distinct from the *particular* problems which are the province of the individual business technician and engineer.'[1] More specifically, he refused to distance himself from the two policies, tariffs and public works, which had previously found justification under the 'special case' of the *Treatise*, even though this reason for sanctioning them had disappeared when Britain left the Gold Standard in September

---

[1] *JMK* xxi. 87.

1931. Although he had thereupon published a formal withdrawal of his support for a general tariff, a few months later he declared himself 'still not prepared to oppose it today with any heat of conviction'.[2]

The timing of this comment is significant, coming in a public lecture given on the very day (4 February 1932) that the National Government's Import Duties Bill was introduced in the House of Commons. Here, declared the Chancellor of the Exchequer, Neville Chamberlain, in a rare display of emotion, was the vindication of his father's crusade for Tariff Reform. For many of those Liberals who had initially supported the National Government, Free Trade was still a great principle which could not be compromised; and the Cabinet had almost broken up on this issue before MacDonald temporarily papered over the cracks by abandoning collective responsibility in favour of an agreement to differ.[3] For Keynes, by contrast, who had never had much time for the National Government in the first place, the abandonment of Free Trade was the least of its defects. 'A year ago,' he wrote in April 1932, 'I was maintaining that the case for a revenue tariff was made out, and the Chancellor's figures show that the same is true today.' His dissent here was limited to the caveat that 'the depreciation of sterling readjusts British costs to world costs far more effectively than a tariff could, and has greatly weakened the case for protective duties'.[4]

For the rest of 1932, Keynes's initiatives were not in the field of policy but in the realm of theory. To be sure, he was ready to 'join in' when, in June 1932, Meade and Harrod organized a letter to *The Times*, signed by virtually all the economists at Oxford and Cambridge (though rather few from London), urging expansionary measures.[5] The desirability of private as well as public spending was the current theme of newspaper debate, in the course of which Pigou was prepared to claim that 'economic opinion is practically unanimous' in not enjoining personal abstinence as an appropriate response to the slump.[6] Indeed, Pigou drafted a further letter to *The Times* in October 1932, in which he stated the general case for pressing on with useful spending, whether public or private. Keynes

[2] *JMK* xxi. 57 (Halley-Stewart lecture, first given 4 Feb. 1932).
[3] See C. L. Mowat, *Britain between the Wars, 1918–40* (1955), 415 ff.; David Marquand, *Ramsay MacDonald* (1977), 709–13.
[4] *JMK* xxi. 103 (*Evening Standard*, 20 Apr. 1932).
[5] *JMK* xxi. 125–6: Elizabeth Durbin, *New Jerusalems* (1985), 140–1.
[6] Letter to *The Times*, 7 June 1932.

was one of six signatories to this letter, which was countered by four Professors at the LSE (T. E. Gregory, F. A. von Hayek, Arnold Plant, and Lionel Robbins). The original six thereupon wrote again, denying that the implementation of plans to utilize resources—say, to build libraries or museums—would, in effect, crowd out the funds needed for spontaneous recovery, 'This conception,' claimed Pigou's group, 'though since its burial by Adam Smith it has enjoyed many resurrections, is an illusion.'[7]

Keynes's distinctive voice comes through in a letter of July 1932 to the *Manchester Guardian*. 'It is often said by wiseacres that we cannot spend more than we earn,' he commented. 'That is, of course, true enough of the individual, but it is exceedingly misleading if it is applied to the community as a whole.' The fallacy of composition was thus central to his argument, permitting him to anticipate in a vernacular form the propositions he was to develop in his university lectures of the following term. 'For the community as a whole,' he argued, 'it would be much truer to say that we cannot earn more than we spend.'[8]

Such interventions, however, even including those instigated by others, were fitful and spasmodic. They were not a part of a sustained public campaign, still less one concerted with his old friends in the Liberal party. Mosley's New Party had been annihilated in the 1931 General Election and its leader was now marching in step with fascism. It may be that it was Keynesianism which made Mosley's version of fascism distinctively English; but Keynes's own aim in this new phase was, as he told Mosley in 1933, 'not to embrace you but to save the country from you'.[9] The National Government was entrenched in power, with a predominantly Conservative composition and outlook. As Keynes saw it, 'we are now in the grip of reactionary forces'; and he told Harold Macmillan in September 1932: 'There is probably no practical good sense in any efforts except those deliberately aimed at ousting them.'[10] Yet the prospects for doing so were bleak.

Keynes acknowledged that the Labour party 'represents the only organised body of opinion outside the National Government', and would 'therefore be called on some day, presumably, to form an

[7] *JMK* xxi. 140 (*The Times*, 21 Oct. 1932). This episode is covered in T. W. Hutchison, *Economics and Economic Policy* (1968), 287–8.

[8] *JMK* xxi. 126.

[9] See Robert Skidelsky, *Oswald Mosley* (1975), 302, 305–6 n.

[10] *JMK* xxi. 127.

alternative government'.[11] His younger professional colleagues, like Richard Kahn, Austin and Joan Robinson, James Meade, and Roy Harrod, were all generally sympathetic to the Labour Party. Indeed, Meade and Harrod were notable for carrying Keynesianism into the deliberations of the New Fabian Research Bureau, where many of Labour's future economic policies were now being thrashed out. Hugh Dalton became the patron of these activities, observing that his former protégé Robbins had 'stiffened in an old-fashioned *laissez-faire* attitude of approach to current problems', and concluding that, under Hayek's influence, Robbins, 'over-cultivates his feud with Keynes'.[12] To Dalton it now seemed 'curious that this movement should have set in at the London School, when both at Oxford and Cambridge there is a distinct movement among the younger teachers of economics in the opposite direction'.[13] The New Fabians' efforts evoked interest and sympathy from Keynes, who saw it as the Labour party's task 'to become intellectually emancipated as to what is economically sound, without losing either its political strength and its political organisation, which goes so deep into the social and economic life of England, or its ideals and ultimate goals'.[14]

It is, however, Keynes's total lack of party affiliations at this stage which stands out. 'My own aim is economic reform by the methods of political liberalism,' he affirmed in 1934;[15] but the Liberal party lay in ruins and it is a mistake to identify Keynes as a partisan supporter in this period. In October 1935, Herbert Samuel, as leader of the Liberal party, sent out the usual pre-election appeal for funds. Now Keynes's generosity for public objects is well attested, and his personal assets were in a very healthy state at the time (around a quarter of a million pounds). Yet he turned Samuel down flat, primarily 'because I do not really agree with what you quite properly stress in your letter, namely, the question of maintaining the separate identity of the Liberal Party'.[16] Conversely, Keynes likewise resisted the plea put by A. L. Rowse, as a sympathetic Labour student of his ideas, that it was necessary 'to place yourself in touch with the group

---

[11] *JMK* xxi. 128 (*New Statesman*, 17 Sept. 1932).

[12] Pimlott, 165 (Dalton diary, 6–8 Jan. 1932). See Ben Pimlott, *Hugh Dalton* (1985) 212–19, and Durbin, *New Jerusalems*, 135–40.

[13] Quoted in Pimlott, *Hugh Dalton*, 215.

[14] *JMK* xxi. 36 ('The dilemma of modern socialism', *Pol. Quarterly*, Apr.–June 1932).   [15] *JMK* xxviii. 29 (letter to *New Statesman and Nation*, 11 Aug. 1934).

[16] *JMK* xxi. 373 (Keynes to Samuel, 23 Oct. 1935); cf. *JMK* xii. 11, Table 3, showing Keynes's assets.

interest which will make your views, when right, effective'—that is, to throw in his lot with Labour.[17]

When Keynes re-entered the debate on economic policy, it was as a free-lance. An article in the *Daily Mail* on New Year's Day 1933 was a curtain-raiser. In it he applauded the steps that had been taken towards recovery—the escape from 'the impediments of a moribund gold system' and, in consequence, the successful establishment of cheap money to encourage enterprise, and the conversion of the War Loan to lower interest rates. But the signs of improvement were 'partial and precarious, relative not absolute'. He accused the Ministry of Health of undoing the good effects on employment of tariffs and devaluation by its policy of restricting local authority borrowing for capital schemes. 'The total unemployment thus caused is much greater than the direct unemployment, since each man whose purchasing power is curtailed by his being put out of work diminishes the employment he can give to others, and so on in a vicious circle.' The same mode of argument was then applied to the forthcoming Budget: 'Aggressive taxation may defeat its own ends by diminishing the income to be taxed.'[18] The underlying analysis was once more based on the income–expenditure link.

Broadcasting with his old friend Stamp later in the same week, Keynes began briskly by demanding, 'today isn't it getting realised pretty generally that one man's expenditure is another man's income?' Starting from this 'central truth, never to be forgotten', he went on to the offensive against the policy of cuts and restriction by public authorities, especially the Ministry of Health. In this sense, 'every pound saved puts a man out of work'. It followed that measures which reduced the national income could not be a sensible strategy for balancing the Budget. 'Look after the unemployment, and the budget will look after itself,' he urged. What Keynes had in mind was a more flexible attitude towards providing for the sinking fund during a period of depression, and thus countenancing a Budget which the purists would have regarded as unbalanced. Keynes himself, no doubt for reasons of prudence, did not explicitly recommend the Chancellor deliberately to budget for a deficit, but 'to take a rather optimistic view'. A relaxation of fiscal stance might

---

[17] See Peter Clarke, *Liberals and Social Democrats* (Cambridge, 1978), 268.
[18] *JMK* xxi. 141–5 (*Daily Mail*, 1 Jan. 1933); for the conversion of the War Loan, see Susan Howson, *Domestic Monetary Management in Britain* (Cambridge, 1975), 88–9.

itself lead to a self-fulfilling buoyancy in revenue and thus in fiscal outcome. 'But that is not really what I want,' he added. 'It is loan expenditure I am wanting.' Public investment not deficit finance remained at the heart of Keynes's message.

The sort of public works he had in mind, however, had somewhat changed in character since 1929–30, when the argument had been almost exclusively about road-bulding. Good schemes of this kind were as desirable as ever, and it was folly for Whitehall to abandon them on the plea of 'hard times'—'forgetting that our income is only another name for what we produce when we are employed'—but there was no master-plan for a new autobahn network. Keynes's priority was to 'increase individual incomes by setting on foot large-scale capital developments which are capable of causing the stagnant savings of the community to circulate again'. The outstanding need here, he suggested—'it is obvious, beyond controversy, what it is'— was to provide at least a million new houses to be let. This might be achieved through a national housing board, working with building societies and local authorities, and backed by guaranteed borrowing powers of, say £100 million.[19] In commending this scheme privately to Hilton Young, the Minister of Health, Keynes added that Pigou was in favour. Young, not unnaturally, was not disposed to let private emollience or old Cambridge associations assuage the stinging public criticisms of his Ministry and made a blunt reply to Keynes: 'Clearly you are in radical disagreement with the policy of the Government in this matter.'[20] Keynes might claim with some justice not to have been moved by party considerations but the instincts of party none the less militated against him.

'The Means to Prosperity'

On 13–16 March 1933 *The Times* published four articles by Keynes under the title 'The Means to Prosperity'. As an argument for loan-financed public works, the series (and eponymous pamphlet) was a better-mounted case along the lines of *Can Lloyd George Do It?*, now that Keynes felt he had a convincing answer to his critics. He was

---

[19] *JMK* xxi. 145–54 ('Spending and saving', *Listener*, 11 Jan. 1933).
[20] *JMK* xxi. 162 (Young to Keynes, 6 Feb. 1933). For Pigou, see also his article 'Price policy: Sterling and its task', *The Times*, 6 Jan. 1933. Young had left the Liberals for the Conservatives in 1926.

ready to explain to them not only what would be the cumulative effect upon employment but also where the money was to be found.

The general political context, however, was wholly different from that of 1929, and, in particular, Keynes's relations with Lloyd George had become frosty. The publication on 14 March of Keynes's *Essays in Biography*, including his much rewritten rehabilitation of Malthus, was seized upon in the press for its arresting portrait of Lloyd George, which created a minor sensation. The *Daily Mail*, for example, carried a headline.

MR LLOYD GEORGE—'THIS SYREN'
MR J. M. KEYNES'S ATTACK

When its reporter asked Lloyd George for a comment, he replied scornfully, 'That was written in 1919', perhaps supposing that it merely reprinted material from *The Economic Consequences of the Peace*.[21] True, Keynes's sketch did date from 1919, but he had decided not to include it in his book at the time because of 'a certain compunction'. The fragment now published spoke of 'this syren, this goat-footed bard', redolent of a 'flavour of final purposelessness, inner irresponsibility'—sufficient, perhaps, to justify Keynes's admission in 1933: 'I feel some compunction still.'[22] In fact, he omitted an even more offensive paragraph referring to Lloyd George's 'methods of untruthful, indeed shameless, intrigue which must lead to ultimate ruin any cause entrusted to him'.[23] But enough had been said to provoke, in due course, a withering blast of retaliation in the memoirs which Lloyd George was currently composing. Keynes was dismissed there as 'an entertaining economist whose bright but shallow dissertations on finance and political economy, when not taken seriously, always provide a source of innocent merriment to his readers'.[24] Readers of *Can Lloyd George Do It?* had, of course, been spared this advice in 1929.

The Means to Prosperity, then, had to make its impact on the strength of Keynes's authorship alone. Its case for public works rested squarely on the multiplier in explaining how additional expenditure would expand income (rather than put up prices) in a situation where resources were far from fully employed. It followed

---

[21] *Daily Mail*, 14 Mar. 1933; Harrod, *Life*, 440–1.
[22] *JMK* x. 20 n., 23 (*Essays in Biography*).
[23] Ibid. 21 n.
[24] David Lloyd George, *War Memoirs*, 2-vol. edn. (1938; first pub. Nov. 1933), i. 410.

through the effect of public (or other new) expenditure; it dealt with the relief to the Exchequer, via savings on the dole; it pointed to the revenue benefit of raising national income. The suggestion was also made at one point that tax cuts could be used to the same ends, with the implication of an unbalanced Budget, and it was even said that 'in some ways this method of increasing expenditure is healthier and better spread throughout the community'.[25]

Keynes maintained that aggregate spending power within a country could only be raised either through increased loan expenditure or by improving the foreign balance (so that a larger proportion of domestic expenditure became domestic income). The first had been tried—albeit half-heartedly and under adverse circumstances—in the Labour Government's public works programme; the second—with more success—through the National Government's tariff policy. 'We have not yet tried both at once,' Keynes commented, before pointing out that there was 'a great difference between the two methods, in as much as only the first is valid for the world as a whole.' Whereas he used to believe that Free Trade was the only theoretically sound policy, whether for one country or for all, he had now come to see that it was theoretically sound for one country to use tariffs to improve its trade balance (and thus raise its national income) but that it could only do so by inflicting an equal disadvantage upon another country.[26]

Before publication, Keynes had submitted his articles to Hubert Henderson, whose reaction was complex. He willingly accepted Keynes's point that the policy of cutting back public works schemes ought now to be thrown in reverse; and he was ready, after three years in which prices had undergone a dramatic fall, to contemplate measures to boost consumption 'by frankly inflationary means'. But he had theoretical reservations—'I don't like the approach of the Kahn calculations'—which reinforced his practical scepticism about 'a splash grandiose programme' of public works. As before, he felt Keynes showed himself not only innocent of the administrative implications but also heedless of the risks in upsetting confidence.[27] Having tried to convey the preoccupations of the Treasury to

---

[25] *JMK* ix. 335–66, at 348 (*The Means to Prosperity*, American edn., but substantially following *The Times*).

[26] Ibid. 352; cf. *JMK* xxi. 204 ff., and *JMK* vii. 338–9.

[27] *JMK* xxi. 164–6 (Henderson to Keynes, 28 Feb. 1933).

Keynes, Henderson soon found himself trying to convey his interpretation of Keynes to the Treasury. It indicates how seriously Keynes was taken that the Treasury response, under the direction of Frederick Phillips, was put through so many drafts: the first of which was sent for comment to none other than the joint secretary of the EAC, Hubert Henderson.

Phillips demanded where the inflationary stimulus necessary to increase employment was to come from, only to affirm that there was 'no doubt' that Keynes would assert that there were 'very large amounts of unused savings deposits lying idle in the country'. Indeed Phillips concluded: 'This is the crux of the matter.' But against this passage Henderson wrote: 'this is not what he would say.'[28] Henderson supplied a better account of Keynes's current thinking: 'His favourite theme is that the expenditure would serve to create most of the savings requisite to finance the public works.' So whereas Phillips had tried to confute Keynes by arguing that savings were insufficient because they came out of incomes which were themselves depressed, Henderson indicated that the converse was nearer to Keynes's actual meaning—in effect, savings represented the tail not the dog. If investment, and hence income, were raised, sufficient savings would thereby be generated.[29] In short, Henderson felt that Phillips's draft did not grasp the real point, which was that world conditions were a constraint upon *any* sort of trade revival, but that, within these limits, many of Keynes's suggestions were valid.

The argument against Keynes on the proposition about idle deposits, which Hopkins and Phillips had considered 'conclusive against any large scale adoption of his ideas',[30] thus turned out to be misconceived. But if this critique proved ultimately inconclusive— 'While it whittles down his argument, it does not get rid of it'—the Treasury, not for the first time, found it prudent to retreat from the ground of economic analysis to that of administrative feasibility. Hopkins endorsed the view that 'the only gilt-edged argument in the present collection is that relating to *delay*'. When it came to elaborating upon the cumbersome recalcitrance of the machinery of

[28] Phillips to Henderson, 15 Mar. 1933, encl. 'Mr Keynes's First and Second Articles', Henderson Papers, box 10.

[29] Henderson to Phillips, 16 Mar. 1933, Henderson Papers, box 10. The quotation from Phillips is in the first draft, as sent to Henderson, and also in the revise in T. 171/309. The Treasury response is fully examined in Howson and Winch, *EAC* 128–30.

[30] 'Suggestions as to policy arising out of Mr Keynes's articles', T. 175/17, Pt. I.

government, the tone of world-weary scepticism which infused all the Treasury memoranda found its *métier*.[31]

How far the Bank of England was now of a different persuasion is not wholly clear. Once the obligations of the Gold Standard had been removed, it was no longer 'under the harrow'; its policy was now to create the monetary conditions for revival, especially through the lower interest rates which it was at last free to engineer. What was needed next was an effective move to make use of this room for expansion. It is a mark of how far the argument had moved on that the issue should now have been posed in these terms. In 1930 there had been widespread agreement that, if only Bank rate could come down, cheap money would do the trick. It had been Robertson not Keynes who was egregious in resisting this point. The *Treatise* did not doubt that investment would be stimulated by a sufficiently low interest rate—this was implicit in its equilibrating role. Once effective demand was instead assigned this role, interest rate in itself was no longer crucial. A more direct stimulus might be needed if the expectations of entrepreneurs were not robust enough to generate a spontaneous revival of investment. If Keynes's new theory suggested this, so did the brute facts of the slump.

In this situation, Henry Clay took the lead within the Bank in pushing for public works on the ground that 'when trade is depressed the trouble is not scarcity of money, but disinclination to use what money there is.'[32] Sprague, too, who gave up the post of Economic Adviser in the spring of 1933, had latterly become sympathetic to Keynes's ideas. 'Were I a British subject,' he told him, 'I think I might be tempted to resign from the Bank and associate myself with you should you be willing, in a public campaign.'[33] As it was, he became a New Dealer on his return to the USA. This left Clay tugging Norman in one direction, while the Australian R. N. Kershaw, acting as Adviser on Commonwealth affairs, was more inclined to drag his feet. Having worked closely with Phillips at the Ottawa Conference, he must have been fully apprised of the Treasury position, and Kershaw's own international responsibilities made him worried about

[31] Hopkins to Fisher and Ferguson, 15 Mar. 1933, T. 171/309; Phillips, 'Mr Keynes's Articles', 21 Mar. 1933, T. 171/309 (also in Hawtrey Papers, HTRY 11/5).

[32] Clay (Sept. 1933, after Sprague's departure), quoted in Howson, *Domestic Monetary Management*, 198 n. 38. On the shift in Bank policy see Sayers, *Bank of England*, 461–3.

[33] Sprague to Keynes, 18 Jan. 1933, quoted in Howson, *Domestic Monetary Management*, 95; and see Sayers, *Bank of England*, 417 n.

'the repercussion on the balance of payments of greatly stimulated loan expenditure in one country'.[34]

In a characteristically taut analysis, Hawtrey likewise argued that 'if currency depreciation is to be avoided, then revival in this country must not outstrip revival elsewhere'. But, as usual with Hawtrey, it was important to identify the premiss from which he was working before taking a conclusion logically derived from it as his own preference. For Hawtrey was quite ready to turn this argument on its head and *advocate* depreciation of the currency. His reasoning was that *any* plan for increasing employment (unless by cutting wages) would increase the national income and would thus be inflationary. The effect of stimulating purchasing power in one country would be to suck in extra imports; so the *success* of the scheme *required* the pound to depreciate. 'That is the question that must be faced before anything is done to promote revival,' claimed Hawtrey.[35]

The option of allowing sterling to find its own level was commended by Hawtrey as 'an obvious and easy alternative to the whole elaborate programme of capital outlay'.[36] He had, as usual, managed to turn a debate about the desirability of public works into one which turned on what he saw as the real underlying issue: whether government was prepared to follow an inflationary policy which would make public works irrelevant as a means of expansion. In the deflationary conditions of the early 1930s, Hawtrey favoured manipulating the tap of inflation in this way. His Treasury colleagues gleaned what they could from his arguments while resisting his conclusions.

In the considered view of the authorities, Keynes was judged unrealistic on the scope and schedule of public works; over-optimistic on the scale of secondary employment and the likely savings on the dole; and insufficiently mindful of the effect on international confidence of efforts to finance such a programme. 'It is no good saying that the works will produce the savings for investment,' Phillips noted, 'for *ex hypothesi* the borrowing preceded the works.'[37] This common-sense remark identified a missing link between Keynes's theory and the implementation of a Keynesian policy in the

[34] Kershaw, 'The Means to Prosperity', 5 Apr. 1933, Bank of England archives, G1/15; cf. J. A. C. Osborne, 'The Means to Prosperity', ibid., which was also sceptical.
[35] Hawtrey, 'The Means to Prosperity', Hawtrey Papers, HTRY 11/5.
[36] Ibid.
[37] 'Questions for Keynes', T. 171/309; and see the discussion by Roger Middleton, *Towards the Managed Economy* (1985), 167–8.

real world where the problem of initially financing it would have to be faced.

As a result of the controversy, Keynes was invited to meet the Chancellor of the Exchequer. 'Could it be that the walls of Jericho are flickering?' Keynes speculated, and reported to Kahn after the interview that Chamberlain appeared 'to hear everything with an open mind and an apparently sympathetic spirit, but quite for the first time'.[38] It is difficult to believe that the economic ingenuousness ostensibly displayed by the Chancellor exceeded the political ingenuousness apparently manifested by his visitor. Can Keynes have supposed that the 'reactionary forces' of whom he had written only six months previously would simply capitulate to his advocacy? Chamberlain's public response in fact stuck closely to the line developed within the Treasury—not surprisingly, since the official brief embodied the policy outlook of the administration of which he was a leading member. On unbalancing the Budget, for example, it reiterated that 'it is certain that once a method of evading current obligations had been discovered repeated recourse would be had to the latter and we should be back in the same condition of affairs from which the National Government extricated the country in 1931'.[39]

When it came to the issue of confidence, to be sure, what was seen to be done was as crucial as what was actually done. In this sense, the crisis months of late 1931, when the response of the National Government was under a spotlight partly of its own devising, represented a peak of orthodoxy, from the rigours of which it was subsequently safe to retreat. The Treasury may have wanted to improve profitability through a carefully controlled rise in domestic prices; but the danger of an exchange crisis made it determined not to take any risks. Talk of deficits, it believed, spelt ultimate ruin to confidence, and this external constraint was regarded as overriding. The consequent effort to balance the Budget during a major slump meant that the Government's fiscal stance continued to tighten until the benefits of cheap money started to come through in the 1933–4 financial year. Since the *raison d'être* of the National Government was to restore confidence as a means of inducing soundly based long-

---

[38] *JMK* xxi. 168 (to Kahn, 16 and 20 Mar. 1933).
[39] Phillips, 'Mr Keynes' Articles', T. 171/309.

term recovery, its main priority was to keep its nerve until the economy revived—as eventually it did.[40]

Under the National Government, it could be claimed, things were getting better. The official unemployment figures, after all, were already touching 22 per cent when the Government was formed and never went above the level of 23 per cent registered in January 1933. Thereafter, there was a virtually uninterrupted fall until the proportion dipped briefly below 10 per cent in the summer of 1937. This laid the foundation for a successful defence of the Government's record in economic policy; in the 1935 General Election the Conservative party and its National allies found little difficulty in claiming that tariffs and cheap money had proved the true means to prosperity. If unemployment remained stubbornly high in the depressed areas, these were, for the most part, incorrigible Labour bastions, not marginal constituencies. Even so, it was with the election campaign in mid-course that Chamberlain capitalized upon a new commitment to undertake a road-building programme, costing £100 million, to be spread over five years.[41]

With the loosening of the external economic constraints, Hopkins was perfectly agreeable to such initiatives. He had not been converted to Keynesian policies, but he told the Chancellor in January 1935 that 'the stage now reached in the general recovery is one at which an expansion of public borrowing would be useful for keeping up the impetus'.[42] Phillips agreed with him, both in countenancing and in circumscribing public works; though whether Niemeyer and Leith-Ross would have taken the same view if still in their shoes may be thought more doubtful. Moreover, the authorities were united in

[40] See the good treatment of these matters in Middleton, *Towards the Managed Economy*, esp. 102, 113–15, 136; and the perceptive interpretation by F. M. Miller, 'The unemployment policy of the National Government, 1931–6', *Hist. Jnl.*, 19 (1976), 477–99. Alan Booth usefully identifies the external constraints, 'Britain in the 1930s: A managed economy?', *Econ. Hist. Rev.*, 2nd ser., 40 (1987), esp. 500–10; and John Stevenson appraises domestic pressures in 'The Making of Unemployment Policy, 1931–1935', in Bentley and Stevenson (eds.), *High and Low Politics in Modern Britain*, 182–213.

[41] On the 1935 General Election see Tom Stannage, *Baldwin Thwarts the Opposition* (1980), esp. 144–5, 159; for the retention of the Labour vote in 1931 in constituencies with high unemployment, see John Stevenson and Chris Cook, *The Slump* (1979), 109, Table 6.4.

[42] Howson and Winch, *EAC* 130–1. The best perspective on this episode is offered by G. C. Peden, 'Keynes, the Treasury and unemployment in the later nineteen-thirties', *Oxford Econ. Papers*, 33 (1980), esp. 2–6.

their advice since the Bank of England was already persuaded that public works could serve as a timely adjunct to cheap money—indeed Norman confided that 'this was almost the only point on which he seriously disagreed with the Chancellor'.[43] It only remained for Chamberlain to lift his own veto. Thus the pillars of sound finance were no longer set in stone once Britain had abandoned both the Gold Standard and Free Trade. The balanced Budget convention remained a salutary discipline which had to be observed, albeit with the help of window-dressing (especially over provision for the sinking fund). Given this, Hopkins evidently thought it expedient that the Treasury View, which he had been largely responsible for reformulating in 1929–30, could now be further relaxed as part of a cautious and pragmatic policy. It was his strategy, not that of Keynes, which succeeded in capturing the political mood of the period.

'The whole bundle of associated ideas'

In writing the *General Theory*, Keynes explicitly turned upon the 'classical' tradition of Marshall and Pigou, in which he had been brought up, and implicitly jettisoned much of his own *Treatise*. There he had spoken as an 'imperfectionist', identifying the actual obstructions in the real world which thwarted the tendency of the market towards equilibrium. Equilibrium meant that all markets cleared—prices were found at which every seller found a buyer and all factors of production were fully employed. Now, instead, Keynes contested the whole set of logically interdependent assumptions on which the market-clearing model was premised. He challenged the doctrine (dating from the time of Say and Ricardo) that the process of supply created its own demand—or would do so given sufficiently flexible prices. For in a money economy it was possible for the costs and the market value of output to diverge. True, at the end of the day, income was necessarily the same as output; but since not all income was spent on consumption of that output, investment had to fill the gap if full employment were to be maintained. When this happened, the classical postulates were fulfilled and the result was a unique position of equilibrium. But a deficiency in effective demand was all too likely, with a reduction in overall output then dragging

---

[43] Per Jacobsson diary, 1 Jan. 1935, quoted in Sayers, *Bank of England*, 463.

down the level of aggregate income until saving and investment found an equilibrium point at some sub-optimal level. The rationality of individual agents in the market could not avert an outcome which was in aggregate self-defeating—the fallacy of composition saw to that. In three crucial areas, moreover, decisions were strongly influenced by psychological factors: by the propensity to consume, by the degree of liquidity preference, and by entrepreneurs' expectations about investment.

The earliest drafts of the book (still called *The Monetary Theory of Production*) date from 1932. Here already are a number of sweeping propositions: that, on certain assumptions, '*any* level of output is a position of stable equilibrium'; that 'there is no presumption whatever that the equilibrium output will be anywhere near the optimum output'; that 'it might be truer to say that the amount of saving over a period of time depends on the amount of investment, than the other way around'; that 'there is no presumption that an *all-round* reduction of the variable costs of production will prove favourable to the volume of employment'; that 'the market rate of interest is a thing in itself, dependent on liquidity preference and the quantity of money'. Moreover, Keynes claimed 'that the above analysis furnishes us with a hint, and a partially correct picture, of the nature of the economic world in which we actually live'.[44]

It was a world in which the teaching of orthodox theory—postulating natural forces which tended to restore equilibrium at the optimum level—had long offended common sense, which tended to see protection and cheap money and free spending as good for trade. Keynes confessed that 'it now seems to me that the economists, in their devotion to a theory of self-adjusting equilibrium, have been, on the whole, wrong in their practical advice and that the instincts of practical men have been, on the whole, sounder.' To this discrepancy he attributed 'the low standing of economists regarded as practical experts and the unwillingness of statesmen and business men to accept their advice'.[45] For his own part, he wrote in 1934, while he had not yet convinced either the expert or the ordinary man that he was right, 'it is, I feel certain, only a matter of time before I convince

---

[44] *JMK* xiii. 387–8, 394, 399, 388. For the authoritative account of the drafting process see D. E. Moggridge, 'From the *Treatise* to the *General Theory*: An exercise in chronology', *Hist. of Pol. Econ.*, v (1973), esp. 79–87, and Moggridge's additional comments in Patinkin and Leith, *Keynes, Cambridge and the General Theory*, 64–71.

[45] *JMK* xiii. 406 (draft of 'Historical Retrospect', probably 1932).

both; and when both are convinced, economic policy will, with the usual time lag, follow suit'.[46]

The hard slog of getting the *General Theory* into shape occupied Keynes during most of 1933 and 1934. He did much of the writing during the university vacations at his country home at Tilton, where Kahn would join him for long spells. They would talk over problems as they arose, whether in the study or over the morning's task of picking vegetables for lunch. Keynes wrote privately of Kahn that 'there never was anyone in the history of the world to whom it was so helpful to submit one's stuff'.[47] Because of this close collaboration, face to face, Kahn's contribution can never be precisely assessed; but his role was essentially as critic of an exercise in exposition by which Keynes set great store. Once in proof in 1935, the book was also subjected to criticism at length from Robertson, Hawtrey, Harrod, and Joan Robinson.

In Keynes's own four-stage account of the inception of the *General Theory*, it was only 'after an immense lot of muddling and many drafts'—in the course of 1934–5—that he reached stage (iv), when 'the proper definition of the marginal efficiency of capital linked up one thing with another'. Though he told Harrod that 'in my own progress of thought it was absolutely vital', it was the least innovative of Keynes's four 'moments of transition'.[48] It took him so long to hit upon a suitable definition because he wished to stress the expected yield on new assets and to differentiate this—as he insisted Marshall had failed to do—from the rate of interest. The underlying tension was between a concept of *productivity* (which, along with thrift, was the determinant of interest in neo-classical theory) and an emphasis upon *expectations*. Harrod thought there was still much to be said for Marshall's view and had some success in producing emendation of the proofs of chapter 11, 'The marginal efficiency of capital'. Kahn, by contrast, with his inclination towards emphasizing risk and uncertainty, thought this chapter, as finally printed, 'one of the most confused'. He was better pleased by the remarks in chapter 12, 'The state of long-term expectation', which, with a lighter touch, linked enterprise to 'animal spirits'.[49]

The high stakes for which Keynes was playing provide part of the

---

[46] *JMK* xxviii. 35 (letter to *New Statesman and Nation*, 21 Nov. 1934).

[47] *JMK* xiii. 422 (to Joan Robinson, 29 Mar. 1934); cf. Kahn, *Making of General Theory*, 114–18.

[48] *JMK* xiii. 549 (Keynes to Harrod, 27 Aug. 1936) and see above, ch. 11 at n. 14.

[49] *JMK* vii. 161–2; Kahn, *Making of General Theory*, 145–8, 254–6, at 145.

explanation for his toils in composition; he was determined not to fail, as he now felt the *Treatise* had failed, in making his ideas fully coherent and convincing. Yet the theory of effective demand proved unaccountably elusive when it came to introducing and developing it as a theme of a book. 'This is probably not the clearest approch to the fundamental idea of this book,' ran one draft; 'but it may help the reader in the long run if we approach it gradually and from various angles as opportunity offers.'[50] There were, Keynes discovered, half a dozen striking ways in which he could outline or adapt his basic concepts. In a draft preface, he suggested that it was 'of the essential nature of economic exposition' that it gave, not a perfectly complete account, 'but a sample statement, so to speak, out of all the things which could be said, intended to suggest to the reader the whole bundle of associated ideas, so that, if he catches the bundle, he will not be in the least confused or impeded by the technical incompleteness of the mere words which the author has written down, taken by themselves'.[51]

It is not altogether surprising that different readers of the *General Theory*, convinced that they had caught the bundle, turned out not to have caught the same bundle. The role of J. R. Hicks, who had moved from the LSE to become a Fellow of Gonville and Caius College, Cambridge, in 1935, has been particularly controversial. As the ostensible progenitor of the 'neo-classical synthesis', Hicks has sometimes been portrayed as the bad fairy in a changeling story— visiting the cradle of the *General Theory* and, while nobody was looking closely enough, substituting for it 'Mr Keynes's special theory'. It was Hicks's influential review in 1937, 'Mr Keynes and the "Classics"', which published a diagram (later known as IS–LM) which simplified the relationship between saving and investment, income and interest. Hicks, contending that the liquidity preference doctrine was vital, showed how this new concept might be incorporated into the neo-classical model where saving and investment were equilibrated by variations in interest rate. 'With this revision,' he claimed, 'Mr Keynes takes a big step back to Marshallian orthodoxy ...'[52] For liquidity preference now became only another imperfection, like sticky wages, thwarting the tendency

---

[50] *JMK* xiii. 429–30.   [51] *JMK* xiii. 470.
[52] John Hicks, *Critical Essays in Monetary Theory* (Oxford, 1967), 134: reprinting 'Mr Keynes and the "Classics"', first given at the Oxford conference of the Econometric Society (Sept. 1936), from *Econometrica*, 5 (1937).

of the system towards equilibrium; and unemployment, however intractable in the real world, was thus in theory a symptom of disequilibrium.

Several points are now clear. In the first place, it has been established that Hicks wrote his famous paper (for delivery at a conference attended by many of the younger British economists) only after reading papers on somewhat similar lines by Meade and Harrod. Each of them presented, moreover, a set of four simultaneous equations, showing how the equilibrium levels of interest, income, investment, and saving were determined. When Hicks drew the investment–savings curve intersecting with the liquidity–money curve in a scissors diagram—'Hicks did a Marshall,' commented one economist—he focused the whole discussion of the *General Theory*.[53] As another participant put it, Hicks enabled 'those who found sets of simultaneous equations indigestible to digest instead a diagram which he obtained by eliminating one or two variables from the set of simultaneous equations'.[54] Furthermore, it is also clear that Hicks had reasonable grounds for maintaining 'that Keynes accepted the IS–LM diagram as a fair statement of his position—of the nucleus that is, of his position'. At any rate, Keynes told Hicks at the time that he had 'next to nothing to say by way of criticism' of the paper he had been shown.[55]

Meade's view of the *General Theory* was as 'a determined system given expectations';[56] Harrod thought likewise; indeed he had conducted a lengthy correspondence with Keynes over the proofs in 1935, as a result of which almost sixty per cent of the published text of chapter 14, 'The classical theory of the rate of interest', had been spliced into the previous draft at the final stage. Harrod was arguing for a synthesis between Keynes's approach and that of the classical theory, and it was these changes which paved the way for the sub-

[53] For a definitive treatment on all these points see Warren Young, *Interpreting Mr Keynes: The IS–LM enigma* (Oxford, 1987), esp. 28, 33–4, 42–5, and quotation from Arthur Brown at 88–9.

[54] Ibid. 85 (quoting David Champernowne). Much the same point is made by Hyman P. Minsky, who goes on, however, to criticize IS–LM as 'an unfair and naive representation of Keynes's subtle and sophisticated views'. *John Maynard Keynes* (New York, 1975), 14, 38.

[55] John Hicks, *Economic Perspectives* (Oxford, 1977), 146; *JMK* xiv. 79 (Keynes to Hicks, 31 Mar. 1937). See Alan Coddington, *Keynesian Economics* (1983), 64–91, for a sympathetic account of Hicks's contribution.

[56] Quoted in Young, *Interpreting Mr Keynes*, 15; and see J. E. Meade, 'A simplified model of Mr Keynes's system', *Rev. of Econ. Studies*, 4 (1936–7), 98–107.

sequent assimilation to a Marshallian account. For if (*given* the level of income) interest measures liquidity preference, then (*given* liquidity preference) there is surely a determinate relationship between income and interest—and this can be drawn as the curve LM. Thus if investment and saving are equilibrated at a certain level of *income*, it is one which is related to *interest*—and this can be drawn as the curve IS. The result can be seen as modifying the neo-classical theory (that interest rate equilibrates saving and investment) by acknowledging a hitherto unsuspected importance for Keynes's concept of liquidity preference.[57]

Disagreements over how far the *General Theory* could be assimilated to the neo-classical tradition of Marshall stemmed as much from temperamental as from intellectual differences. Keynes himself may have been a natural iconoclast but he also had the skills of a conciliator when he chose to deploy them. It was a deliberate decision on his part to intensify the assault on the classical school in order to forestall attempts at accommodation which might sap the force of his doctrine. 'I *want*, so to speak, to raise a dust,' he told Harrod; 'because it is only out of the controversy that will arise that what I am saying will get understood.'[58] Keynes well recognized how alien such a course was to Robertson ('So unlike me!') whose own conceptual innovations, he told him, seemed to crave the sanction of ostensible continuity: 'But you won't slough your skins, like a good snake!' Robertson, responding, admitted having 'gone through real intellectual torment trying to make up my mind whether, as you often seem to claim, there is some new piece on the board or rather a rearrangement, which seems to you superior, of existing pieces'. Hence the relief with which he discovered Hicks and Harrod 'both taking the latter view, though agreeing far more with you than with me about the merits of the re-arrangement'.[59]

The Hicks–Harrod–Meade approach, which became IS–LM, may be regarded as a bridge leading back to the conventions of neo-classical economics, and one which Keynes himself had chosen not to construct. It should, however, be remembered not only that it is possible to cross a bridge in either direction but also that the less

---

[57] See the Keynes–Harrod correspondence, *JMK* xiii. esp. 547–57; Hicks, *Critical Essays*, 134–5; Young, *Interpreting Mr Keynes*, 20–1. Milgate has traced the impact on ch. 14 as redrafted, *Capital and Employment*, 118–22.

[58] *JMK* xiii. 548 (Keynes to Harrod, 27 Aug. 1935).

[59] *JMK* xiv. 94–5 (Keynes to Robertson, 13 Dec. 1936; Robertson to Keynes, 29 Dec. 1936).

athletically intrepid may find it easier to walk over a bridge than to jump over an abyss. Such bridge-building, however, depends on taking the *General Theory*—at least on given assumptions—as a determinate system, in this sense like the neo-classical system. How far this premiss is vitiated by Keynes's introduction of uncertainty raises a further issue about the nature of his revolution in economic theory.

'So far as I myself am concerned, I am trying to prevent my mind from crystallising too much on the precise lines of the *General Theory*,' Keynes told Joan Robinson in December 1936. 'I am attentive to criticisms and to what raises difficulties and catches people's attention—in which there are a good many surprises.'[60] He seems at this stage to have maintained a degree of ambivalence which in a lesser mortal might be termed muddle. It is certainly too late now to extricate the historical Keynes from inconsistency, for example by reconstructing chapter 14 on the basis of the 1934 drafts rather than the final published text.[61] At any rate, it is clear that Keynes did not insist on others 'learning the Russian' so long as they showed signs of engaging with his basic ideas. If he tacitly accepted IS–LM as one possible exposition of his theory, albeit in the sort of stylized model which he had himself forsworn, he did not endorse it as the authorized version.[62] There is, indeed, good reason to suppose that his article, 'The general theory of employment', which was written before the end of 1936, was intended as a counterweight to the IS–LM approach as endorsed by Meade, Harrod, and Hicks.

'The general theory of employment' is the *locus classicus* for the interpretation favoured by Joan Robinson, and by Richard Kahn, who approved it for publication, saying, 'I like this very much and I think it is definitely helpful.'[63] For here Keynes put the emphasis upon

[60] *JMK* xxix. 185.
[61] This is essentially the task—which may have a legitimate *economic* justification—attempted by Milgate, *Capital and Employment*, 122–3. Coddington upholds the view that, in his theory of interest, Keynes 'got himself into a muddle which he induced the major part of the profession to share': *Keynesian Economics*, 78.
[62] Vicarelli argues that 'those who construe him in these limited equational terms . . . have done Keynes a disservice' by contributing to 'a systematic elimination of any strand in Keynes's thinking that cannot be rendered in a stylized model of the economic system'; *Keynes: The instability of capitalism*, 182. Hicks himself never claimed to have captured all the strands in two curves.
[63] *JMK* xiv. 108. Cf. Kahn's later view that it was 'tragic' that Keynes failed to make a 'public protest' against Hicks: *Making of General Theory*, 160–1. Young is surely right to suggest that the article was a response to IS–LM, but one which maintained an 'agnostic' ambivalence: *Interpreting Mr Keynes*, 9–10, 178.

uncertainty and hence upon expectations within a money economy. He suggested that 'our desire to hold money as a store of wealth is a barometer of the degree of our distrust of our own calculations and conventions regarding the future'. He summed up his theory by saying 'given the psychology of the public, the level of output and employment as a whole depends on the amount of investment'; but it is the very factors determining the rate of investment 'which are most unreliable, since it is they which are influenced by our views of the future about which we know so little.'[64]

According to Joan Robinson, recognition of uncertainty or indeterminacy was the essence of Keynes's revolution in theory, and it was only in this article that 'he got it into focus'.[65] Yet if this is the lens through which the *General Theory* must be read, it is a pity that readers were not authoritatively prescribed it at the outset. The reason seems to be that uncertainty infused the theory of effective demand at a fairly late stage. In his university lectures for 1932–3 and 1933–4 Keynes did not talk in this way. R. B. Bryce, who had sat through them attentively, summarized his understanding of their drift in the summer of 1935 in a seminar paper which had Keynes's blessing. While acknowledging that 'the theory held "that money is of considerable significance in determining employment"', Bryce added: 'On reflection I think it only has this importance because labour so often sets its supply price in money rather than real terms—or else custom or policy prevents reductions in money wage rates.'[66] Not until the Michaelmas Term of 1935, obviously lecturing from the page-proofs, did Keynes's pregnant remarks—'money links the changing expectations re future to the present'—promote the theme to prominence.[67] It was well after publication that Keynes ventured the further speculation that 'in a world ruled by uncertainty with an uncertain future linked to an actual present, a final position of equilibrium, such as one deals with in static economics, does not

---

[64] *JMK* xiv. 109–23 (*Quarterly Jnl. of Econ.*, Feb. 1937), at 116, 121.
[65] 'What has become of the Keynesian revolution?', in M. Keynes (ed.), *Essays*, 125; but see the section on expectations, *JMK* vii. 148–53. Shackle, *The Years of High Theory*, esp. chs. 11 and 18, provides a brilliant account in terms of uncertainty; and, largely influenced by it, my treatment in *Liberals and Social Democrats*, 271, lent more credence to this interpretation than I now think historically justified.
[66] *JMK* xxix. 133 (Bryce's paper as sent to Keynes, 3 July 1935).
[67] Tarshis notes, 2 Dec. 1935; cf. *JMK* vii. 293.

properly exist'.[68] Was Keynes's restless mind now toying with a generalization of the *General Theory?* If so, he was moving beyond the theory of effective demand which he had formulated, not providing the key to its historical elucidation.

Policy and theory

In the period between the controversy over *The Means to Prosperity* in March–April 1933 and the publication of the *General Theory* in February 1936, Keynes again withdrew from active advocacy of a change of course in British economic policy. His commendation of Roosevelt's New Deal in the USA naturally had a domestic resonance but, equally naturally by this time, he did not become enlisted in Lloyd George's final crusade for a 'British New Deal'. More surprisingly, when, in 1935, Keynes was approached by the Next Five Years Group—an eminently congenial gathering of *bien-pensant* liberal intellectuals—he refused to endorse their manifesto in favour of economic expansion, saying: 'whilst I thought that the proposals and the sort of ideas which your book contains was my job two years ago, and I daresay it was, I now consider my job is rather different.'[69] He seems, in fact, to have been convinced that 'we are ... at one of those uncommon junctures of human affairs where we can be saved by the solution of an intellectual problem, and in no other way'.[70] In telling Bernard Shaw that 'I believe myself to be writing a book on economic theory, which will largely revolutionise—not, I suppose, at once but in the course of the next ten years—the way the world thinks about economic problems', he was not simply humouring the old jester. The impression his claim made on Virginia Woolf—'a gigantic boast; true I daresay'—suggests that Keynes's most perceptive friends knew him to be in deadly earnest.[71]

[68] *JMK* xxix. 222 (Keynes to Henderson, 28 May 1936). Thus, from a slightly different angle, I share Milgate's view that 'the fundamental proposition of the *General Theory*, that decisions to save are adjusted to decisions to invest *via* changes in the level of income (output), is entirely independent of the existence of uncertainty and expectations.' *Capital and Employment*, 90; cf. 102, 144–52; and see *JMK* xiv. 181.

[69] *JMK* xxi. 355 (Keynes to Arthur Salter, 10 July 1935). For a critical account of the Next Five Years Group, see Alan Booth and Melvin Pack, *Employment, Capital, and Economic Policy* (Oxford, 1985), 64–7.

[70] *JMK* xiii. 492 ('Poverty in plenty', Nov. 1934).

[71] Anne Olivier Bell (ed.), *The Diary of Virginia Woolf*, iv (Penguin edn., 1983), 272 (6 Jan. 1935); *JMK* xxviii. 42 (Keynes to Shaw, 1 Jan. 1935).

In one crucial respect, Keynes remained totally consistent and unambiguous in the claims he made. Obviously his theory was intended to offer an explanation of fluctuations in employment and output. 'It does not offer', he added, 'a ready-made remedy as to how to avoid these fluctuations and to maintain output at a steady optimum level.' His suggestions for a cure were thus 'on a different plane from the diagnosis' and subject to all sorts of qualifications; whereas he maintained that 'my main reasons for departing from the traditional theory go much deeper than this'.[72] Getting the theory right, however, was the pre-condition for finding a remedy—a proposition best attested in the 1934 university lecture notes:[73]

Once we have grasped the nature of the social machine, there is no reason why it should be recalcitrant. Without this knowledge of controls you will get all kinds of random dislocations and maladjustments in our economy. With an understanding of the essential nature of the beast, and the concomitant knowledge of its controls, it is entirely possible to raise output to the neighbourhood of the optimum.

There is almost nothing in the *General Theory* that speaks directly to the 'Keynesian' policy agenda—barely a mention of emergency public works, nothing on fiscal methods of demand management, nor on deficit budgeting. Instead, even in the final chapter, it simply gestures towards structural problems in contemporary society— notably its failure to provide full employment and its inequitable distribution of wealth—and suggests that the two problems could now be solved together. Redistribution of income, in short, by stimulating effective demand, could make investment more profitable and thus help capital growth; and as capital ceased to be scarce, the *rentier* could be rewarded less, and the entrepreneur more appropriately. 'In some other respects the foregoing theory is moderately conservative in its implications,' Keynes continued— though since he immediately suggested that 'a somewhat comprehensive socialisation of investment will prove the only means of securing an approximation to full employment',[74] not all moderate Conservatives might be expected to agree. The necessity of central controls to govern the volume of output as a whole was his theme; but he did not develop it into a policy blueprint in the *General Theory*.

---

[72] *JMK* xiv. 121–2 ('The general theory of employment').
[73] Fallgatter notes, 20 Nov. 1934.   [74] *JMK* vii. 377–8.

Its claims to supersede previous theory, however, rested not only on the cogency of its internal logic but on its congruence with external facts. ('Not only is the old theory faulty. The facts of the world shift.')[75] A new theory was needed, with greater verisimilitude. 'Economics is a science of thinking in terms of models joined to the art of choosing models which are relevant to the contemporary world,' Keynes suggested to Harrod in 1938.[76] His growing irritation with Robertson and Pigou, as it became clear that they could not accept the *General Theory*, did not arise from policy disagreements— 'when it comes to practice, there is really extremely little between us'—but from Keynes's sense that the premises upon which they worked were obsolete and inappropriate. 'Why do they insist on maintaining theories from which their own practical conclusions cannot possibly follow?'[77]

In his conception of the nature and function of economics, Keynes remained recognizably a pupil of Marshall; and it is ironic that some of his most wounding academic quarrels should have been with old colleagues from the same stable. When Hubert Henderson, now a Fellow of All Souls College, Oxford, visited Cambridge in May 1936, these differences came to a head. In his paper to the Marshall Society, he said that Keynes had invited the world 'to throw upon the scrap-heap a large part of the orthodox economic theory in which I still believe, to discard the methods of analysis which I intend to continue to employ, and to substitute a new theoretical system of his own which seems to me in its main outlines a farrago of sophisticated confusion.' Henderson acknowledged that all social theories were influenced by the circumstances of their time, but claimed that this was true of the *General Theory* to an exceptional degree. 'His book is a child of the slump which began in 1929,' Henderson concluded. 'It represents the results of the conflict between the actual phenomena of that slump and the ideas of economic policy which Mr Keynes entertained before it began.'[78]

Those who were present at this meeting have testified to the violence of Henderson's attack and the furore it created. Henderson

[75] *JMK* xxviii. 32 (*New Statesman and Nation*, 10 Nov. 1934); cf. *JMK* vii. 378.
[76] *JMK* xiv. 296.
[77] *JMK* xiv. 259 (Keynes to Kahn, 20 Oct. 1937).
[78] 'Mr Keynes's Theories', Henderson Papers, box 10. The quotations are from 'Version 2' which is in fact the original, as delivered to the Marshall Society, 2 May 1936. Thus 'Version 1' is the revision, as printed in Henderson, *The Inter-War Years*, 160–77.

explained his intention in advance to Harrod by saying: 'I have allowed myself to be inhibited for many years from publishing many things by a desire not to quarrel in public with Maynard.'[79] Harrod thought he had now over-reacted, with intemperate remarks which ignored the force of the *General Theory* as a coherent alternative to the notion of a self-equilibrating system: 'It certainly won't live unless a large number of people not merely pay lip-service to it, but are able to take up its ideas into their mental stock in trade and work with them.'[80]

Keynes, too, claimed that Henderson had not 'really tackled it as being what it claims to be, namely, a complete theory with far-reaching implications and connections'. Henderson countered by saying that it was just this claim that had made him react so strongly against it, because 'it seems to me essentially false and likely to lead to the misunderstanding rather than the illumination of the economic problems that confront us'.[81] Keynes later acknowledged to Robertson that 'you and Hubert think me very wicked!—for being so cocksure and putting all the driving force I know how behind arguments which for me are of painfully practical importance'.[82]

Henderson reaffirmed his analysis of unemployment under three categories—minimum, transfer, and cyclical—and argued 'that an attempt to make effective demand stronger would not in the long run reduce unemployment under any one of these heads'. His own support for public works, going back to *Can Lloyd George Do It?*, had rested on cyclical and transfer arguments, not on any need to bolster demand 'in the long run'. In confronting Keynes with this phrase, Henderson confessed himself 'frankly baffled by your attitude'. Keynes seemed to him to be generalizing from an anomalous period of slump toward conclusions about maintaining investment which would merely fuel inflation if applied when conditions were tending towards boom. 'Rejecting this contention,' Henderson wrote, 'I necessarily reject everything that turns on it, the doctrine of the multiplier, the insistence that there is an equation missing in the

[79] Henderson to Harrod, 2 Apr. 1936, Henderson Papers, box 10. For the meeting see E. D. Simon to J. Jewkes, 4 May 1936, copy, ibid.; Michael Straight, *After Long Silence* (1983), 57; and *JMK* xxix. 218.

[80] Harrod to Henderson, 9 Apr. 1936, Henderson Papers, box 10.

[81] *JMK* xxix. 224 (Keynes to Henderson, 28 May 1936; Henderson to Keynes, 4 June 1936).

[82] *JMK* xiv. 88 (Keynes to Robertson, 20 Sept. 1936).

orthodox theory of interest etc.'[83] Since it was liquidity preference that the 'missing equation' introduced, it is noteworthy that Henderson allowed some relevance to the concept, though not as the basis for a new theory.

In mounting his attack on the *General Theory*, Henderson privately admitted to finding 'intensely exasperating the tacit assumption that prevails in certain circles that those who do not accept its general doctrine are to be regarded as intellectually inferior beings'. Harrod's attempted belittlement of the grounds for this view—'Perhaps 2 people in Cambridge together with a few undergraduates'—cannot dispel the suspicion that party lines were indeed forming in this way.[84] Whether the '2 people in Cambridge' should be identified as Richard Kahn and Joan Robinson must remain a matter for speculation, but certainly Keynes turned increasingly towards them for the sort of support that was not forthcoming from his own contemporaries. 'The whole business is of course devastating educationally,' Robertson reflected, '—but I suppose if they really think they have saved the world by finding that missing equation, they are entitled to ignore that!'[85]

Keynes has often been criticized for supposedly believing that his theory would achieve a purely intellectual triumph over intractable political, social, and economic obstacles. The final passage of the *General Theory*, with its theme that 'soon or late, it is ideas, not vested interests, which are dangerous for good or evil', can be cited in support of this contention. To Rowse, this clearly exemplified the 'rationalist fallacy, the fatal defect of the liberal mind'.[86] Whether Keynes should be seen as whistling in the dark in the mid-1930s is partly a matter of perspective. Less than two years previously, Lionel Robbins had concluded his own book on the slump by writing that 'the ideas which, for good or for bad, have come to dominate policy are the ideas which have been put forward in the first instance by detached and isolated thinkers'. From his point of view, the 'overwhelmingly socialist' cast which policy had assumed had come about

[83] *JMK* xxix. 230 (Henderson to Keynes, 18 June 1936); see also 'Do we want public works?' (May 1935), *The Inter-War Years*, 151–60.

[84] Henderson to Harrod, 2 Apr., 1936; Harrod to Henderson, 9 Apr., Henderson Papers, box 10.

[85] Robertson to Henderson, 21 June 1936, Henderson Papers, box 10; cf. *JMK* xiv. 95–6 (Robertson to Keynes, 29 Dec. 1936).

[86] A. L. Rowse, *Mr Keynes and the Labour Movement* (1936), 60–2, citing *JMK* vii. 384.

because 'men of intellect, with powers of reason and persuasion' had proved so plausible. 'In the short run, it is true,' Robbins conceded, 'ideas are unimportant and ineffective, but in the long run they can rule the world.'[87]

Even in these terms, Keynes's enterprise in the *General Theory* did not seem wholly unpropitious. The questions which he himself posed about the potential efficacy of his ideas were, moreover, slightly different. 'Have they insufficient roots in the motives which govern the evolution of political society?' he queried. 'Are the interests which they will thwart stronger and more obvious than those which they will serve?' To provide a proper answer, he wrote, 'would need a volume of a different character from this one';[88] but, in admitting this, he should surely be read as acknowledging the problem of ideology, not dismissing it. The sort of revolution he hoped to bring about—'not, I suppose, at once but in the course of the next ten years'—indisputably looked less chimerical, for good or evil, in 1945 than in 1935. If this was for reasons which he did not predict, it was less because he misguidedly subscribed to an intellectualist fallacy than because he correctly sensed that there would be more to it than that. His letter to Shaw, often cited against Keynes on this score, in fact continues: 'When my new theory has been duly assimilated and mixed with politics and feelings and passions, I can't predict what the final upshot will be in its effect on action and affairs.'[89] Keynes sensed the intuitive truth of his 'gigantic boast', confident that, like many of his intuitions, it would turn out to be well-founded—in the long run, of course.

'At this stage of the argument', Keynes wrote in his preface, 'the general public, though welcome at the debate, are only eavesdroppers at an attempt by an economist to bring to an issue the deep divergences of opinion between fellow economists which have for the time being almost destroyed the practical influence of economic theory, and will, until they are resolved, continue to do so.' Rarely innocent of some ulterior purpose in his writing, Keynes had not abjured the ambition to effect a change in economic policy while he applied his main energies to issues of economic theory, but he now sought to achieve the one through the other. In one sense, his theory

[87] *The Great Depression* (1934), 199–200.
[88] *JMK* vii. 383.
[89] *JMK* xxviii. 42, largely repeated in *JMK* xxi. 347–8 (Keynes to Susan Lawrence, 15 Jan. 1936).

was undeniably, as Henderson said, 'a child of the slump': because any theory that could not account for the slump would *ipso facto* have demonstrated that it had lost touch with the real-world problems to which it should be addressed.

It was the theory on which Keynes had been brought up which now seemed susceptible to this charge. He had himself deployed its analytical resources with unrivalled lucidity, notably in expounding the *modus operandi* of Bank rate. In the 1920s he argued that in practice the economy was regulated by the level of employment and output, but accepted that this was so only because of rigidities which impaired the postulate of price flexibility. In the 1930s his great intellectual coup was to disclose that in theory, too, the economy was regulated by the level of employment and output, and to argue that this was so regardless of any rigidities in wage rates. Little wonder that Keynes, conscious of the distance he had travelled, claimed this as a revolution: or, for the same reason, concluded that he had 'no companions, it seems, in my own generation, either of earliest teachers or of earliest pupils'.[90] The zest and vitality of the *General Theory* tell their own story about the man who made it; about his own animal spirits in investing so much in it; and corroborate his vibrant sense of elation—'I am shaking myself like a dog on dry land'[91]—over what he had accomplished.

[90] *JMK* xiv. 85 (Keynes to Harrod, 30 Aug. 1936).
[91] *JMK* xxix. 165 (Keynes to Robertson, 6 Dec. 1937).

PART V

Conclusion

13

Keynes and Keynesianism

The historical Keynes

In the theory of effective demand Keynes had fashioned a new pair of economic spectacles; but what use were they? He was himself partly responsible for raising unrealistically high hopes about the immediate practical efficacy of Keynesianism, through the cocksure manner which he had always been prone to adopt. Faced by the world slump in December 1930, he reached resourcefully for a mechanical metaphor appropriate to the current state of the art. 'We have magneto trouble,' he wrote. 'How, then, can we start up again?'[1] Keynesian policies, both at the time and subsequently, were often displayed as a magic tool-kit which could not only patch up the engine but, with fine tuning, keep it running at maximum horse-power in a trouble-free way. In the enlightened post-war world, right up to the end of the 1960s, nearly everyone swore by the magic tool-kit; thereafter, faced with an old-fashioned breakdown, they swore at it.

Most of the extravagant claims about Keynesianism, however, were generated posthumously rather than by the historical Keynes. True, he lent his sanction to a prospectus to 'conquer' unemployment in 1929. This was, however, defined as reducing unemployment to the level considered normal before 1914—something under 5 per cent on the official figures, as compared with 10 per cent in 1929. The Treasury View at the time maintained that, while public works might redistribute the unemployed, they were not capable of reducing the overall level of unemployment; and this was the official line followed by the Conservative Government.[2] As a general proposition, it was soon rendered untenable, not least through Keynes's efforts, and it is now generally agreed that in principle there was

[1] *JMK* ix. 129 ('The great slump of 1930').

[2] Readers of ch. 3 above must judge whether, as Roger Middleton now claims, there has been 'a complete misspecification of the Treasury view' and that its strong version—*in 1929*—is simply 'myth': 'Treasury policy on unemployment', in Glynn and Booth (eds.), *Road to Full Employment*, 109–24, at 115. For the potential impact on unemployment, see above, ch. 4 nn. 77–8.

room for some reduction in unemployment. But how much? Other things being equal, could Lloyd George have carried out his famous pledge? Or would he have failed to 'do it'? And if so, by what order of magnitude? These are legitimate historical questions, and econometric analysis is certainly useful here in suggesting that the Liberal pledge was rather too optimistic.

Whether the proposals would have been worth trying is a question which also involves more imponderable factors, such as the effect on confidence in the City, the utility of such measures in promoting welfare, and the general political desirability of such an initiative. There were, too, practical administrative constraints, summed up in the Treasury's 'gilt-edged argument' of 1933 about delay. It may well be that a road simply could not be built within twelve months, as proposed in 1929; though if the same road could not be built *for the same reason* in 1933, it was surely because preparatory work had not been started in the years since 1929.[3] In this sense, Lloyd George's emphasis on the lack of political will to overcome difficulties was not wholly misconceived. These were all issues which contemporaries had to resolve according to their own values and priorities, under conditions of imperfect knowledge.

The 1929 programme was a real historical option. So was the strategy which Keynes advocated in 1930–1, when, faced with a rise in unemployment towards 20 per cent, he supplemented public works with other policies. The confidence factor had meanwhile become more pressing, though it is not conclusive simply to cite the crisis of August 1931 as proof that any earlier departures from the principles of sound finance would not have been viable. Tariffs, in particular, were specifically designed to buttress confidence and protect the international position. Keynes's objective was to avoid drifting into the sort of crisis which ultimately supervened. Even under adverse conditions, he obviously hoped it would be possible to check rising unemployment, but did not specify by how much.

In *The Means to Prosperity* in 1933, when the figures still stood at over 20 per cent, Keynes spoke of a target of one million new jobs— implying a residual unemployment level of at least 12 per cent. This claim, too, is worth testing as a counter-factual alternative to the progress actually achieved under the National Government. But to

---

[3] Again, compare Middleton: 'All subsequent programmes in the 1930s suffered from a similar problem of credibility over the time-scale of their execution' (ibid. 113); and see above, ch. 12 n. 31.

test whether a so-called 'Keynesian solution' of deficit-financed public works could by itself have cut unemployment from its peak in 1932 (23 per cent) back to the target level specified in 1929, is a calculation which may be of methodological interest to econometricians but does not bear upon any real historical issue.[4]

In recent years it has become commonplace to assert that Keynes misunderstood the difficulties faced by the British economy between the wars—perversely ignoring the real structural problems and instead simplistically opting for an increase in overall demand.[5] This has led to an overdue reassessment of the work of pre-Keynesian economists, especially Pigou, whose cogency within an implicit disequilibrium approach has been brought out.[6] Yet the differences between the pre-Keynesians and Keynes can easily be exaggerated. In 1930 he too spoke in terms of an unemployment disequilibrium and he too agreed that there were structural causes for British unemployment in a competitive world market, implying that wages must be too high. But identifying the *causes* of the malady did not peremptorily imply the appropriate *remedies*. Neither Keynes nor Pigou actually recommended cutting wages. The issue was, what could best be done?

The centrality of the (labour) transfer problem was explicitly acknowledged in *Can Lloyd George Do It?* The argument was that it was more likely to be solved, through the stimulus of public works, within a context of expansion. Empirical evidence on the narrowing of regional disparities during economic recovery suggests that this view was well founded.[7] Moreover, the pre-Keynesian economists Pigou and Clay, for all their emphasis on structural problems, are

---

[4] This is the project undertaken in S. Glynn and P. G. A. Howells, 'Unemployment in the 1930s: The Keynesian solution reconsidered', *Aust. Econ. Hist. Rev.*, 20, 28–45; it is incisively criticized in T. J. Hatton, 'Unemployment in the 1930s and the "Keynesian solution": Some notes of dissent', *Aust. Econ. Hist. Rev.*, 25 (1985), 1–30. See also Hatton, 'The outlines of a Keynesian solution', in Glynn and Booth (eds.), *Road to Full Employment*, 82–94.

[5] Work in this field is surveyed in Sean Glynn and Alan Booth, 'Unemployment in inter-war Britain: A case for re-learning the lessons of the 1930s?', *Econ. Hist. Rev.*, 2nd ser., 36 (1983), 329–48; T. J. Hatton, *The Analysis of Unemployment in Inter-War Britain* (Centre for Economic Policy Research, 1985); and Patrick O'Brien, 'Britain's economy between the Wars: A survey of a counter-revolution in economic history', *Past and Present*, 115 (May 1987), 107–30.

[6] See Mark Casson, *Economics of Unemployment: An historical perspective* (Oxford, 1983), esp. 147–9. Despite its subtitle, this is less a historical study than a reconstruction of a viable line of argument, which is not in all respects faithful to the historical Pigou; see above, ch. 8 n. 73.

[7] Hatton, 'Unemployment in the 1930s', 133–4.

both to be found supporting public works in 1933. Henderson, too, continued to argue that expansionary measures were the best means of solving the transfer problem, though by 1935 he favoured increasing consumption through spending on the social services rather than public works.[8] Nor did his former co-author Keynes lose sight of the structural constraints upon an expansion of demand.

How the real world looked through the new economic spectacles of the *General Theory* to Keynes himself does not have to be a matter of guesswork. His 1937 articles in *The Times*, 'How to avoid a slump', subsequently slipped out of sight for many years but have been the focus of considerable interest since their retrieval by Hutchison. For in them, Keynes declared that 'we are approaching, or have reached, the point where there is not much advantage in applying a further general stimulus at the centre.' He wrote this at a time when unemployment was still 12 per cent nationally, though of course concentrated in the distressed areas. Indeed his point was that there was now more need of 'a rightly distributed demand than of a greater aggregate demand'. In short, he showed himself acutely aware of those regional peculiarities and economic bottle-necks—'the economic structure is unfortunately rigid'—which Keynesianism has often been accused of ignoring. Moreover, he now advised the Government to take measures 'temporarily to damp down aggregate demand, with a view to stabilising subsequent activity at as high a level as possible'. This meant austerity at the Treasury, procrastination on public expenditure, and relaxation of protective measures on the international front.[9]

There is no need to conclude that Keynes supposed 12 per cent was the limit of full employment, conceived in the *General Theory* as the point at which prices rather than output would rise. His 1937 measures were broached in a context where a further fall in the official figures to 10 per cent was already in prospect. Even so, these were similar to the levels current when he had produced *Can Lloyd George Do It?* in 1929. It is true that in 1937 he was aware that resources would have to be found for the rearmament programme; but Kahn's subsequent interpretation of *The Times* articles in terms

---

[8] Henderson, *The Inter-war Years*, 160; for Pigou and Clay, see above, ch. 12 nn. 20, 32.

[9] *JMK* xxi. 384–95, at 385, 390 (*The Times*, 12–14 Jan. 1937). The articles are discussed (and reprinted) in T. W. Hutchison, *Keynes versus the 'Keynesians' . . .?* (Inst. of Econ. Affairs, 1977), which includes comments by Lord Kahn and Sir Austin Robinson.

of this motive lacks corroborative evidence and hardly seems convincing.[10]

The fact is that the historical point in contention here has become a proxy for a more wide-ranging dispute about the figure which Keynes thought practicable as a full-employment target. Sir Willam Beveridge's book, *Full Employment in a Free Society* (1944) was to introduce a norm as low as 3 per cent. 'No harm in aiming at 3 per cent unemployed,' Keynes responded, 'but I shall be surprised if we succeed.'[11] (It may be added that Meade thought Beveridge was shamelessly 'playing to the gallery'.)[12] Even this target seemed embarrassingly conservative in retrospect to many Keynesians during the post-war boom, when even 2 per cent came to be regarded as high; but it was almost certainly more optimistic than Keynes himself thought possible on the basis of pre-war experience. 'It is easy to employ 80 to 90 per cent of the national resources without taking much thought as to how to fit things in,' he wrote in 1937. '... But to employ 95 to 100 per cent of the national resources is a different task altogether.'[13] The *General Theory*, in short, does not seem to have altered Keynes's view of the 'normal proportion' of unemployment—perhaps 5 per cent—at which *Can Lloyd George Do It?* had thought it reasonable to aim.

In 1929, when he was fundamentally orthodox in his economic theory, Keynes had propounded a radical critique of prevailing economic policy. He had perfectly good arguments—often similar to those of Pigou and Robertson—to justify the expedients he proposed, under conditions of disequilibrium, as the *Treatise* explained. The shift to the *General Theory* cannot simply be inferred from the polemical requirements of the debate over policy. It was not, as Hayek alleged, 'a tract for the times', even though it may have been, as Henderson surmised, 'a child of the slump'.[14] This lack of correlation is shown by the fact that once Keynes had developed his radical theory, he became, if anything, more cautious and pragmatic in the economic policy he advocated. His own analysis disclosed how

[10] Ibid. 49–50; and see Moggridge, *Keynes*, 2nd edn. (1980), 185 n. 24.

[11] *JMK* xxvii. 381 (to Beveridge, 16 Dec. 1944).

[12] Meade diary, 25 Nov. 1944, Meade Papers 1/3, LSE. Meade thought it more reasonable to aim at getting back to the pre-1914 figure of 6 per cent.

[13] *JMK* xxi. 409 ('Borrowing for defence: is it inflation?', *The Times*, 11 Mar. 1937); and see his comments of 1943, *JMK* xxvii 335–6.

[14] See above, ch. 10 n. 2 and ch. 12 n. 78.

deep-seated and intractable the problem of unemployment was, rather than how easy it would be to conquer it.

Over the years, views of the relationship between Keynes and the Treasury up to the Second World War have swung from the complaint that he was shamefully disregarded to the verdict that the walls of Jericho had suffered a discreet collapse. There is now a fair measure of agreement that the Treasury had become more open-minded in what it was prepared to consider.[15] Clearly, the Government's acceptance of loan finance for rearmament from 1935 made a considerable difference; but acknowledgement of the macro-economic impact of such measures did not necessarily imply conversion to a Keynesian perspective.

The role of Hawtrey, who wrote a sceptical appraisal of the *General Theory* for Treasury consumption, bears examination. Not for the first time, caution is needed before his policy advice is inferred from his theoretical analysis. For he saw the merit of what was coming to be called 'reflation' to counteract deflation, while remaining as unconvinced as ever that public works in themselves made any difference. In discussing Keynes's articles in 1937, therefore, he argued that, since an inflationary increase in credit was the only means by which trade recovery was brought about, the logical way to control trade fluctuations was by resorting to cheap money in a slump and applying a credit squeeze when boom conditions developed. It was, he held, a central banking question. To the Bank of England, where all this was noted with interest, this seemed to make sense of actual Treasury priorities—Leith-Ross's faith in cheap money, for example. It suggested that, 'whatever they may say about Hawtrey, his theories in fact fill the vacuum left in their minds by the lack of economic theories on this subject of their own'.[16]

This percipient remark helps explain some difference of emphasis in Phillips's comments, which may otherwise seem puzzling. In 1938, for instance, he advised against raising taxes in the Budget, despite the common allegation that government borrowing led to inflation. 'There is not in fact grave danger of inflation until we shall be much nearer than at present to a state of full employment,' he argued.

---

[15] See Howson and Winch, *EAC* 134–52; Peden, 'Keynes, the Treasury and unemployment'; Middleton, *Towards the Managed Economy*, chs. 6–8; Booth, 'Britain in the 1930s: A managed economy?', esp. 499–500, 506–10, 519–20.

[16] Memo. for B. G. Catterns (Deputy Governor), 12 Feb. 1937, G1 1/15; authorship obscure (?Clay). For a revised version of Hawtrey's paper, see his *Capital and Employment* (1937), ch. 7.

'Inflation is a thing which is inconsistent with the existence of 1,800,000 unemployed.'[17] So far, so Keynesian. Yet Phillips revealed his underlying view in advising on the line to be taken in Parliament in April 1939:[18]

I agree with Mr Hawtrey that the real stimulus comes from reflationary finance. If there were no reflationary finance, the government works would tend merely to replace private works without much effect on employment. But this is the famous or infamous 'Treasury view', still a most bitter subject of controversy which it would be a great mistake to raise.

Perhaps Hawtrey's long years in the dungeon in which his Treasury colleagues had immured him had, in the end, given him a more subtly insidious influence in the 1930s than has usually been supposed.

If rearmament was important in Britain, in Hitler's Germany it was crucial in stimulating and sustaining economic growth. 'Fundamentally, the Nazis "solved" only one economic problem: unemployment,' James has concluded.[19] Everything else was subordinated to this single priority. No such charge could be levelled against the National Government which, rightly or wrongly, took cognizance of other priorities. In Germany, it appears, rearmament had to be passed off as work creation. (Even the famous autobahn network was not all it seemed: net spending on transport in fact declined between 1928 and 1936.) In Britain, by contrast, work creation had to be passed off as rearmament—or, at any rate, any explicit linkage between them was officially resisted.

Hopkins was concerned lest 'the country began to think of a Defence Loan as a comfortable Lloyd-Georgian device for securing not only larger forces but also lower estimates, Budget surpluses and diminishing taxation'.[20] To some extent, his fears were justified by the sort of arguments which began to be used by Labour spokesmen in the House of Commons: 'If you can do that for armaments you

---

[17] Quoted in Middleton, *Towards the Managed Economy*, 118.

[18] Quoted in Peden, 'Keynes, the Treasury and unemployment', 6.

[19] James, *The German Slump*, 419; and see 371–87, 413–14, for other points in this paragraph. For the impact on the British economy, see G. C. Peden, *British Rearmament and the Treasury* (Edinburgh, 1979), ch. 3, and Mark Thomas, 'Rearmament and economic recovery in the late 1930's, *Econ. Hist. Rev.*, 2nd ser., 36 (1983), 552–73.

[20] Hopkins (Oct. 1935), quoted in Peden, *British Rearmament*, 74. He meant a surplus on the revenue account if defence spending were classed as capital expenditure.

are going to have great difficulty in persuading the working men of the country that it is a wrong policy to borrow for real assets in public works.'[21] There were, of course, valid admininstrative differences which made a rearmament programme easier to mount, even though the economic return to the community on the assets created might not be appreciably greater than that from digging holes in the ground and filling them in again.

It was the Second World War which resolved many of these dilemmas. 'It is, it seems, politically impossible for a capitalistic democracy to organize expenditure on the scale necessary to make the grand experiments which would prove my case—except in war conditions,' Keynes wrote in June 1940.[22] By the time his words were published, Keynes had himself received an invitation to join the Treasury, in which he was to occupy a peculiar and elevated position—'he was just "Keynes"'—for the rest of his life. In 1941 he became a Director of the Bank of England and Lord Keynes the following year. The fact that he was now himself an important figure in Whitehall is one reason for the rapid transmission of his views. He formed a close and effective working relationship with Hopkins, who often took the advice of the author of the *General Theory*—with a grain of Treasury salt, of course—and eventually read the book on his retirement. Keynes found, too, that he warmed to the laconic Phillips on closer acquaintance. Moreover, Keynes was not alone in exerting a personal influence—of his circle, Richard Kahn, Austin Robinson, Richard Stone, and, above all, James Meade, were all temporary Civil Servants in key positions. The chief counterweight was not Robbins—much chastened in his views by the time he was working in the Cabinet Office—but Henderson, as economic adviser to the Treasury.[23]

The actual immediate problems of wartime generally speeded up change by requiring improvisation and superseding precedent. The

---

[21] A. V. Alexander (Oct. 1937), quoted in Middleton, *Towards the Managed Economy*, 170.

[22] *JMK* xxii. 149 (*New Republic*, 29 July 1940); see also *JMK* ix. 354 (*Means to Prosperity*).

[23] D. E. Moggridge, 'Economic policy in the Second World War', in M. Keynes (ed), *Essays*, 177–201; Alan Booth, 'The "Keynesian revolution" in economic policy-making', *Econ. Hist. Rev.*, 2nd ser., 36 (1983), 103–23; Peden, 'Sir Richard Hopkins and the "Keynesian Revolution"', ibid. 281–96. See also Keynes's appreciation of Phillips, *JMK* x. 330–1; Clay's introduction to Henderson, *The Inter-War Years*, xxii–xxv; Lord Kahn, *On Re-reading Keynes*, Fourth Keynes Lecture, from *Proc. Brit. Acad.*, 60 (1974), esp. 25–6; Robbins, *Autobiography*, 154–5, 193.

war economy, too, presented crucially different macro-economic problems from those of peacetime: the symptoms were those of inflation not deflation. Whereas Keynes had encountered resistance from the Treasury to his arguments for remedial reflationary measures, it was much easier to win assent for anti-inflationary expedients like his proposals in *How to Pay for the War* (1940). Again, if 1941 can be regarded as the occasion of the first Keynesian Budget—presented in terms of national-income accounts, not just government revenue and expenditure—this too must be seen in the context of restraining rather than stimulating aggregate demand.[24]

Perhaps most important, the war transformed the ideological climate. Keynesian ideas had made a fair amount of headway in the Labour party in the late 1930s. To Rowse, who regarded the *General Theory* as 'the complete vindication of the Labour Movement', its prospects of translation into action were enhanced 'since there is a generation of young men in the Labour Movement already thinking on these lines'.[25] The book by Douglas Jay, *The Socialist Case* (1937), acknowledging Meade's influence, exemplifies the point. Keynes himself remained uncommitted. 'The Liberal party is the centre of gravity and ought to be the focus of a new alignment of progressive forces,' he told the incoming Liberal leader, Sinclair, in 1938, adding: 'In practice, of course, the Labour Party has to be the predominant member.'[26] Here was a pipe-dream of the revival of the progressive movement of his youth under new conditions—and one which, unexpectedly quickly, the political revolution of 1940 was to fulfil. With the replacement of the National Government by the Churchill Coalition, the centre of gravity indeed shifted to the left, while party political considerations ceased to be overriding.[27] These were highly

[24] R. S. Sayers, '1941—the first Keynesian Budget', reprinted from his official history, *Financial Policy*, in Charles Feinstein (ed.), *The Managed Economy* (Oxford, 1983), 107–17; cf. Booth, 'Keynesian revolution', 106–7.

[25] Rowse, *Mr Keynes and the Labour Movement*, 66; and see Durbin, *New Jerusalems*, esp. 147–59, 243–64.

[26] *JMK* xxviii. 107 (Keynes to Sinclair, 4 Apr. 1938). On Keynes's general sympathy for the left in the 1930s, Winch provides an excellent corrective to Harrod's 'establishment' view: *Economics and Politics*, 350–60. In the 1930s Harrod had himself been ready to work with the New Fabian Research Bureau: Durbin, *New Jerusalems*, esp. 98, 105–6, 162. By 1951, however, Keynes's official biographer was seeking to become Conservative candidate for Bournemouth: see Harold Nicolson, *Diaries and Letters, 1945–62* (1968), 214 (30 Dec. 1951).

[27] Paul Addison, *The Road to 1945: British Politics and the Second World War* (1975) remains the most persuasive account; see also the compatible interpretation of the war's role in Robert Skidelsky, 'The reception of the Keynesian revolution', in M. Keynes (ed.), *Essays*, 89–107.

favourable conditions for the exertion of Keynes's own influence and for the ideological diffusion of his ideas.

Neither the 1941 Budget nor the Coalition Government's White Paper on Employment Policy (1944) in itself marks an unconditional surrender by the Treasury to Keynesian ideas; but their incremental encroachment was certainly gathering pace. The fact that the White Paper, though modified in its thrust by the circumspect Hoppy, was in effect competing with Beveridge's own manifesto underlines the point. To Meade, the agreement on basic principles in both schemes was 'a most remarkable fact if one casts one's memory back to the doctrinal bedlam of the nineteen-thirties'.[28] Their congruence is hardly surprising in view of the contribution of Meade to the one and that of Joan Robinson and Nicholas Kaldor to the other. This obliquely reflects the emerging academic consensus around the *General Theory*. In the Cambridge Economics Tripos, so Pigou told Keynes, 'the parrot-like treatment of your stuff is due to the lectures and supervisions of the beautiful Mrs R' but even where 'this drill-sergeant business' was less conspicuous, the indoctrination of the young in what was to become the conventional wisdom of the 1950s and 1960s was afoot.[29] After all, the *General Theory* itself had surmised that 'in the field of economic and political philosophy there are not many who are influenced by new theories after they are twenty-five or thirty years of age, so that the ideas which civil servants and politicians and even agitators apply to current events are not likely to be the newest'.[30]

It should be added that the Treasury's adoption of Keynesianism in the post-war period was more faltering than used to be supposed. As Chancellor of the Exchequer in the Labour Government, Dalton showed himself still resistant to the spell cast by his old teacher, and it was not until 1947 that the younger Keynesian ministers, especially Jay and Gaitskell, started to come into their own.[31] The continuity of approach when Butler went to the Treasury in the 1951 Conservative

[28] Meade diary, 25 Nov. 1944; and see Booth, 'Keynesian revolution', 107–17; Peden, 'Sir Richard Hopkins', 285–94; Josè Harris, *William Beveridge*, (Oxford, 1977), 435–41.

[29] Pigou (n.d.), quoted in Collard, 'A. C. Pigou', 130.

[30] *JMK* vii. 383–4.

[31] Booth, 'Keynesian revolution', 118–23; Pimlott, *Hugh Dalton*, 386–7, 397, 452–3; Alec Cairncross, *Years of Recovery: British economic policy, 1945–51*, (1985), 54–7, 299–310, 318–32, 409–26, 502; Kenneth O. Morgan, *Labour in Power, 1945–51* (Oxford, 1984), 363 ff.

Government—the 'Butskellite consensus'—was tempered by a new willingness to supplement fiscal with monetary policy.[32] The Conservatives wished to operate a policy of counter-cyclical macroeconomic demand management at arm's length instead of through direct controls. But the salience of Bank rate in this strategy was such that old Treasury hands might well have associated it not with Keynes but with Hawtrey. The policy of reflating and deflating in a cycle governed by unemployment on the one hand and the balance of payments on the other, came to be known pejoratively under Macmillan as 'stop-go'. Whether it should be identified as bastard Keynesianism of the right or whether a paternity suit should also cite the name of Hawtrey—to add to his putative record in promiscuously fathering the Treasury View and the multiplier—is a matter for innocent speculation.

In the long run

In retrospect, the 1960s can be seen as the peak of Keynesian prestige, from which there was nowhere to go but down. The post-war consensus in economic policy, maintaining full employment by demand management through fiscal changes and control of credit, ostensibly derived from Keynes. The pedagogic triumph of the IS–LM diagram legitimized this approach. The 'neo-classical synthesis' thus allowed a sort of peaceful coexistence. In the real world Keynesian policies could be justified by claiming that rigid wages and a 'liquidity trap' were facts of life, preventing full flexibility of prices and interest rates; but in a frictionless realm of theory the neo-classical postulate of equilibrium was not challenged. In 1968, however, this era of coexistence was notably disrupted by Milton Friedman's opening shots in the monetarist counter-revolution— shots which echoed round the world—and it was more discreetly subverted by the work of Leijonhufvud which fuelled controversy about the identity of 'Keynesianism' as against 'the economics of

---

[32] G. C. Peden, *British Economic and Social Policy* (1985), 165–70; Winch, *Economics and Policy*, 299–305; Samuel Brittan, *The Treasury under the Tories* (Harmondsworth, 1964), esp. ch. 6, and the revised edn., *Steering the Economy* (Harmondsworth, 1971), 448–56; J. C. R. Dow, *The Management of the British Economy, 1945–60* (Cambridge, 1964), ch. 3; Anthony Seldon, *Churchill's Indian Summer: The Conservative Government, 1951–5* (1981), ch. 5, parts 1 and 2.

Keynes'.[33] Both in theory and in practice, then, the consensus was challenged.

The monetarist critique of Keynesianism was successful in shifting the terms of debate away from demand to the supply side and in particular to the price of labour. When the Institute of Economic Affairs came to commemorate the fiftieth anniversary of the publication of the *General Theory*, many economists thought it time to bury Keynes not to praise him. 'The fundamental issue', as Beenstock puts it, 'is why wages and prices do not adjust themselves as fluidly as exchange rates. The rigidity of wages and prices is a basic premise in the *General Theory*.' Hence his statement that 'the Keynesian counter-revolutionaries have long since pointed out that wage–price flexibility completely undermines the Keynesian paradigm'.[34] This reading of the *General Theory* is, of course, quite unhistorical in imputing to Keynes a premiss about wages and prices which he did not, in fact, hold. Beenstock, though, is certainly right to comment that 'we have come full circle', because the position he now defends is precisely that 'classical' postulate which Keynes criticized. He wrote that it was 'accustomed to rest the supposedly self-adjusting character of the economic system on an assumed fluidity of money wages; and, when there is rigidity, to lay on this rigidity the blame of maladjustment.'[35] It is simply incorrect to regard the *General Theory* as an imperfectionist account, in the neo-classical tradition, postulating a market-clearing equilibrium which is unfortunately frustrated (by the persistence of sticky wages or the operation of a liquidity trap) in doing the trick.

The alternative to Keynes is illuminated by Yeager's concise exposition of 'a sound approach to macro-economics':[36]

Fundamentally, behind the veil of money, people specialize in producing particular goods and services to exchange them for the specialized outputs of other people. Any particular output thus constitutes demand for other (non-competing) outputs. Since supply constitutes demand in that sense, there can

---

[33] See Leijonhufvud, *On Keynesian Economics and the Economics of Keynes*, esp. 6–8; also his *Keynes and the Classics* (Instit. of Econ. Affairs, 1969); the illuminating study by Gordon Fletcher, *The Keynesian Revolution and its Critics* (1987), chs. 16–18; and Gilbert, *Keynes's Impact on Monetary Economics*, chs. 6–8, 12.

[34] Michael Beenstock, 'The *General Theory*, secular stagnation and the world economy', in John Burton (intro.), *Keynes's 'General Theory': Fifty years on* (Instit. of Econ. Affairs, 1986), 119–35, at 134.   [35] *JMK* vii. 257.

[36] Leland B. Yeager, 'The Keynesian heritage in economics', in Burton *et al.*, *Keynes's General Theory*, 25–44, at 28.

be no fundamental problem of deficiency of aggregate demand. Even in a depression, men and women are willing to work, produce, exchange and consume. In particular, employers are willing to hire more workers and produce more goods if only they could find customers, while unemployed workers are willing and eager to become customers if only they could be back at work earning money to spend.

Thus the real problem is why and how people are obstructed in making the transactions which would allow the markets to clear. But the revolution of the *General Theory* was to repudiate the assumption of Say's Law and thus to deny the natural tendency towards a market-clearing equilibrium at full employment. The theory of effective demand, whatever its deficiencies, cannot be undermined by simply willing Say's Law back to life again.[37]

Such points were not incidental but integral to Keynes's enterprise. The earliest drafts of his *magnum opus*, dating from 1932, already contain his essential doctrine on the efficacy of the 'obvious' exit from the vicious circle of depression by means of reductions in wages:[38]

Now the leading characteristic of this remedy, which is commonly overlooked, is that it is, taken absolutely and apart from consideration of its indirect reactions, what we may call a *competitive* remedy. That is to say, it is calculated to help any given entrepreneur who has the advantage of it, or indeed the entrepreneurs of any given group or country, provided the same advantages are not extended to *all* entrepreneurs in the closed system under examination. For the expected benefit is based on the assumption, which each entrepreneur looking only to his own affairs naturally makes, that entrepreneurs' outgoings will be diminished per unit of output without this having the effect of reducing their incomings to an equal extent.

This insight was at the heart of his theory. He saw that wage cuts *all round* sustained a self-defeating process, feeding a cycle of deflation. Obviously his eyes were fixed upon the conditions of his own day, but he was advancing a theoretical explanation, not a policy precept. The simple basic idea was, of course, an application of the fallacy of composition—that it does not follow that what one can do,

---

[37] This point is well made in Fletcher, *Keynesian Revolution and its Critics*, esp. 304. As Frank Hahn puts it: 'The overwhelmingly most important postulate of the Monetarists is that the invisible hand works and that it works pretty swiftly, although not instantaneously.' 'Monetarism and economic theory', *Economica*, 47 (1980), 1–17, at 16.

[38] *JMK* xiii. 390.

all can do simultaneously. As a theoretical axiom, therefore, the same point is surely applicable to the very different conditions of our own day. It is a straightforward inference from what Keynes said that wage *increases* all round sustain a self-defeating process, feeding a cycle of inflation.

The incapacity of the free market, unaided and uncontrolled, to guarantee full use of resources, whether in conditions of deflation or of inflation, is thus an inescapable implication of the theory of effective demand. In this sense, changes in price, which are what mainly affect the individual, may be less important in regulating the economy as a whole than changes in income and output. Since all bargains are two-sided, there is obviously an identity in aggregate between what is sold and bought—but an identity required by certain levels of income. Aggregate income, in short, has to change until the bargains can be accommodated.

Though any individual may be able to carry out his initial decision, he may find at the end of the day that it does not deliver the full prospective advantage. Now Leijonhufvud recognizes the centrality of the fallacy of composition to this dilemma, but he argues, with Yeager, that when plans cannot mesh in this way, the result is a *disequilibrium* position. It should, however, be observed that this is only true in the sense that it violates the formal condition of general equilibrium (that all plans can simultaneously be carried out at ruling prices and therefore that all markets clear). This might, in fact, usefully be distinguished as the *formal* concept of equilibrium. Its basis is essentially that the system be 'in balance'; if this condition is violated, then the public is 'wrong' about prices. But Leijonhufvud's central contention is not that individuals behave irrationally in maintaining this 'disequilibrium' but that their information is imperfect. If only they knew the 'right' prices, the system would necessarily be in equilibrium![39] But there is no implication that market adjustments will in fact get it right.

It will be apparent that such a model must be distinguished from the (more usual) *operational* sense of the term equilibrium, which implies corrective change. It implies, in fact, that disequilibrium prices, being necessarily unstable, will change in *a process of equilibration*; and, conversely, that the system is 'at rest' when this process exerts no further pressure for change. Such a position may well fall

---

[39] *On Keynesian Economics and the Economics of Keynes*, 262, 267, 333, 379, 381, 385, 397.

short of full employment—to that extent prevailing prices are 'wrong'—but it must, to be faithful to the *General Theory*, be understood as one of equilibrium.[40]

Keynes's point is that the *extent* to which agents fail to carry out their plans in the market—through consequent price or income or output changes—is determined in ways which do not necesssarily bear directly upon the individuals concerned. Hence the putative role of uncertainty or imperfect information or the rationality of expectations is not operationally crucial. The fact is that the market does not provide individuals with incentives to change irreconcilable plans which are collectively incompatible with a full-employment equilibrium. It is still rational for us as individual agents to adopt competitive strategies which we can perfectly well understand to be collectively self-defeating if adopted all round. This may be defensive, through a Hobbesian mistrust of our fellows; or aggressive, in the pursuit of *relative* advantage; or unconscious, in following market pressures.

These are surely valid insights into the world in which we live—and they derive from the Keynesian revolution in economic theory, which discloses the possibilities of sub-optimal equilibrium. But though these ideas still possess analytical power, they do not carry prescriptive authority, because solutions are not inherent in problems. The historical Keynes, of course, was deeply interested in policy as well as theory, but his own suggested remedies, while sometimes of surviving relevance, must be considered within the context of his own era, not least its political context. For the application of Keynes's theory to the real world was, as he foresaw, to be inextricably intertwined with politics and feelings and passions.

It would be an odd reading of Keynes which acknowledged the cogency of his explanation of the workings of the economy without raising the issue of whether unemployment can in practice be alleviated. Keynes clearly envisaged a bigger role for government in managing the economy. The political consequences of Mr Keynes have accordingly been the focus of much discussion, especially within the framework of 'public choice' theory. For has not Keynesianism

---

[40] Instead of my distinction of operational/formal models of equilibrium, one might explore the differences between a Marshallian partial equilibrium model and a Walrasian general equilibrium model, as Patinkin does. I share Patinkin's doubts whether Keynes did 'in his own mind draw a sharp distinction between the Marshallian and Walrasian approaches'. See Patinkin, *Keynes's Monetary Thought*, 98–101; and above, ch. 11 at nn. 95 ff.

validated a political regime ostensibly aiming at full employment but in fact leading to the edge of an economic precipice? As Buchanan puts it: 'Budget deficits, inflation and the growth of government—all are intensified by the Keynesian destruction of former constitutional principles of sound finance.'[41]

There are two distinct issues here. The first concerns the attitude of the historical Keynes, up to his death in 1946. The 'Keynes' of much recent public choice analysis is a callow rationalist and élitist who seems to have lacked the wit to venture beyond the end of Harvey Road or to tumble to the way the world wagged. It has, however, been suggested in the course of this book that the famous 'presuppositions' have had too much thrust upon them in explaining Keynes's own political views. He was not simply naïve, though he may have been optimistic, in thinking that his ideas could improve the world. He was, however, a man of his time, with a political outlook which had, in crucial respects, been formed before the First World War. If his exchange with Hayek in 1944, which has become well known, is read in this light, it will perhaps be better understood. In contesting Hayek's minimalist conception of the role of the state, Keynes wrote:[42]

I should therefore conclude your theme rather differently. I should say that what we want is not no planning, or even less planning, indeed I should say we almost certainly want more. But the planning should take place in a community in which as many people as possible, both leaders and followers, wholly share your own moral position. Moderate planning will be safe if those carrying it out are rightly orientated in their own minds and hearts to the moral issue.

It is tempting to suggest that, at the end of his life, Keynes reverted instinctively to the 'moral reformist' values which infused the New Liberalism of his youth.[43]

The second issue arising out of public choice analysis is not only historical but concerns its own (often implicit) ideological bearings. It is certainly true that the planks of the fiscal constitution fitted tightly

---

[41] James M. Buchanan, Richard E. Wagner and John Burton, *The Consequences of Mr Keynes* (Inst. of Econ. Affairs, 1978), 23. This tract restates, with special reference to Britain, the argument in Buchanan, *Democracy in Deficit: The political legacy of Lord Keynes* (1977).

[42] *JMK* xxvii. 387 (Keynes to Hayek, 28 June 1944).

[43] See above, ch. 1. Such conceptions, however, may not have been specific to his own generation. Joan Robinson wrote to Beveridge in 1943: 'Everything depends on the moral atmosphere.' (Harris, *Beveridge*, 437.)

together in the late nineteenth and early twentieth centuries, with the balanced Budget convention in pride of place. The notion that the system could work in a self-acting manner, rendered 'knave-proof' through its insulation from the temptations of democratic politics, was admittedly one which Keynes challenged, initially in his attack upon the Gold Standard. This system, he maintained, 'with its dependence on pure chance, its faith in "automatic adjustments", and its general regardlessness of social detail, is an essential emblem and idol of those who sit in the top tier of the machine'.[44] Sound finance is not a painless means of running the economy—only painless for those in 'the top tier' who do not bear the brunt of the 'automatic adjustments'. What Keynes did was to demystify this system by letting the cat out of the bag. Sound finance may well be a valid political option, but it took Keynes to make it clear that a choice between options was available. It is never true that there is no alternative, and it is historically implausible to suppose that the cat can now be put back into the bag.

The politics of Keynesian economics look different in the late 1980s from even a few years ago. The leading protagonists of public choice theory in the late 1970s displayed no doubt that, unless the fiscal constitution were itself reformed, political pressures would continue to militate against unemployment but to condone inflation, with the result that British democracy would crumble under the influence of the corruption of Keynesianism.[45] Even after Mrs Thatcher's installation as Prime Minister, it still seemed axiomatic to an economist studying the 1930s that pre-Keynesian policies, though cogent, were 'vote-losers'.[46] The General Elections of 1983 and 1987, however, have surely helped historians to appreciate why Keynesian policies did not make greater political headway between the wars and to understand how the National Government remained impregnable in that period. As so often, the present throws as much light upon the past as vice versa.

Now that Thatcher has become the longest-serving Prime Minister of the twentieth century, these are good conditions under which to locate the historical significance of the Keynesian revolution. For it is the *political* success of Thatcherism, not the economic success of

---

[44] *JMK* ix. 224 (*Economic Consequences of Mr Churchill*); cf. Buchanan *et al.*, *Consequences of Mr Keynes*, esp. 37–41.

[45] Buchanan *et al.*, *Consequences of Mr Keynes*, 71, 74–5, 81–2.

[46] Casson, *Economics of Unemployment*, 162, 164.

'monetarism', which seems more obvious and more thought-provoking. In the 1970s, to be sure, the claim was that Keynesianism simply did not work. But how far does experience since 1979 show that Thatcherism 'works'? It has indeed worked on inflation, first through intensifying and then through perpetuating unemployment —a demonstration which would not, it is safe to say, have undermined Keynes's intellectual self-confidence or caused him to doubt the validity of his own analysis. Yet the populist appeal of Thatcherism shows that such policies have a wide appeal (albeit one exaggerated by the distortions of the electoral system). Just as the historic transformation of the Conservative party between the nineteenth and twentieth centuries was from a largely landed party to one based upon the middle classes, so a further fundamental change may be under way in the late twentieth century: the emergence of a party appealing to strong bargainers in *all* classes. Such a party can well satisfy its own constituency by running the economy at the sub-optimal levels of output and employment which are all that market forces may be capable of producing. The notion that the democratic process itself axiomatically enshrines Keynesian policies may serve as an example of a rationalist fallacy as naïve as any contained in the writings of the historical Keynes.

BIBLIOGRAPHY

London is the place of publication unless otherwise stated.

Abbreviations

EAC	S. Howson and D. Winch, *The Economic Advisory Council, 1930–9* (Cambridge, 1977)
5 Hansard	Parliamentary Debates, 5th series
JMK	*The Collected Writings of John Maynard Keynes*, 29 vols. to date (1971–); managing editors, Donald Moggridge and Sir Austin Robinson
Jones, *Whitehall Diary*	Keith Middlemas (ed.), *Thomas Jones: Whitehall Diary 1916–30*, 2 vols. (1969)
Macmillan Report	Committee on Finance and Industry, Report, Cmd. 3897 (1931)
Macmillan Evidence	Committee on Finance and Industry, Minutes of Evidence, 2 vols. (1931)
Pimlott	Ben Pimlott (ed.), *The Political Diary of Hugh Dalton, 1918–40, 1945–60* (1986)

For reference

Craig, F. W. S. (ed.), *British Parliamentary Election Results, 1918–49* (Glasgow, 1969)
Dictionary of National Biography
HMSO, *British Labour Statistics, 1886–1968* (1971)

Public Record Office

CAB 23	Cabinet conclusions
CAB 24	Cabinet memoranda (CP papers)
CAB 58/150–1	EAC committee of economists
T. 160/426, file 11548	Macmillan Committee
T. 171/309	Chancellor of the Exchequer's Office: Budget
T. 172	Chancellor of the Exchequer's office: misc., Files 1502, 1516, 1652, 1662, 1734, 2095.

T. 175   Hopkins Papers, Files 1, 17, 26, 41–3, 46, 50–2
T. 176   Niemeyer Papers, Files 13, 21.
T. 177/4   Phillips Papers
T. 188   Leith-Ross Papers, Files 28, 263, 274–5
T. 200   Macmillan Committee, Files 1–6

Bank of England

ADM 20   Norman diaries
EID 1/2   Intelligence department: Macmillan Committee
G1/15–16   'Keynes files'
OV/9   Niemeyer Papers
S 44/1   Macmillan Committee

Other archives

Dalton Papers, London School of Economics
Hawtrey Papers, Churchill College, Cambridge
Henderson Papers, Nuffield College, Oxford
Keynes Papers, King's College, Cambridge
Meade Papers, London School of Economics

Published works cited

ADDISON, P., *The Road to 1945: British politics and the Second World War* (1975)
ANON., 'Sir Richard Hopkins', *Public Administration*, 34 (1956), 115–23
ANYADIKE-DANES, M. K., 'Dennis Robertson and Keynes's General Theory', in Harcourt, G. C. (ed.), *Keynes and His Contemporaries* (1985), 105–40
ASIMAKOPULOS, A., 'Keynes, Patinkin, historical time, and equilibrium analysis', *Can. Jnl. of Econ.*, 6 (1973), 179–88.
—— 'Anticipations of Keynes's General Theory', *Can. Jnl. of Econ.*, 16 (1983), 517–30
BEENSTOCK, M., 'The *General Theory*, secular stagnation and the world economy', in Burton, J., *et al.*, *Keynes's 'General Theory': Fifty years on* (Institute of Economic Affairs, 1986), 119–35
BELL, A. O. (ed.), *The Diary of Virginia Woolf*, ii–v (Harmondsworth, 1981–5)
BENTLEY, M., and STEVENSON, J. (eds.), *High and Low Politics in Modern Britain* (Oxford, 1983)
BLACK, R. D. C., 'R. G. Hawtrey', *Proc. Brit. Acad.*, 63 (1977), 363–407

BOOTH, A., 'The "Keynesian revolution" in economic policy-making', *Econ. Hist. Rev.*, 2nd ser., 36 (1983), 103–23

—— 'Defining a "Keynesian Revolution"', *Econ. Hist. Rev.*, 2nd ser., 38 (1984), 263–7

—— 'Britain in the 1930s: A managed economy?', *Econ. Hist. Rev.*, 2nd ser., 40 (1987), 499–522

—— and PACK, M., *Employment, Capital, and Economic Policy* (Oxford, 1985)

BOYLE, A., *Montagu Norman* (1967)

BRITTAN, S., *The Treasury under the Tories*; 3rd edn., entitled *Steering the Economy: The Role of the Treasury* (Harmondsworth, 1964; 1971)

BUCHANAN, J. M., *Democracy in Deficit: The political legacy of Lord Keynes* (1977)

——, WAGNER, R. E., and BURTON, J., *The Consequences of Mr Keynes* (Institute of Economic Affairs, 1978)

BULLOCK, A., *The Life and Times of Ernest Bevin*, i (1960)

BURK, KATHLEEN, 'The Treasury: From impotence to power', in Burk (ed.), *War and the State* (1982), 84–107

BURTON, J., *et al.*, *Keynes's 'General Theory': Fifty years on* (Institute of Economic Affairs, 1986)

BUTLER, D. E., *The Electoral System in Britain, 1918–51* (Oxford, 1953)

CAIN, N., 'Cambridge and its revolution: A perspecive on the multiplier and effective demand', *Economic Record*, 55 (1979), 108–17

—— 'Hawtrey and multiplier theory', *Australian Economic History Review*, 22 (1982), 68–78

CAIRNCROSS, A., *Years of Recovery: British economic policy, 1945–51* (1985)

CAMPBELL, J., *Lloyd George, The Goat in the Wilderness, 1922–1931* (1977)

CAPIE, F., *Depression and Protectionism: Britain between the Wars* (1983)

CASSON, M., *Economics of Unemployment: An historical perspective* (Oxford, 1983)

CHURCHILL, W. S., 'Parliamentary government and the economic problem', in Churchill, *Thoughts and Adventures* (1932)

CLARKE, P. F., *Lancashire and the New Liberalism* (Cambridge, 1971)

—— *Liberals and Social Democrats* (Cambridge, 1978)

CLAY, H., *Lord Norman* (1957)

CODDINGTON, A., *Keynesian Economics: The search for first principles* (1983)

COLLARD, D., 'A. C. Pigou, 1877–1959' in O'Brien, D. P., and Presley, J. R. (eds.), *Pioneers of Modern Economics in Britain* (1981), 105–39

COLLINI, S., WINCH, D., and BURROW, J., *That Noble Science of Politics* (Cambridge, 1983)

COOK, C., *The Age of Alignment, 1922–9* (1975)

CRANSTON, M., 'Keynes: His political ideas and their influence', in Thirwell, A. P. (ed.), *Keynes and Laissez-Faire* (1978), 101–15

DAVIS, E. G., 'The correspondence between R. G. Hawtrey and J. M. Keynes on the Treatise: The genesis of output adjustment models', *Can. Jnl. of Econ.*, 13 (1980), 716–24

—— 'R. G. Hawtrey', in O'Brien, D. P., and Presley, J. R. (eds.), *Pioneers of Modern Economics in Britain* (1981), 203–33

DONOUGHUE, B., and JONES, G. W., *Herbert Morrison: Portrait of a Politician* (1973)

DOW, J. C. R., *The Management of the British Economy, 1945–60* (Cambridge, 1964)

DURBIN, E., *New Jerusalems* (1985)

EATWELL, J., and MILGATE, M. (eds.), *Keynes's Economics and the Theory of Value and Distribution* (1983)

EICHENGREEN, B. (ed.), *The Gold Standard in Theory and History* (1985)

EINZIG, P., *Montagu Norman* (1932)

—— *In the Centre of Things* (1960)

FEINSTEIN, C. (ed.), *The Managed Economy* (Oxford, 1983)

FLETCHER, G., *The Keynesian Revolution and its Critics* (1987)

FLOUD, R., and McCLOSKY, D. (eds.), *The Economic History of Britain since 1700*, ii (Cambridge, 1981)

FREEDEN, M., *The New Liberalism* (Oxford, 1978)

—— *Liberalism Divided* (Oxford, 1986)

GILBERT, J. C., *Keynes's Impact on Monetary Economics* (1982)

GILBERT, M., *Winston S. Churchill*, v (1976)

GLYNN, S., and BOOTH, A., 'Unemployment in inter-war Britain: A case for re-learning the lessons of the 1930s?', *Econ. Hist. Rev.*, 2nd ser., 36 (1983), 329–48

——, —— (eds.), *The Road to Full Employment* (1987)

—— and HOWELLS, P. G. A., 'Unemployment in the 1930s: The Keynesian solution reconsidered', *Aust. Econ. Hist. Rev.*, 20 (1980), 28–45

GREEN, E. H. H., 'Radical Conservatism in Britain, 1899–1914', Ph.D. thesis (Cambridge, 1986)

GRIGG, P. J., *Prejudice and Judgement* (1948)

HMSO, *Memoranda on certain proposals relating to unemployment*, Cmd. 3331 (1929)

HAHN, F. H., 'Monetarism and economic theory', *Economica*, 47 (1980), 1–17

HANCOCK, K. J., 'Unemployment and the economists in the 1920's', *Economica*, NS 27 (1960), 305–21

—— 'The reduction of unemployment as a problem of public policy; 1920–9', in Pollard, S. (ed.), *The Gold Standard and Employment Policies between the Wars* (1970), 99–121

HARCOURT, G. C. (ed.), *Keynes and his Contemporaries* (1985)

—— and O'SHAUGHNESSY, T. J., 'Keynes's unemployment equilibrium: Some insights from Joan Robinson, Piero Sraffa and Richard Kahn', in Harcourt (ed.), *Keynes and his Contemporaries* (1985), 3–41

HARGRAVE, J. G., *Professor Skinner alias Montagu Norman* (n.d.)

HARRIS, J., *William Beveridge* (Oxford, 1977)

HARROD, R., *The Life of John Maynard Keynes* (1951)

HART, M., 'The decline of the Liberal Party in Parliament and in the Constituencies, 1914–31', D.Phil. thesis (Oxford, 1982)

HATTON, T. J., *The Analysis of Unemployment in Inter-War Britain* (Centre for Economic Policy Research, 1985)

—— 'Unemployment in the 1930s and the "Keynesian solution": Some notes of dissent', *Aust. Econ. Hist. Rev.*, 25 (1985), 1–30

—— 'The outlines of a Keynesian solution', in Glynn, S., and Booth, A. (eds.), *The Road to Full Employment* (1987), 82–94

HAWTREY, R. G., 'Public expenditure and the demand for labour', *Economica*, 5 (1925), 38–48

—— *Currency and Credit*, 3rd edn. (1928)

—— *The Art of Central Banking* (1933)

—— *Capital and Employment* (1937)

HAYEK, F. A., *A Tiger by the Tail*, ed. Shenoy, S. R. (Institute of Economic Affairs, 1972)

HENDERSON, H. D., *The Inter-War Years* (1955)

HESSION, C., *John Maynard Keynes* (1984)

HICKS, J., 'Mr. Keynes and the "Classics"', in Hicks, *Critical Essays in Monetary Theory* (Oxford, 1967), from *Econometrica*, 5 (1937)

—— *Economic Perspectives* (Oxford, 1977)

HOWSON, S., '"A dear money man"? Keynes on monetary policy, 1920', *Econ. Jnl.*, 83 (1973), 456–64

—— *Domestic Monetary Management in Britain, 1919–38* (Cambridge, 1975)

—— 'Hawtrey and the real world', in Harcourt, G. C. (ed.), *Keynes and his Contemporaries* (1985), 142–88

—— and WINCH, D., *The Economic Advisory Council, 1930–9* (Cambridge, 1977)

HUBBACK, D., *No Ordinary Press Baron: A Life of Walter Layton* (1985)

HUME, L. J., 'The Gold Standard and deflation: Issues and attitudes in the 1920s', in Pollard, S., *The Gold Standard and Employment Policies between the Wars* (1970), 122–45

HUTCHISON, T. W., *Economics and Economic Policy in Britain, 1946–66* (1968)

—— *Keynes versus the 'Keynesians'...?* (Institute of Economic Affairs, 1977)

INTERNATIONAL LABOUR OFFICE, *Unemployment and Public Works* (Geneva, 1931)

JACKMAN, R., 'Keynes and Leijonhufvud', *Oxford Econ. Papers*, NS 36 (1974), 259–72

JAMES, H., *The German Slump* (Oxford, 1986)

JOHNSON, E. S., and JOHNSON, H. G., 'The social and intellectual origins of the *General Theory*' reprinted in Johnson and Johnson, *The Shadow of Keynes* (Oxford, 1978), 65–83, from *Hist. of Pol. Econ.*, vi (1974), 261–77

——, —— *The Shadow of Keynes* (Oxford, 1978)

JOHNSON, H. G., 'Keynes and British economics', in Keynes, M. (ed.), *Essays on John Maynard Keynes* (1975), 108–202, reprinted in Johnson, *The Shadow of Keynes* (Oxford, 1978), 203–20

—— 'Cambridge as an academic environment in the early 1930s: A reconstruction from the late 1940s', in Patinkin, D., and Leith, J. C. (eds.), *Keynes, Cambridge and the General Theory* (1977)

JONES, THOMAS, *A Diary with Letters, 1931–50* (1954)

KAHN, R. F., 'The relation of home investment to unemployment', reprinted in Kahn, *Selected Essays in Employment and Growth* (Cambridge, 1972), 1–27, from *Econ. Jnl.*, 41 (1931), 173–98

—— 'The financing of public works: A note', *Econ. Jnl.*, 42 (1932), 492–5

—— 'John Maynard Keynes', *Proc. Brit. Acad.*, 32 (1946), 395–414

—— *On Re-reading Keynes*, Fourth Keynes Lecture, from *Proc. Brit. Acad.*, 60 (1974)

—— *The Making of Keynes's General Theory* (Cambridge, 1984)

KEYNES, M. (ed.), *Essays on John Maynard Keynes* (1975)

KLEIN, L. R., *The Keynesian Revolution* (New York, 1947; London, 1952)

LAMBERT, P., 'The evolution of Keynes's thought from the *Treatise on Money* to the *General Theory*', *Annals of Public and Cooperative Economy*, 40 (1969), 243–63

LEIJONHUFVUD, A., *On Keynesian Economics and the Economics of Keynes* (1968)

—— *Keynes and the Classics* (Institute of Economic Affairs, 1969)

—— 'Schools, "revolutions" and research programmes in economic theory', in Leijonhufvud, *Information and Co-ordination* (1981)

LEITH-ROSS, F. W., *Money Talks* (1968)

LIBERAL PARTY, *We Can Conquer Unemployment* (1929)

LLOYD GEORGE, D., *War Memoirs*, 2 vols., 2-vol. edn. (1938)

LOWE, R., *Adjusting to Democracy* (Oxford, 1986)

MCKENNA, R., *Post-War Banking Policy* (1928)

MCKIBBIN, R., 'The economic policy of the second Labour Government, 1929–31', *Past and Present*, 68 (Aug. 1975), 95–123

MACMILLAN, H. P., *A Man of Law's Tale: The reminiscences of Lord Macmillan* (1952)

MARQUAND, D., *Ramsay MacDonald* (1977)

MATTHEWS, K. G. P., 'Was sterling overvalued in 1925?', *Econ. Hist. Rev.*, NS 39 (1986), 572–87

MEADE, J. E., *Public Works in their International Aspect* (1933)

—— 'A simplified model of Mr. Keynes's system', *Rev. of Econ. Studies*, 4 (1936-7), 98–107

MEADE, J. E., 'The Keynesian Revolution', in Keynes, M. (ed.), *Essays on John Maynard Keynes* (1975), 82–8

MIDDLETON, R., 'The Treasury in the 1930s: Political and administrative constraints to acceptance of the "new" economics', *Oxford Econ. Papers*, NS 34 (1982), 48–77

—— 'The Treasury and public investment: A perspective on inter-war economic management', *Public Admin.* 61 (1983), 351–70

—— *Towards the Managed Economy* (1985)

—— 'Treasury policy on unemployment', in Glynn, S., and Booth, A. (eds.), *The Road to Full Employment* (1987), 109–24

MILGATE, M., *Capital and Employment* (1982)

—— 'Keynes on the "classical" theory of interest', in Eatwell, J., and Milgate, M. (eds.), *Keynes's Economics and the Theory of Value and Distribution* (1983), 79–89

—— 'Keynes and Pigou on the Gold Standard and monetary theory', *Contribs. to Pol. Econ.*,2 (1983), 39–48

—— 'The "new" Keynes papers', in Eatwell, J., and Milgate, M. (eds.), *Keynes's Economics and the Theory of Value and Distribution* (1983), 187–99

MILLER, F. M., 'The unemployment policy of the National Government, 1931–6', *Hist. Jnl.*, 19 (1976), 477–99

MINSKY, H. P., *John Maynard Keynes* (New York, 1975)

MOGGRIDGE, D. E., *British Monetary Policy, 1924–31* (Cambridge, 1972)

—— 'From the *Treatise* to the *General Theory*: An exercise in chronology', *Hist. of Pol. Econ.*, 5 (1973), 72–88

—— 'Economic policy in the Second World War', in Keynes, M. (ed.), *Essays on John Maynard Keynes* (1975), 177–201

—— 'Cambridge discussion and criticism surrounding the writing of *The General Theory*: A chronicler's view', in Patinkin, D., and Leith, J. C. (eds.), *Keynes, Cambridge and the General Theory* (1977)

—— *Keynes*, 2nd edn. (1980)

—— and HOWSON, S., 'Keynes on monetary policy, 1910–46', *Oxford Econ. Papers*, NS 26 (1974), 226–47

MOMMSEN, W. J. (ed.), *The Emergence of the Welfare State in Britain and Germany, 1850–1950* (1981)

MORAN, LORD, *Winston Churchill: The struggle for survival, 1940–65* (1966)

MORGAN, K. O., *Labour in Power, 1945–51* (Oxford, 1984)

MOWAT, C. L., *Britain between the Wars, 1918–40* (1955)

MURRAY, B. K., *The People's Budget, 1909–10* (Oxford, 1980)

NICOLSON, H., *Diaries and Letters*, 3 vols. (1966–8)

O'BRIEN, D. P., and PRESLEY, J. R. (eds.), *Pioneers of Modern Economics in Britain* (1981)

O'BRIEN, P. K., 'Britain's economy between the Wars: A survey of a counter-revolution in economic history', *Past and Present*, 115 (May 1987), 107–30

O'HALPIN, E., 'Sir Warren Fisher, head of the civil service', Ph.D. thesis (Cambridge, 1982)

PATINKIN, D., *Keynes's Monetary Thought: A study of its development* (Durham, NC, 1976)

—— 'Keynes and the multiplier', *Manchester School*, 45 (1978), 209–23

—— *Anticipations of the General Theory?* (Chicago, 1982)

—— and LEITH, J. C. (eds.), *Keynes, Cambridge and the General Theory* (1977)

PEDEN, G. C., *British Rearmament and the Treasury* (Edinburgh, 1979)

—— 'Keynes, the Treasury and unemployment in the later nineteen-thirties', *Oxford Econ. Papers*, 33 (1980), 1–18

—— 'Sir Richard Hopkins and the "Keynesian Revolution" in employment policy, 1929–45', *Econ. Hist. Rev.*, NS 36 (1983), 281–96

—— 'The Treasury as the central department of government, 1919–39', *Public Admin.* 61 (1983), 371–85

—— 'The "Treasury View" on public works and employment in the interwar period', *Econ. Hist. Rev.*, 2nd ser., 37 (1984), 167–81

—— *British Economic and Social Policy* (1985)

PELLING, H., *Winston Churchill* (1974)

PIGOU, A. C., *The Theory of Unemployment* (1933)

PIMLOTT, B., *Hugh Dalton* (1985)

POLLARD, S., *The Gold Standard and Employment Policies between the Wars* (1970)

PRESLEY, J. R., 'D. H. Robertson, 1890–1963', in O'Brien and Presley (eds.), *Pioneers of Modern Economics in Britain* (1981), 175–198

ROBBINS, L., *The Great Depression* (1934)

—— *Autobiography of an Economist* (1971)

ROBERTSON, D. H., 'Mr Keynes's theory of money', *Econ. Jnl.*, 41 (1931), 395–411

ROBINSON, E. A. G., 'John Maynard Keynes, 1883–1946', *Econ. Jnl.*, 57 (1947)

—— 'Keynes and his Cambridge colleagues', in Patinkin, D., and Leith, J. C. (eds.), *Keynes, Cambridge and the General Theory* (1977), 25–38

ROBINSON, J., 'What has become of the Keynesian revolution?', in Keynes, M. (ed.), *Essays on John Maynard Keynes* (1975), 123–301

—— and WILKINSON, F., 'Ideology and logic', in Vicarelli, F. (ed.), *Keynes's Relevance Today* (1985), 73–98

ROSEVEARE, H., *The Treasury* (1969)

ROWSE, A. L., *Mr Keynes and the Labour Movement* (1936)

RYMES, T. K., 'Keynes's lectures, 1932–5: Notes of a representative student. A prelude: Notes for the Easter Term, 1932', *Eastern Econ. Jnl.*, 12 (1986), 397–412

SAYERS, R. S., 'The return to gold, 1925', in Pollard, S. (ed.), *The Gold Standard and Employment Policies between the Wars* (1970), 85–98

SAYERS, R. S., *The Bank of England, 1891–1944* (Cambridge, 1976)
—— '1941—the first Keynesian Budget', in Feinstein, C. (ed.), *The Managed Economy* (Oxford, 1983), 107–17
SCHUMPETER, J. A., 'John Maynard Keynes, 1883–1946', reprinted from *Am. Econ. Rev.*, 36 (1946) in Schumpeter, *Ten Great Economists* (1952), 260–91
—— *History of Economic Analysis* (New York, 1954)
SELDON, A., *Churchill's Indian Summer: The Conservative Government, 1951–5* (1981)
SHACKLE, G. L. S., *The Years of High Theory* (Cambridge, 1967)
SHORT, M., 'The politics of personal taxation: Budget-making in Britain, 1917–31', Ph.D. thesis (Cambridge, 1985)
SKIDELSKY, R., *Politicians and the Slump* (1967)
—— *Oswald Mosley* (1975)
—— 'The reception of the Keynesian revolution', in Keynes, M. (ed.), *Essays on John Maynard Keynes* (1975), 89–107
—— 'Keynes and the Treasury View: The case for and against an active unemployment policy, 1920–1929', in Mommsen, W. J. (ed.), *The Emergence of the Welfare State in Britain and Germany, 1850–1950* (1981), 167–87
—— *John Maynard Keynes*, i, *Hopes Betrayed, 1883–1920* (1983)
STANNAGE, T., *Baldwin Thwarts the Opposition* (1980)
STEINDL, J., 'J. M. Keynes: Society and the economist', in Vicarelli, F. (ed.), *Keynes's Relevance Today* (1985), 99–125
STEVENSON, J., 'The Making of Unemployment Policy, 1931–1935', in Bentley, M., and Stevenson, J. (eds.), *High and Low Politics in Modern Britain* (Oxford, 1983), 182–213
—— and COOK, C., *The Slump: Society and Politics during the Depression* (1979)
STEWART, M., *Keynes and After*, 1st and 2nd edns. (Harmondsworth, 1967; 1972)
STRAIGHT, M., *After Long Silence* (1983)
TARSHIS, L., 'Keynes as seen by his students in the 1930s', in Patinkin, D., and Leith, J. C. (eds.), *Keynes, Cambridge and the General Theory* (1977), 39–63
THIRWELL, A. P. (ed.), *Keynes and Laissez-Faire* (1978)
THOMAS, M., 'Rearmament and economic recovery in the late 1930s', *Econ. Hist. Rev.*, 2nd ser., 36 (1983), 552–73
THOMAS, T., 'Aggregate demand in the United Kingdom, 1918–45', in Floud, R., and McCloskey, D. (eds.), *The Economic History of Britain since 1700*, ii (Cambridge, 1981), 332–406
TOMLINSON, J., *Problems of British Economic Policy, 1870–1945* (1981)
VICARELLI, F., *Keynes: The instability of capitalism* (Milan, 1977; London 1984)
—— (ed.), *Keynes's Relevance Today* (1985)

WARMING, J. 'International difficulties arising out of the financing of public works during depression', *Econ. Jnl.*, 42 (1932), 211–24

WILLIAMSON, P., ' "Safety First": Baldwin, the Conservative Party, and the 1929 General Election', *Hist. Jnl.*, 25 (1982), 385–409

—— 'Financiers, the Gold Standard and British politics, 1925–31', in Turner, J. (ed.), *Businessmen and Politics* (1984), 105–29

—— 'A "bankers' ramp"? Financiers and the British political crisis of August 1931', *EHR* 99 (1984), 770–806

—— 'The formation of the National Government, 1929–31', Ph.D. thesis (Cambridge, 1987)

WINCH, D., *Economics and Policy*, revised edn. (1972)

YEAGER, L. B., 'The Keynesian heritage in economics', in Burton, J., *et al.*, *Keynes's General Theory: Fifty years on* (Institute of Economic Affairs, 1986), 25–44

YOUNG, W., *Interpreting Mr Keynes: The IS–LM enigma* (Oxford, 1987)

YOUNGSON, A. J., *The British Economy, 1920–1957* (1960)

INDEX

Keynes's *Treatise on Money* (1930) is referred to below as *Treatise* and the *General Theory* (1936) as *GT*.